Journal of Semitic Studies Supplement 11

JEWISH WAYS OF READING
THE BIBLE

Edited by
George J. Brooke

Published by Oxford University Press
on behalf of the University of Manchester

2000

OXFORD
UNIVERSITY PRESS

Great Clarendon Street, Oxford OX2 6DP

Oxford University Press is a department of the University of Oxford.
It furthers the University's objective of excellence in research, scholarship,
and education by publishing worldwide in

Oxford   New York

Athens Auckland Bangkok Bogotá Buenos Aires Calcutta
Cape Town Chennai Dar es Salaam Delhi Florence Hong Kong Istanbul
Karachi Kuala Lumpur Madrid Melbourne Mexico City Mumbai
Nairobi Paris São Paulo Shanghai Singapore Taipei Tokyo Toronto Warsaw

with associated companies in Berlin Ibadan

Oxford is a registered trade mark of Oxford University Press
in the UK and in certain other countries

Published in the United Kingdom
by Oxford University Press, Oxford

A catalogue for this book is available from the British Library

Library of Congress Cataloguing in Publication Data
(Data available)

ISSN 0022-4480
ISBN 0-19-850918-9

Subscription information for the *Journal of Semitic Studies* is available
from

Journals Customer Services	Journals Marketing Department
Oxford University Press	Oxford University Press
Great Clarendon Street	2001 Evans Road
Oxford OX2 6DP	Cary, NC 27513
UK	USA

Printed by the Charlesworth Group, Huddersfield, UK, 01484 517077

Contents

Jewish Ways of Reading the Bible

Reading the Bible in the Modern Age

Indexes

Preface

The papers collected in this volume were all presented in some form at the annual meeting of the British Association for Jewish Studies held at Ashburne Hall in the University of Manchester in July 1999. The theme of the meeting was 'Jewish Ways of Reading the Bible'. Although papers on other topics were welcome at the meeting itself, all of the contributions to this collection fall broadly within the overall theme. As President of the Association in 1999 I owe thanks to many people, especially those who made the annual conference a very enjoyable occasion. Not least I am indebted to several colleagues, all of whom are part of the University of Manchester's Centre for Jewish Studies: Philip Alexander, Bernard Jackson, Brian Lancaster, Harry Lesser, and Alexander Samely. Their contributions to the 1999 annual meeting appear in this volume. For several years Philip Alexander has taught a course at Manchester entitled 'Jewish Ways of Reading the Bible' and, both for the annual meeting and also for this volume of papers, I have borrowed that course title from him with permission. The University of Manchester's Centre for Jewish Studies also generously hosted a reception for the Association during the annual meeting.

Two particular features of the 1999 annual meeting deserve special mention. Firstly, it was very good to have in our midst, as guest of the Association, Professor Moshe Bernstein of Yeshiva University, New York. His paper appears in this volume, but he is also a lively and generous conversation partner and he contributed much else to the meeting as well. Secondly, one afternoon session was held at the John Rylands University Library on Deansgate in Manchester. In addition to the opportunity for those attending to see some of the library's rich collection of Hebrew manuscripts, the Association was treated to a very memorable virtuoso presentation by Professor Raphael Loewe, which is also printed in this collection. After his lecture, the Association presented Professor Loewe with a small gift to mark his 80th birthday and as a token of very sincere gratitude for all that he has done for Jewish Studies in the United Kingdom and beyond.

In addition to those already mentioned, this volume contains some papers by other well-established scholars: Nina Collins and Eva Frojmovic (both from Leeds), Heather McKay (Ormskirk) and Christine Pilkington (Canterbury). There are also a few short contributions from other members of the Association who may be less well-known in Jewish Studies circles: Siam Bhayro (Sheffield), Clive Fierstone (London), Niclas Förster (Göttingen), and Moshe Ish-Horowicz (London).

For the most part the presentations here follow the style of the *Journal of Semitic Studies*, but some measure of freedom has also been granted each author. In particular, most authors have adopted a minimalist approach to the transliteration of Hebrew and Aramaic, and many Hebrew words appear in their readily recognisable English forms. Abbreviations have been kept to a minimum.

I am grateful to my colleagues on the editorial committee of the *Journal of Semitic Studies* for welcoming this collection of essays into the Supplement Series of the Journal and for providing financial assistance for its production.

George J. Brooke
Manchester

Reading the Bible in the Classical Age

The Original Oral Law

Bernard S. Jackson

We are all familiar with the (or a) rabbinic conception of the oral law: it can be sketched roughly as having the following characteristics: God gave to Moses on Mount Sinai not only the written law but also an oral law, which was originally intended never to be written down, and which was not in fact written down until the end of the tannaitic period. That oral law had two principal elements: on the one hand, it provided the authorised interpretation of the written law; on the other, it contained further material not within the written law at all. Of these two elements, the rabbis ultimately accorded equal status with the written law to at least the first, the authorised exegesis of the written law, terming it *de'oraita* as opposed to *derabbanan*.[1]

The whole notion of the oral law is viewed by scholars as postbiblical; indeed, it can be located within the controversies which divided the different Jewish sects within the second commonwealth period.[2] How far it was originally conceived to

---

[1] But subject to some dispute as to whether everything deduced by the *middot* is even presumptively *de'oraita*. See Maimonides, *Sefer Hamitsvot,* 2nd princ., Kafih p. 11: 'We therefore conclude: Anything not explicit in Scripture, but deduced in the Talmud by means of one of the thirteen canons, is *de-oraita* if the talmudic sages specifically so state or state that it is essentially biblical. In such a case, it is entitled to biblical status because the receivers of the tradition have stated it to be biblical; but if they have not made a clear and specific statement designating the rule as Biblical, then it is considered *de-rabbanan*, since there is no verse that teaches it.' *Aliter,* Nahmanides, Commentary, ad loc.: 'Thus, it is proper to say that the opposite is true, i.e. that every matter deduced in the Talmud by means of one of the thirteen canons is biblical, unless the talmudic sages have specifically stated that the textual connection is *asmakhta.*'

[2] Normally associated with the Pharisee-Sadducee divide, but b. Shab. 31a provides a story suggesting that gentile converts might also (wrongly, in the view of the Talmud) have suspected a difference even between Hillelites and Shammaites.

extend,[3] and what was the original meaning of the 'ban' on writing it down,[4] are beyond the scope of the present paper. Suffice it to note its specific identification by R. Judah b. Shalom with the Mishnah.[5]

In this paper, I want to suggest that, from a critical point of view, there must have existed in biblical times something which we might, rather tendentiously, call an 'oral law', on the basis of a *modern* understanding of how language works, and in particular of the nature of sense construction processes within orality. I shall sketch the theory, provide a number of illustrations, and indicate some differences between this scholarly construction and the traditional rabbinic view.

Modern conceptions of meaning seek a very close relationship between *verba* and *voluntas*: we (normally) are expected to mean what we say, and to say what we mean. In principle, there should be no gap between the meaning we intend and the meaning of the words we utter. If there is, we are judged incompetent. Another way of expressing this notion is through the conception of literal meaning. But that very expression gives the game away. 'Literal' meaning is a conception of meaning bound to writing, not just words; it is a form of meaning construction associated with literacy.[6]

But literacy, as scholars like Walter Ong and Jack Goody stress, is not simply an alternative channel of transmission of meaning; it is a way of thought. 'Writing restructures consciousness.'[7] Two aspects of the transformation of structures of

---

[3] The *halakhot,* according to b. Tem. 14b; 'General principles', according to *Exod. Rabb., Ki Tissa* 41:6; cf. Eliezer Berkovits, *Not in Heaven. The Nature and Function of Halakha* (New York 1983), 71, on Albo; M. Elon, *Jewish Law, History, Sources, Principles* (Philadelphia 1994), I.225f.

[4] The dictum of R. Judah b. Nahmani, 'Matters that are written you are not at liberty to recite orally; matters transmitted orally, you are not at liberty to recite from a writing' (b. Git. 60b), is sometimes taken as indicating that there was no original ban on writing down the 'Oral Law' as such; only a ban on a *tanna* using a written text, rather than his memory of the oral tradition, to verify it. See José Faur, *Golden Doves with Silver Dots* (Bloomington 1986), 135-38; Elon, *Jewish Law,* I.224-27.

[5] *Tanḥuma, Ki Tissa* 34.

[6] For debate within linguistics and the philosophy of language on 'literal meaning', see B. S. Jackson, *Making Sense in Law* (Liverpool 1995), 42-45.

[7] The title of ch. 4 of W. Ong, *Orality and Literacy* (London and New York 1982); see also J. Goody, *The Domestication of the Savage Mind* (Cambridge 1977); Jackson, *Making Sense in Law,* 79-83.

consciousness, between orality and literacy, are particularly relevant here. First, orality favours events rather than concepts or system; the kind of connections we can best process through speech are those of narrative rather than logical sequence. We can tolerate a complex story told orally, but not a complex legal document. Secondly, the distinction between orality and literacy very frequently coincides with that which the linguist Basil Bernstein has termed 'restricted code' rather than 'elaborated code'.[8] In restricted code we need *not* say everything which we mean, because we can rely upon the shared social knowledge within a small community to fill in what, at the explicit level, would be gaps; elaborated code, by contrast, makes no such assumptions. Everything we want to say must be elaborated; the people with whom we are communicating are not expected to share our cultural, contextual assumptions; any such assumptions therefore need to be spelled out.

These two facets of the distinction between orality and literacy come together in the following opposition: literal meaning assumes elaborated code and is applicable in principle to any content, so long as we spell it out and expect the reader to pay full attention to everything we have written (and no attention to what we have not written); narrative meaning, by contrast, consists not in a paraphrase, the substitution of one set of words by another, but rather the typical stories, or narrative images evoked by the words within a group which shares the social knowledge necessary to evoke those images without fully spelling them out.[9] Such a conception of narrative meaning is not, however, lost the moment speech is reduced to writing: from the early stages of literacy, we encounter what has been termed 'oral residue'.[10]

This brings me to the biblical text. Biblical form criticism stresses particularly the existence of oral antecedents to the texts of biblical law. It is still worth asking

---

[8] B. Bernstein, *Class, Codes and Control* (London 1971), Vol. I, chs 5-7, esp. pp. 108f., 123-37.

[9] For the interdisciplinary narrative theory, deriving from Greimassian semiotics, psychology (Bartlett, Bruner) and the later Wittgensteinian philosophy of language, which provides the theoretical foundations of this conception of meaning, see further Jackson, *Making Sense in Law,* esp. ch. 5 and §§ 6.4, 10.2-3; idem, *Making Sense in Jurisprudence* (Liverpool 1996), §§ 7.5, 9.2, 4.

[10] Narrative images still underlie much of our case law and jurisprudential theorising about it: see B. S.

whether different forms – the broad classes of the casuistic and apodictic and the internal variations of which they admit – correspond with different *Sitzen im Leben*, with which we can associate different uses. Yet Alt 'read' the apodictic form in a strikingly 'literal' way: his stress upon setting and origin was at the expense of any attention to structures of meaning. The problematisation of meaning itself – the appreciation that words uttered orally might have a different meaning from those same words when written down – was not yet on the agenda. We shall see the effects of this in a moment, when considering Alt's account of one example of 'apodictic' law. I start, however, with two casuistic examples. My argument is that the meaning of these rules, even when first written down, would have been constructed in a narrative rather than a literal sense.

Exod. 22:2-3 (= MT 22:1-2):
22:2 If a thief is found breaking in, and is struck so that he dies, there shall be no bloodguilt for him;
22:3 but if the sun has risen upon him, there shall be bloodguilt for him.

22:1 אם במחתרת ימצא הגנב והכה ומת אין לו דמים:
22:2 אם זרחה השמש עליו דמים לו

This biblical provision has appeared to many as badly drafted: the first verse, which allows self-help, makes no explicit mention of the time of the incident; the only explicit reference to the time occurs in the second verse, which denies the legitimacy of self-help during the day. It is in the light of that qualification, apparently, that the permission of self-help has to be restricted to the nocturnal incident. This would appear at first sight to be a very strange type of drafting. Apparently, the audience is first given the impression that self-help is *always* available, then this is qualified by denying its availability when the incident occurs during the day. Indeed, some scholars have wondered whether the second verse may be a later addition: originally the householder was entitled to kill the intruding thief at any time of day or night; later this form of self-help was restricted to the daytime intruder.[11]

Jackson, *Law, Fact and Narrative Coherence* (Merseyside 1988), esp. chs 3-5.
[11] Discussed and rejected in my *Theft in Early Jewish Law* (Oxford 1972), 204-206.

This argument, we may note, derives from a 'semantic' or 'literal' reading of the first verse: 'If a thief is found breaking in, and is struck so that he dies, there shall be no bloodguilt for him'. If we pose the question of meaning in the (semantic) form: 'what situations do the words of this rule cover?', then since the provision makes no mention of day or night, we infer that this is irrelevant, so that the rule 'covers' the intruder both by day and night. If, on the other hand, we pose the question of meaning in the (narrative) form: 'what typical situations do the words of this rule evoke?', then we are entitled to take into account the image of typical thieving presented in the book of Job:

Job 24:14, 16

The murderer rises in the dark;
    that he may kill the poor and needy
        and in the night he is as a thief.

24:14 לאור יקום רוצח יקטל עני ואביון ובלילה יהי כגנב:

In the dark they dig through houses;
    by day they shut themselves up;
        they do not know the light.

24:16 חתר בחשך בתים יומם חתמו למו לא ידעו אור:

This indicates that nocturnal activity was the primary image of acting like a thief. The first verse did not have to make that explicit: it was part of the narrative image evoked by the words. Such a rule, when orally transmitted, would be understood as evoking that situation.

In the rabbinic oral law, a further step was taken. Not only was the first verse interpreted as limited by the second – an example of what today might be termed 'backward scanning';[12] the whole distinction between day and night was treated – exceptionally – as a *mashal*, indicating not the time at which the killing took place,

---

[12] Goody, *The Domestication of the Savage Mind*, 128; Ong, *Orality and Literacy*, 104: we are prompted to read the first provision again, in the light of what comes later. We can do this only because the text of the first provision is still in front of us, available for 'backward scanning'. Suppose, however, that these rule were communicated in speech, not writing. Speech is 'evanescent': it disappears as soon as it is uttered. Any cognitive difficulty of reconciling the two texts thus depends upon having retained the *words* of the first rule in memory. Exact words are more difficult to retain in memory than are images: hence the greater likelihood that in an oral society, the meaning of the first rule would have been identified with its typical image – here, that of the nocturnal intruder – and thus no cognitive conflict between the two rules will have been perceived.

but rather a test of whether the intruder's intention (to kill or simply to steal) was 'as clear as the sun'.[13]

My second example, however, is one where we may oppose an original 'narrative' oral law with a rabbinic 'literal' oral law reading. I refer to one of the rules concerning goring oxen :

Exod. 21:35

When a man's ox hurts another's, so that it dies, then they shall sell the live ox and divide the price of it; and the dead beast also they shall divide.

21:35 וכי יגף שור איש את שור רעהו ומת ומכרו את השור החי וחצו את כספו

The object, here, is to achieve an 'equitable distribution of loss when the circumstances of the case suggest that there was no clear justification for shifting the burden of the loss from one party to the other.'[14] But how was such 'equitable distribution' to be achieved? As has been widely observed from the time of the earliest rabbinic commentaries, an equal division of the loss results from the *literal* application of the ancient procedure (dividing the carcass and dividing the price of the live ox) only if the two oxen had been of equal value before the incident. If the dead ox had been worth more than the live, then the result of the procedure of division is that the owner of the dead ox will lose more than the owner of the live, since half the price of the live ox is less than half the price the dead ox would have commanded, had it been sold live.[15] Conversely, if the surviving ox had been the more valuable of the two, its owner loses half its value, whereas the owner of the dead ox is compensated by more than half his loss.[16] Indeed, in the highly unlikely case of the surviving ox being worth more than double the value of the dead ox when alive, the owner of the dead ox makes a profit.[17] There is even a theoretical possibility that the

---

[13] *Mekhilta* ad loc.; see further Jackson, *Theft in Early Jewish Law*, 209-12, for parallels and variants.

[14] J. J. Finkelstein, 'The Ox That Gored', *Transactions of the American Philosophical Society* 72:2 (1981), 36.

[15] Example: Value of dead ox when alive: 300; value of carcass: 50; value of goring ox when sold: 200. Each party gets equivalent of 125; owner of dead ox has thus lost 175, owner of gorer has lost 75.

[16] Example: Value of dead ox when alive: 200; value of carcass: 50; value of goring ox when sold: 300. Each party gets equivalent of 175; owner of dead ox has thus lost 25, owner of gorer has lost 125.

[17] Example: Value of dead ox when alive: 200; value of carcass: 50; value of goring ox when sold: 500. Each party gets equivalent of 275; owner of dead ox has thus gained 75, owner of gorer has lost 225.

owner of the gorer could make a profit, if the value of the carcass were worth more than the value of the gorer.[18]

To avoid such results, the rabbis[19] add a condition which is not found in the text: this procedure applies only when the two oxen (when both were alive) were indeed of equal value. Where this was not the case, a court would have to calculate what sum of money would in fact produce equal loss division.[20] But the rule produces the consequences to which the Rabbis object only if it is read 'semantically' (literally), i.e. as covering *all* cases which may be subsumed under its language. Since no mention is made of the relative values of the two animals, the literal argument goes, that factor is irrelevant, and the rule applies whatever the relative values of the two animals. If, however, we adopt a narrative rather than a semantic approach to the meaning of the biblical text, then this problem largely disappears.[21] It applied to the typical cases whose images are evoked by the words of the rule, and these typical cases will, indeed, be those where the relative values of the two animals are equal or roughly equivalent. The more distant the circumstances (here, the relative values) from that typical case, the less the rule would have appeared applicable, and the more likely resort would have been made to some other (no doubt equally informal) method of dispute resolution, such as ad hoc settlement or some form of third party arbitration. Here again, the rule, when orally transmitted, would be understood as evoking the typical situation of its use, and the conventions of common sense applied in such situations by its users.

---

[18] Example: Value of dead ox when alive: 600; value of carcass: 150; value of goring ox when sold: 100. Each party gets equivalent of 125; owner of dead ox has thus lost 475, owner of gorer has gained 25!

[19] And with some minor qualification Finkelstein.

[20] I.e. the difference between the dead animal's value before and after the incident: the plaintiff retained the carcass of his dead ox, and deducted the whole of its value from that of the ox when alive, in order to ascertain the loss which should be divided. See, e.g., Maimonides, *The Book of Torts,* trans. H. Klein (New Haven 1954), 4 (*Hilkhot nizke mamon* 1:3): 'Thus, if an ox worth one hundred *denar* gores an ox worth twenty and kills it and the carcass is worth four, the owner of the ox must pay eight, this being half of the residual damage.' The rabbis expressed this as 'half damages from its body': m. B.Q. 1:4; *Mekhilta,* Exod. 21:29 (Lauterbach iii 82-83). In this case, a literal application of Exod. 21:35 would have given each party fifty denar plus half the actual carcass, thus considerably profiting the owner of the dead ox.

[21] As I argued in 'The Goring Ox Again', *Journal of Juristic Papyrology* 18 (1974), 55-93, at 74-77; reprinted in my *Essays in Jewish and Comparative Legal History* (Leiden 1975), 130-35.

Jewish Ways of Reading the Bible

I turn next to an 'apodictic'[22] example from the Covenant Code:

Exod. 21:12-14
21:12 Whoever strikes a man so that he dies shall be put to death.
21:13 But if he did not lie in wait for him, but God let him fall into his hand, then I will appoint for you a place to which he may flee.
21:14 But if a man wilfully attacks another to kill him treacherously, you shall take him from my altar, that he may die.

21:12 מכה איש ומת מות יומת:
21:13 ואשר לא צדה והאלהים אנה לידו ושמתי לך מקום אשר ינוס שמה:
21:14 וכי יזד איש על רעהו להרגו בערמה מעם מזבחי תקחנו למות:

Verse 12 is the first of a series of four 'participial' provisions, which continues in vv.15-17; vv.13-14 are generally viewed as a 'casuistic' interpolation. Alt's identification of a cultic Sitz im Leben for the form has been widely challenged: a setting in domestic discipline and teaching has attracted significant support.[23] But what was the meaning of verse 12, when it stood alone? A 'literal' (semantic) reading might lead us to conclude that the provision is 'absolute', applying to anyone 'who strikes a man so that he dies': no qualifications having been stated, it may be argued, none apply. Alt put the argument thus:

> It refers to homicide; but it makes no distinction between murder and manslaughter, using expressions, indeed, which seem deliberately chosen to leave no doubt that both are included. It treats every killing as a crime punishable by death — and it does not restrict this by any reference to the possibility of allaying one's guilt by paying an indemnity or seeking sanctuary. Its content, then, is as unconditional as its form, and this is what distinguishes it so sharply from what follows. We must ask why it allows of no conditions. The outlook of the whole Old Testament leaves us in no doubt of the answer: it is Yahweh who demands a stern retribution for every drop of blood that is spilt ...[24]

---

[22] At least according to Alt's classification of the participial form: A. Alt, 'The Origins of Israelite Law', reprinted in *Essays on Old Testament History and Religion* (Sheffield 1989), 111-14; *aliter,* G. Wenham, 'Legal Forms in the Book of the Covenant', *Tyndale Bulletin* 22 (1971), 97, 102; J. M. Sprinkle, *The Book of the Covenant – A Literary Approach* (ISOTSup 174; Sheffield 1994), 74: R. Westbrook, 'What is the Covenant Code?', in B.M. Levinson (ed.), *Theory and Method in Biblical and Cuneiform Law* (JSOTSup 181; Sheffield 1994), 32.

[23] E. Gerstenberger, *Wesen und Herkunft des "apodiktischen Rechts"* (WMANT 20; Neukirchen-Vluyn 1965). See further my *Wisdom-Laws: A Study of the Mishpatim*, Vol. I, ch. 2 (forthcoming).

[24] Alt, 'Origins', 110; cf. B. S. Childs, *Exodus. A Commentary* (London 1974), 469f.; as regards the exclusion of composition: M. Greenberg, 'Some Postulates of Biblical Criminal Law', in M. Haran (ed.), *Yehezkel Kaufman Jubilee Volume* (Jerusalem 1960), 13f.; *contra,* H. McKeating, 'The Development of the Law of Homicide in Ancient Israel', *Vetus Testamentum* 25 (1975), 66-68.

Against this, Schenker has recently argued that vv.13-14 should be viewed not as a correction of verse 12, but rather as a process of making it more explicit:[25] the institution of (altar) refuge in Israel is ancient, as is shown by the narratives regarding Adonijah and Joab.[26] Exod. 21:12 should be understood against the background of the contemporaneous institution of places of refuge, and the distinction between intentional and unintentional killing is implicit in that institution. Such an approach rightly takes account of the institutional context and use of Exod. 21:12. That is part of the social knowledge which we rightly impute into the meaning of the provision when we apply the notions of 'narrative reading' and 'restricted code'.[27] If, then, we ask what was the typical narrative image evoked by the words, the case of homicide which would typically generate a demand for death, the most likely answer is a direct,[28] deliberate assault probably accompanied by an intention to kill. The further we move away from the case of the typical killer, the less strongly will the normal expectation regarding the penalty hold good.[29] Again, we may reasonably assume such implications as to the typical case and its typical treatment to have been encoded in the original, oral use of the apodictic formulation.

Similar arguments may be applied to the talionic formula:

Exod. 21:24-25
21:24 Eye for eye, tooth for tooth, hand for hand, foot for foot,
21:25 burn for burn, wound for wound, stripe for stripe.

21:24 עין תחת עין שן תחת שן יד תחת יד רגל תחת רגל:
21:25 כויה תחת כויה פצע תחת פצע חבורה תחת חבורה:

---

[25] A. Schenker, 'Die Analyse der Intentionalität im Bundesbuch (Ex 21-23)', *Zeitschrift für Altorientalische und Biblische Rechtsgeschichte* 4 (1998), 210f.

[26] 1 Kgs 1:50-53; 1 Kgs 2:28-35. See further my *Wisdom-Laws,* ch. 4, forthcoming.

[27] Schenker, 'Die Analyse der Intentionalität', 211, however, adopts a semantic approach in arguing that Exod. 21:12-14 distinguishes three cases: unintentional (verse 13), intentional (verse 12), premeditated (verse 14).

[28] B. S. Jackson, 'Murder', in P. J. Achtemeier (ed.), *Harper's Bible Dictionary* (San Francisco 1985), 663; cf. E. Otto, *Körperverletzungen in den Keilschriftrechten und im Alten Testament* (Neukirchen-Vluyn 1991), 162f.

[29] This is, in principle, different from the approach which views Exod. 21:12 as a 'guiding principle' (e.g. Alt, 'Origins', 109: 'Whoever placed it in this prominent position must have regarded it as the guiding principle for the treatment of the whole matter' of murder and manslaughter). A principle, as understood in the context of a literate society, is a formulation whose meaning is semantic, but whose application may nevertheless not be rigid.

It is partly through the Sermon on the Mount[30] that this provision has been taken as representative of a crude and cruel legalism attributed to Jewish law. What Matthew understood as the meaning of 'An eye for an eye' is beyond the scope of the present paper.[31] Suffice it to say that readers of the New Testament have adopted a 'literal' reading of it, which makes, *inter alia*, the following assumptions: (a) it applies whatever the circumstances of the injury (deliberate or accidental); (b) it applies whatever the relative bodily conditions of offender and victim (c); the remedy is mandatory: you have to apply it.[32]

In what circumstances may talionic punishment be demanded? Are we to take a 'literal' (semantic) view, and say that because the formula does not address the circumstances of the offence, the latter are irrelevant, so that the provision 'applies' whether the injury was inflicted deliberately or accidentally?[33] Or are we to understand it narratively,[34] in terms of the typical image of the infliction of bodily injury, which is a deliberate[35] attack? In fact, in all the narratives of the Bible, there is only one mention of the actual *practice* of *talio* as a measure of human justice (though even there justified in terms of divine justice). That is the story of the king Adoni-Bezek in the first chapter of the book of Judges.[36] The king says, in reaction to his mutilation by the Judaites, who had cut off his thumbs and large toes: '70 kings with their thumbs and their great toes cut off used to pick up scraps under my table; as I have done, so God has requited me' (Judg. 1:7).[37] Adoni-Bezek's offence was

---

[30] 'You have heard that it was said, "An eye for an eye and a tooth for a tooth." But I say to you, Do not resist one who is evil. But if any one strikes you on the right cheek, turn to him the other also...' (Matt. 5:38-39).

[31] D. Daube, *The New Testament and Rabbinic Judaism* (London 1956), 255-59, argues from the antithetical examples Jesus provides that he is arguing not against mutilation for bodily injury but rather against suing for damages for insult.

[32] See further my 'An Aye for an I?: the Semiotics of Lex Talionis in the Bible', in W. Pencak and J. Ralph Lindgren (eds), *Semiotics and the Human Sciences: New Directions – Essays in Honor of Roberta Kevelson* (New York and Bern 1997), 127-50.

[33] The immediate context of this occurrence of the formula is indeed accidental injury (Exod. 21:22-23). But it is probable that this context is not original: on the interpolation of these verses, see further my *Essays in Jewish and Comparative Legal History*, 96-107.

[34] Finkelstein, 'The Ox That Gored', 34f., wrote that *talio* should be regarded as a 'paradigm'.

[35] Cf. Philo's rendition: *De Specialibus Legibus* III.195.

[36] See further Jackson, *Essays*, 83f.

[37] The words put into the mouth of Adoni-Bezek are similar to the language used to express *talio* in Deut. 19:19, 'Then you shall do to him as he had meant to do to his brother' and also to the formula in Lev. 24:19, 'As he has done it shall be done to him'. On the history of this (distinct) version of the

clearly deliberate. Whether talionic punishment could ever have been applied where the injury was caused accidentally is a matter for speculation. If the text is read narratively, we do not have to assume that it was intended for application way beyond the scope of the typical narrative image it evoked. That would be a matter for debate.

Similar considerations apply to the relative bodily conditions of offender and victim. Arguing that *'ayin taḥat 'ayin* refers to compensation rather than bodily retaliation, the rabbis asked:

> What then will you say where a blind man put out the eye of another man, or where a cripple cut off the hand of another or where a lame person broke the leg of another. How can I carry out in this case [the principle of retaliation of] 'eye for eye', seeing that the Torah says, 'Ye shall have one manner of law', implying that the manner of law should be the same in all cases.[38]

Since the biblical text stated no limitations on the relative bodily conditions of offender and victim, the rabbis understand that no such limitations can apply. But such a 'literal' application of *talio* would mean that the eye of the offender must be taken, notwithstanding the fact that he will thereby be rendered completely blind, etc., whereas his victim was left half-sighted. Such a conclusion is rejected as self-evidently[39] impossible. The range of the biblical provision cannot however be restricted to exclude such cases (while preserving it for the 'normal' case), in the light of the 'one law' principle. If we cannot modify the range of the principle, we must then seek an alternative meaning for the penalty, one where the blind, crippled or lame offender will suffer no more than the able-bodied offender. *'Ayin taḥat 'ayin* must therefore mean compensation rather than retaliation.

This rabbinic argument, we may note, depends upon two aspects of the literary presentation of talion. First, the range of application of the formula is given a 'literal' reading: no limitations on the relative bodily conditions of offender and victim having been stated, no limitations apply. Second, the justification for not making an exception for the untypical (blind, crippled, lame) offender is taken from the literary

---

formula, see my *Wisdom-Laws,* ch. 4 (forthcoming).

[38] b. B.Q. 84a (Soncino translation). See also Aristotle, Nik. Eth. V.5; H. H. Cohn, 'Talion', *Encyclopedia Judaica* (Jerusalem 1973), XV.741.

[39] Unless we take the 'one law' principle to refer to equivalence between offender and victim. But this does not appear to be its function in the talmudic argument.

association between the talionic formula as it appears in Lev. 24:20 and the 'one law' principle (Lev. 24:22), even though the latter is actually used in the biblical text for a quite different purpose: to stress that the law of blasphemy applies equally to the *ger*, here the son of an Israelite woman and an Egyptian man. If, by contrast, we replace this by asking what would have been the meaning of the talionic formula as transmitted orally, and thus replace a literal by a narrative reading, we can hardly suggest that the image of the typical offender was that of the blind, crippled or lame! The exception to which the Rabbis objected would have been implicit: physical retaliation (subject to the argument below) could be applied to the typical case; it need not be applied to the atypical case, notwithstanding the unqualified range of the words.

Such an argument would appear to support what is generally viewed as a 'literal' approach to the penalty: bodily retaliation rather than monetary compensation. But there is a further issue to be considered: whether such a sanction was mandatory or not. The view that talionic punishment is here presented as mandatory cannot in fact be based upon any notion of literal meaning, since there is no linguistic expression in the text on which it can be based. The Hebrew formula has no verb at all.[40] Without a verb, there is nothing explicit to indicate what modality – prescription or permission – is intended. It is simply the assumption of a (modern, positivist) reader that 'an eye for an eye' means 'you *must* give/take an eye for an eye', rather than 'you *may* give/take an eye for an eye'.[41] In short, the mandatory character of talionic punishment derives from discourse assumptions, not literal meaning. And the particular discourse assumption here made turns out to be unjustified. Even in some capital crimes, such as murder and adultery, we hear of the institution of 'ransom' (*kofer*), whereby the victims may agree to accept financial compensation and thereby relieve the offender of capital punishment.[42] Indeed, in the

---

[40] That is clear in Deut. 19:21 and Lev. 24:20, in the light of which any argument that the formula in Exod. 21:24-25 was originally governed by the verb in the previous verse (ונתתה נפש תחת נפש) is much weakened. The relationship of Exod. 21:24-25 to Exod. 21:22-23 is discussed in my *Wisdom-Laws*, ch. 5 (forthcoming).

[41] In fact, even where (as normal) verbs are present, Biblical Hebrew grammar does not have any clear or regular way of distinguishing these modalities. The attribution of the correct modality is a matter of 'restricted' rather than 'elaborated' code.

[42] On David's offer of *kofer* to the Gibeonites (2 Sam. 21:3) and the proverbial advice against relying upon a cuckolded husband's acceptance of *kofer* (Prov. 6:32-35) – both matters of some controversy, see further my *Wisdom-Laws*, ch.4 (forthcoming).

case of murder such 'ransom' appears to have been banned only at a late stage in the history of biblical law (Num. 35:31-32), and in the case of adultery it does not appear to have been banned in biblical times at all.[43] If ransom was available for capital crimes, it must surely have been available also for non-capital crimes. Indeed, Josephus later explicitly reads this into the talionic formula: 'He that maimeth a man shall undergo the like, being deprived of that limb whereof he deprived the other, unless indeed the maimed man be willing to accept money.'[44]

The ultimate rabbinic view on this matter is well known. The oral law did not leave the victim with a choice between retaliation and a monetary settlement (*kofer*): *'ayin taḥat 'ayin* meant monetary compensation, and this would be assessed by a court, according to a sophisticated regime for assessment of damages for personal injury laid down by the Mishnah.[45] It is worth looking at the way in which the rabbis justified this conclusion, since it points to an important conceptual distinction between their notion of oral law and that advanced in this paper:

> 'An eye for an eye' – that means money. You say it means money, but perhaps you are wrong and it really does mean an eye? – Rabbi Ishmael used to say: 'Behold it says, "And he that killeth a beast shall make it good and he that killeth a man shall be put to death" (Lev. 24:21). The Torah compares damage caused to a man to damage caused to a beast, and damage caused to a beast to damage caused to a man. Just as in the case of damage caused to a beast there is a monetary payment, so in the case of damage caused to a man there is also monetary payment.' (Mekhilta, Exod. 21:24)

The comparison (*hekesh*) of Rabbi Ishmael is based upon the following sequence of rules, stated in Leviticus 24 in the wake of the adjudication of the case of the 'blasphemer':

Lev. 24:17-21
17 He who kills a man shall be put to death.
18 He who kills a beast shall make it good, life for life.

---

[43] See further my *Essays*, 41-50, 59-62.
[44] Ant. 4.8.35.280, contrary to the opinion of Daube, *The New Testament and Rabbinic Judaism*, 256, who sees Josephus as reflecting the (similar) provision of the Twelve Tables (VIII.2): *si membrum rupsit, ni cum eo pacit, talio esto.*
[45] m. B.Q. 8:1 (*hahovel ...*).

19 When a man causes a disfigurement in his neighbour, as he has done it shall be done to him,
20 fracture for fracture, eye for eye, tooth for tooth; as he has disfigured a man, he shall be disfigured.
21 He who kills a beast shall make it good; and he who kills a man shall be put to death.

24:17 איש כי יכה כל נפש אדם מות יומת:
24:18 ומכה נפש בהמה ישלמנה נפש תחת נפש:
24:19 ואיש כי יתן מום בעמיתו כאשר עשה כן יעשה לו:
24:20 שבר תחת שבר עין תחת עין שן תחת שן כאשר יתן מום באדם כן ינתן בו:
24:21 ומכה בהמה ישלמנה ומכה אדם יומת:

nefesh taḥat nefesh, in this context, means not killing a beast of the offender, but rather compensation with a (live) beast (or its value). The rest of the talionic formula, which immediately follows, is to be interpreted in that context, and this is then applied from Leviticus 24 to Exodus 21.[46] The rabbis are not concerned simply with the meaning of any particular provision in isolation: they are concerned with its integration within a *system* of consistent meaning, a system of intertextuality in which the meaning of one pentateuchal text must be consistent with the meaning of every other. By contrast, the 'narrative' interpretation of the oral law seeks to reconstruct the social knowledge assumed in (original) individual texts on the basis of such *evidence* of that social knowledge as may be provided by other biblical texts (and any other available evidence, such as that of archaeology). Whereas the rabbinic conception of the oral law postulates a single textual system, the narrative conception must always evaluate the evidence of other biblical texts, for their relevance, dating, etc. For there may well be more than a single 'restricted code' reflected in biblical literature: that literature emerges from a variety of groups whose narrative and semiotic structures cannot be assumed to have been identical.

There is one further distinction to be drawn between the original 'oral law' and that of the rabbis: in every one of the examples I have given, the rabbinic reading is one which implies a form of institutionalisation of the law which, I would maintain, is quite different from the manner in which these disputes were originally resolved.

---

[46] Logically, it could equally have been reversed: interpret *'ayin taḥat 'ayin* in Exod. 21:24 in the light of *nefesh taḥat nefesh* in v. 23, then apply the result to the killing of an animal by a man in Leviticus 24! Such an approach was, indeed, adopted by H. F. Jolowicz, 'The Assessment of Penalties in Primitive Law', in *Cambridge Legal Essays* (Cambridge 1926), 207; *contra,* Daube, *Studies in Biblical Law* (Cambridge 1947), 114f.

In the case of the intruding 'thief', the processes are those of self-help: the owner is entitled to kill the thief found at night, not entitled so to do during the day. The killing of the intruder does not lead to an adjudication, unless the family of the victim pursues the matter through a *go'el hadam*, and even that, for much of the biblical period, remained a form of self-help without institutional control. The effect of the rabbinic interpretation was to require an adjudication, to determine what the intruder's intention had been, and therefore whether the owner was subject to punishment. The case of the goring ox equally generated a new need for adjudication: *hatsi nezek migufo* required a determination of how much the dead ox had been worth when alive, something unnecessary to decide according to the original, where the farmers simply took the survivor to the market, divided its price and carved up the carcase of the dead ox. The homicide provision of Exod. 21:12, for the rabbis, would never have been read in isolation; for them, the problem was reconciling the altar and the *makom* (of Exod. 21:13) with the city of refuge, in its fully institutionalised form in Numbers 35 (with adjudication by an *'edah*). The *makom*, they argued, referred precisely to the city of refuge, and if anyone did take refuge at an altar, he could be handed over to the *go'el* without any trial,[47] not because the homicide was premeditated but because he had gone to the wrong place! Finally, the rabbinic interpretation of talion was one, as already noted, which led to an adjudication in terms of the five headings of damages in m. B.Q. 8:1, involving similar (partially speculative and thus contestable) 'before and after' calculations to those required in the case of the goring ox. It is hardly coincidental that this institutionalisation of dispute resolution goes hand in hand with the professionalisation of meaning – the application of the structures of literacy to a vast textual universe.

Is there any biblical support for the conception of a 'narrative' oral law which I have outlined in this paper? The biblical account(s) of the Sinaitic revelation(s) are complicated, but they do seem to indicate separate processes of oral and written communication. The entire set of *devarim* and *mishpatim* of Exod. 20:23-23:39 were (according to the final form of the text) first orally recited by Moses to the people and accepted by them on the basis of that oral recitation (Exod. 24:3), before being (immediately) written down (Exod. 24:4) in order to form the basis of a covenantal

---

[47] *Mekhilta*, Exod. 21:14 (Lauterbach iii 40): *velo ladun.*

17

approval of that written text, which was once again read out (Exod. 24:7). There is no hint, of course, that any difference in sense was perceived as between the first recitation, not from a written text, and the second, from a written text. But that second reading was an oral 'reading out' to the people, not a modern 'reading from' the text by the people. Both this and the narrative context should caution against concluding that the written version was originally conceived as anything other than the best evidence of what was essentially an oral revelation.

In all this, the Decalogue stands out as distinct. According to the present text, the 'direct' oral communication of the Decalogue to the entire people long preceded its delivery in written form on the tablets (at least 40 days later), and, unlike the *sefer haberit*, there is no suggestion that the Decalogue was ever 'read out' from the *luḥot* (not even after the giving of the second set). What follows from conceiving of the Decalogue in terms of orality rather than literacy? I confine myself to just one point, the meaning of *lo tirtsaḥ*. Even today, there are still those who debate issues such as capital punishment in terms of whether the phrase means 'You shall not kill' or 'You shall not murder.' At a purely philological level, there is no doubt that the semantic range of *ratsaḥ* favours 'kill': even the offender who is to be protected in the cities of refuge is classified as a *rotseaḥ* (Num. 35:12); indeed, the verb is used even of the (justified) action of the blood-avenger who catches the manslayer outside the city of refuge (Num. 35:27).[48] But what does this prove? Are we to say that the Decalogue is really saying to the *go'el hadam*: you are entitled to pursuit, but (morally) you ought not to do it? A better approach is narrative: to ask not what is the full range of situations which, semantically, *lo tirtsaḥ* might 'cover', but rather what typical situations it might evoke? The typical situation evoked in this context is surely 'murder', in the sense of premeditated homicide. The further one departs from that typical case, the more the issue becomes not one of narrative sense but literary interpretation.[49]

---

[48] Cf. H. H. Cohn, 'Homicide', *Encyclopedia Judaica* (Jerusalem 1973), VIII.945; A. Rofé, 'The History of the Cities of Refuge in Biblical Law', in S. Japhet (ed.), *Studies in Bible* (Scripta Hierosolymitana XXXI; Jerusalem 1986), 232-34; P. Haas, '"Die He Shall Surely Die": The Structure of Homicide in Biblical Law', *Semeia* 45 (1989), 78.

[49] On Wittgenstein's distinction between the unreflective following of a rule and the reflective process of interpreting it, see my *Making Sense in Jurisprudence*, 186f.

I conclude by noting that at least one modern Orthodox scholar has depicted the original *rabbinic* conception of the oral law in terms not dissimilar to mine, and has seen its development into its classical form as an unfortunate response to historical circumstances. Eliezer Berkovits, the author of *T'nai be'Nisuin uveget*, wrote in his *Not in Heaven* of the:

> mutuality of the covenant concluded with Israel by means of the *Torah she'baal'Peh*. Halakha is the result of the cooperation between the eternal written word and the timely spoken one. A text solidifies a meaning; the spoken word of wisdom carries within itself the awareness of its situation-dependent validity as well as vitality of self-renewal. Therein lies the significance of the law that forbade entrusting the *Torah she'baal'Peh* to writing ... Such is the ideal situation. Unfortunately ... the situation changed radically. Because of external necessities, a process or solidification of the Oral Torah set in ... As a first step, the *Torah she'baal'Peh* had to be systematised ... the transforming of the halakhic tradition into a systematic and authoritative work was in itself a revolutionary departure from the prevailing norm.[50]

---

[50] E. Berkovits, *Not in Heaven: The Nature and Function of Halakha* (New York 1983), 87f.

Who Wanted a Translation of the Pentateuch into Greek?

Nina L. Collins

I. Why was the Pentateuch translated into Greek?

Why was the Pentateuch translated into Greek? According to the Letter of Aristeas, probably the source for all ancient accounts, Ptolemy II accepted the suggestion of Demetrius of Phalerum that the king should acquire a translation of the Hebrew Pentateuch, in order to increase his collection of worthy books.[1] In other words, the translation was made solely because the king wanted a copy of a particular book, the Hebrew Pentateuch in Greek.

This simple explanation was accepted and repeated in the nearly fifty or so accounts from ancient times. But a new theory gained hold over the last two hundred years, which almost completely rejects the account of Aristeas. This is due mainly to the work of the Oxford Regius Professor of Greek, Humphrey Hody, who dissected and dismissed Aristeas in his book *Contra Historiam LXX Interpretum Aristeae nomine inscriptuam Dissertatio*, published in 1684. Since this publication, most scholars insist that, contrary to Aristeas, the translation was initiated by the Jews, perhaps with the help of Ptolemy II. This was because a large majority of Egyptian Jews could not understand Hebrew, and therefore requested a written translation of the

---

[1] For a comprehensive list of texts, translations and studies on Aristeas, see S. P. Brock, C. T. Fritsch, S. Jellicoe, *A Classified Bibliography of the Septuagint* (Leiden 1973), 44-47; C. Dogniez, *Bibliography of the Septuagint* (Leiden 1955), 18-22.

Bible, particularly for liturgical use.[2] Although this explanation is only supposition, is not supported by any ancient text, and contradicts Aristeas who probably provides the only ancient and independent account, it has become almost a credo of Hellenistic history, and is almost always stated by historians of the event. There is no doubt moreover that it is based on a truth – the majority of Jews living in Hellenistic Egypt in the third century BCE were probably unable to read or understand the Hebrew biblical text. But how relevant is this fact? The evidence that exists suggests not only that the Jewish knowledge of Hebrew is irrelevant to the decision to translate the Hebrew Pentateuch into Greek, but that the Jews were actively opposed to the plan and tried to thwart it as far as they could. The subject as a whole will now be discussed.

II. Details from Aristeas for a Greek Initiative for the Translation

(1) The Basic Truth of Aristeas

If Aristeas is correct when he claims that the translation was inspired by Demetrius of Phalerum, acting with the support of Ptolemy II, it must be shown with evidence independent of Aristeas that the Pentateuch was translated in the reign of Ptolemy II and that Demetrius of Phalerum could have worked for this king. This has been done. Using evidence which is independent of Aristeas, I have shown that the insinuations of Diogenes Laertius against Demetrius of Phalerum, which imply that Demetrius was murdered by Ptolemy II, are based on a mistake in chronology which was probably made in the 2nd century BCE. This means that Aristeas must be believed

---

[2] E.g., W. W. Harvey, *Sancti Irenaei: Libros quinque adversus Haereses*, Vol. 2, (Cambridge 1857), 112; H. B. Swete, *An Introduction to the Old Testament in Greek* (Cambridge 1900), 20; S. Jellicoe, *The Septuagint and Modern Study* (Oxford, 1968), 55. The comment of N. Walter, 'Jewish Greek Literature of the Greek Period', in W. D. Davies & L. Finkelstein (eds), *The Cambridge History of Judaism, Volume 2, The Hellenistic Age* (Cambridge 1989), 385-408, p. 385, is typical: 'The Jews of the Diaspora, especially in Egypt, felt the need of a Greek translation of their Holy Scripture, because *obviously* only a minority of Jews in that Greek-speaking environment were still capable of reading and understanding Hebrew' (my italics). One relatively modern dissenting voice is that of M. Gaster, *The Samaritans* (London, 1925), 112ff, who suggests that the request of an Egyptian king for a copy of the Jewish Law for an enrichment of his library must be assigned 'to the domain of legend', its presence forming part of the 'apologetic tendency so characteristic of the whole of Hellenistic literature'.

when he states that Demetrius of Phalerum worked in the court of Ptolemy II.[3] The case against Demetrius been previously based merely on a subjective evaluation of evidence between the hints of Diogenes compared with the evidence of Aristeas, while the external evidence assembled in this book mean that the historical situation can be objectively judged. As a result, the case for Aristeas – at least concerning his assertion that Demetrius of Phalerum worked in the court of Ptolemy II – is difficult to refute.

(2) The Detail of Demetrius in Aristeas

It is undoubtedly true that many details in Aristeas may not be historically correct. But a mixture of fact and fantasy is not unknown in ancient texts, for example, the Greek apocryphal books of Esdras I and II, so that Aristeas cannot be dismissed for this reason alone. In any case, the historically dubious sections of Aristeas are mainly peripheral to the main theme of his tale, which is the story of the translation of the Pentateuch into Greek. For example, it is not important to the story of the translation if the alleged victory at Cos of Ptolemy II was actually a defeat or if the presence of Menedemus is an anachronism, or that the historical Theopompus and the tragedian Theodectus relate stories which are difficult to believe.[4] This also applies to events which occupy even more space in the Letter than the main theme of the tale, such as the speech of the High priest regarding the Jewish dietary laws. Similarly, the fact that Aristeas lived after the events he relates is irrelevant to this discussion – most ancient histories were written by men who lived after the events they record.

There is however one exception to this general rule. This occurs in the main theme of Aristeas. The detail is peripheral to the main theme in the sense that it could be omitted without leaving a gap. On the other hand, if only for the reason that it occurs within the main theme, it is highly significant for the discussion here. This is the 'detail' of the involvement of Demetrius of Phalerum, which could be omitted from

---

[3] See N. L. Collins, The Library in Alexandria and the Bible in Greek (Leiden 2000); a preliminary study came to the same conclusions: see N. L. Collins, '281 BCE: The Date of the Translation of the Pentateuch into Greek under Ptolemy II', in G. J. Brooke & B. Lindars (eds), *The Septuagint and its Relations to the Dead Sea Scrolls and Other Writings* (SBLSCS 33; Atlanta 1992), 403-503.
[4] Let.Aris.180, 200, 318. For a fuller list of objections to the historicity of Aristeas, see P. W. Wendland, 'Aristeas, Letter of', in *The Jewish Encyclopedia*, Vol. 2 (New York-London, 1903), 92-93.

the story without leaving a trace by assigning all responsibility for the translation to Ptolemy II as Philo has shown.[5] For Philo therefore, Ptolemy is the only Greek in the tale, while for Aristeas, it is Demetrius who both inspires and ensures the project's success, while Ptolemy provides only the resources which facilitate the deed. Unless therefore the description by Aristeas of Demetrius was an historical fact, it is difficult to explain why he features at all, and especially why he plays so prominent a role. Needless to say, the detractors of Aristeas and the role of Demetrius have an explanation to hand. According to their theory, Demetrius is merely a symbol of Hellenistic approval for the literature of the Jews.[6] But then why does his role in Aristeas eclipse that of Ptolemy II? Did the king need the prior approval of his Demetrius? The description of Demetrius by Aristeas, along with the fact that there is little reason to doubt the claim of Aristeas that Demetrius was employed by Ptolemy II, increase the probability that Demetrius of Phalerum played a major role in the translation of the Hebrew Pentateuch into Greek.

(3) The Translation was Destined for a Non-Jewish Source

A further indication of the non-Jewish, Greek inspiration for the translation project is indicated by the fact that the translation was destined for the library in Alexandria. This is recorded by Aristeas, Josephus, and also Epiphanius, the only source to note specifically that the completed translation was deposited in the library.[7]

The library was part of the Temple of the Muses, a religious institution in the eyes of the Greeks.[8] For the Jews however, it could only have been considered a most heathen place. It is thus unlikely that they would have joyfully translated their most holy book for eventual storage in a Greek temple, where it would be treated like any secular book. Although there is no ultimate proof for this view, and we are dealing

---

[5] Philo, Mos. II.31-44.
[6] For example, J. F. J. Foakes and K. Lake, *The Beginnings of Christianity*, Vol. 1 (London, 1920), 153; H. M. Orlinsky, 'The Septuagint and its Hebrew Texts', in W. D. Davies and L. Finkelstein (eds), *The Cambridge History of Judaism*, Vol. II (Cambridge 1989), 141-42.
[7] Let. Aris. 10; Josephus, Ant. 12.36,48; Epiphanius, 'On Weights and Measures', in J. E. Dean, *Epiphanius' Treatise on Weights and Measures* (Chicago 1935), § 53c.
[8] R. Pfeiffer, *History of Classical Scholarship* (Oxford 1968), 98.

here with a translation rather than the Hebrew Pentateuch itself, our knowledge of the veneration of Judaism for the Pentateuch, a text transmitted directly from God, strongly suggests that this is the case.[9] In addition to the yet unexplained observation of the tannaim that the rolls of Scripture render the hands ritually unclean, this veneration also included practical rules (m.Yad. 3.5). The special rules for writing the Torah are well known – Aristeas himself notes that at a time when other 'books' were written on parchment, the Hebrew Pentateuch was still written on skins (Let. Aris. 4). Less familiar perhaps are the practical directives on how the Torah should be stored and even how it should be opened and read for private study. The text of Masseketh Sefer Torah, a work said to antedate the second century CE, thus cites a statement attributed to the tanna Rabbi Nehemiah: 'It is not permissible to place it [=a Torah scroll] over a chair [with its sheets] hanging down while it is read in the manner of ordinary documents because [sacred] books must not be treated with disrespect'.[10] Similar veneration of a practical kind is shown in an unattributed and therefore possibly early mishnah, which directs that the strict sabbath rule prohibiting the carrying of objects on the sabbath must be relaxed in order to save a sacred book from fire (m. Shab.16.1).[11] The surprising, complete absence of any reference to Torah scrolls in accounts of the sacking of the first Temple by Nebuchadnezzar or the second by Titus (including the absence of the scrolls on Titus' Arch) may suggest that special arrangements were made to prevent non-Jewish possession of this sacred text. It may of course be argued that a copy of the translation in the library was the price extracted by Ptolemy for his help in the task. Even so, it is difficult to believe that Jewish co-operation would have been willingly offered to make a carefully prepared version of the most sacred of Jewish texts, which would be housed in a building which promoted practices and ideas abhorrent to Judaism, and which would be handled (in Jewish eyes) in a way that could

---

[9] For the transmission of the Pentateuch, see m. Avot 1.1.
[10] I. Slotki, 'Sefer Torah', Chapter 3, Rule 9, in A. Cohen (ed.), *The Minor Tractates of the Torah*, Vol. 2 (London 1965), 638.
[11] For the many customs recorded in the Jerusalem and Babylonian Talmuds reflecting the sanctity of the written Hebrew Pentateuch, see *Enclyclopaedia Judaica*, Vol. 14 (1971), s.v. 'Sepher Torah'.

not reflect Jewish veneration and belief. On these considerations alone it is unlikely that the project of the translation was conceived by the Jews.

III. Evidence for Jewish Opposition to the Translation

In addition to his claim that the translation was the result of a project of the Greeks, a careful examination of Aristeas also records hints of Jewish opposition to the plan that Ptolemy proposed, whose evidence and implications scholars have simply ignored. These can be found in (1) the letter of the High Priest Eleazar to Ptolemy II, (2) the role of Demetrius, especially in the ceremony on the Pharos, when he read the Greek text to the Jews, (3) the famous incident of the freeing of the Jewish slaves, (4) the mixed Jewish reception to the translation, (5) the changing Jewish attitude to the translation and (6) the contradictions in Aristeas.

(1) The Words of the High Priest

According to the words of the High Priest Eleazar writing in response to Ptolemy's command, the translation was 'unnatural', the Jews would co-operate only to fulfil Ptolemy's 'desire' and the translation would be made in the way that Ptolemy proposed – or, as stated in the text, the way that was 'expedient' to him – that is, not in the way that the Jews would have liked. The relevant sections are italicized below:

> ... Everything which is to your advantage, *even if it is unnatural* (εἰ παρὰ φύσιν), we will carry out ... The whole multitude [of the Jews] made supplication that it should come to pass *for you entirely as you desire* (σοι γένηται καθὼς προαιρῇ) ... and that the translation of the sacred Law should come to pass in a manner *expedient to you* (σοι συμφερόντως) (Let. Aris. 4).

These phrases may be considered as diplomatic politeness from the priest to the king. But as one scholar is reluctantly forced to note, 'we may see [here] a hint of misgivings at the prospect of translating Scriptures into an alien language.'[12] In any case, the speech of the priest hardly expresses the positive sentiments of those who were pressing for a translation to be made. Even if the wishes of the king were conceded by

---

[12] M. Hadas, *Aristeas to Philocrates (Letter of Aristeas)* (New York 1951), 117, in relation to 'even if it is unnatural'.

the Jews as the price of his cooperation (although it might be expected that for a project designed for Jewish religious needs, the work would be done in a way pleasing to the Jews), why should the translation be described as 'unnatural'? At the very least, it must be assumed that the High Priest was opposed to the proposal of the king.

(2) The Role of Demetrius of Phalerum

Unless the inspiration for the translation came from a non-Jewish source and was composed originally for a non-religious use, it is difficult to explain why, according to Aristeas, it was the *non*-Jewish Demetrius, rather than an official Jewish spokesman, who read the words of the translation to the Jewish congregation which assembled on the Pharos when the work was complete (Let. Aris. 308). If the Jews needed the translation for liturgical use (as is fashionably alleged), this ceremony must represent the acceptance or sanctification of the text. But apart from the fact that no ancient religious system would be likely to allow a complete outsider to take a major role in even one of its ceremonies, there is otherwise no other record within Judaism which implies that the authority for a Jewish religious text was accepted by Jews from a non-Jewish source, which Demetrius represents here. This is all the more unlikely when the text in question is the most sacred of all – the Pentateuch itself. The role of Demetrius thus only makes sense if the translation was not intended for holy use. It is even possible that the Jews exploited a natural wish of Demetrius to play a major role at the final event, in order to make this fact clear.

Similarly, it is difficult to accept that any religious group would allow an outsider a role in the composition of a major religious text, as is described for Demetrius when he took part in the actual act of translation by recording what the translators had agreed: 'The result of their [=the translators'] agreement was thus made into writing under the direction of Demetrius' (Let. Aris. 302).

It could be argued that the involvement of Demetrius reveals Ptolemy's price for his cooperation with the Jews. But why should Demetrius be involved in a translation that the Jews wanted for themselves? The incongruity of this role of Demetrius may have been recognised by Josephus, who therefore omitted this detail.

The role of Demetrius in coordinating the text of the translation strongly suggests that there was no Jewish intention to use the text for themselves. This being the case, the motivation for making the translation could not have been religious, as far as the Jews were concerned, but that ultimate responsibility for the project lay with Demetrius and the Greeks, rather than the Jews, who only facilitated the task.

(3) The Freeing of the Jewish Slaves

Perhaps the clearest evidence for the wish of the Jews not to translate the Pentateuch into Greek can be seen in the famous story of the liberation of the Jewish slaves by Ptolemy II. If the original request for a translation came from the Jews (as it is fashionable to allege), it is then rather odd that having gained at least a hint of royal cooperation for the translation, the Jews then made a second demand *which had already been refused several times in the past* which was breathtaking in extent, both financially and economically, namely, when they asked for the freedom of over 100,000 Jewish slaves, including 30,000 trained, working soldiers (Let. Aris. 12-27).[13] At the very least, the Jewish courtiers who made this request must have been aware of the great expense this would entail, which, in the event, amounted to around 660 talents (Let. Aris. 27).[14] Considered merely from a diplomatic point of view, it was surely unwise to anticipate the cooperation of the king in the translation, and then to make a further request which might endanger the earlier pledge of co-operation by the king, especially since it was likely to be dismissed, having already been refused several times in the past (Let. Aris. 12). This reaction is confirmed by noting that the cooperation of the Jews to their own request was conditional on Ptolemy's acquiescence to their further demand. In other words, fashionable theory suggests that the Jews made a request which Ptolemy granted. They then made a further, outrageous request, whose compliance by Ptolemy was conditional for their own cooperation to their first request. This is a nonsense. However these events are viewed, they do not make sense if the request for the translation came from the Jews.

---

[13] See Hadas, *Aristeas to Philocrates*, 104.
[14] For the total cost see W. L. Westermann, *Upon Slavery in Ptolemaic Egypt* (New York 1929), 40.

Jewish Ways of Reading the Bible

The only logical explanation for the extraordinary Jewish request to free the Jewish slaves must be deduced directly from the facts that Aristeas states. According to Aristeas Ptolemy II asked the Jews to translate their holy text. Compliance with this request would fulfil Ptolemy's desire for 'great glory' (μεγάλην δόξαν), achieved in this case by the acquisition of books (Let. Aris. 39).[15] The Jews however wanted to refuse, but could not, or did not wish refuse in an obvious way. They were, after all, the subject people of a king whose ruthlessness is revealed by the execution of two of his own elder brothers, probably early in his reign, because, as elder brothers, they had a better claim to the throne (Appian xi 10.62). The Jews could not therefore openly refuse Ptolemy's request. What could they do? Before replying to Ptolemy's command, they asked Ptolemy a favour in return. The favour they asked was one which Ptolemy had several times refused, and was likely therefore to refuse once again (Let. Aris. 12). This would provide an excellent excuse for the Jewish refusal for Ptolemy's request. Ptolemy however unexpectedly agreed. As a result, the Jews had little option but to comply with his request. The Jewish appeal for the freedom of the slaves was thus a subtle attempt to refuse Ptolemy's command, which failed.

The Jewish demand for the freedom of the slaves thus reveals the strength of Jewish opposition to Ptolemy's request. As will be increasingly evident as this study proceeds, the Jews did not want or need a written translation of the Pentateuch into Greek, and Ptolemy's request was not a task that they wished to undertake. It is not relevant here whether the Jewish request for the slaves reflects an historical fact, a question which has received much attention in the past. Such a debate has diverted attention from the equally important question – what is the underlying reason for the Jewish demand in the context of the tale that Aristeas relates?[16] The reason behind the Jewish request outlined above makes sense in the context that Aristeas provides, whether or not the event actually took place. If it did not, Aristeas may be commended

---

[15] For the books, see Let. Aris. 9; Josephus, Ant. 12.16.
[16] Hadas, Aristeas to Philocrates, 28-32, suggests that the decree of Ptolemy II (Let. Aris. 22-25) may be based on P. Rainier 24,552.

for the invention of a story which subtly concealed the Jewish opposition to Ptolemy's request for the Jews to translate the Pentateuch into Greek.

(4) A Mixed Jewish Reception to the Completed Translation

According to Aristeas, the Jewish leaders did not even expect to keep a completed copy of the translation for themselves. It seems that a group of Jewish people, named earlier by Aristeas as τὸ πλῆθος (Let. Aris. 308), asked Demetrius to supply their leaders with a copy after they had heard a reading of the completed work: 'And they [τὸ πλῆθος] asked him [=Demetrius] to have a transcription of the entire Law made and to present it to their leaders' (Let. Aris. 309).

If the Jews needed the translation, why did they not make a copy for themselves? It is also rather strange that the copy was requested by those for whom Aristeas uses the possibly derogatory term τὸ πλῆθος, 'the mob', rather than by the Jewish leaders.[17] It can only be assumed that those who were influential in the community were not concerned with the translation, and that interest in the text came from another source. Finally, it is odd that Demetrius was asked to arrange a copy of the text. Even if Ptolemy II had demanded the original text of the translation as a price for his cooperation, surely the Jews would have made a copy for themselves, if this is what they originally planned? It was moreover well known that copies of a text were inferior to the original, because of the changes, both deliberate and accidental, that could arise during the copying of a text. Such changes were thus avoided by Ptolemy III, who decided to keep the originals of a text and to return only the copies.[18] The Jews had their own system for preventing alterations when copying texts.[19] If they indeed had to make do with a copy, they would hardly have asked the Greek Demetrius to organize the work. These details however make perfect sense if it was Ptolemy who originally wanted the translation, and if, when the work was complete, the Jewish people, perhaps recognising only the potential use of the translation, asked Demetrius

---

[17] Galen, Comm. in Hipp. Epidem. 3, reprinted by P. M. Fraser, *Ptolemaic Alexandria*, Vol. 2 (Oxford 1972), 480-81.
[18] Galen, Comm. in Hipp. Epidem. 3.
[19] t. Sof. 1-10; t. Meg. 18b.

for a copy for their leaders.

Further dissent of Jewish leaders is implied by Aristeas when he gives a list of those who publicly declared that the translation should not be changed (on the significance of this declaration, see below), 'the priests and the elders of the translators, and *some of* (τῶν ἀπο) the corporate body and the leaders of the people' (Let. Aris. 310). Why not 'all of' rather than 'some of'? The detail must be significant because Josephus takes the trouble to remove 'some of' and to include 'all' the corporate body (see below). Aristeas thus suggests that some of the officials of the Jewish people in Alexandria (the politeuma) did not even want to take part in a declaration for the preservation of the translated text. They may have included those who had originally opposed the translation, but who were eventually overruled.

(5) Changing Status of the Completed Translation (Let. Aris. 308-11)

The initiative of Ptolemy rather than the Jews is also indicated by a comparison of the two Jewish declarations that (according to Aristeas) were made at the ceremony on the Pharos, to celebrate the completion of the translation (Let. Aris. 308-11). A close examination suggests that these two declarations come from two different times, and show a dramatic change in attitude to the translation, of a type that makes it unlikely that the translation was originally intended for liturgical use. This being the case, it is unlikely that the translation was made at the request of the Jews. Rather, the initiative came from Ptolemy II.

Aristeas implies that although the Jewish leaders may have been initially reluctant to comply with Ptolemy's request (as can be seen by the speech of the High Priest and by the story of the freeing of the Jewish salves), the final translation aroused respect. This is suggested not only by those ordinary Jews who asked Demetrius for a copy (see above) but by the presence of the translators and the Jewish dignitaries of Alexandria at the ceremony to celebrate the translation (Let. Aris. 308). But this official Jewish presence does not mean that the translation was intended for Jewish liturgical use. The latter has been deduced from the fact that the ceremony was held on the Pharos, rather than in Alexandria, which would probably have been more convenient (in view of the difficulties in approaching the Pharos), in view of the alleged Jewish tradition that a ceremony of commemoration should take place on the same spot as the original event as for example, the ceremony for the acceptance of the Hebrew Pentateuch was conducted where it was offered by God (Let. Aris. 308).[20] But this is a distracting, irrelevant observation, which gives the misleading impression that some kind of religious ceremony also took place on the Pharos. If indeed this were the case, the ceremony would have celebrated the translated text and would have canonised its religious use in some way. But this is impossible in view of the fact that the non-Jewish Demetrius of Phalerum read the translation to the assembled crowd. As noted above, the idea that an ancient and conservative religious organisation such as Judaism would allow its holiest text to be read aloud at a ceremony *for the religious acceptance of that very text*, by an outsider of the group, who actively subscribed to a pagan cult (as can be seen from the paeans that he composed to Sarapis) must be dismissed. The major participation of Demetrius proves that the ceremony on the Pharos was not a Jewish religious ceremony of any kind. It was merely a ceremony of respect for the newly translated, written text.

It is against this background that we must evaluate the significance the first declaration of the Jews at the ceremony on the Pharos: 'Inasmuch as the translation has been well and piously made and is in every respect accurate, it is right that it should remain in its present form and that no revision should take place [μὴ γένηται μηδεμία διασκευή]' (Let. Aris. 310). In the context that it stands, this declaration is evidence only of respect for the integrity and preservation of the text. There is no indication here that the translation was intended for liturgical use, or was given divine status of any kind. This is in accord with common sense. The many modern corrections of ancient texts show that there was no guarantee that a text would be preserved in its pristine state, and that changes, both deliberate and accidental could occur. Reference has already been made to the fact that Ptolemy III tried to avoid the

---

[20] Exod. 24:1ff.; cf. Exod. 19:1ff.; this point is observed by H. M. Orlinsky, 'The Septuagint and its Hebrew Texts', 543-44.

changes that might arise through the copying of a text, by keeping the originals and returning only the copies.[21] It is well known also that changes occurred when texts were cited from memory. In addition, a special danger of *deliberate* change surely existed in relation to the translation. When it was first complete, however elaborate and costly its production, and however much ceremony heralded its fruition, the translation was still essentially an offshoot of a more illustrious work, rather than a text within its own right. The words of the translation were thus entirely dependent on whatever single meaning was attributed to its underlying Hebrew source. At such a time, the translation was surely prone to as many deliberate changes in its text as there were differences of opinion on its underlying source. Hence the first Jewish declaration reported by Aristeas reveals nothing more than recognition of the dangers that awaited a newly-born text, coupled with a respect for the translation as a translation, which should be preserved as it stood.

This is confirmed when we consider the second Jewish declaration cited by Aristeas. This appears at first sight to be a mere elaboration of the first. But in the light of Jewish commentaries and belief, the differences are more significant than they first appear. This second declaration specifies precisely that there should be no 'addition', 'transposition' or 'excision' of the translated Greek text, and warns that such changes will be punished by a curse: '[The Jewish community] bade that a curse be pronounced regarding to their custom, upon any who should revise (διασκευάσαι) the text [of the translation] by adding (προστιθεὶς) or transposing (μεταφέρων) anything whatever in what had been written down, or by making any excision (ἀφαίρεσιν)' (Let. Aris. 311).

As scholars have noted, the words of Aristeas echo the text of Deut. 4:2 and Deut. 12:32, 'Ye shall not add (προσθήσεις) unto the word which I command you, neither shall you diminish (ἀφελεῖς) it'. Jewish tradition understands this edict as an absolute command to preserve, *inter alia*, the integrity of the Hebrew Pentateuch which

---

[21] Galen, Comm. in Hipp. Epidem. 3 (see n. 17).

according to traditional Jewish belief) records the original, spoken words of God.[22] In typical rabbinic style, which gives an example instead of stating a principle, the tannaitic commentary Sifre Deuteronomy thus notes:

> Whence do we learn that if one has already commenced to recite the priestly blessing, he should not say, 'Since I have already commenced the blessing, I will go on to say, "The Lord, God of you fathers, make you a thousand times (so many more as ye are, and bless you)"[Deut. 1:11]'? From the expression 'this word' [at Deut. 4:2] – [therefore] do not add even one word (Sifre [Deut.], Piska 82).

The application of this principle to the text of the Pentateuch is manifest particularly in the strict precautions which are taken to preserve the text. Philo thus notes in his comment on Deut. 12:32,

> '... all the laws originally ordained should be kept unaltered just as they were. For what actually happens, as we clearly see, is that it is the unjust which is added and the just which is taken away, for the wise legislator has omitted nothing [from the text] which can give possession of justice whole and complete' (Spec. IV.143).

The transference by Aristeas of this statement from the Hebrew to the Greek Pentateuch thus indicates a belief that both the Hebrew and Greek texts should be venerated in the same way.[23] This can only mean that according to Aristeas, the Greek translation was divinely inspired, in a way similar to the Hebrew Pentateuch itself.

The fact that Aristeas does not express this declaration in exactly the same words as the Greek Pentateuch does not negate this view. Philo, who certainly believed in the divine origin of the translation, also expresses the same prohibitions which themselves appear to add to the Pentateuchal text, and thus also contradict the very command that he claims to observe.[24] Philo however uses similar vocabulary as Aristeas for individual prohibitions, although he presents them in a different order. The variation in order may suggest that Aristeas and Philo are using versions of a Jewish Greek, oral commentary on Deut. 4:2.

---

[22] See Hadas, *Aristeas to Philocrates*, 221, and the rabbinic references to Deut. 4:2 at m. Zev. 8:10; t. Zev. 8.22; b. 'Eruv. 96a, 100a; b. R. ha-Sh. 28b; to Deut. 12:32 at Sifre (Deut.), Piska 82.

[23] Hadas, *Aristeas to Philocrates*, 69.

[24] Philo, De Vit.Mos.II.34: 'Reflecting how great an understanding it was to make a full version of the laws given by the Voice of God, where they could not take away or add or transfer anything (μήτ' ἀφελεῖν τι μήτε προσθεῖναι ἢ μεταθεῖναι) but must keep the original form and shape.'

The second Jewish declaration in Aristeas thus suggests that the translation was now regarded as similar in sanctity to the text from which it was derived. Since divine creations must ultimately be the responsibility of God, it is clear that the translation was no longer considered as a mere offshoot of its parent, but as an independent text in its own right. This is emphasised by the curse expressed by Aristeas, which is not present in any relevant rabbinic Jewish commentaries, and suggests an even stricter attitude (if this can be imagined) to the preservation of the Greek Pentateuch than the corresponding Hebrew text. The change from polite respect for the translation in the first Jewish declaration, to a belief that the translation was divinely inspired is dramatic, and can only have come about with the passage of time. It is thus reasonable to assume that the first declaration belongs to the time of the translation (probably in 281 BCE), and the second probably to the later time of Aristeas.

This conclusion explains several difficulties in the text: (1) If both declarations were intended as commands to preserve the integrity of the text, and one is simply an elaboration of the other, why are there two? Surely only one, the second more elaborate declaration, would have sufficed? The presence of two when only the second would suffice can be explained on the basis that Aristeas has recorded the history of the event in which the first declaration was made, and has added later material from his own time. (2) This also accounts for the fact that the declarations are not continuous, but are separated by a short break. (3) It also accounts for the illogical content of the break, which consists of the assent of the people and the curse. As a result, only the first declaration is given assent, while only the second is affected by the curse. Logically, the assent and the curse should apply to both declarations, and should therefore either preface or follow both. Again, this can be explained on the basis that Aristeas inherited an account of the ceremony on the Pharos which included the first declaration and its assent, to which he then added the second declaration and its accompanying curse, so that the assent and the curse became a bridge between the two. (4) This also accounts for the brevity of his references to the assent and the curse, which unlike the declarations are not quoted verbatim. As they appear, however, they give the impression of continuity for the two declarations, which implies that they were part of the same prayer and made at the same time. This is a mark of the technique of Aristeas, which is revealed by a close analysis of his text. The first declaration probably originally ended with the words 'And all assented to what had been said'. When the second declaration was added, the conjunction was removed and a genitive absolute put in its place so that 'When they had all assented to what had been said' became the seamless introduction to the second declaration.

Seen in this way, the two Jewish declarations highlight a fundamental change in attitude and use towards the Greek translation. The first shows an attitude of simple respect for the text, and the second, a belief in the sacred nature of the text. The latter is bolstered by the feeling of awe for the translation that pervades Aristeas, and by his allusions to the mysterious coincidences of the number seventy-two – the seventy-two translators, the seventy-two questions of the king and the seventy-two days in which the translation was made – which give the impression that the translation was miraculous, and must therefore have been divinely inspired. These details are however superfluous to the tale. It seems that Aristeas has reported the history of an event which was based on a written source, on to which he imposed his own later belief.[25]

If the translation was used in the synagogue as soon as it was complete, why was it later given divine status of some kind? If it later needed this status to enable its use in the synagogue, why was it not given to the translation when the work was first made? The change in status of the translation, from a secular to a divine book, suggests that it was not originally conceived for liturgical use.

(6) The Contradictions in Aristeas

The discussion so far suggests that Aristeas has recorded several different Jewish attitudes towards the translation of the Pentateuch into Greek, of which none are in accord with his own. His story concerns the initiative of Demetrius of Phalerum, who suggested to his employer Ptolemy II that he should acquire a translation of the

---

[25] Thus, H. M. Orlinsky, 'The Septuagint and its Hebrew Texts', 542-48.

Hebrew Pentateuch in Greek to add to his stock of library books. The Jews were thus faced with a request from Ptolemy II, to translate the Pentateuch into Greek. The Jewish leaders, including the High Priest of Jerusalem, wanted to refuse, and Jewish officials in Ptolemy's court tried to create a situation in which they would be able politely to decline. Their subterfuge failed when Ptolemy agreed to their outrageous request (which had several times already been refused) to free the Jewish slaves, and the Jews were thus obliged to fulfil the royal demand. Having promised their cooperation, it seems that the project was then given whole-hearted support. When the translation was complete, a majority of the Jewish leaders showed their respect, and in an age when texts were liable to alterations, both deliberate and accidental, declared that the completed text should be permanently preserved. But the Jews did not even keep a copy of the work for themselves, and a group of people who tried to remedy this lack by asking Demetrius for a copy for their leaders are deprecatingly called 'the mob'. There is thus no indication at this stage in its history that the translation was intended for religious use or that it was honoured in any way as sacred.

On to this story, Aristeas then imposed his own later belief in the sanctity of the text. This can be seen in the second declaration of the Jews on the Pharos, the three allusions to the number seventy-two, and a general feeling of awe for the translation which pervades his account.

It is obvious however that in accordance with this belief, Aristeas would have preferred a basic history of the text in which, from the very beginning, the Jews wanted the translation and considered the translation as divinely inspired, and in which the role of the Greeks was much reduced. What religious group would admit to the possession of a holy book that was inspired by a complete outsider to that religion, and was reluctantly compiled by the members of the religious group? Aristeas however does not alter his history, perhaps in the interests of historical accuracy. But the fact that he retains details in his account which do not support his own attitude and are therefore not in his interests to retain suggests that those details which conflict with his ideas are indeed details from an earlier written history of the event. The many hints in Aristeas noted above which suggest that the Jews were reluctant to make the translation, and that the translation was the initiative of the Greeks, are thus probably correct.

One other of these contradictions can now be discussed. This is the fact that according to Aristeas, a group identified as τὸ πλῆθος ask Demetrius to give the Jewish leaders a copy of the translation (Let. Aris. 309). The identity of these people is unclear. This is because Aristeas arranges his text to make it seem that the translators themselves ask for a copy of the text. This is achieved by distancing the term πλῆθος from the specific request, and also by an intervening reference to 'the translators':

> When the work was completed, Demetrius assembled the community of Jews (τὸ πλῆθος τῶν Ἰουδαίων) at the place where the translation was made, and read it out to the entire gathering, *the translators too being present*. These received a great ovation from the community also in recognition of the great service for which they were responsible, and they accorded Demetrius a similar reception, and requested him to have a transcription of the entire Law made and to present it to their rulers (Let. Aris. 308-309).

Why does Aristeas arrange the text in this way? The answer may lie in the superimposition of his beliefs on an earlier account, which Aristeas used as his source. In this earlier account, the official Jewish community took no interest in the translation, other than according it nominal respect. There were however a group of people who opposed this stance (perhaps they realised the potential use of the translation) and asked for a copy of the translated text. Since they opposed the official attitude of the Jews, they are identified with the neutral, bordering on non-complimentary term τὸ πλῆθος. Aristeas however would have commended the action of this group because their request for a copy complimented his own belief in the sanctity of the text (who would not want a copy of a divinely inspired text?). Aristeas therefore distracted attention from the derogatory nature of this term by constructing his text to give the impression that τὸ πλῆθος was in some way allied with the translators, who are likely to have wanted a copy of their text. Hence the obscurity in Aristeas of the identity of those who asked for a copy of the text. It is interesting that Josephus removes the obscurity of Aristeas and makes it perfectly clear that the πλῆθος wanted a copy, because this suits his aim in presenting the unanimous opinion of the Jews that the translation was not divinely inspired (see below).

There is little doubt therefore that although the history of the translation was written by an author who would have supported the idea that the translation was the result of Jewish initiative and need, the history written by this author indicates that the Jews did not want or request a translation of the Hebrew Pentateuch into Greek, for liturgical or any other use. The claim of Aristeas for divine status for the text does not however prove that even by the time of Aristeas, the translation had passed into liturgical use. If indeed this was the case, it is possible that the translation was used as a kind of Targum, in place of (or alongside) the Aramaic Targum, which was used as a translation for the Pentateuchal portion read in the synagogue every week.[26] Targum however, although used in the synagogue, never acquired a sacred status. On the other hand, Targum had been introduced apparently with no opposition by Ezra the Scribe, and was not a written, literal text. Perhaps therefore Targum did not need the endorsement of divine origins for its use, unlike the literal, written Greek translation which the Jewish leaders had tried to suppress. Although therefore an equation between the alleged sanctity of the translation and its use in the synagogue should not automatically be assumed, it possible that by the time of Aristeas, when sacred status of some kind was finally accepted for the translation by a majority of the Jewish leaders, the translation was incorporated into liturgical use.

The later perceived sanctity of the translation is important for a question which no one would have asked when the translation was made: 'Who wanted the Hebrew Pentateuch in Greek?' If a history of the translation shows the initial opposition of the Jews, with the result that a copy of the translation was not even owned by the Jewish leaders when it was first made, and if the text achieved or needed to achieve divine status of some kind before it was used in the synagogue, it can be concluded, yet again, that it is unlikely that the translation was used in the synagogue when it was first

---

[26] The translation may also have been used as a substitute for the Shema, which consists almost solely of quotations from the Pentateuch.

complete, so that it is unlikely that the translation was requested by the Jews. In other words, the request for the translation came from the Greeks, as Aristeas records.

IV. Philo's Account of the Translation

As will be seen below, Philo continues the fight to prove the divine origins of the translation, but at the cost of sacrificing the logic of his account. Philo, along with Josephus, also tries to answer the question posed here: 'Why was the translation made by the Jews?' Both writers offer different explanations, but neither confirm that the translation was made for liturgical use. This lack of corroboration for the modern theory in sources which were relatively close to events should be a cause of concern to those who are content to repeat the theory that the translation was made at the request of the Jews, because they had forgotten 'their holy tongue'. If this is true, why did Philo and Josephus conceal this fact, and why did they provide alternative views? It is interesting to note that the Jews never concealed the use of the Aramaic targum.

Unlike Aristeas, Philo's motivation in referring to the translation was not basically historical, but coincides with the reason he offers for the making of this text. Philo thus claims that the translation was made to show how 'the greater part, or even the whole of the human race might be profited and led to a better life by continuing to observe such wise and truly admirable ordinances' (Mos. II.32, 36). This is in accord with Philo's mission of Jewish apologetic to the Hellenistic world. In contrast with Aristeas who tries to justify Jewish practice (for example, in the speech of the High Priest, which rationalises the dietary laws [Let. Aris. 128-71]), Philo suggests that the Greek Pentateuch was produced in order to spread the ideas of Judaism in the non-Jewish world. This idea is implicitly supported by Philo's allusions to the divine origin of the Pentateuchal text.

The reason suggested by Philo for the origin of the translation indicates the two major constraints on his history of this work. Firstly, if indeed the Pentateuch was divinely inspired and was translated by the Jews in order to spread knowledge of Judaism within the Greek world, Philo must suggest that the Jews were always totally committed to the task. Secondly, since is unlikely that Ptolemy II wished to bring about the adoption of Judaism in his realm (which Philo proclaims was the reason for translating the Pentateuch into Greek), if the Ptolemy or the Greeks contributed to the translation in any way, the Greek contribution must be seen to be minimal in extent.

The first of these requirements – to show the constant enthusiasm of the Jews – is realised by Philo in several ways. Philo claims that the high priest at the time of the translation supported the project from the very first. Apparently, he was 'naturally pleased' at Ptolemy's request, and 'thinking that God's guiding care must have led the king to busy himself in such an undertaking', sought out the best translators whom he 'joyfully' sent to the king (Mos. II.32). This contrasts sharply with the muted criticism and distinct lack of enthusiasm of the High Priest in Aristeas. Philo also omits the Jewish request to free the slaves, probably the incident which more than any demonstrates the reluctance of the Jews to comply with the request of Ptolemy to translate the Hebrew text. But this reluctance is not in Philo's interests to show. In view of the popularity of this story in the many accounts, there is little doubt that he knew the story of the slaves, and his omission was deliberate, motivated by his understanding of the significance of this event. What could be more damaging to Philo's claim that the Jews wanted to make a translation but yet adopted a strategy which would defeat this aim, if Ptolemy II had refused their outrageous request?

Similarly, Aristeas' description of the ceremony on the Pharos posed a problem for Philo. On the one hand it fits with Philo's desire to show a positive Jewish attitude towards the translation. Nevertheless, the presence of Demetrius of Phalerum, whose involvement may have become a traditional part of the story (since he appears in Aristeas) suggests that the project of the translation was, at the very least, partly an initiative of the Greeks, an impression that Philo would have wished to avoid. This problem was solved by omitting the ceremony completely from his work. This facilitated his omission of the first Jewish declaration, which, apart from suggesting (to those who knew) a less than adulatory Jewish attitude to the translation, is also superfluous in view of the second declaration of the Jews. The latter however, as described above, which prohibited 'removal' or 'addition' or 'transposition' of the Greek text, was in Philo's interests to retain, because it reveals the Jewish belief in the divine origin of the Hebrew text, and thus by transference, of the Greek text as well. Philo therefore took what he may have considered this one important detail of the ceremony on the Pharos, which he placed in the minds of the translators, even before the work was begun. This was because the translators are the only group of Jews who appear in his account, and therefore the only group of people to whom this declaration could apply. There is moreover no other place in Philo's account for them to make this declaration, because Philo has no gathering of the translators after the translation is complete. But, as the following paragraphs will show, this placement produces several problems in his text.

Philo thus claims that when the translators planned their translation, they anticipated that their text would be preserved with the same strict prohibitions as the Hebrew Pentateuch itself. By transference of this thought to the as yet unwritten Greek Pentateuch, they therefore expected, like prophets, to produce a divinely inspired text:

> Reflecting how great an undertaking it was to make *a full version of the laws given by the Voice of God, where they could not add or take away or transfer anything*, but must keep the original form and shape, they [=the translators] proceeded to look for the most open and unoccupied spot in the neighbourhood outside the city. For, within the walls, it was full of every kind of living creatures, and consequently the prevalence of diseases and deaths and the impure conduct of the healthy inhabitants made them suspicious of it. In front of Alexandria lies the island of Pharos, stretching with its narrow strip of land towards the city, and enclosed by a sea not deep but mostly consisting of shoals, so that the loud din and booming of the surging waves grows faint through the long distance before it reaches the land ... [The resulting Greek text corresponded so perfectly with the Hebrew text that] people speak of the authors not as translators but as prophets and priests of the mysteries, whose sincerity and singleness of thought has enabled them to go hand in hand with the purest of spirits, the spirit of Moses (Mos. II.34,40).

Philo's reference to the search of the translators for the 'most open and unoccupied spot' is a clear allusion to the traditional Jewish justification for the fact that the Jews received the Pentateuch from God in the open desert of Sinai, and implies Philo's belief that the Greek translation was similarly inspired and therefore sacred.[27] For Philo, the question 'Why was the Torah received at Sinai?' had become, 'Why was the Greek Pentateuch received on the Pharos?', and the answer to the first question provided the answer to both. But unfortunately for Philo, although fulfilling the requirement of an 'open, unoccupied and healthy place', the situation ultimately chosen for the translation to emerge (according to Aristeas) was 'close to the shore' (Let. Aris. 301). This feature is important in Aristeas because it enabled the translators to perform the ritual washing of their hands before they started to translate the Hebrew Pentateuchal text (Let. Aris. 306). It was unfortunate for Philo therefore that the area on the Pharos where the translators 'received' their text was very different to the dry, waterless desert of biblical Sinai. Philo attempted to minimize this discrepancy by noting that the sea was 'not deep but mostly consisting of shoals', and far enough from the water so that only a faint sound of the waves reached the place where the translators worked. Although possibly true if there are different tides around the Pharos (of which Philo of Alexandria would have been aware), this contradicts not only Aristeas, but also Philo himself, when he later refers to the yearly festival that was held on the Pharos, at 'the place in which the light of that version first shone out', namely 'the seaside' and the sandy beach (Let. Aris. 301; Mos. II.41-42).

Furthermore, although Philo's attempted link between Sinai and the Pharos is logical in the light of traditional Jewish belief - Philo's argument is that since the Torah was given by God at Sinai, a deserted, open place, it follows therefore that since the translation was made in an open deserted place, it was also given by God - the assumed sanctity of the unwritten text has no direct connection with the prohibitions against changes to the text, defined by Philo in the quotation above as 'addition, removal or transference'. The latter does not prove that the text was holy, but only how those by whom the book was regarded as holy took precautions to ensure it was preserved. It is moreover illogical to prohibit changes to a text that has not yet been produced. A

---

[27] J. Lauterbach, *Mekilta de-Rabbi Ishmael*, Vol. 2 (Philadelphia 1933), 198: Bahodesh 1, commentary on Exod. 19:2.

prohibition against change is only relevant for a text that exists.

A further illogicality in Philo's account stems from the fact that the prohibitions against change are only 'reflections' of the translators, so that the declaration has no communal force. This is the price that Philo must pay for omitting the description by Aristeas of the ceremony on the Pharos. As a result, Philo's translators are the only group of Jews who appear in his account, who declare their opposition to the change of a text that they have not yet even composed. In any case, in such cases where Jewish tradition requires communal assent, it requires the spoken assent of a majority, not merely the thoughts of a section of the community. This appears to go back to Sinai itself: 'And Moses came and called for the elders of the people and set before them all these words which the Lord had commanded him. And *all the people* answered *together* and said: All that the Lord has spoken we will do ... And Moses took the book of the covenant and read it in the hearing of the people, and they said, 'All that the Lord has spoken will we do and obey' (Deut. 19:7, 24:7). Similarly, at the ceremony to confirm the reaping of the Omer in post biblical times, it is the people who are required to voice their consent (m. Men.10:3).

Philo's belief in the divine origins of the translation comes to a climax when he describes the translators at the completion of their task:

> Sitting here in seclusion with none present same the elements of nature, earth, water, air, heaven, the genesis [γενέσεως] of which was to be the first theme of their sacred revelation, for the laws begin with the story of the world's creation, they [=the translators] became as it were possessed, and, under inspiration, wrote, each one something different, but the same word for word, as though dictated [ἐνηχοῦντος] to each by an invisible prompter (Mos. II.37).

At this point in his account, Philo refers to the Jewish belief that there were two major creations of God, the creation of the world, and the creation of the Pentateuch which God conveyed to Moses at Sinai. According to Philo, both these events were echoed when the Pentateuch was translated into Greek. The idea of the translation as a divine creation is conveyed by Philo's claim that each of the men involved with the translation emerged with the same translation, as though 'dictated to each [translator] by an invisible prompter'. It is significant moreover that Philo never refers directly to the

43

translators as 'translators'. The closest they come to any named role is when Ptolemy II asks the High priest to send men who 'expound the [Jewish] law' (τοὺς τὸν νόμον διερμηνεύσοντας, Mos.II.31).[28] Otherwise, Philo never even refers to their facility in Greek. For Philo the translators are simply an anonymous 'they' or 'their', the latter implicit in the person of the verb or number of the participle or noun. In the one instance that he used the term 'translators' (ἑρμηνέας) in the context of the story of the translation, Philo claims that such men should be regarded 'as prophets and priests of the mysteries, whose sincerity and singleness of thought has enabled them to go hand in hand with the purest of spirits, the spirit of Moses' (Mos. II.40). It is clear that Philo wishes to avoid the idea that the translation was achieved though human agents, but stresses that it arose through the intervention of the Divine, and therefore was itself divine. Aristeas, by contrast, wished to write a history of the text, and his reverence for the translation has not obscured his description of the role of the men who gave it birth. Aristeas thus either implies that the men were translators, through their ability in Hebrew and Greek (for example §32, §121) or refers to them specifically as 'translators' (§310, τῶν ἑρμηνέων).

The second act of creation by God – the creation of the world – is evoked by Philo's reference to 'the elements of nature, earth, water, air, heaven', and by the term 'genesis' (the Greek name for the first book of the Pentateuch). Concerning the reception of the Pentateuch by Moses from God, Philo alludes to his traditional Jewish belief that the Hebrew Pentateuch was given 'by the voice of God' to which nothing could be added or subtracted (Mos. II.34).[29] This is indicated by the verb ἐνηχεῖν, 'to teach by word of mouth'.[30]

Philo's further reference to a yearly 'festival and assembly' which had been established by the Jews to celebrate the completion of the translation, shows that his

---

[28] The Loeb translation may be misleading here, giving 'persons to make a full rendering of the Law into Greek'.
[29] Also Migr. 130 which cites LXX Deut. 33:3 (ἐδέξατο ἀπο τῶν λόγων αὐτοῦ) suggesting that the laws of God were received through 'His words'.
[30] H. G. Liddell, R. Scott and H. S. Jones, *A Greek English Lexicon* (Oxford 1968), s.v. ἐνηχεῖν.

attitude to the translation follows a trend of his time. His description refers to 'prayers and thanksgivings', suggests a religious festival of some kind (Mos. II.41). Perhaps the curse, and the second Jewish declaration mentioned by Aristeas at the ceremony on the Pharos after the completion of the translation is a quotation from the liturgy to which Philo refers.

As far as the second of Philo's requirements is concerned – a reduction of the contribution of the Greeks – this is also a problem for those who proclaim that the translation was made on the initiative of the Jews. A recent, scholarly explanation of events which grapples with the problem of how Ptolemy could have been involved if the initiative came from the Jews thus suggests that: 'The translation was an official undertaking, initiated by Jewish rather than Egyptian authority, though it might have been undertaken with the good will, and conceivably the good offices, of Philadelphus'.[31] Why else for example would Ptolemy have brought translators from Jerusalem, whom he housed at Alexandria at great expense? If the Jews had wanted to make a translation, they would surely have made simpler and less costly arrangements, perhaps even writing the translation in Jerusalem, rather than importing translators from Jerusalem to Egypt. This alone helps to confirm that Ptolemy II was somehow involved and must thus somehow be included in the answer to the question 'Why was the Pentateuch translated into Greek?'

Philo must therefore accept the contribution of the Greeks, but minimise it as far as he can. For this reason he chose to omit Demetrius completely from the story and to attribute the undeniable role of the Greeks solely to the King. This delegation to a figurehead of major traditions and events is within the tradition of biblical historiography, in which a king may be held responsible for all the events of his reign, although he may not have suggested or performed them himself. Moreover, as noted above, the absence of Demetrius facilitates the omission of the final ceremony held on the Pharos when the Jews approved of the text which Demetrius read aloud. As

---

[31] S. Jellicoe, *The Septuagint and Modern Study* (Oxford 1968), 55.

noted above, Philo thus loses an opportunity to show general Jewish approval of the translation. Perhaps the connection between Demetrius and the ceremony had become a traditional part of the story, so that Philo could not refer to the ceremony without Demetrius, so that, from Philo's point of view, it was better not to mention the ceremony at all. Similarly, the nonsensical supposition that Ptolemy II would want to place a book in his library which was intended to persuade the Greeks of the advantages of Judaism, and thereby seduce them away from the official cult indicates clearly why Philo makes no mention of the library of the king.

The internal illogicialites noted above are also reflected in the overall account, which is based by Philo on the following plan: Ptolemy II asked the High Priest in Jerusalem to make a translation; the High Priest welcomed the opportunity of spreading Jewish ideas and the final result was a work which was divinely inspired and widely used amongst Jews. However, it is more reasonable to assume that, if Ptolemy asked for a translation, it was for his own secular benefit and use and would not have been considered as divinely inspired. That inspired quality of the translation, as is intimated by Aristeas, came later in the history of the text. As far as the anticipation of the High Priest is concerned, his expressed hope is more likely to reflect the intention of Philo, who devoted his life to the dispersal of Jewish ideas among the Greeks. Perhaps such aims were current among the Jews at the time of the translation. But it is more than suspicious that they coincide with the purpose of the author of the text in which they appear.

In the light of the discussion above, the only historical scenario that makes sense is based on a story in which Ptolemy requested the Jews to make a translation, which they did. The translation was duly given to Ptolemy. The Jews however eventually had a copy made for themselves, which was probably used in the synagogue, thereby changing its status in the eyes of many in the Jewish community from a secular work to a divinely inspired book.

Philo thus wrote to show his belief in the divine inspiration of the text, along with his opinion that it was translated in order to show the wisdom of Judaism to the outside world, a task to which Philo devoted his life. Taken together, they create a strong impression that Philo was dependent on Aristeas, who must therefore precede him in time. Otherwise, it is difficult to explain the overwhelming coincidence of changes made in relation to Aristeas that suit the purpose of Philo, and cause such illogicalities in Philo's text. The latter arise from the fact that, rather than rethinking the history of the translation painted by Aristeas, Philo was content to use Aristeas as a base from which to construct his own account. This suggests that as far as concerns the historical implications of any differences between Philo and Aristeas, the account of Aristeas should be preferred.

The earlier date of Aristeas in relation to Philo is also indicated by a comparison between the main themes of their accounts. Aristeas wrote a history of the text which indicated that the Jews had not wanted to translate the text and that it was not welcomed by all the community even when it was complete. On to this history he superimposed his own belief in the divine inspiration of the text. Philo however minimised the history of the text, eliminating any hint of the opposition of the Jews, and focused his account on displaying the divine inspiration of the text from the moment it was conceived, and even before it was composed. Unlike Aristeas, moreover, he gives a purpose for the divine inspiration, claiming that its function was to spread Judaism to the outside world. Philo thus develops the theme of the divine inspiration of the text, whereas Aristeas simply alludes to the fact.

All in all therefore, Philo confirms the history of the translation given by Aristeas. In spite of Philo's efforts to prove the contrary, the Jews did not want to produce a translation of the Hebrew Pentateuch into Greek.

V. The Attitude of Josephus to the Translation

Josephus also bases his knowledge and account of the translation on Aristeas. However, unlike Aristeas and Philo, who both believed that the Greek translation was divinely inspired, Josephus was of the opinion that the translation was merely an excellent, man-made work. This explains the changes made by Josephus to the account of Aristeas.

Josephus repeats the bulk of Aristeas, including details referring to the involvement of the Greeks, all omitted by Philo, such as the role of Demetrius, the actions of Ptolemy II, and references to the library, where Ptolemy II intended to deposit the translated text (Ant. 12.36, 49). One detail on Demetrius omitted by Josephus is the allegation of Aristeas that Demetrius coordinated the work of the translators while they were working on their text (Let. Aris. 303). Perhaps even Josephus was reluctant to admit that the pagan Demetrius had helped in this way. But in relation to the role of Demetrius, this omission is adequately redressed when Josephus praises Demetrius as the man who 'conceived the idea [of the translation] through which he [=Demetrius] had become the originator of great benefits to them' (Ant. 12.108). The comment is not found in the account of Aristeas.

Josephus conveys the initial reluctance of the Jews to comply with Ptolemy's request through a speech of the High Priest. Whereas this speech in Aristeas gives reasons for the non-compliance of the Jews, Josephus offers a positive explanation for why the Jews ultimately agreed to Ptolemy's request, namely that they wanted to prove that they had nothing to hide (Ant. 12.11). Josephus thus suggests that external pressure on the Jews forced them to comply with a request they would have preferred to decline. Predictably also, Josephus retains the story of the liberation of the Jewish slaves, along with the detail that a request for their freedom had 'often' been made (Let. Aris. 12; Ant. 12.17). For Josephus, this story, evaluated against the background of his refusal to believe in the divine inspiration of the translation, must have confirmed his opinion that the Jews did not want to translate the holy text.

Significant changes made by Josephus to Aristeas occur in those sections in which Aristeas promotes the divine inspiration of the text. Of the three references by Aristeas to the number seventy-two, only one is repeated in Josephus, namely the reference to the seventy-two days. It is possible that by the time of Josephus, this detail had become an integral part of the story which Josephus had little choice but to retain.

But for the seventy-two questions of the king, Josephus refers his reader to Aristeas, and although he mentions six translators from each tribe, he does not give the number of the tribes, and refers to only seventy translators (Ant. 12.100).

Similarly, Josephus also changes details in Aristeas' description of the Jewish request to Demetrius for a copy of the completed text to be given to their leaders. As noted above, since Aristeas wanted to show broad support for the translation, he blurs the identity of those who requested a copy of the translation with the identity of the translators themselves. Josephus however corrects this ambiguity and makes it perfectly clear that all the Jewish people express their approval of the text, which he has taken care to describe without the trappings of divine inspiration. The Jewish people are thus unanimous in their approval of an *un*inspired text. According to Josephus, the Jewish leaders were not interested in the translation and certainly did not consider that it was divinely inspired. Josephus thus 'proves' his opinion by showing that it was confirmed by the people, the sages and leaders at the time that the translation was made (Ant. 12.108). Further evidence of the determination of Josephus to remove any idea that the text of the translation was divinely inspired can be seen from other changes that he made to Aristeas' description of the ceremony on the Pharos (Ant. 12.108). In particular he omits the adulatory comments of Aristeas that the translation was 'well and piously expounded' and 'in every respect accurate', and instead more reservedly states that it was 'successfully made'.

All in all, therefore, Josephus gives a version of Aristeas which tells the astonishing story of the translation, while removing – as far as possible – the idea that it was divinely inspired. As far as the history of the translation is concerned, the evidence of Josephus merely repeats Aristeas. It is interesting, however, that Josephus knows no conflicting account. Therefore, as far as Josephus is concerned, the translation was made on the initiative of the Greeks.

VI. Different Jewish Attitudes to the Translation

The discussion above suggests that the earliest account of the translation (partially preserved by Aristeas) shows that the work was written at Ptolemy's request by Jewish translators who were reluctant to perform the royal command. Their resulting translation could scarcely have been considered as a holy text, and any question of such sanctity is unlikely to have been voiced. Later, however, such belief arose, and Aristeas altered the original story of the translation to suggest that the Alexandrian work was a holy text. This attitude is upheld and intensified by Philo, who all but eliminated the role of the Greeks, and declared that the Jewish translation was divinely inspired. That this echoed the belief of many Jews in Alexandria can be seen from Philo's reference to the yearly festival that was held on the Pharos to celebrate the translation of the Pentateuch into Greek.[32] But was this attitude universal among the Alexandrian Jews? Were there a group of Jews who never overcame their initial aversion to a translation of the Pentateuch, or who never considered the text to be divinely inspired?

While it could be claimed that the most appropriate place to hold the ceremony which celebrated the completion of the translation was on the Pharos where the translation was made, this argument is less convincing for the yearly festival which commemorated the translation of the Pentateuch into Greek (De Vit. Mos. II.41). Philo's reference to the 'prayers and thanksgivings' that took place suggests a religious festival of some kind. But apart from the fact that the creation of an extra-Pentateuchal festival was a remarkable event – Channukah and Purim are the exceptions which prove the rule – no regular festival in mainstream Judaism – not even Channukah or Purim – is celebrated entirely outside the synagogue or home in the way Philo describes.[33] It is moreover difficult to understand why the celebration for the translation did not take place in the synagogue, especially if the translation was destined for use in the synagogue, as is commonly claimed.

---

[32] Jewish celebration of the completion of the translation may be an echo or an inspiration for the link between the Jewish festival of Shavuot ('Weeks') which celebrates the giving of the Hebrew Pentateuch on Sinai. This link is not biblical.

[33] A unique exception concerns the Samaritans who celebrated (and celebrate today) the first night of the seven days of Passover on Mt Gerizim.

The celebration of this religious festival outside an official place of prayer may indicate that although Philo and others held the Greek Pentateuch in great esteem, there were others who did not. These may have included officials who were in charge of the synagogues, since only such people could have prevented a celebration of the festivity in the synagogue itself. This being the case, those who believed in the sanctity of the Greek Pentateuch chose a location on the Pharos – a logical alternative – to celebrate the event. Philo's description of the festival thus hints at dissent within the Jewish community regarding the translation of the Pentateuch into Greek.

Some confirmation for the identity of early dissenters comes from Aristeas. In addition to those who originally objected to a translation of the text, of whom some may have changed their opposition for genuine respect after the translation was complete, Aristeas also hints at those who did not recognise the translation even after it was complete, and would not even join in the declaration to preserve the text. This is hinted by Aristeas when he notes the identity of those who assented to the first of the Jewish declarations, 'the priests, the elders of the translators, and *some of* the corporate body and leaders of the people (Let. Aris. 310). The 'some' is expressed in Greek as a partitive genitive. This hint that the Jewish politeuma was not united in their approval of the translation is intriguing. Aristeas would probably have preferred to show complete harmony among the Jews in support of his claim of the divine inspiration of the text, as Josephus does (Ant. 12.108). If some of the leaders of the community were also those who controlled what took place in the synagogues, then it is at least problematic to surmise that the existence of the festival on the Pharos indicates proof that all the Jews wanted a translation of the Pentateuch in Greek.

This hint of disunity by Aristeas needs to be associated with the implications of Philo's claim that there was absolutely no disagreement on the text when the translation was first produced. According to Philo, the translators miraculously produced identical Greek texts, which they received from an 'invisible prompter' (De Vit. Mos. II.37-39). This rather conveniently disposes the claim that there were initial differences of opinion regarding the text, which was thus not divinely inspired. But the very existence of such a protestation suggests the existence of another which denied such a claim. Why bother to claim the unity of the text unless the unity of the text was in dispute? The underlying implication of Philo's narrative thus suggests that there were those in Alexandria who considered that the text of the Greek Pentateuch was not universally agreed and divinely inspired

Although Josephus did not consider that the translation was divinely inspired in any way, he does not express disapproval of the text. This neutral attitude was however later followed by the bitter resentment of later Jews against the very existence of the translation. The Megillat Ta'anit (written in the 1st or 2nd century CE) thus states that after the completion of the translation, 'darkness came upon the world for three days'.[34] As there is no evidence of such a heavenly portent in earlier Greek accounts of the translation, including that of Aristeas, and no evidence of an eclipse of the sun over Alexandria in the years 281/0 BCE (the probable dates for the translation), it appears that these three days of darkness were used as a symbol for the future suffering of the Jews at Christian hands.[35] It is indeed ironic that a holy book composed and preserved by the Jews, which was regarded as divinely inspired, and which the Jews themselves (through the orders of Ptolemy II) had been persuaded to open to the scrutiny of the world, was later turned in evidence against them and used for their harm. Likewise, the rabbis after the fourth century CE noted that the translation of the Law was as 'ominous for Israel as the day on which the golden calf was made, since the Torah could not be accurately translated' (Masseket Sophrim1.7). This is clearly articulated in Albîrûnî's *The Chronology of the Ancient Nations*, written around 1000 CE, who commented that:

---

[34] A. Neubauer, *Mediaeval Jewish Chronicles* II (1895), 24.

[35] No eclipse of the sun of significant magnitude, visible from Alexandria, is reported around 280 BCE, see J. K. Fotheringham, 'A Solution of Ancient Eclipses of the Sun', *Monthly Notices of the Royal Astronomical Society* 81 (1921), 104-26, on p. 111. Similarly, there is no eclipse for Babylon or Palestine in 281 (astronomical year -281), see T. R. von Oppolzer, *Canon of Eclipses* (trans. O. Gingerich; New York 1962). A total eclipse took place over Babylon in 280 BCE. Could this have been remembered in connection with the translation?

> The Jews, however, give a quite different account [of the reason for the translation compared with Aristeas], viz. that they made the translation under compulsion and that they yielded to the king's demand only from fear of violence and maltreatment, and not before having agreed upon inverting and confounding the text of the book.[36]

This very negative attitude of the Jews to the translation is of a different order of intensity, and undoubtedly provoked by historical circumstances which could never have been imagined by those who originally opposed the making of the translation, or those who did not join in the general veneration of the text. It is nevertheless interesting to note that, as far as the Jews were concerned, Jewish opposition to the translation of the Pentateuch was fully vindicated in later times.

VII. Pre-Septuagint Translation of Jewish Sacred Texts

The persistence of the theory that the Jews needed a translation because the majority could no longer read and understand the Pentateuch in Hebrew is undoubtedly due at least partly to the fact that the latter is true. As is well known, after their return from Babylon and the time of Ezra in the fifth century BCE, a large number of Jews spoke Aramaic and could not understand Hebrew, and this situation naturally continued in Hellenistic times. Unfortunately however for those who maintain the theory mentioned above, the loss of Hebrew among the Jews is almost irrelevant to the question of the translation, and does not account for the production of a literal, written translation of the Hebrew Pentateuch into Greek.

The return from Babylon in 538 BCE, when a large majority of Jews no longer spoke or understood Hebrew, seems to have been followed by the development of the Aramaic Targum. But this was not a written translation in the modern sense of this word, or in the sense of the translation of the Hebrew Pentateuch into Greek. Unlike the latter, which was written, literal and composed in Greek, the earliest targum was oral, discursive, and composed in Aramaic. The latter were thus used in a way which would be impossible or inappropriate for a fixed, written text. The occasion and

---

[36] Albîrûnî, *Athâr-Ul-Bâkiya*; trans. C. E. Sachau, *The Chronology of the Ancient Nations* (London 1979), 24

procedure of the Aramaic translation is described in the Mishnah, in possibly one of the oldest sections of this work (m. Meg. 4:4). At a certain time in a service, a reader would read aloud one verse from the Hebrew Pentateuch – or three verses at a time from the Prophets – after which the translator would give an oral version in Aramaic, apparently spontaneously, without recourse to any written text. The prohibition against a written text is expressly stated, although in later times (j. Meg. 4:1 74d). The earliest surviving written targumic text is the Targum of Job discovered at Qumran, which has been dated to the late second century BCE. If the translation of the Pentateuch into Greek took place in the early third century BCE – probably in 280 BCE –, the Greek translation was made before any other written translation of the Pentateuch, and certainly before any other *literal* translation of the Pentateuchal text.

The Greek translation was thus the first of its kind and fundamentally different from earlier translations. Little wonder therefore that it was given the respect of the Jews, as Aristeas suggests in his description of the ceremony on the Pharos. But this should not distract us from the fact that the emergence of this translation does not show a development of Jewish practice but marks a complete and fundamental change. It is reasonable to assume that a change of this magnitude was not internally motivated but was imposed from without. If the Jews of Egypt in Hellenistic times had wanted to understand the Bible in Greek, it is far more likely that they would have prepared an oral Greek version on the pattern of a Targum – a genre apparently already established for over one hundred years – rather than the translation that was actually produced, a single, written scroll, with a literal translation, which was deposited in a pagan building for the use of non-Jews. All this further indicates that the motivation for the Greek translation did not come from the Jews.

The popularity of the claim that the Jews needed a translation because a substantial number no longer understood their holy tongue is thus based on a fact which is largely true but probably irrelevant to the question in hand. The translation was produced because the Greeks, rather than the Jews, did not understand the Hebrew words of the Pentateuchal text.

VIII. The Language of the Jews in Early Ptolemaic Times

The improbability of a Jewish initiative for the translation is also apparent when we consider the history and language of the majority of Jews in Egypt from the sixth century BCE, particularly in relation to the date of the translation deduced in this book. Many Jews seem to have fled to Egypt in the thirty year period between the accession of Jehoiakim in Jerusalem in 609 BCE and the assassination of Gedaliah, the governor set up by Nebuchadnezzar. Jeremiah implies that the size of the Jewish community in Egypt in his time was similar to the size of the remnant in Jerusalem and in the rest of Judaea (Jer. 24:8). Until the invasion of Alexander, these Jews were exposed to the culture of Egyptians, Ethiopians and Persians and, as far as is known, they spoke Aramaic. It is hardly necessary to note that they would not have needed a biblical version in Greek and it must be assumed that they continued to use the Aramaic targum.

A theoretical need for a Greek version of the Pentateuch could only have arisen after Alexander invaded Egypt in 332/1 BCE. A substantial influx of Jews probably occurred in 312 BCE, when Ptolemy I brought over the Jewish captives (who, according to Aristeas, his son later released) (Let. Aris. 12). These Jewish immigrants into Egypt used Aramaic in their everyday life, although many knew Hebrew as well. The first authentic evidence of Jews in Alexandria in early Ptolemaic times appears in Greek and Aramaic inscriptions probably from the reign of Ptolemy II. However, the use of Aramaic by the Jews continued 'during the entire third century, and perhaps the first half of the second, [when] Egyptian Jews continued to speak Aramaic, as is shown by papyri and ostraka in that language'.[37] Subsequently, for many centuries, no Aramaic documents are found. But if a majority of Jews spoke Aramaic in early Ptolemaic times, why would they have wanted a version in Greek of the Pentateuchal text?

---

[37] Tcherikover and Fuks (1957), p. 3 with p. 30, n. 8.

This may also be deduced from the history of the Jews. It is reasonable to assume that a large majority of the Jews who settled in Alexandria with Ptolemy I were drawn from among the 100,000 people who were brought to Egypt by Ptolemy in 312 BCE. If furthermore the translation was completed in 281 BCE, there was a maximum of thirty years between the arrival of these Jews in Egypt and their request for a translation. This allows for one new generation. Observation suggests – and this is confirmed by the archaeological records of Aramaic described above – that the first generation of immigrants are familiar with the language of their parents, in this case Aramaic. Without even considering the different nature of the written, literal Greek translation compared with the discursive, oral targum, it must be asked how likely it was that this first generation, or their parents, many of whom could have still been alive, clamoured for a translation of the Pentateuch into Greek because they had forgotten their native tongue.

But it is moreover important to remember that although the initial effects of the translation are probably over-stressed, the very existence of the translation must have encouraged the use of Greek among the Jews in relation to their holy texts.[38] But the anticipated demand for a product before it is produced may bear no relation to the demand after it appears. Modern history is littered with examples of modern inventions whose widespread use could never have been anticipated by their inventors. Similarly with the first, written, literal translation of the Pentateuch: how could the Jews of Egypt have realised the impact the translation before such a work had ever been produced?

IX. Conclusion

The discussion above has challenged the attractive, but deeply flawed modern opinion – prevalent only in the last two hundred or so years – that the translation of

---

[38] Such statements as the following are surely an exaggeration: 'From the moment of translation [of the Pentateuch] the study of Hebrew became obsolete, and since it was not (as was Aramaic) a language of everyday use, it disappeared wholly from Jewish life in Egypt' (in Tcherikover and Fuks [1957], 31).

the Hebrew Pentateuch into Greek arose on the initiative of the Jews, because the Jews had forgotten their holy tongue. The latter is correct, but essentially irrelevant to the question in hand. Rather, the employment of Demetrius of Phalerum by Ptolemy II, combined with a detailed examination of Aristeas, suggests that the translation was made, as Aristeas describes, at the request of Demetrius of Phalerum, working in the service of Ptolemy II. This is confirmed by the accounts of Philo and Josephus in the sense that they offer no alternative explanation for events. This history of the translation also makes sense in the light of the use of Aramaic translations by the Jews before the second century BCE, and from the Jewish knowledge of Aramaic (rather than Greek) in early Ptolemaic times. It can safely be concluded that the Jews of early Ptolemaic times would not have wanted or needed a written, literal translation of the Pentateuch in Greek.

This understanding of the origin of the translation must profoundly affect the way it is viewed. If the Greek biblical text was composed by Jewish translators working reluctantly in Alexandria in the third century BCE, for the benefit of the Greeks rather than the Jews, then, the text must be regarded primarily as a document in which, for the first time in history, the inner sanctum of Judaism was exposed to the curious gaze of the pagan world. This could not have been easy for a religious system whose many social rituals tended to keep it apart.

Apart from the complete break with Jewish tradition in producing a written, literal translation of their holiest text into an alien language which was strongly associated with idolatrous cults, these problems alone account for the fact that the Jews were opposed to Ptolemy's demand to translate the Pentateuch into Greek. The Jews did not need or request the translation, and only reluctantly agreed to Ptolemy's request for a translation of the Hebrew Pentateuch into Greek.

Daniel's 'Watchers' in Enochic Exegesis of Genesis 6:1-4

Siam Bhayro

The First Book of Enoch, or the Ethiopic Book of Enoch, is a composite work made up of five 'books':[1] the Book of Watchers (1 En. 1-36); the Similitudes or Parables (1 En. 37-71); the Astronomical Book (1 En. 72-82); the Book of Dreams (1 En. 83-90); and the Epistle (1 En. 91-108). The first of these, the Book of Watchers, describes the judgement of the so-called Watchers, the angels who sinned by fornicating with human women and producing giant offspring. This Book of Watchers is also a composite, and can be divided as follows:[2] Introduction (1 En. 1-5); the Story of the Fallen Angels (1 En. 6-11); the Petitions of the Giants (1 En. 12-16); and Enoch's Journeys (1 En. 17-36).

It is likely that the section comprising chapters 6-11 is the earliest part of the Book of Watchers, as it forms the basis for the rest of the narrative which is built around it. The relationship between chapters 6-11 and the rest of the Book of Watchers is

---

[1] This division was first suggested by R. H. Charles, who argued against the consensus of the day which considered chapters 1-36 and 72-104 as being of the same stratum: cf. R. H. Charles, *The Apocrypha and Pseudepigrapha of the Old Testament*, II: *Pseudepigrapha* (Oxford 1913), 168-70. Due to the lack of any fragments from the Similitudes being discovered among the Enochic fragments from Qumran, and the discovery of fragments of a Qumran Book of Giants, it is thought that the Similitudes displaced the Book of Giants at some point in late antiquity. For recent discussions on 1 Enoch and the Book of Giants, cf. John C. Reeves, *Jewish Lore in Manichaean Cosmogony* (Cincinnati 1992); John J. Collins, *The Apocalyptic Imagination* (2nd edn; Cambridge 1998), 43 ff. The designation of these five books as an Enochic Pentateuch should be considered in the light of the helpful comments made by D. Dimant, 'The Biography of Enoch and the Books of Enoch', *Vetus Testamentum* 33 (1983), 14-29.

[2] Cf. the discussion of these sections in Collins, *The Apocalyptic Imagination*, 47-59.

worthy of detailed examination,[3] but these chapters themselves, chapters 6-11, comprise a distinct narrative and merit an examination on that basis.[4]

Before we examine this narrative, let us first summarise its contents. 1 Enoch 6-11 retells Gen. 6:1-4 to introduce the angels who descend in order to fornicate with human women. These angels teach mantic skills and other arts of civilisation to humanity. Giant offspring of the illicit union between the angels and human women devour the earth and its inhabitants causing mankind to cry out. The four archangels petition the Most High on behalf of the earth and its inhabitants. The Most High responds through his archangels, pronouncing judgement upon the Watchers and their giant offspring. The survival of Noah and his offspring upon a cleansed earth is promised.

The first striking thing about this narrative is that it contradicts the Bible in two obvious ways. Firstly, in Genesis, mankind is the object of God's wrath in the flood narrative, whilst in this Enoch passage, it is the Watchers and the giants who are the object of God's wrath, and mankind is their victim.[5] Thus the role of mankind is changed from judged sinner to victim. Furthermore, in Genesis the descent of the sons of God and the birth of the giants are neutral events, mentioned with no further comment. Thus these events are not presented negatively, whereas in the Enoch

---

[3] This was attempted by C. A. Newsom, 'The Development of 1 Enoch 6-19: Cosmology and Judgement', *Catholic Biblical Quarterly* 42 (1980), 310-29. Newsom, however, argues that the mantic element in 1 Enoch 6-11 was a secondary development which occurred following its incor-poration into the Enochic corpus. The present author considers the mantic element to be part of the base stratum of 1 Enoch 6-11, and that its role within the Enochic corpus should be analysed in this context.

[4] Previous analyses of this section include P. D. Hanson, 'Rebellion in Heaven, Azazel, and Euhemeristic Heroes in 1 Enoch 6-11', *Journal of Biblical Literature* 96 (1977), 195-233; G. W. E. Nickelsburg, 'Apocalyptic and Myth in 1 Enoch 6-11', *Journal of Biblical Literature* 96 (1977), 383-405; C. Molenberg, 'A Study of the Roles of Shemihaza and Asael in 1 Enoch 6-11', *Journal of Jewish Studies* 35 (1984), 136-46; D. Dimant, '1 Enoch 6-11: A Methodological Perspective', in P. J. Achtemeier (ed.), *Society of Biblical Literature 1978 Seminar Papers,* I (Missoula 1978), 323-39; J. J. Collins, 'Methodological Issues in the Study of 1 Enoch: Reflections on the Articles of P. D. Hanson and G. W. E. Nickelsburg', in Achtemeier (ed.), *Seminar Papers*, I, 315-22; G. W. E. Nickelsburg, 'Reflections upon Reflections: A Response to John Collins' "Methodological Issues in the Study of 1 Enoch"', in Achtemeier (ed.), *Seminar Papers*, I, 311-4; P. D. Hanson, 'A Response to John Collins' "Methodological Issues in the Study of 1 Enoch"', in Achtemeier (ed.), *Seminar Papers*, I, 307-9.

[5] Nickelsburg, 'Apocalyptic and Myth', 386-8.

narrative, they are most certainly a negative event worthy of God's unbridled wrath.[6] These contradictions have never been satisfactorily explained; they have just been observed as an interesting feature of 1 Enoch 6-11.[7] But these contradictions must be there for a purpose. There must be a point being made by such a startling deviance from the biblical account.

We shall shed light on this problem by examining another contradiction between the Enoch narrative and the Bible, this time regarding the mantic arts: divination.[8] Whilst divination is condemned in the Torah, particularly in Deut. 18:10-14,[9] a slightly different attitude can be discerned in the books of Genesis and Daniel, in the Joseph and Daniel narratives. In Genesis 41, Joseph is able to interpret the two dreams of Pharaoh, a feat which all the magicians and wise men of Egypt were unable to do. Furthermore, in Gen. 44:5, Joseph himself mentions the cup which he uses for divining.[10] Similarly, in Daniel 2, Daniel can tell and interpret the dream of the great statue. In chapter 4, Daniel can interpret the dream of the tree when the other wise men cannot. In chapter 5, Daniel can interpret the writing on the wall. In each of these occurrences, Daniel explains an omen to the king, while the rest of the wise men of Babylon are unable to do likewise.

What is interesting about these narratives, particularly the Daniel narrative, is that the narrator is not antagonistic towards the mantic arts; rather, the point of the

---

[6] James C. VanderKam, *Enoch and the Growth of an Apocalyptic Tradition* (Catholic Bibilical Quarterly Monograph Series 16; Washington 1984), 125-6.

[7] For example, in reference to the contradiction regarding the mixing of the sons of God with the daughters of men and the subsequent birth of the giants, VanderKam simply observes that one result of the negative account in 1 Enoch 6-11 is to 'cast a negative light on the crafts and arts - the secrets - which the angels revealed'; cf. *Enoch and the Growth of an Apocalyptic Tradition*, 126. Nickelsburg offers no explanation for the contradiction concerning the roles of humanity and the angels.

[8] Cf. *Enoch and the Growth of an Apocalyptic Tradition*, 71-75. This section, entitled 'Divination in the Old Testament', gives an excellent account of the issues discussed below.

[9] VanderKam observes that the Hebrew Bible's anti-divination passages are especially found in the prophetic literature of the exilic period, and concludes that the conflict was between Jewish prophecy and the divination of the pagans the Jews found themselves amongst: cf. *Enoch and the Growth of an Apocalyptic Tradition*, 71-73.

[10] *Enoch and the Growth of an Apocalyptic Tradition*, 74.

Daniel narrative is that the wisdom of Daniel's God enables Daniel to employ these arts better than his contemporaries (cf. Dan. 2:20, 47; 4:3-5; 5:11-12, 14-16).[11]

This contrasts greatly with 1 Enoch 6-11 which condemns outright the practise of the mantic arts. This is done by asserting that such skills were given to humanity by the wicked angels who, by mixing with humanity, brought upon the earth all of the ills which now afflict it (cf. 1 En. 9:6-8). This contrast in attitude to the mantic arts between the Daniel and Enoch narratives was the main theme behind the composition of 1 Enoch 6-11,[12] and this can be demonstrated through an analysis of the Aramaic term עירין, 'Watchers'.

The Aramaic term עיר (pl. עירין) occurs only three times in the Bible, all in the book of Daniel. It occurs in the singular twice (Dan. 4:10, 20) and in the plural once (Dan. 4:14). In every case, it occurs in conjunction with the term קדישין/קדיש.[13]

What is apparent from the ancient Bible translations is that the use of these phrases was problematic for translators:

LXX	ἄγγελος	angel
Theodotion	ιρ (or ειρ) καὶ ἄγιος	'ir and a holy one
Peshitta	'yr' wqdyš'	watcher and holy one
Aquila/Symmachus	ἐγρήγορος	watcher

---

[11] For Daniel's role as a mantic sage, and the relationship between Jewish apocalyptic literature and mantic wisdom, cf. H. P. Müller, 'Mantische Weisheit und Apokalyptik', in *Congress Volume, Uppsala 1971* (Vetus Testamentum Supplement 22; Leiden 1972), 268-93. VanderKam discusses other mantic methods such as the ephod and the urîm and tummîm, and how the method of dream interpretation continued after the others ceased; cf. *Enoch and the Growth of an Apocalyptic Tradition*, 74.

[12] It is probably more accurate to speak of the contrast between the Daniel narrative and 1 Enoch 6-11, because the rest of the Enoch narrative appears to have a contrary attitude towards the mantic arts than 1 Enoch 6-11. The reasons for this are beyond the scope of this article, but the present author hopes to discuss this elsewhere. For the sake of convenience, terms such as 'Enoch narrative' are used in reference to 1 Enoch 6-11.

[13] It is not certain from the text whether עיר וקדיש and עירין וקדישין are intended to refer to the same being, but this assumption appears to have received almost universal acceptance. For example, Montgomery suggested that they refer to the same being, the watcher being 'an importation from the current syncretistic religion' with the addition of an 'epexegetical "and holy", to secure the identification with the angelic category': J. A. Montgomery, *A Critical and Exegetical Commentary on the Book of Daniel* (Edinburgh 1927), 231-22. Likewise Charles, noting the existence in Enochic literature of good and evil watchers, asserts that 'there are not two heavenly beings who are referred to here but one only ... "the watcher and that a holy one"': R. H. Charles, *A Critical and Exegetical Commentary on the Book of Daniel* (Oxford 1929), 91.

The LXX translates עיר וקדיש both times as ἄγγελος, choosing to merge the עיר and the קדיש into one being. The merging aspect of the LXX's interpretation is explicable: the עיר and the קדיש could be understood as a couplet. What is more difficult to explain, however, is why the term ἄγγελος was used. Whilst it may be argued that the context implies that the being was an angel, the LXX's identification of the עיר וקדיש as an angel is still rather bold, perhaps attributable to the translators' knowledge of the traditions extant in the Book of Watchers, which identifies the עירין as being fallen angels. Theodotion chooses to avoid the hazards of translation and characteristically simply gives ιρ (or ειρ) καὶ ἅγιος for עיר וקדיש. Thus the structure of the Aramaic text is preserved and the problematic עיר simply transliterated. Similarly, the Peshitta gives 'yr' wqdyš', although it is possible that the Syriac 'yr' was already a loaded term equated with watcher-angels. Aquila and Symmachus both use ἐγρήγορος.

As mentioned above, the explanation of why the עירין were identified with angels by early translators is probably due to the Book of Watchers, in which one encounters the earliest explicit identification of the עירין with angels.[14] This identification is not made in the Aramaic text of Daniel 4 and may not have been the original meaning. Thus prior to analysing the use of the term עירין in the Book of Watchers, we must first examine its use in Daniel 4, and attempt to discern its original intended meaning.

The context of the use of עירין in Daniel 4 is striking. Firstly, one notes that the passage is explicitly Babylonian in setting. Thus we should consider the narrative in its Babylonian context. Secondly, one notes that the narrative, like so much of the Book of Daniel, revolves around contrasting the God of Daniel with the gods of Babylon. This

---

[14] The Enoch fragments from Qumran provide a *terminus ad quem* for the final form of the Book of Watchers. The earliest of the Enoch manuscripts containing the Book of Watchers is dated palaeographically to the first half of the second century BCE; this manuscript, however, was probably made from an older copy dating from the third century. Cf. J. T. Milik, *The Books of Enoch: Aramaic Fragments of Qumran Cave 4* (Oxford 1976), 22, 140-41.

contrast is illustrated through the superior wisdom and mantic skills of Daniel with respect to the wise men of Babylon.

The narrator skilfully illustrates this contrast between the God of Daniel and the Babylonian pantheon. In Dan. 4:14, Nebuchadnezzar states that the omen is 'by the decree of the watchers and the word of the holy ones'.[15] In verse 21, however, Daniel contradicts the king, and states that 'this is the decree of the Most High'. Thus Daniel's point to the king is that his fate is not determined by the watchers and holy ones, but by the Most High. Precisely who these עירין and קדישין are, of whom one is described as descending with the omen, remains to be established. It is clear from the contrast described above, however, that they belong to the Babylonian omen system. They are not angels.[16] Nebuchadnezzar describes the omen being brought by one of them, and he affirms his belief that his fate has been determined by them.

Thus we are left to consider to whom the narrator is referring by the term עיר/עירין. This term is derived from the root עיר which pertains to 'being awake' or 'watchful'. Although not cognate, the Akkadian root *barû* is related in meaning to the root עיר, since *barû* also means to watch over.[17] From the root *barû*, the term *bārû* is derived, referring to the Babylonian diviner who engaged in haruspexology, the art of extracting an omen from animal organs. The *bārû* was known especially for extispicy, reading omens from the liver of a sacrificial sheep.[18]

---

[15] Quoted according to the American Jewish Version. See below, however, where this phrase is discussed in more detail.

[16] Contrary to the current consensus; cf. for example J. J. Collins, 'Watcher', in K. van der Toorn, B. Becking and P. W. van der Horst (eds), *Dictionary of Deities and Demons in the Bible* (Leiden 1995), 1681-85.

[17] *Chicago Assyrian Dictionary* 2.115-8.

[18] *Chicago Assyrian Dictionary* 2.121-5. For detailed discussions on the *bārû*, cf. Ivan Starr, *The Rituals of the Diviner* (Malibu 1983); Ulla Jeyes, *Old Babylonian Extispicy: Omen Texts in the British Museum* (Leiden 1989); Ivan Starr, *Queries to the Sungod* (Helsinki 1990). VanderKam discusses Mesopotamian divination, in particular the *bārû*, at length: cf. VanderKam, *Enoch and the Growth of an Apocalyptic Tradition*, 52-62. According to VanderKam's hypothesis, Enoch is the Jewish version of the mythological seventh antediluvian king Enmeduranki. A text published by Lambert tells how Enmeduranki, king of Sippar, was taught various methods of divination by Šamaš and Adad, which he in turn taught to the men of Sippar, Nippur and Babylon; cf. W. G. Lambert, 'Enmeduranki and Related Matters', *Journal of Cuneiform Studies* 21 (1967), 126-38, 127. In the course of his excellent analysis of 1 Enoch 1-36, however, VanderKam fails to identify the Watchers with the *bārû* (c.f. especially

The highest position which a *bārû* could attain within his profession was that of court diviner. Such a position would involve administrative and diplomatic duties.[19] This is of particular interest for our investigation which concerns divination in the royal court.

Also of interest is the status afforded the practise of extispicy in relation to other mantic methods such as the observation of astronomical phenomena and the interpretation of dreams. The latter methods were considered to be somewhat insecure and in need of confirmation by the more secure method of extispicy. It is for this reason, as Starr notes, that the dream interpreter and the *bārû* often appear together.[20] This again relates to our investigation of Daniel 4 which concerns the *bārû* and dream interpretation.

Thus we are left with the prospect of identifying the עיר with a *bārû*. This would lead us to conclude that the narrator of Daniel 4 was not referring to angels, but to the receiving or confirmation of an omen by one particular *bārû*. In order to do this, the narrator is faced with the problem of translating the Akkadian *bārû*, but with having no suitable cognate root. Thus he translated *bārû* into עיר.

This identification of עיר with *bārû* appears to be confirmed when analysed in reference to Dan. 4:14: 'The message is in the cutting of the watchers, and the word of the priestesses is the dream portent' (בגזרת עירין פתגמא ומאמר קדישין שאלתא). This verse is brimming with mantic terminology. From the root גזר, 'to cut', come the גזרין, 'the soothsayers' (cf. Dan. 2:27; 4:4; 5:7, 11). The root גזר, 'to cut', was used because they cut open animals and inspected their internal organs in order to find the omen. Thus it is possible that the term בגזרת, as used in Dan. 4:14, is to be understood as being what is determined by mantic arts specifically through cutting. This understanding of the root

---

VanderKam, *Enoch and the Growth of an Apocalytpic Tradition*, 110, note 1). Such an identification would help to explain why 1 Enoch 6-11 contradicts the rest of the Book of Watchers in its attitude towards the mantic arts.
[19] Jeyes, *Old Babylonian Extispicy*, 16.
[20] Starr, *The Rituals*, 7.

גזר and the noun גזרת coincides with the Akkadian use of the root *parāsu* which also means 'to cut/divide'. From the root *parāsu*, the noun *purussû* is derived which, although literally meaning 'cutting', has the meaning 'decision' or 'oracular answer'.[21] Thus the first stanza of the above phrase would mean 'the message (i.e. omen) is in the oracle (lit. cutting for the purpose of confirming the message by mantic arts) of the watchers (i.e. the *bārû*)'. Furthermore, the word שאלתא is also a mantic term, being related to the Akkadian *šā'ilu*, 'a dream interpreter'. Thus the pairing of the *bārû* with the method of dream interpretation, as discussed above, occurs in Dan. 4:14.[22]

What of the identity of the קדישין? From the description of one of the קדישין descending from heaven (see below), this could refer to the Babylonian pantheon. This is unlikely, however, as the Babylonians never refer to their gods in this way. Instead, they used the term *qadištu* to refer to a class of priestess set apart for temple service.[23] Thus whilst the first stanza tells how the omen was confirmed, by *a watcher*, the second tells who received it, it was a saying of *the holy ones*, the priestesses.

This leaves the question as to why the עירין וקדיש, whom we identify with a *bārû* and a priestess, are pictured as having descended from heaven in both Dan. 4:10 ('a watcher and a holy one descended', עיר וקדיש מן שמיא נחת) and 4:20 ('the king saw a watcher and a holy one descend from heaven', חזה מלכא עיר וקדיש נחת מן שמיא). The answer to this is given, in part, by the text published by Lambert which describes the *bārû* as 'an expert in oil, *of abiding descent*, offspring of Enmeduranki ...'[24]

The *bārû* were considered to be descended from Enmeduranki, the legendary king of Sippar who was brought up to heaven into the presence of Šamaš to receive instruction in the mantic arts. Thus it was held that the mantic arts descended from

---

[21] Rykle Borger, *Babylonisch-Assyrische Lesestücke* (Rome 1979), 264.
[22] The pairing of the roots גזר and שאל

65

heaven,[25] and those who practised them were referred to as being of abiding descent of the one who first received them, Enmeduranki.[26]

We must now consider how such an understanding of the עירין helps us explain 1 Enoch 6-11. As noted above, the Enoch narrator is seeking to present a condemnation of the mantic arts, in order to contradict an apparently positive attitude to divination in such accounts as the Joseph and Daniel narratives.

He does this using the Genesis narrative about the sons of God and adds to the Genesis narrative the negative aspect of their descent, and makes his anti-divination point by stating that it was the sons of God who taught the mantic arts to mankind, thus bringing evil to the earth. In order to identify his opponents specifically, and to leave no ambiguity as to whom he is condemning, he adds to his manipulation of the Genesis narrative a key element in the Daniel narrator's presentation of the Babylonian omen system: the עירין/bārû. In the Enoch narrator's polemic, the only ones who survive God's wrath are those pure from contamination with the Watchers, i.e., those who have not engaged in divination.

One needs to consider why the Enochic author chose to write an anti-divination polemic based upon Genesis 6. The answer is that the Genesis narrative is unique in detailing the crossing of the boundaries between the terrestrial realm and the divine realm – the natural and the supernatural – a key aspect to divination.[27] Thus the use of Genesis 6 in relation to divination is certainly understandable.

In conclusion, 1 Enoch 6-11 is a polemic against the mantic arts, which uses the Genesis narrative as its foundation. In order to appreciate the depth of this polemic, we have to revise our understanding of who Daniel's עירין, 'watchers', are – they are not angels, but part of the Babylonian mantic system.

---

[25] The same idea occurs in reference to kingship which is also stated to have descended from heaven; cf. S. N. Kramer, *The Sumerians* (Chicago 1963), 328-31.

[26] Lambert, 'Enmeduranki', 127.

[27] Hanson discusses how the transgression of the boundaries between heaven and earth was built upon the Genesis narrative by the Enochic author; Hanson, 'Rebellion in Heaven', 198-99.

Reading the Plain Meaning of Scripture in the Dead Sea Scrolls

George J. Brooke

I. Introduction

Refer to almost any study of biblical interpretation in the Dead Sea Scrolls and much of the discussion will be taken up with consideration of the form and overall characteristics of the so-called pesharim, the biblical commentaries.   Usually this discussion is concerned to point out that the author (even the Teacher of Righteousness himself) or authors of the pesharim ignored the plain or literal meaning of the prophetic texts which they were interpreting; instead they identified particular words or phrases in the texts as veiled references to their own circumstances.   This process of identification is commonly understood to have been more or less inspired, as God made known to the interpreter all the mysteries of the words of his servants the prophets (1QpHab 7:4-5).   For example, Jacob Neusner has commented that 'the forms of Midrash in the Dead Sea Scrolls reveal to us a sustained effort to identify contemporary events with the scriptural prophetic passages of the past.   The self-evident purpose of the exegete is to allow for further inquiry into the near future.'[1]   Many other examples could be cited from scholars of all persuasions.[2]

---

[1] J. Neusner, *What is Midrash?* (Philadelphia 1987), 32

[2] The scholarly literature on biblical interpretation in the Dead Sea Scrolls is vast.   Good surveys can be found in M. Fishbane, 'Use, Authority and Interpretation of Mikra at Qumran', in M. J. Mulder (ed.), *Mikra: Text Translation, Reading and Interpretation of the Hebrew Bible in Ancient Judaism and Early Christinaity* (Compendia Rerum Judaicarum ad Novum Testamentum 2/1; Assen-Philadelphia 1988), 339-77; J. Maier, 'Early Jewish Biblical Interpretation in the Qumran Literature', in M. Sæbø, *Hebrew Bible/Old Testament: The History of Its Interpretation*, Vol. I, *From the Beginings to the Middle Ages (Until 1300)* (Göttingen 1996), 108-29; M. J. Bernstein, 'Pentateuchal Interpretation at Qumran', in P. W. Flint and J. C. VanderKam (eds), *The Dead Sea Scroll after Fifty Years: A Comprehensive Assessment*

Jewish Ways of Reading the Bible

There seem to be three principal reasons for this. (1) To begin with, the accidents of discovery are not unimportant. Most obviously, of the seven principal manuscripts found in Cave 1 two were copies of Isaiah whose variants were initially considered from the perspective of the standard approaches of text criticism,[3] one was a collection of non-biblical hymns replete with biblical phraseology but not considered initially as exegetical,[4] one was a community rule book with virtually no explicit dependence on scripture,[5] one was a somewhat enigmatic eschatological cultic battle manual,[6] and one (the Genesis Apocryphon[7]) could not initially be unrolled. Only one text was clearly an interpretation of a biblical book, the Commentary on Habakkuk, and that had such a distinctive appearance that its form and content immediately came to control all the descriptions of the community's exegetical assumptions and methods.

(2) Secondly, the immediate and continuing dating of the finds to the late second temple period caused Christian scholars in particular to notice that the closest parallels to the explicit biblical interpretation in the scrolls were to be found in the New

---

(Leiden 1998), 1.128-59; G. J. Brooke, 'Dead Sea Scrolls', in J. H. Hayes (ed.), *Dictionary of Biblical Interpretation* (Nashville 1999), 253-56; M. J. Bernstein, 'Interpretation of Scriptures', in L. H. Schiffman and J. C. VanderKam (eds), *Encyclopedia of the Dead Sea Scrolls* (New York 2000), 1.376-83; G. J. Brooke, Biblical Interpretation in the Qumran Scrolls and the New Testament', in L. H. Schiffman, E. Tov, and J. C. VanderKam (eds), *The Dead Sea Scrolls Fifty Years After Their Discovery: Proceedings of the Jerusalem Congress, July 20-25, 1997* (Jerusalem 2000), 60-73. Other items can be found in the standard bibliographical resources for the study of the Dead Sea Scrolls, especially F. García Martínez and D. W. Parry, *A Bibliography of the Finds in the Desert of Judah 1970-1995* (Studies on the Texts of the Desert of Judah 19; Leiden 1996) and for studies published since 1995 at www.orion.mscc.huji.ac.il.

[3] The first major corrective to this approach to the Isaiah scrolls was the monograph by W. H. Brownlee, *The Meaning of the Qumrân Scrolls for the Bible with Special Attention to the Book of Isaiah* (New York 1964).

[4] A full appreciation of the exegetical character of 1QH was offered by S. Holm-Nielsen, *Hodayot: Psalms from Qumran* (Acta Theologica Danica 2; Aarhus 1960), 301-15.

[5] Amongst the studies on scriptural interpretation in 1QS see G. J. Brooke, 'Isaiah 40:3 and the Wilderness Community', in G. J. Brooke with F. García Martínez (eds), *New Qumran Texts and Studies: Proceedings of the First Meeting of the International Organization for Qumran Studies, Paris 1992* (Leiden 1994), 117-32; and S. Metso, 'The Use of Old Testament Quotations in the Qumran Community Rule', in F. H. Cryer and T. L. Thompson, *Qumran Between the Old and New Testaments* (Journal for the Study of the Old Testament Supplement 290; Sheffield 1998), 217-31.

[6] But see J. Carmignac, 'Les citations de l'Ancien Testament dans la Guerre des Fils de Lumière contre les Fils de Ténèbres', *Revue Biblique* 63 (1956), 234-60, 375-90.

[7] Now see M. J. Bernstein, 'Re-arrangement, Anticipation and Harmonization as Exegetical Features in the Genesis Apocryphon', *Dead Sea Discoveries* 3 (1996), 37-57.

Testament, especially in the use of so-called proof texts, notably by Matthew in his infancy and passion narratives.[8] Indeed through being brought to the American School of Oriental Research in Jerusalem in February 1948 the Habakkuk Commentary was first described and discussed by Christian scholars and the first extensive treatments of its exegesis were also produced by Christian scholars.[9] Through juxtaposition with New Testament interests in the fulfilment of prophecy, the primary characteristics of the exegesis of the community that produced the sectarian scrolls was assumed to be of a similar sort. It is really only since the publication of the Temple Scroll in 1977 that a proper balance has begun to emerge in the understanding of the exegetical concerns of the Qumran community and the wider movement of which it was a part, as can be seen, for example, in the short but significant contribution by Philip Alexander in *The Oxford Companion to the Bible.*[10] Apart from the 'mantological' interpretation of the pesharim, of all the many exegetical com-positions found at Qumran, in the limited space allotted to him Alexander refers only to the Temple Scroll in relation to early Jewish biblical interpretation.

(3) Thirdly, the canons of the textual criticism of the Hebrew Bible as these were generally formulated by western scholars in the middle of the twentieth century prevented the immediate recognition, for example, that some variants in the Isaiah manuscripts from Qumran, and other biblical manuscripts made available since, could be suitably described as exegetical. In general, variants were characterized as corruptions rather than as expositions or clarifications, and whole manuscripts disdainfully referred to as 'vulgar'.

---

[8] Note, e.g., the landmark study by K. Stendahl, *The School of St. Matthew and its Use of the Old Testament* (Acta Seminarii Neotestamentici Upsaliensis 20; Uppsala-Lund 1954).

[9] Amongst others see the studies by W. H. Brownlee, 'Biblical Interpretation among the Sectaries of the Dead Sea Scrolls', Biblical Archaeologist 14 (1951), 54-76, and 'The Habakkuk Midrash and the Targum of Jonathan', *Journal of Jewish Studies* 7 (1956), 169-86; and K. Elliger, *Studien zum Habakuk-Kommentar vom Toten Meer* (Beiträge zur historischen Theologie 15; Tübingen 1953).

[10] P. S. Alexander, 'Jewish Interpretation', in B. M. Metzger and M. D. Coogan (eds), *The Oxford Companion to the Bible* (New York-Oxford 1993), 305.

Jewish Ways of Reading the Bible

In light of the continuing assumption in many quarters that the biblical interpretation in the scrolls is primarily or exclusively concerned with the atomistic interpretation of the prophets and closely related texts, such as unfulfilled promises, blessings and curses, the purpose of this paper is to draw attention to some of the ways in which the Qumran scribes and their contemporaries whose work is represented in the Dead Sea Scrolls were interested in the plain meaning of the text itself, as they received it. It seems that in a wide range of matters the scribes of the late second temple period implicitly respected the plain meaning of the authoritative texts with which they were dealing. Amongst these scribes were those who might be most closely associated with the so-called Qumran scribal school.[11] At the same time it will be suggested that it is not always easy or even proper to distinguish between interest in the plain meaning and other attitudes towards scriptural texts.

II. What is meant by 'Plain Meaning'?

Those who concern themselves with Jewish ways of reading the Bible may find it odd that any time should be spent considering what is meant by 'plain meaning'.[12] However, it is important to clarify precisely what is at stake, since it will be argued in this study that even in the pesharim there is attention to the surface or literal details of the authoritative scriptural text being used as the basis of the exegesis. To focus on the plain meaning of scripture is not to be equated with restricting oneself to the literal meaning of the text alone. Paying attention to the plain meaning is far more than being

---

[11] The existence of such a scribal school has been most thoroughly proposed, especially in relation to the scriptural manuscripts found in the Qumran caves, by E. Tov, 'The Significance of the Texts from the Judean Desert for the History of the Text of the Hebrew Bible: A New Synthesis', in F. H. Cryer and T. L. Thompson, *Qumran Between the Old and New Testaments* (Journal for the Study of the Old Testament Supplement 290; Sheffield 1998), 277-309, esp. 294-96.

[12] Since the important study by R. Loewe, 'The "Plain" Meaning of Scripture in Early Jewish Exegesis', *Papers of the Institute of Jewish Studies*, Vol. 1 (Jerusalem 1964), 140-85, scholars have been wary of talking of *peshaṭ* and *derash* as explicitly distinct types of exegesis. Loewe asserts with much justification that there is no 'self-conscious positive concept of plain exegesis up to the end of the talmudic period' (p. 183).

concerned with literalism.[13]   Rather, it is being concerned with understanding the text as it is received, being concerned with the way in which the authoritative scriptural text presents itself, rather than focusing on the text solely from the point of view of the interpreter.[14] Nevertheless, issues of plain meaning cannot be described or investigated apart from the stances of particular readers, hearers or copyists, whether ancient or modern.[15] So the first step in appreciating the plain meaning of the text as understood by the early Jewish interpreters, whose works are now found in the Qumran caves, is to attempt to describe some of the assumptions which the scribes and commentators of the late second temple period may have had towards the scriptural texts which they encountered. At least five matters should be considered briefly.

(1) To begin with, it is axiomatic that the Jewish scribes and interpreters whose work is represented in the Qumran library were interested *both* in the *texts* of certain authoritative scriptures *and also* in the *interpretation* of those scriptures. In many ways the two matters cannot be divorced, since often the interpretation is contained within what the modern interpreter may take to be the authoritative scriptural text and very often the interpretation is riddled with quotations and allusions to scriptural antecedents which function not only as the basis of exegesis but also as the ongoing inter-texts for the interpretation. However, too often the focus of studies of biblical interpretation in the scrolls proceeds immediately to make statements based in the close reading of

---

[13] It has often been pointed out that the very term 'Dead Sea Scrolls', if taken literally, is a bad misnomer; 'Judaean Wilderness Scrolls' would be a more accurate label. The literalists also enjoyed teasing us when the journal *Dead Sea Discoveries* was launched: was it to be a journal on marine biology or nautical archaeology, and if the former, did we not know that the journal would barely have a single article to publish, since there were not many signs of life in the Dead Sea?

[14] R. Loewe has made this distinction thus: 'the true distinction to be drawn is between exegesis that is concerned constantly to enlarge the significance of a given text by relating it to new ideas, conditions, or associations in the mind of the exegete himself, and a concentration on the text that would eschew such accretions' ('The "Plain" Meaning of Scripture in Early Jewish Exegesis', 183). He also argued that the term פשט

exegetical compositions from the interpreter's point of view; too little is said about the character of the authoritative text which itself lies behind any interpretation.[16]

For example, it is commonly pointed out that in several places the Damascus Document insists not on obedience to the Law but on the pursuit of a lifestyle in accordance with the appropriate interpretation of the Law (לעשות כפרוש התורה CD 4:8 and 6:14; ולשמור את יום השבת כפרושה CD 6:18).[17] But attention to the correct interpretation of the Law should not be deemed as in some way exclusively more important than attention to the scriptural texts which the interpretation naturally accompanies. The Rule of the Community refers to those who study the Law continually ('day and night' in 1QS 6:6-7[18]) and who read 'the book', whatever that may be. It is not just a matter of exegetical results; the authoritative text is given some sort of priority. As such, every exegete, both ancient and modern, has a view about the plain meaning of the text.

(2) A second set of assumptions which needs to be factored in to any account of the attitude to scripture amongst those responsible for collecting the Qumran library together surround the attitude to various authoritative *texts as artifacts*. The Qumran manuscript collection shows that authoritative scriptural texts exist in several forms and

---

[16] In two studies in particular I have raised some of the intertextual issues related to these matters: G. J. Brooke, 'The Biblical texts in the Qumran Commentaries: Scribal Errors or Exegetical Variants?' in C. A. Evans and W. F. Stinespring (eds), *Early Jewish and Christian Exegesis: Studies in Memory of William Hugh Brownlee* (Society of Biblical Literature Homage Series 10; Atlanta 1987), 85-100; G. J. Brooke, 'Shared Intertextual Interpretations in the Dead Sea Scrolls and the New Testament', in M. E. Stone and E. Chazon (eds), *Biblical Perspectives: Early Use and Interpretation of the Bible in Light of the Dead Sea Scrolls* (Studies on the Texts of the Desert of Judah 28; Leiden 1998), 35-57, now reprinted and slightly revised in 'Interprétations intertextuelles communes dans les manuscrits de la Mer Morte et le Nouveau Testament', in A. H. W. Curtis and D. Marguerat (eds), *Intertextualités: La Bible en échos* (Le Monde de la Bible 40; Geneva 2000), 97-120.

[17] L. H. Schiffman, *The Halakah at Qumran* (Studies in Judaism in Late Antiquity 16; Leiden 1975), 32-41, has argued cogently that פרוש is not merely the exact statement of a text, but sectarian interpretation which is integrally connected to a text; he has commented, pertinently for this study, that '*perush* afforded the Qumran sect the same escape from the literal word that the dual-Torah concept gave the Rabbinic Jews' (p. 41).

[18] 4QS[d] 1 ii 10 represents the sentence differently. In a badly damaged context, in order to fit the available letter spaces, the editors propose omitting the phrase 'day and night': P. S. Alexander and G. Vermes, *Qumran Cave 4.XIX: Serekh ha-Yaḥad and Two Related Texts* (Discoveries in the Judaean Desert 26; Oxford 1998), 99-100.

their contents are presented in a variety of ways.[19]   Though much preliminary work has

been done in describing much of the data, it is clear that we are still a long way from

understanding fully why the so-called biblical manuscripts at Qumran have such a wide

range of sizes and formats.[20]   It is possible that amongst other matters the variety

represents an ongoing concern with the plain meaning of the text.

The contemporary function of a particular copy of a scriptural book may explain

the size and layout of some manuscripts, such as the way in which most of the *megillot*

texts are presented in relatively small columns both in width and height.[21]   But for the

most part, the presentation of the biblical books shows various attempts at assisting the

reader with the plain meaning of the text.   So, for example, the paragraph divisions in

many of the biblical scrolls are indications of how the scribe or his predecessors

understood the sense-units in the authoritative text which was being copied.   Often these

paragraphs correspond with what is found in the later Massoretic Bibles, but often there

are differences.[22]   It mattered to scribes how the authoritative text appeared on the sheet

---

[19] See the helpful introductory comments by M. Fishbane, 'Use, Authority and Interpretation of Mikra at Qumran' (see n. 2), 342-47. E. Tov has written most on this matter: see, for example, his 'Scribal Practices Reflected in the Texts from the Judaean Desert', in P. W. Flint and J. C. VanderKam (eds), *The Dead Sea Scrolls after Fifty Years: A Comprehensive Assessment* (Leiden 1998), 1.403-29; 'Scribal Practices and Physical Aspects of the Dead Sea Scrolls', in J. Sharpe and K. Van Kampen (eds), *The Bible as Book: The Manuscript Tradition* (London 1998), 9-34.

[20] On why the term 'biblical' is somewhat anachronistically inappropriate for the period of the scrolls found at Qumran, see especially E. Ulrich, 'The Bible in the Making: The Scriptures at Qumran', in E. Ulrich and J. VanderKam (eds), *The Community of the Renewed Covenant: The Notre Dame Symposium on the Dead Sea Scrolls* (Christianity and Judaism in Antiquity 10; Notre Dame, IN 1994), 77-93; reprinted as ch. 2 in E. Ulrich, *The Dead Sea Scrolls and the Origins of the Bible* (Studies in the Dead Sea Scrolls and Related Literature; Grand Rapids, MI 1999).

[21] The possible liturgical use of the *megillot* (apart from Esther) is described by J. Jarick, 'The Bible's "Festival Scrolls" among the Dead Sea Scrolls', in S. E. Porter and C. A. Evans (eds), *The Scrolls and the Scriptures: Qumran Fifty Years After* (Journal for the Study of the Pseudepigrapha Supplement 26; Sheffield 1997), 170-82.

[22] See J. M. Oesch, *Petucha und Setuma: Untersuchungen zu einer überlieferten Gliederung im hebräischen Text des Alten Testaments* (Freiburg-Göttingen 1979), 165-314; 'Textgliederung im Alten Testament und in den Qumranhandschriften', *Henoch* 5 (1983), 289-321. An overall survey of paragraph markings in both the biblical and non-biblical scrolls found at Qumran is offered by E. Tov, 'Scribal Markings in the Texts from the Judean Desert', in D. W. Parry and S. D. Ricks (eds), *Current Research and Technological Developments on the Dead Sea Scrolls: Conference on the Texts from the Judean Desert, Jerusalem, 30 April 1995* (Studies on the Texts of the Desert of Judah 20; Leiden 1996), 41-77.

of leather, and it mattered not primarily for aesthetic reasons but rather for reasons of comprehension.

Another piece of evidence to be appreciated from the manuscripts as artefacts concerns corrections. In many of the biblical manuscripts there is ample evidence of alterations being made. Sometimes the principal scribe of the manuscript makes these corrections to his own work, sometimes the corrections are in another hand.[23] Whereas the standard reaction amongst modern commentators is to count how many corrections are being made to the text to bring it into line with what may be supposed to be some form of the proto-Massoretic text, the first matter to notice is that corrections are made at all.[24] This is all the more intriguing since in many manuscripts which contain texts which may have had some authority, even scriptural authority, for their scribes, virtually no corrections are made. The number of corrections in the copies of the Rule of the Community or of the Damascus Document is insignificant compared with the number made in the so-called 'biblical' manuscripts. It seems that the practice of scrutinising and correcting manuscripts shows a concern for the status of the text in them and for the attention that some thought should be given to the actual letters of the text therein. Thus, the proportionately greater number of corrections in many of the scriptural manuscripts is suggestive of the greater authority of their contents. The actual manuscript evidence, therefore, shows us that the authoritative scriptural text was taken very seriously.

(3) This recognition of the status of the wording of scriptural texts may be confirmed by a third matter. It is clear that Moses and the prophets were in some fashion viewed as directed by God in their writings; the scriptures are considered to be *divinely inspired*. It is not Moses who speaks on his own authority; rather, God speaks

---

[23] It is probable, for example, that the scribe who wrote out 1QS-1Qsa-1QSb also inserted some of the corrections in 1QIsa[a].

[24] See the significant survey by E. Tov, The Textual Base of the Corrections in the Biblical texts Found at Qumran,' in D. Dimant and U. Rappaport (eds), *The Dead Sea Scrolls: Forty Years of Research* (Studies on the Texts of the Desert of Judah 10; Jerusalem/Leiden 1992), 299-314, who also states that 'much importance should be attached to the fact that many of the corrections happen to agree with the proto-Masoretic Text' (p. 306).

through Moses as is explicit, for example, in 1QM 10:7, 'They [the officers] shall recount that which You said through Moses (אשר ד]בר[תה ביד מושה)'. Even when the compositions ascribed to Moses and the prophets were understood to contain divine mysteries which only the well-trained and inspired exegete could expound, the writings in themselves commanded respect; there was attention to the words of the text. To some extent this attitude to the text is attested in the use of the introductory formula 'as it is written (כאשר כתוב)' which is only commonly used for introducing those authoritative scriptures whose every word is important.[25]

(4) Nevertheless, some place is also to be given to the one who was thus inspired. It is not uncommon to read before a scriptural quotation that it was written in the book of the Law (CD 5:2), or in the book of Isaiah the prophet (4Q174 1-2 iii 15[26]), or in the book of Daniel the prophet (4Q174 1-3 iv 3). Thus it is also clear that in some fashion the inspired authors were respected for their compositional activities. It is thus common to find that the various scriptures are referred to as what was commanded 'by the hand of Moses and all His servants the prophets' (1QS 1:3). Or again, in CD 5:8 'whereas Moses said' introduces the scriptural quotation, 'You shall not approach your mother's sister, she is your mother's near kin.' Or again, in CD 8:20 there is reference to 'the word which Jeremiah spoke to Baruch son of Neriah'. The spoken word seems to be acknowledged as carrying authority, even though it is only known in what was subsequently written down.

We should not overstate the case to insist that the scribes of the manuscripts found at Qumran were fully conversant with what we might label authorial intention. Indeed, there is some interchangeability in the very phraseology to which reference is being made: sometimes there is reference to a written artefact, sometimes to an author. So, for example, the range of authoritative scriptural texts is referred to in 4QMMT as

---

[25] For a comprehensive analysis of the significance of these formulae in the pesharim, see M. J. Bernstein, 'Introductory Formulas for Citation and Re-citation of Biblical Verses in the Qumran Pesharim', *Dead Sea Discoveries* 1 (1994), 30-70.

[26] Using the column numbers proposed by A. Steudel, *Der Midrasch zur Eschatologie aus der Qumrangemeinde (4Qmidrschat*[a.b]*)* (Studies on the Texts of the Desert of Judah 13; Leiden 1994).

'in the book of Moses [and] in the book[s of the pr]ophets and in Davi[d ...'[27] However, the point of importance is that the writers of the late second temple period realised they were copying texts written by their predecessors, the great men of the past, and as such they would have assumed that, even though inspired, the meaning had been or was obvious to them. Thus, for some Qumran interpreters of scripture it became necessary from time to time to signal that the author had not been fully aware of what he was writing, since the assumption was that the plain meaning of the text was the starting point of comprehension. When the author of the Habakkuk Commentary asserts that it is only the Teacher of Righteousness who can make known the mysteries of God's servants the prophets, the assertion seems to be made because the reader or hearer of Habakkuk would naturally assume otherwise.

(5) This respect for the role of the supposed author in presenting the text together with the concern with the text as artifact, to be corrected as appropriate, leads us to comment on an assumption which the Temple Scroll has brought to the fore. The overall attitude of respect for the authoritative scriptural text makes one suppose that such texts were not considered to be replaceable.[28] When the Temple Scroll reworks sections of the Torah and combines similar items of legislation for its own purposes, it could be considered to be making a re-presentation which renders its scriptural sources no longer necessary. Moshe Bernstein makes the same point with regard to the Book of Jubilees: 'was the goal of the author of Jubilees to interpret the book of Genesis or to replace it? Parts of Jubilees seem to rewrite Genesis for the purpose of clarifying it or of choosing among various understandings of the biblical text, while other, often halakhic, sections are superimposed on the narrative framework of Genesis externally

---

[27] 4Q397 frgs 16-18, line 10, a very fragmentary portion of text, is published in E. Qimron and J. Strugnell (eds), *Qumran Cave 4.V: Miqsat Ma'aśe Ha-Torah* (Discoveries in the Judaean Desert 10; Oxford 1994), 27, and plate VI.

[28] In commenting on the so-called 'Rewritten Bible' compositions P. S. Alexander similarly observes that 'despite the superficial independence of form, these texts are not intended to replace, or to supersede the Bible': 'Retelling the Old Testament', in D. A. Carson and H. G. M. Williamson (eds), *It is Written: Scripture Citing Scripture* (Cambridge 1988), 116.

and can in no way be regarded as interpretation of that pentateuchal book'.[29] Bernstein prefers to focus on the ways that Jubilees explains Genesis, rather than on the supplementary material, and so he concludes that it is primarily an exegetical work which does not in itself displace Genesis. With regard to the Temple Scroll the same can be observed. When the text's purpose is explanatory and clarificatory (which is most of the time), its purpose is not to replace its sources but to be the authoritative guide to them.

In sum, those at Qumran who collected, copied, and interpreted authoritative scriptural texts were concerned with understanding the text in itself and not just in reading their own concerns into the text. As such their understanding is represented in the ways in which the scriptural texts were copied and transmitted, ways which often attempted to clarify the meaning of the text. These interpreters assumed that, even if inspired, those who had written these authoritative texts knew what they meant; it was the responsibility of the text's transmitters to continue to present something of that meaning, whilst obviously having interpretative concerns of their own. The scriptural text as received had been and remained largely intelligible; it was not primarily or even at all a giant puzzle waiting to be decoded, by computer or by any other means. There was no short cut to correct interpretation; the scriptural text remained a constant element which had to be negotiated with directly through constant study.

III. Examples of the place of the plain meaning in scrolls from Qumran

In 1976 Geza Vermes proposed in a summary form that there were three kinds of biblical interpretation evident in the Qumran scrolls: midrashic supplementation of stories, halachic reinterpretation, and the fulfilment of prophecy.[30] In the first two types he noted that there was both pure and applied exegesis. His definition of pure exegesis can provide us with a starting point for our quest for defining the place of the plain

---

[29] M. Bernstein, 'Pentateuchal Interpretation at Qumran' (see n. 2), 136.
[30] G. Vermes, 'Interpretation, History of: At Qumran and in the Targums', *The Interpreter's Dictionary of the Bible: Supplementary Volume* (Nashville 1976), 440-41.

meaning of scripture within the discourse about biblical interpretation which is visible in the scrolls found at or near Qumran. Vermes defines pure exegesis as 'rendering the message of the text intelligible, coherent, and acceptable'.[31]

(1) *Intelligibility* is above all a matter of lexicography, appreciating the meaning of individual words and phrases. Such appreciation depends to a large extent on paying attention to the original context of such words. Vermes himself offers no examples of such a process, but the following may help illustrate this point for the surface meaning of the text.

It is well known that in the creation account in Genesis 1 the word יום is used in two different ways, predominantly in the formulaic phrase 'it was evening and it was morning day (יום) x'. Here יום obviously refers to the whole twenty-four hour period, a complete day. But in Genesis 1:5 after God has separated the light from the darkness, he calls the light 'day' (יום). In 4QGen[g] at Gen. 1:5 the text reads יומם. יומם is defined by the lexicographers and grammarians as an abstract noun (or sometimes an adverb) derived from יום. The reading of יומם in this place is reflected in the translations of all the Aramaic targumim and the Peshitta. Indeed these translations use יומם in Gen. 1:14, 16, and 18 as well, none of which verses happen to be preserved in 4QGen[g].

Though the reading of יומם is clearly secondary, it seems to be an alteration of the text to clarify the distinction between the two meanings of יום, 'day' and 'daytime'. James Davila, the editor of the Qumran cave four Genesis manuscripts, has pointed all this out, both in a preliminary study and in the principal edition.[32] However, he also comments that 'it is possible that the alteration arose from a dittography of *mem* in an early MS or one written in the Palaeo-Hebrew script. In either case there would have been no distinction between medial and final *mem*. Once the error was present it could

---

[31] G. Vermes, 'Interpretation, History of: At Qumran and in the Targums', 440.
[32] J. A. Davila, 'New Qumran Readings for Genesis One' in H. W. Attridge, J. J. Collins and T. H. Tobin (eds), *Of Scribes and Scrolls: Studies on the Hebrew Bible, Intertestamental Judaism, and Christian Origins* (Resources in Religion 5; Lanham MD 1990), 5-6; '4QGen[g]', in E. Ulrich (ed.), *Qumran Cave 4.VII: Genesis to Numbers* (Discoveries in the Judaean Desert 12; Oxford 1994), 58-59.

easily have spread to other passages where it seemed appropriate.'[33] What some might consider to be a deliberate clarificatory alteration becomes, in one scholar's view, a textual error. Here we see at work the assumption of the modern biblical interpreter who is somewhat reluctant to recognise how scribes in late antiquity might have adjusted the plain text in front of them with a particular exegetical purpose in mind; rather, for Davila, this variant is to be seen as coming about by scribal error.

A clearer example of lexical clarification occurs in the diglossic evidence of 11QtgJob. Michael Sokoloff has characterised the Qumran targum as providing a 'more readable and internally consistent text'[34] than the Masoretic and Daniel Harrington has noted that the targum was probably made 'because readers found the Hebrew so hard and needed help in understanding the text'.[35] In Job 42:11 those who come to console Job present him with קשיטה. This presents modern lexicographers with a challenge: as Harrington has noted, suggestions range 'from the vague "something valuable" to the very specific ("a weight of silver used in financial transactions," see Gen 33:19)'.[36] The ancient translator may have been similarly perplexed by the term and was equally determined to make some sense of it: the Qumran Job targumist rendered it as 'ewe lamb (אמרה)'.[37] Whether he was right or wrong, the targumist displays the concern of those who are determined to offer intelligibility to their hearers and readers.[38]

Intelligibility often goes beyond the search for the suitable meaning for a difficult word or the clarification of an ambiguity. The targumist often introduces small changes into his rendering in order to clarify the purpose of the text for his audience or

---

[33] J. Davila, '4QGen[g]', 59.

[34] M. Sokoloff, *The Targum to Job from Qumran Cave XI* (Ramat Gan 1974), 8.

[35] D. J. Harrington, *Wisdom Texts from Qumran* (London 1996), 19; following J. A. Fitzmyer, 'Some Observations on the Targum of Job from Qumran Cave 11', *Catholic Biblical Quarterly* 36 (1974), 503-24; reprinted in *A Wandering Aramean: Collected Aramaic Essays* (Missoula MT 1977), 161-82.

[36] D. J. Harrington, *Wisdom Texts from Qumran*, 22.

[37] 11QtgJob is presented in a fresh edition in F. García Martínez, E. J. C. Tigchelaar, and A. S. van der Woude, *Qumran Cave 11.II (11Q2-18, 11Q20-31)* (Discoveries in the Judaean Desert 23; Oxford 1998); here p. 170.

[38] D. J. Harrington, *Wisdom Texts from Qumran*, 22: 'clear (though not necessarily correct) translation'.

readership along particular theological lines; at this point the distinction between text and interpreter is much less clear. A well-known example of the targumist at work is cited by Lawrence Schiffman: 'For the verse "Who closed the sea behind doors, when it gushed forth out of the womb ... ?" (38:8), the translator translated "out of the womb" as "the womb of the deep," thus explaining that the "womb" from which the sea gushed forth was the depths of the sea itself, so that no one would mistakenly think that this verse referred to the mythological birth of the sea god, Yamm, prominent in ancient Near eastern mythology.'[39]

Thus clarifications of the plain meaning of the text can often carry theological interpretations too. Another example can be noted at Job 38:7, which in the Hebrew has all the morning stars sing together and the sons of God shouting for joy. The targumist renders this as 'when the morning stars shone together, and all of God's angels shouted together'.[40] The rendering rids the text of an anthropomorphism, as the stars no longer sing, and it puts the sons of God in their place as angels, thus protecting God himself.

This attention to the plain meaning of the text could be combined with other interpretative purposes too. A fine example of how the scribes of the late second temple period were aware of the polyvalence of some biblical words and phrases is to be found in the Rule of the Community. Isaiah 40:3 is cited and interpreted explicitly in 1QS 8:13-16:

> And when these become members of the Community in Israel according to all these rules, they shall separate from the habitation of unjust men and shall go into the wilderness to prepare there the way of Him; as it is written, *Prepare in the wilderness the way of* ••••, *make straight in the desert a path for our God* (Isa. xl, 3). This (path) is the study of the Law which he commanded by the hand of Moses that they may do according to all that has been revealed from age to age, and as the Prophets have revealed by His Holy Spirit.[41]

---

[39] L. H. Schiffman, *Reclaiming the Dead Sea Scrolls: The History of Judaism, the Background of Christianity, the Lost Library of Qumran* (Philadelphia-Jerusalem 1994), 215.
[40] F. García Martínez, E. J. C. Tigchelaar, and A. S. van der Woude, *Qumran Cave 11.II (11Q2-18, 11Q20-31)*, 150.
[41] Trans. G. Vermes, *The Complete Dead Sea Scrolls in English* (London 1997), 109. It is important to note that Vermes specifies in brackets to what the demonstrative might refer; perhaps it refers to the whole verse.

It is possible to acknowledge that the preparation in the wilderness has two meanings. On the one hand in the preamble to the quotation it refers to a literal withdrawal into the wilderness which is a separation from the habitation of unjust men; on the other hand in the interpretation which follows the quotation the demonstrative implies that preparation of the way in the wilderness is a metaphor for the study of the Law.[42] Not to see that the plain meaning of the text is retained alongside the more figurative interpretation has been the cause of some strange arguments. Norman Golb, for example, has insisted vehemently and somewhat arbitrarily that the metaphorical interpretation entirely overrides the literal meaning. Thus for him the community referred to here never separated itself off into a wilderness area, but only kept itself apart for its own study of the Law: in other words, for Golb, the men of the community never went to Qumran.[43]

(2) Vermes' second aspect of pure exegesis is *coherence*. Under this label can be grouped a number of strategies which are employed in some biblical manuscripts as well as in explicitly or implicitly exegetical texts. Here we should consider all those aspects of scribal practice which seek to render the authoritative scriptural texts magisterially coherent in themselves. There are three principal aspects to this handling of the plain meaning of the text: harmonisation, consistency, and what Michael Fishbane has called 'logical extension'.[44]

Harmonisation is visible in several biblical manuscripts and related texts.[45] This occurs chiefly where there are two versions of the same text. In the pentateuchal manuscripts found at Qumran there are many examples where the parallels in Exodus and Deuteronomy infect one another. Sometimes this might have come about because a text is being copied from memory, but it could also be the case that rendering the two

---

[42] My arguments for this are laid out in G. J. Brooke, 'Isaiah 40:3 and the Wilderness Community' (see n. 5).

[43] N. Golb, *Who Wrote the Dead Sea Scrolls? The Search for the Secret of Qumran* (New York-London 1995), 93-94.

[44] M. Fishbane, 'Use, Authority and Interpretation of Mikra at Qumran' (see n. 2), 369-70.

[45] See E. Tov, 'The Nature and Background of Harmonizations in Biblical Manuscripts', *Journal for the Study of the Old Testament* 31 (1985), 3-29.

versions of the same narrative or the same speech in similar phraseology was done deliberately to bring about a sense of internal coherence in the Torah. Clear examples can be seen in the phylacteries. In Phylactery G Deut. 5:1-21 is being followed closely for the most part as the base text, but in several places the language of Exodus 20 is plain to see.[46] Thus the justification of the sabbath commandment of Deut. 5:15 is replaced with the reasoning from Exod. 20:11: 'For in six days the Lord made the heaven and earth, the sea and all that is in them, but rested the seventh day; therefore the Lord blessed the sabbath day and consecrated it'. In the same phylactery the next commandment reads 'Honour your father and your mother so that your days may be long in the land which the Lord your God (gives you), as the Lord your God commanded you'. The first part comes from Exod. 20:12, but the final phrase reverts to the text of Deut. 5:16, though the phrasing is now in a different order than that represented in the Masoretic text. The character of what is taking place here and what kind of interpretation it represents can be debated at length: for example, does the new scriptural text to be placed in the phylactery case represent a deliberate attempt to suggest that the Decalogue of Exodus in some way takes precedence over that in Deuteronomy, for all that it is the Deuteronomy text which lies at the base of what is being included? Whatever the case, at the least the cross-fertilisation of the two versions of the Decalogue is plain to see. It is difficult to determine whether the scribe who painstakingly copied this material was aware of the composite character of what he was producing.

Consistency is most apparent in those pentateuchal manuscripts and their relations, such as the Reworked Pentateuch texts,[47] which are akin in many ways to the

---

[46] See J. T. Milik, 'Tefillin, Mezuzot et Targums (4Q128-4Q157)', in R. de Vaux and J. T. Milik (eds), *Qumrân Cave 4.II* (Discoveries in the Judaean Desert 6; Oxford 1977), 58-60.

[47] For the so-called Reworked Pentateuch texts, see 4Q158 in J. M. Allegro with A. A. Anderson, *Qumrân Cave 4.I* (Discoveries in the Judaean Desert of Jordan 5; Oxford 1968), 1-6, and 4Q364-67 in E. Tov and S. White, 'Reworked Pentateuch', in H. Attridge et al. (eds), *Qumran Cave 4.VIII* (Discoveries in the Judaean Desert 13; Oxford 1994), 187-351.

Samaritan Pentateuch in which consistency plays a major part.[48] For the Qumran biblical manuscripts it is most obvious in 4QpaleoExod^m, a text of a type akin to the non-sectarian sections of the Samaritan Pentateuch, which has been analysed most extensively by Judith Sanderson.[49] This manuscript in palaeo-Hebrew from about 150-50 BCE contains many expansions of the text of Exodus, expansions which seem intended deliberately to improve the flow of the text. As Sanderson has exhaustively shown, these expansions are not created at the whim of the scribe, but are nearly always couched in biblical phraseology from a parallel passage somewhere else in Exodus itself or perhaps in Deuteronomy or another pentateuchal book. Sanderson found only two expansions using non-pentateuchal language, one from Ezekiel and one from Job. She concurs overall with S. Talmon's description of the scribe of the second temple period as one who felt competent to be 'a minor partner' together with the author 'in the creative literary process'.[50] Minor variations could be introduced to improve the text and add to its appeal. Sanderson also surmises that some of the variations in 4QpaleoExod^m may result from the use of the text in various liturgical settings. Sanderson's analysis raises acutely the issue concerning whether any scribe in the late second temple period would have considered himself to have been a mere copyist; they were expositors of the plain meaning of the text, copying it out verbatim for the most part, but enhancing it in many small but intriguing ways.[51]

Logical extension is apparent in those retellings of narrative texts in which clarification is given to the story line through the inclusion of an incident so that actions seem logical. Vermes himself provides a neat example from the Genesis Apocryphon.[52]

---

[48] On the overall character of the exegesis apparent in 4Q158 and 4Q364-367, see E. Tov, 'Biblical Texts as Reworked in Some Qumran Manuscripts with Special Attention to 4QRP and 4QParaGen-Exod', in E. Ulrich and J. VanderKam (eds), *The Community of the Renewed Covenant: The Notre Dame Symposium on the Dead Sea Scrolls* (Christianity and Judaism in Antiquity Series 10; Notre Dame IN 1994), 111-34.
[49] J. E. Sanderson, *An Exodus Scroll from Qumran: 4QpaleoExod^m and the Samaritan Tradition* (Harvard Semitic Studies 30; Atlanta 1986), esp. 261-306.
[50] S. Talmon, 'The Textual Study of the Bible: A New Outlook', in F. M. Cross and S. Talmon (eds), *Qumran and the History of the Biblical Text* (Cambridge, MA 1975), 381.
[51] J. E. Sanderson, *An Exodus Scroll from Qumran*, 299-306.
[52] G. Vermes, 'Interpretation, History of: At Qumran and in the Targums', 449.

In the Genesis account of Abram's journey to Egypt, the biblical author fails to indicate how the patriarch learned of the danger that he would incur should he and his beautiful wife cross the southern frontier of Canaan. The Genesis Apocryphon introduces a premonitory dream as a result of which Abram keeps his wife out of the sight of the Egyptians for five years. Her attractions are discovered only when three princes of Pharaoh are dispatched explicitly to make inquiries concerning the foreign couple (1QapGen 19:14-24). Abram's dream explains why the events take the course that they do.

(3) Rendering the text *acceptable*, Vermes' third category of pure exegesis, is more problematic in relation to understanding the status accorded to the plain meaning of the text. Acceptability is a matter which rests more with the interpreter and his audience than with the scriptural text itself. From the example which Vermes gives to illustrate his point it seems as if by 'acceptability' he means to suggest that some re-presentation of texts is done to make them practical. Vermes mentions the use of Num. 30:9 in CD 16:10-12; the scriptural text is given in the Damascus Document in a slightly paraphrased form, 'it is for her husband to cancel her oath'. The commentator respects the original text's concern with oaths but whereas in Numbers the husband may nullify any oath of his wife at his discretion, the Damascus Document restricts the husband's right only to those oaths which he deems never should have been made in the first place. This could be categorised as applied exegesis, rather than what Vermes labels pure exegesis, since the original context in the Book of Numbers is not respected in a thoroughgoing manner, but its legislation becomes practical for the community members (and possibly others), when it is restricted as the Damascus Document suggests.

The notion that pure exegesis can involve making the scriptural text acceptable shows us again that the borderline between text and interpreter is very indeterminate. Just as copyists of biblical texts in the late second temple period considered themselves part of the dynamic of the text they were passing on, so those who read these

84

authoritative texts found that when they took the plain meaning seriously they inevitably recontextualized it for themselves. This conundrum can be seen in the handling of narrative texts too. The most extensively preserved of the Genesis Commentaries from cave four, 4Q252, Commentary on Genesis A, contains much which falls in this category of expounding the plain meaning of the text, though this complex commentary is not yet fully understood.[53] The text deserves the title 'commentary' because it contains references to parts of Genesis from chapter 6 through to chapter 49. Only a few passages of Genesis are selected for comment and the manner of comment varies from passage to passage: sometimes there is retelling, what can be called rewritten Bible,[54] sometimes straight quotation without even any glossing, sometimes citation together with pesher-interpretation.[55] Why the commentator chose the passages he did is still not clear, though various attempts have been made to discern a pattern in the selection of texts and the choice of genres in the various parts of the commentary.[56]

The opening sections of the commentary seem particularly concerned to sort out various chronological and calendrical problems in the text of Genesis; the scriptural text is obscure, imprecise, or ambiguous at several points.[57] It is clear that the commentator's attention to the text of Genesis is motivated in no small measure by

---

[53] See G. J. Brooke, '4QCommentary on Genesis A', in G. J. Brooke et al., *Qumran Cave 4.XVII: Parabiblical Texts Part 3* (Discoveries in the Judaean Deseret 22; Oxford 1996), 185-207.

[54] On the meaning of this term see especially G. Vermes, *Scripture and Tradition in Judaism: Haggadic Studies* (Studia Post-Biblica 4; 2nd edn; Leiden 1983), 67-126; P. S. Alexander, 'Retelling the Bible', in D. A. Carson and H. G. M. Williamson (eds), *It is Written: Scripture Citing Scripture* (Cambridge 1988), 99-121; and G. J. Brooke, 'Rewritten Bible', in L. H. Schiffman and J. C. VanderKam (eds), *Encyclopedia of the Dead Sea Scrolls* (New York 2000), 777-81.

[55] Preliminary genre analysis is in G. J. Brooke, 'The Genre of 4Q252: From Poetry to Pesher', *Dead Sea Discoveries* 1 (1994), 160-79; and M. Bernstein, '4Q252: From Re-Written Bible to Biblical Commentary', *Journal of Jewish Studies* 45 (1994), 1-27.

[56] See especially, G. J. Brooke, 'The Thematic Content of 4Q252', *Jewish Quarterly Review* 85 (1994-95), 33-59; I. Fröhlich, 'Themes, Structure and Genre of Pesher Genesis', *Jewish Quarterly Review* 85 (1994-95), 81-90; 'Narrative Exegesis in the Dead Sea Scrolls', in M. E. Stone and E. G. Chazon (eds), *Biblical Perspectives: Early Use and Interpretation of the Bible in Light of the Dead Sea Scrolls: Proceedings of the First International Symposium of the Orion Center for the Study of the Dead Sea Scrolls and Associated Literature, 12-14 May, 1996* (Studies on the Texts of the Desert of Judah; Leiden 1998), 81-99.

[57] As highlighted especially by M. Bernstein, '4Q252: From Re-Written Bible to Biblical Commentary' (n. 55), 5-9.

some of the calendrical preferences of the Qumran community and the wider movement of which it was a part. Thus the flood narrative is retold to fit in with the 364-day calendar of the community, a calendar which in one sense is implied by the various dates in the text of Genesis itself.[58] The concern with chronology more generally is also reflected in other community texts (such as CD 1:1-10 and 11QMelch 2:5-8), not least in the attention the community seems to have paid to the Book of Jubilees.

However, there are several places where the interpretation in the Genesis Commentary (4Q252) seems less motivated by partisan views than by a more neutral desire to clarify what may be deemed the plain meaning or intention of Genesis itself. The Commentary refers to the problem that when Noah awoke from his drunken sleep he cursed Canaan rather than Ham who had seen his nakedness. Why Canaan? The commentary explains: 'But he did not curse Ham, but his son, because God blessed the sons of Noah' (4Q252 2:6-7). Noah's action is explained through reference to an earlier part of Genesis 9 (Gen. 9:1): because Ham was already blessed, God could not reverse his blessing. 'The simplicity and directness of this answer and of other explanations given in this text have led one scholar to suggest that this is the first biblical commentary attempting to provide the plain sense of the biblical text'.[59] Lawrence Schiffman thereby alludes to the detailed work on this text by Moshe Bernstein, who has commented on this particular instance that the interpretation offered as to why Noah cursed Canaan 'is coherent with all the parameters of literal exegesis'.[60] It is in instances like this that the scriptural text is rendered *acceptable* to the reader, to return to Vermes' term.

(4) But concern with the plain meaning of the text has a place beyond these kinds of exegetical practices in biblical manuscripts, their reworked forms, and certain

---

[58] MT Genesis implies that the flood lasted for 364 days; all 4Q252 does is say that that number of days is a year. The chronological compatability of Genesis and 4Q252 on 364 days has given rise to suggestions that behind everything lies a text-critical problem: R. S. Hendel, '4Q252 and the Flood Chronology of Genesis 7-8: A Text-Critical Solution', *Dead Sea Discoveries* 2 (1995), 72-79.

[59] L. H. Schiffman, *Reclaiming the Dead Sea Scrolls*, 216. Schiffman's book is one of the few which contains a section on what he calls 'Plain Sense Commentary', pp. 215-17.

[60] M. Bernstein, 'From Re-Written Bible to Biblical Commentary' (n. 55), 10; cf. Gen. Rab. 36:7.

kinds of early commentary. In addition to *intelligibility*, *coherence*, and *acceptability* (in some sense), there is a fourth area to which attention should be drawn, since it is usually overlooked or not considered as having much to do with the plain meaning of the text or literal exegesis. This fourth area we might label *respect* for the overall scriptural text in itself. Something of this has already been implied in what has been said above about scribal practices in the late second temple period, but there is more to be said.

It can be argued that the plain meaning of the text is what is often understood and exploited even in the pesharim, which according to their own self-presentation are supposed to be exclusively about what is not on the surface of the prophetic text. A couple of examples from the Habakkuk Commentary can illustrate this. The plain meaning of the text plays a role both at the macro-level and also at the micro-level. At the macro-level it is important to notice that the author of the Habakkuk Commentary does not break up his biblical source in an arbitrary fashion. In fact in one sense he is less selective in relation to his scriptural source than the author of the Commentary on Genesis to which we have just referred. Thus it is important to realize that the commentator respects the integrity of the text of Habakkuk as he received it: for all that he wished to relate that text to his own experiences that text controlled his immediate exegetical purposes.

Attention to the overall structure of the Book of Habakkuk in itself can be seen in the Commentary. For example, it is well known that Habakkuk 2:6-20 contains five woes: 'Alas for you who heap up what is not your own' (2:6-8); 'Alas for you who get evil gain for your houses' (2:9-11); 'Alas for you who build a town by bloodshed an found a city on iniquity' (2:12-14); 'Alas for you who make your neighbours drink' (2:15-17); and 'Alas for you who say to wood "Wake up!" to silent stone "Rouse yourself!"' (2:18-20). The Qumran commentator is sensitive to this structure as he applies the oracles to his present day; he does not ignore it entirely. Thus the first and second woes are applied to the Wicked Priest. The third is referred to the so-called

Spouter of Lies. The fourth is related again to the Wicked Priest. The fifth is made to refer to the Gentiles, as indeed it seems to do in the prophecy of Habakkuk itself. Thus the commentator pays attention to the structure of the prophecies of Habakkuk at the macro-level, if not always expounding the text in a way which would have been intelligible to Habakkuk's first hearers.[61] The text of Habakkuk does indeed exercise some kind of control over the Qumran commentator.

At the micro-level the same may also be apparent. Vermes has noted that even in the pesharim it is rare to find any liberty being taken with the text of scripture itself. Rather, he has made the telling comment that

> The usual attitude is so respectful that at times it presents the exegete with difficulties. For example, in Hab. 2:16, the commentator reproduces the Hebrew text with a LXX-type variant, "Stagger!" (*hērā'ēl*), instead of the Masoretic reading, "Show your foreskin!" (*he'ārēl*) ... Yet his exegesis shows knowledge of both textual traditions ... This rendering not only implies an acquaintance with the variants; it also shows an inability or unwillingness to choose between them. Both readings are cleverly mingled, revealing that, far from being free with the biblical text, the interpreter held in profound esteem every witness of what in his view was the sacred record of the word of God.[62]

It is this attitude of respect for the text in itself which lies at the heart of coming to terms with the plain meaning of the text. It would have been good if Vermes had categorized this as a kind of pure exegesis within the broad category of fulfilment of prophecy.

This fourth aspect of describing the place of the plain meaning of the text in the exegetical concerns of those responsible for composing the scrolls found at Qumran raises the question of demarcation. What ultimately distinguishes pure from applied exegesis? If clear evidence for respect for the text and its original meaning can be found even in the pesharim, supposedly the very epitome of applied exegesis at Qumran, often

---

[61] See the comments of W. H. Brownlee, 'The Composition of Habakkuk', in A. Caquot and M. Philonenko (eds), *Hommages à André Dupont-Sommer* (Paris 1971), 255-75; many of these insights are repeated in the relevant sections of his detailed commentary on 1QpHab: *The Midrash Pesher of Habakkuk* (SBL Monograph Series 24; Missoula, MT 1979).

[62] G. Vermes, 'Interpretation, History of: At Qumran and in the Targums', 441. See also the discussion of the same issue by T. H. Lim, *Holy Scripture in the Qumran Commentaries and Pauline Letters* (Oxford 1997), 50, in the context of an analysis of features of literalism in which Lim argues that the commentator is not interested solely in reading his own meaning into the text, but is also aware of the textual niceties of the scriptural text itself.

considered to be basically ignoring the original meanings and structures of their base texts, then we are faced with the clear need to rethink categories.

Perhaps a new model is required for understanding what is going on in all these varied materials. This model should not be a crude taxonomy which distinguishes literal from other kinds of interpretation, but rather a kind of double helix. The two strands woven together and interdependent may be considered to represent the text and the interpreter, whether as copyist or commentator. Each strand is made up of patterned intricacy, a kind of pluralism. On the one hand there are multiple text-types and variant readings which nevertheless carry a family resemblance. On the other hand there are sets of interpretative assumptions and prejudices which can be given a set of historical contexts of their own. Neither strand can be divorced from the other without the whole becoming unrecognisable. Of course any particular feature of one strand can be looked at in isolation, so that we may understand it all the better, but in the end it must be put back in place.

IV. Conclusion

To pay attention to the plain meaning of the text in the Qumran scrolls allows one to add an important dimension to how the handling of authoritative scriptural texts took place. For the late second temple period modern scholars should be wary of distinguishing between matters they may deem to be in the realm of textual criticism and the scribal transmission of texts and those which can be more obviously described as exegetical or eisegetical. All the evidence is interrelated. Discussion of literal exegesis is not just about the establishment of an unambiguous surface meaning as intended by the original author; it is also about the status of the scriptural text, and the interpreter's views of God, humanity and the world and their interrelationship. Paying attention to the plain meaning of the text as it is reflected in the Qumran scrolls lets us see that the ancients knew that words are polyvalent, that authoritative texts demand to be made intelligible for those they influence and often control, that the quest for literary coherence is not bland standardisation but a reflection of the text's own integrity, and that respect for the text is part and parcel of making sense of experience. There is really no neat dividing line between pure exegesis and applied exegesis, between the copying of biblical manuscripts and their interpretation and over-interpretation. All handling of scripture in the scrolls from Qumran shows not antiquarian interest but that certain authoritative traditions were understood to be continuously relevant. Of course the understanding of all the finds at Qumran is, like the finds themselves, still very fragmentary, but the rich range of materials now available from one place offers the modern scholar an unequalled opportunity to embark on a comprehensive analysis of the place of authoritative scriptures in a believing community. Any such analysis must give proper place to the texts of the scriptures themselves, which includes their plain sense, as well as outlining the broader exegetical assumptions of those who transmitted and interpreted them.

The Exegesis of Homer and Numerology as a Method for Interpreting the Bible in the Writings of Philo of Alexandria

Niclas Förster

I. Introduction

'... the Homeric poetry that, in my opinion, was tasted by each of the early wise men and especially by all those who drew water for themselves from the external wisdom'.[1] With these words written in the 12th century Eustathius, archbishop of Thessaloniki, praises Homer in his commentary on the Iliad. Almost a thousand years earlier the author of the Essay on the Life and Poetry of Homer went even further. This book survived in medieval manuscripts as a part of Plutarch's Moral Essays, but was probably written two or three generations later than Plutarch in approximately 200 CE.[2] The author of this Essay attempts to demonstrate that Homer is the source of all philosophy – and not only of philosophy, but also of rhetoric and of many other human skills as well. 'Thus,' he writes, 'Homer was the first to philosophize in the areas of ethics and physics. Arithmetic and music, which Pythagoras held in particular honour, belong to the same area of speculation. Let us examine whether or not there is an account of these things in the Poet. Why, there is a very substantial account, indeed! It will suffice to set out a few examples from the

---

[1] *Eustathii Archepiscopi Thessalonicensis Commentarii ad Homeri Iliadem pertinentes*, Volumen primum, *Praefationem et Commentarios ad Libros A-D complectens* (ed. M. van der Valk; Leiden 1971), 1, 7-8.
[2] For the date of the Essay on the Life and Poetry of Homer, cf. R. Lamberton, *Homer the Theologian. Neoplatonist Allegorical Reading and the Growth of the Epic Traditions* (Berkeley-Los Angeles-London 1986), 40; M. Hillgruber, 'Einleitung und Kommentar zu den Kapiteln 1-73', in *Die pseudoplutarchische Schrift De Homero,* Teil 1 (Beiträge zur Altertumskunde 57; Stuttgart-Leipzig 1994), 74-75; [Plutarch], *Essay on the Life and Poetry of Homer,* J. J. Keaney and R. Lamberton (eds) (American Philological Association: American Classical Studies 40; Atlanta 1996), 9.

many available'.[3] He then shows that Pythagorean arithmology is rooted in Homer by quoting certain verses from the Iliad and Odyssey. He further emphasizes that 'Homer demonstrates not only the power of numbers but also the technique of calculation'[4] and gives examples from his poems.

The purpose of the present paper is to examine Philo's arithmological interpretation of the Bible and to demonstrate, if possible, that he was familiar with the exegesis which authors like Pseudo-Plutarch used as proof for Pythagorean arithmology, and that he modelled his interpretation of biblical texts on it. The paper is divided into the following sections: (1) an investigation of the sources which Philo could have drawn on for his understanding of the Bible according to the arithmological interpretation of Homer; (2) an examination of whether Philo knew the kind of exegesis contained in such sources; and (3) a consideration of the extent to which Philo, by using this exegetical method, came to the same results as authors like Pseudo-Plutarch.

II. The Sources for the Arithmological Interpretation of Homer

How could Philo have known about the arithmological interpretation of Homer, and which sources informed him about this way of understanding the poet? In order to answer this question one must bear in mind that Homer played a leading part in Greek culture. This is already apparent from the central position of the Homeric epic in the ancient Greek system of education. The exercises of reading and writing were based on the text of Homer at an early stage. The pupils also learned large portions of the text by heart, and it can be assumed 'that the average Greek who had received some primary education had his head full of Homeric lines'[5]. This role of Homer as the foundation of Greek cultural identity could only remain authoritative

---

[3] For the Greek text cf. J. F. Kindstrand (ed.) [Plutarchi], *De Homero* (Bibliotheca Scriptorum Graecorum et Romanorum Teubneriana; Leipzig 1990), Chs 144-145 (77, 1738-1743). The translation is taken from J. J. Keaney and R. Lamberton (eds), [Plutarch], *Essay on the Life and Poetry of Homer*, 229

[4] Kindstrand (ed.), *De Homero*, Ch. 146 (79, 1795-1796); J. J. Keaney and R. Lamberton (eds), *Essay on the Life and Poetry of Homer*, 233.

[5] Cf. W. J. Verdenius, *Homer, The Educator of the Greeks* (Mededelingen der koninklijke Nederlandse Akademie van Wetenschappen, AFD. Letterkunde [New Series] 33.5; Amsterdam- London 1970), 6.

for centuries, despite all social and cultural change, if the message of the Homeric text could be brought up to date.[6] The method of allegorical interpretation served this purpose. Indeed, philosophers were already using this method in the fifth and fourth centuries BCE for finding their own teaching in Homer, and for legitimating it on behalf of the general public.[7] Relatively early on, some people also supported the view that Homer was in fact the source of all skills. So boasts, for example, Nikeratos in Xenophon's Symposion with his manifold knowledge learned from Homer:[8]

> You may now hear me tell wherein you will be improved by associating with me. You know, doubtless, that the sage Homer has written about practically everything pertaining to man. Any one of you, therefore, who wishes to acquire the art of the householder, the political leader, or the general, or to become like Achilles or Ajax or Nestor or Odysseus, should seek my favour, for I understand all these things.

Schoolteachers, and especially the grammarians who were responsible for teaching the poets, adopted this view in order to justify the leading part that Homer played in education. Therefore, for the majority of pupils who never read the philosophers or specialist literature, for example, 'about the householder', this concentration on Homer was not a deficiency in their studies.[9] In such an environment it seemed natural to interpret Homer in an arithmological way.

The literature that may have informed Philo about the reading of Homer as a source and proof-text for arithmology was divided into three groups:

(a) As in several other technical fields in ancient times there were in circulation handbooks about Pythagorean arithmology. They consisted of an introduction and chapters dealing with the numbers one to ten. In these chapters both the mathematical and symbolical characteristics of the first ten numbers were

---

[6] A. A. Long, 'Stoic Readings of Homer', in R. Lamberton and J. J. Keaney (eds), *Homer's Ancient Readers. The Hermeneutics of Greek Epic's Earliest Exegetes* (Princeton 1992), 41-66, here p. 44.
[7] Cf. M. Hillgruber (ed.), *Die pseudoplutarchische Schrift De Homero,* Teil 1, 16-35.
[8] Xenophon, Symposium, IV. 6. For the translation see: *Xenophon in Seven Volumes* IV, *Symposium and Apology* (trans. O. J. Todd; Cambridge, MA-London 1979), 567. On Nikeratos see: W. J. Verdenius, *Homer*, 15-16 and M. Hillgruber, *Die pseudoplutarchische Schrift De Homero* Teil 1, 14-15.
[9] Cf. G. W. Most, *Ansichten über einen Hund. Zu einigen Strukturen der Homerrezeption zwischen Antike und Neuzeit* (Antike und Abendland: Beiträge zum Verständnis der Griechen und Römer und ihres Nachlebens 37; Berlin-New York 1991), 144-66, here p. 156, and M. Hillgruber, *Die pseudoplutarchische Schrift De Homero,* Teil 1, 34-35.

described. Thus certain numbers were equated with certain gods, and several Homeric verses are quoted by the authors because Homer 'had also known'[10] this form of speculation. The two most important arithmological writers whose treatises are still extant are Nicomachos of Gerasa and Anatolius. Both lived in Roman times, one in the second and the other in the third century CE.[11] Philo was almost certainly familiar with some Hellenistic literature with very similar contents because he was the author of a book About Numbers. This treatise is lost today, but he mentions it by name in his other writings. It probably contained speculations about numbers.[12]

(b) Other writers, like the author of the Essay on the Life and Poetry of Homer, based their teachings on the Iliad and the Odyssey, and developed them as a whole system for all branches of science. The Essay of Pseudo-Plutarch is probably only one surviving example of a much more extensive literature. Similar excerpts can be found in the collection of Stobaius. They are gathered under the headline 'that Homer also understood the theory about the numbers'.[13]

(c) Thirdly also the different Scholia on both epic poems by Homer provide us information about the interpretation of Homer in support of Pythagorean speculations. These Scholia are, in most cases, of a very late origin, so that it cannot be excluded that they used the writings of, for example, Nicomachus or Pseudo-Plutarch as sources from which they drew. Despite this, some of the manuscripts that are preserved today seem to reflect an independent tradition of Pythagorean

---

[10] J. L. Heiberg, 'Anatolius. Sur les dix premiers nombres', in *Annales internationales d'histoire, Congrès de Paris 1900*, 5. Section: *Histoire des sciences* (Paris 1901), 27-41, here p. 30.

[11] The text of Nicomachus' work is largely preserved by the excerpts of Pseudo-Iamblichus, cf. [Iamblichi], *Theologumena Arithmeticae* (ed. V. de Falco [1922]), revised and corrected by V. Klein (Stuttgart 1975). The book of Anatolius was edited by J. L. Heiberg, 'Anatolius. Sur les dix premiers nombres' (see previous note). On Nicomachus of Gerasa see also: F. Kliem, 'Nikomachus', *Paulys Real-Encyclopädie* XVII, 463-64; L. Tarán, 'Nicomachus of Gerasa', *Dictionary of Scientific Biography* X, 112-14; and H. R. Moehring, 'Arithmology as an Exegetical Tool in the Writings of Philo of Alexandria', in J. P. Kenney (ed.), *The School of Moses. Studies in Philo and Hellenistic Religion in Memory of H. R. Moehring* (Brown Judaic Studies 304; Studia Philonica Monographs 1; Atlanta 1995), 148. On Anatolius see: G. Borghorst, *De Anatolii Fontibus*, Ph.D. thesis (Berlin 1905).

[12] Cf. F. E. Robbins, 'Posidonius and the Sources of Pythagorean Arithmology', *Classical Philology* 15 (1920), 309-22, here p. 320 and K. Staehle, *Die Zahlenmystik bei Philon von Alexandreia* (Leipzig-Berlin 1931), who tries to reconstruct this lost essay of Philo.

[13] *Ioannis Stobaei Eclogarum Physicarum et Ethicarum libri duo,* Tom. I (ed. A. Meineke; Leipzig 1860), 1.

exegesis.[14] One Scholion remarks about the Homeric hero Achilles: 'He is more a Pythagorean philosopher than a soldier'.[15] Another manuscript summarizes the following interpretation of Homer: 'For in general Homer considers the odd number more powerful than the even. The Pythagorean philosophers also especially uphold this, because the odd is always indivisible, since the "Monas" (unity) is fallen among it'[16] or: 'Pythagoras speaks about two beginnings: the "one" and the "two", the "one" is the beginning of the good (things) but the "two" is the beginning of the bad (things). This is obvious on the basis of Homer's writings'.[17]

III. Philo's Knowledge of Arithmological Sources

The aforementioned writings could have informed Philo about the interpretation of Homer in accordance with Pythagorean numerology. But did Philo really know this form of exegesis? The starting point of the following considerations is the observation that Philo quoted lines of the Iliad in connection with his arithmological explanations. In his essay On the Confusion of Tongues Philo quotes the verses from the second book of the Iliad: 'It is not well that many lords should rule; Be there but one, one king'[18] for his interpretation of Gen. 3:22:

> And once more, 'God said, "behold Adam has become as one of us by knowing good and evil";' here the 'us' in 'as one of us' is said not of one, but of more than one. Now we must first lay down that no existing thing is of equal honour to God and that there is only one sovereign and ruler and king, who alone may direct and dispose of all things. For the lines: 'It is not well that many lords should rule; Be there but one,

---

[14] On the Pythagorean traditions preserved in the different Scholia see the collection of the most important references by C. Schmid, *Homerische Studien I. Homer, das hellenische Universalgenie nach den Begriffen der antiken Schulerklärung, Schulprogramm* (Landau 1905); cf. also F. Wehrli, *Zur Geschichte der allegorischen Deutung Homers im Altertum*, (Borna-Leipzig 1928), 40; M. Schmidt, *Die Erklärungen zum Weltbild Homers und zur Kultur der Heroenzeit in den bT-Scholien zur Ilias* (Zetemata 62; München 1976), 58-59.

[15] On Iliad I.66c, *Scholia Graeca in Homeri Iliadem (Scholia vetera)*, Volumen primum, *Praefationem et Scholia ad libros A-D* (ed. H. Erbse; Berlin 1969), 30; cf. also *Scholion on Iliad XVI 225, Scholia Graeca in Homeri Iliadem (Scholia vetera)*, Volumen quartum, *Scholia ad libros O-T* (ed. H. Erbse; Berlin 1975), 217.

[16] On Iliad I.53-55, *Scholia Graeca in Homeri Iliadem (Scholia vetera)*, Volumen primum, *Praefationem et Scholia ad libros A-D* (ed. H. Erbse; Berlin 1969), 25, in the notes.

[17] On Iliad XV.138, *Scholia Graeca in Homeri Iliadem (Scholia vetera)*, Volumen quartum *Scholia ad libros O-T* (ed. H. Erbse; Berlin 1975), 39, in the notes.

[18] Iliad II.204-205.

one king,' could be said with more justice of the world and God than of cities and men. For being one it must needs have one maker and father and master.[19]

In the treatise Who is the Heir of the Divine Things he quotes another verse from the ninth book of the same Homeric epic[20] for interpreting Exod. 30:15:

> With reason then will Moses say, 'He that is rich shall not add, and he that is poor shall not diminish, from the half of the didrachmon'. That half, as I said, is both a drachma and a unit, to which every number might well address the words of the poet, 'With thee I'll cease, with thee I will begin'. For the whole series of numbers to infinity multiplied by infinity ends when resolved in the unit and begins with the unit when arranged in an unlimited series. And therefore those who study such questions declare that the unit is not a number at all, but the element and source from which number springs.[21]

In his commentary on Gen. 18:6: 'Abraham hastened to the tent to Sarah and said to her, "Hasten and mix three measures of wheat-flour and make ash-cakes",' Philo remarks:

> And most natural is the passage concerning the three measures, for in reality all things are measured by three, having a beginning, middle and end. And each of these partial things is empty if it does not have (the others), similarly constituted. Wherefore Homer not ineptly says that 'all things are divided into three'. And the Pythagoreans assume that the triad among numbers, and the right-angled triangle among figures are the foundation of the knowledge of all things.[22]

In this passage Philo quotes part of a verse which he found in the fifteenth book of the Iliad,[23] the Homeric epic, which he also quotes in the two other texts given above. The Pythagorean background of these speculations is quite clear, because Philo once explicitly refers to 'the Pythagoreans' and in another case probably alludes to them by mentioning 'those who study such questions'. Furthermore, the books of Pseudo-Plutarch and Nicomachus of Gerasa make it plausible that Philo used an older

---

[19] Philo, On the Confusion of Tongues, 169-70. The translation is taken from *Philo in Ten Volumes (and Two Supplementary Volumes)* IV (with an English translation by F. H. Colson and G. H. Whitaker; Cambridge,MA-London 1985), 103.

[20] Iliad IX.97.

[21] Philo, Who is the Heir, 189-90. The translation is taken from *Philo in Ten Volumes (and Two Supplementary Volumes)* IV (with an English translation by F. H. Colson and G. H. Whitaker; Cambridge, MA-London 1985), 377-79.

[22] Philo, Questions and Answers on Genesis IV.8. The translation is taken from *Philo Supplement I. Questions and Answers on Genesis* (translated from the ancient Armenian version of the original Greek by R. Marcus; Cambridge, MA-London 1961), 279-80.

[23] Iliad XV.189.

tradition for this interpretation of the Bible since both authors quoted the same Homeric verses as he did, among many others, for their own arithmological speculations. Pseudo-Plutarch explains the meaning of the numbers one and three as follows: 'Homer often places the nature of the "one" in the sphere of the good and that of the dyad in the opposite sphere... And he says, "It is no good for many to rule: let there be one chief" and "not to be divided in war or in counsel, but to be of one mind, with one sound opinion".'[24] Homer always takes the odd number as better, for he depicts the entire universe as divided into five parts and then further distinguishes the middle three: 'The universe was divided into three and each had his share of honour. For this reason, Aristotle held the opinion that there were five elements since the odd in its perfection has power in everything. He also assigns the odd to the celestial gods...'[25] In a quite similar fashion Nicomachus of Gerasa argues:

> And somebody may join the words of Homer with this: 'The universe was divided into three', whereas we also find that the virtues are a midway between two badnesses that are opposed to one another and to the virtue, and the ratio agrees, that the virtues are in accordance with the monad defined, knowable and prudent – for the midway is the 'one' – but the badnesses are in accordance with the dyad indeterminate, unknown and foolish.[26]

IV. Philo's Use of Arithmology

The result of this brief survey is that it seems that certain lines of Homer had a significant place in arithmology and that this was also known by Philo. But if Philo was familiar with the arithmological interpretation of Homer, does this imply that he imitated it in his own exegesis of biblical texts? In answering this question it is important to distinguish between the method of Philo's exegesis and its results. The method of speculative exegesis is indeed relatively similar. The interpretation takes its starting point from certain numbers that by chance are mentioned in the text, for example, the 'three measures of wheat-flour' or the 'universe' that 'was divided into

---

[24] Odyssey III.137-38.

[25] Kindstrand (ed.), *De Homero,* Chap. 145 (78, 1760-74); J. J. Keaney and R. Lamberton (eds), *Essay on the Life and Poetry of Homer,* 229-31.

[26] [Iamblichi], *Theologumena Arithmeticae* V. de Falco (ed.), 19, 11-17.

three'. These numbers link the text to the arithmological explanations about their characteristics and symbolical meaning. As a result, the connection between the arithmological teachings and the Homeric or biblical text are relatively loose and often seem arbitrary. This is also apparent, for example, from the fact that Philo could explain the same verse of the Iliad in quite different ways. In the essay On the Confusion of Tongues he applies the line 'It is no good for many to rule: let there be one chief' to God but in his book On the Embassy to Gaius he connects it with the political situation after the unification of the Mediterranean world under Roman rule. He writes about the first emperor, Augustus:

> He was also the first and the greatest and the common benefactor in that he displaced the rule of many and committed the ship of the commonwealth to be steered by a single pilot, that is himself, a marvellous master of the science of government. For there is justice in the saying 'It is not well that many lords should rule', since multiplicity of suffrages produces multiform evils.[27]

With regard to the results of his exegesis, Philo often draws different conclusions from those of authors like Nicomachus of Gerasa or Pseudo-Plutarch. Pseudo-Plutarch, for example, stresses the ethical implications of number symbolism by interpreting the 'one' as a symbol of the good. Philo, however, is more interested in its theological meaning, and applies it to God. In general these differences are not based on profound divergences, but on a different selection and use of common traditions of arithmology.

It therefore seems probable that Philo's arithmological exegesis of the Bible was to some extent influenced by the interpretation of Homer.

---

[27] Philo, The Embassy to Gaius 149. The translation is taken from from *Philo in Ten Volumes (and Two Supplementary Volumes)* X (with an English translation by F. H. Colson; Cambridge, MA-London 1971), 75-77.

Delaying the Progress from Case to Case:
Redundancy in the Halakhic Discourse of the Mishnah

Alexander Samely

This paper explores a number of issues concerning the thematic arrangement of the text of the Mishnah. The ultimate aim is to develop general categories for describing the underlying coherence (or lack of coherence) of the halakhic discourse presented in that text. Our central hypothesis is that the thematic progress of the Mishnah is largely determined by series or clusters of hypothetical legal case schemata, or legal 'cases'. Accordingly, textual material which separates these cases from each other *delays*, textually speaking, the thematic progress. Material appearing between cases takes different forms and contents. It includes halakhic dissent, scriptural quotations, and clauses containing reasons or principles. Despite this variety in form and content, such material shares the effect of creating a hiatus when textually separating two thematically related cases. We are going to suggest that this shared effect points to a more substantive similarity: an implicit concern with the principles of halakhic reasoning which, in the Mishnah, are almost never articulated in absolute terms. The case-separating material points to or implies such principles, but it also limits their scope.

The Mishnah, from a modern point of view, offers a remarkable combination of textual features. On the one hand, it makes no effort to spell out the basics of its subject matter, or articulate its own starting point as a text. On the other hand, the density of information it achieves is very high, i.e. it manages to expend few words while conveying much detail. Although technical vocabulary plays a role in this economy, much of it is achieved by the arrangement of the Mishnaic topics. A text can 'save' words by not repeating information which is already spelled out in the neighbourhood; this is what is known as ellipsis. In this way, parts of a document become dependent on each other in that typical way we call a text, and the Mishnah manifests conspicuous and pervasive ellipsis of this type.[1] But the opposite of ellipsis, namely the repetition of information, or redundancy, can also have the effect of reinforcing the relationships of text parts. Where repetition appears in parts of a document which are in other respects also characterized by the economy of ellipsis, it is conspicuous. Conspicuous repetition of information is one of the phenomena which we are going to investigate in what follows.

One of the main recurrent structures in the Mishnah is the provision of a halakhic or legal case. The information given in the halakhic case is what ought to be done in a given situation, or what is that situation's legal evaluation. We are going to refer to this unit of information as the *case schema* (see below). The recurrence of this unit gives something like a pulse to the Mishnah's text. Often, literary units which contain a case schema do not merely link up with each other by following a common format in the presentation of the case, but also because there are very precise thematic links between the neighbouring case schemata, and thematic progress is visible.[2] Even where that happens, however, other types of material may be found between neighbouring case schemata. These 'interruptions' have their own recurrent patterns, both when compared with each other and with regard to their links to the case schemata. The more complex larger literary units, i.e. series of case schemata plus 'interruptions', are also recognizable through their recurrence. The frequency and regularity of these patterns of interruption educate the reader of the Mishnah to keep track of the way in which the case schemata hang together. The reader can *verify* the progress of case schemata by looking back in the text to the preceding case

---

[1] See N. A. van Uchelen, *Chagigah: The Linguistic Encoding of Halakhah* (Amsterdam 1994); more on this below.

[2] This idea is treated in more depth in an article of mine complementing the present paper, entitled 'From Case to Case. Notes on the Discourse Logic of the Mishnah', in G. R. Hawting, J. A. Mojaddedi and A. Samely (eds), *Studies in Middle Eastern Texts and Traditions in Memory of Norman Calder* (Journal of Semitic Studies Supplement 12; Oxford, forthcoming).

schema, or skipping the interrupting material.[3]

In many cases, the material which interrupts a series of case schemata is also *conspicuously redundant* in the sense explained above. The Mishnah itself is, in a sense, a *repetition* – namely of Scripture, or so it came to be seen. But that repetition is a historical relationship holding between two separate documents. It is a textual phenomenon only where the words of Scripture and the words of the rabbis come to stand next to each other *inside* the Mishnah. The biblical quotation's main function in the Mishnah is to *support* what is said by a rabbinic voice. By its very function, it goes over the same ground as the case schema or norm to which it is attached. And there are other such textual units, which on the one hand separate thematically related case schemata, and on the other cover the same ground as the case schemata with which they are found. There is for example the rabbinic 'precedent' (מעשה) whose report comes to stand next to a hypothetical formulation which makes the same point. Similar in important respects are two further types of material often found attached to case schemata: clauses presenting a *reason* for a halakhic evaluation or consequence; and very importantly, the provision of an *alternative* halakhic decision for a given case schema. Scriptural quotation, precedent, reason clause, dispute, all of these are frequently found *between* case schemata which are thematically related to each other. Thus all of them involve the reader in the work of *constructing the text's thematic progress as different from its textual sequence.* This is helped by the fact that most of them are presented in rigid and highly characteristic literary patterns, or in formulaic language; they are thus easily distinguished from the thematic series of case schemata.

I. The case schema and the dispute as loop and bifurcation

Let us first look more closely at the nature of the case schema. The case schema is one of the main carriers of *thematic* identity, and it deals, usually in a very succinct manner, with a hypothetical halakhic case. It is normally couched in

---

[3] I am explaining this structure as I find it, namely as an optical (or spatial) phenomenon – eminently linked to the processes of reading. But this does not mean that it could not have had a parallel in the realm of hearing and speaking, i.e. linked to processes of oral performance.

descriptive terms,[4] and formulated as a complex sentence. That sentence has an implicit or explicit conditional format (using words corresponding to 'if ... then'). Its function can be defined as linking a set of circumstances on the one hand to a halakhic evaluation, or statement of obligation or permission, on the other. The enunciation of circumstances or of the situation is said to be contained in the protasis of the sentence (the 'if' part), while the halakhic evaluation is given in its apodosis (the 'then' part).[5] Protasis-apodosis units have a fairly high measure of formal identity, i.e. they can occur in different textual environments while retaining a basic integrity. One can visualize the composition of the Mishnah as putting together larger literary units from the semi-independent case schemata, producing a basically *paratactic* structure. Other semi-independent formats can be combined with case schemata, suggesting a 'construction kit' model for the production of the text.[6]

How can a succession of case schemata be used to create thematic *progress*? The short, formulaic answer is: by allowing only a *minimal critical difference* between the protasis of any two neighbouring case schemata. Thus the apodosis changes from one case schema to the next, while only one situational factor named in the protasis will be altered or added.[7] Material coming between case schemata which are only minimally different from each other may obscure the *exact* points of similarity and dissimilarity, and thus obscure the progression between them. This stands in contrast with case schemata which form a thematic series as well as a

---

[4] See J. Neusner, *The Memorized Torah. The Mnemonic System of the Mishnah* (Chico, CA 1985).

[5] For an analysis from the linguistic point of view, see M. Azar, 'The Conditional Clause in Mishnaic Hebrew', in M. Bar-Asher (ed.), *Studies in Mishnaic Hebrew* (Scripta Hierosolymitana 37; Jerusalem 1998), 58-68, in particular pp. 67f. (conditions expressed in non-conditional clause forms). We are going to use the phrase 'case schema' for the hypothetical (i.e. conditional) relationship obtaining between two states of affairs or actions, regardless of whether the surface form is that of a conditional clause. We shall also use the words 'protasis' and 'apodosis' as abstract names for the two components of that hypothetical structure.

[6] This is not a suggestion of how the text of the Mishnah was put together (which requires a different perspective of investigation); the construction kit model is used here to stress certain synchronic relationships.

[7] More on this below, in our discussion of passage (1). The principle 'minimal critical difference' is explained and illustrated in my 'From Case to Case' (note 2 above).

contiguous text.[8] We shall therefore use the device of *eliminating* in some of our examples the 'interrupting' matter, in order to bring this coherence to the surface. Let us first consider the case where case schemata are separated by rival opinions, or the presentation of dissenting voices. Passage (1) below is an example containing several such occurrences of dissent; it deals with the delivery of a valid bill of divorce (*get*) from the husband to the wife through an intermediary. The *mishnayyot* are numbered in square brackets.

> (1) m. Gittin 1:1-3
> [1] *The person who brings a* get *from a province[9] beyond the sea needs to say: In my presence it was written and in my presence it was signed.* Rabban Gamliel says: Also the one who brings it from Reqem and from Hagar. R. Eliezer says: Even from Kefar Ludim to Lod. And the Sages say: He needs to say: In my presence it was written and in my presence it was signed, only if he brings it from beyond the sea or if he takes [it there].[10] *And the person who brings [it] from province to province beyond the sea needs to say: In my presence it was written and in my presence it was signed.* Rabban Shim'on ben Gamliel says: Even from region (*hegemonia*) to region. [2] R. Yehudah says: [The requirement applies] From Reqem eastwards, and Reqem is like the East; from Ashkelon southwards and Ashkelon is like the South; from Akko northwards and Akko is like the North. R. Meir says: Akko is like the Land of Israel for the purposes of the *get*. [3] *The person who brings a* get *within the Land of Israel does not need to say: In my presence it was written and in my presence it was signed – if there are objectors concerning it, let those who signed it confirm it. If a person brings a* get *from a province beyond the sea and cannot say: In my presence it was written and in my presence it was signed, if there are witnesses, let it be confirmed by the persons who signed it.*

The dispute in *mishnayyot* 1 and 2 is about the underlying concept 'land of Israel', in its application to the procedures of a *get*, although that concept is only once mentioned. The notion here used as its opposite, מדינת הים, 'province beyond the sea'.

---

[8] But in such immediate proximity, compositional mechanisms of ellipsis may take effect so that we find a cluster of grammatically complex, integrated units instead of a more numerous series of grammatically independent case schemata.

[9] The word used here, מדינה, does not necessarily mean 'country' in the modern sense (even in the restricted sense in which there were such countries in antiquity); Danby translates the first appearance of the phrase as 'from beyond the sea', and the second as 'from province to province beyond the sea'. The term used in Shim'on ben Gamliel's Dictum, here translated as 'region', is the Greek loan-word 'hegemonia' (ηγεμονια); the word is rendered as 'jurisdiction' by Jastrow (*A Dictionary of the Targumim, the Talmud Babli and Yerushalmi, and the Midrashic Literature* [Philadelphia 1903], p. 331, s.v. הגמוניא). This also represents one of the meanings of *medinah*, cf. op. cit., p. 734a. The English Schürer translates 'hegemonia' as 'province' (E. Schürer, *The History of the Jewish People in the Age of Jesus Christ*, vol. 2 [revised by G. Vermes, F. Millar and M. Black; Edinburgh 1979], 53).

[10] This latter part of the Sages' Dictum, 'or if he takes it there', goes beyond the information contained in the first sentence, while presenting itself merely as its confirmation. It expands the series of case schemata by a new one. See further below.

does not become the explicit subject of the discussion at all; and no particular importance seems to be attached to the geophysical reality of 'sea'.[11] Perhaps originally the question, 'What are the boundaries of the Land of Israel?' formed the co-text of *mishnah* 2. But as placed into the discourse here, it contributes primarily not to that question, but to the question, 'To what regions does the requirement to say: "In my presence..." apply?' All of this has a bearing on the expression 'province beyond the sea', which is necessary for this case schema and the successive ones. But the whole of this discussion does not, as such, have an impact on the thematic direction which the series of case schemata themselves impose. Below in (2) is the series in which the directionality of the discourse manifests itself. The new text is achieved by no operation other than cutting the text that comes between complete case schemata.

> (2) (a) The person who brings a *get* from a province beyond the sea needs to say: In my presence it was written and in my presence it was signed. (b) And the person who brings [it] from province to province beyond the sea needs to say: In my presence it was written and in my presence it was signed. (c) The person who brings a *get* within the Land of Israel does not need to say: In my presence it was written and in my presence it was signed - if there are objectors concerning it, let those who signed it confirm it. (d) If a person brings a *get* from a province beyond the sea and cannot say: In my presence it was written and in my presence it was signed, if there are witnesses, let it be confirmed by the persons who signed it.[12]

We have a very clear topical progression here, achieved by varying *one by one* the

---

[11] That is being done in the Tosefta (t. Giṭ. 1:1, ed. Zuckermandel, p. 232), where it says: 'The one who brings the *get* by ship is like the one who brings it from outside the Land', (המביא גט בספינה כמביא מחוצה לארץ) in other words, the concept of 'province beyond the sea' is wholly replaced by 'outside the Land'; at the same time, the idea of travel by sea is distinguished from it terminologically while being identified with it as an halakhic category.

[12] J. Neusner, in his treatment of this passage (*A History of the Mishnaic Law of Women. Part 4: Sotah, Gittin, Qiddushin* [Leiden 1980]), offers two summaries of the main line of the discourse. In the one he seems to select according to the importance or level of generality of the subject matter, in the other he rearranges the subject matter for the sake of clarity. When summarizing 'how the topic is laid out', he gives the gist of 1:1-3 in three sentences which correspond to our (a), (b) and (c), i.e. leaving out (d) (p. 117). When explaining the text itself, he states 'the rule very simply' in three parts, the first of which combines our segments (a) and (d), while (b) and (c) are given as two further, separate, points (p. 125). This second summary therefore does not follow the sequence of case schemata in the Mishnah. Thus, although Neusner too is interested in the mishnaic structures without the disputes, his concerns are different from ours. In our separation of textual elements, we are not making a distinction between more general/important and less general/important case schemata, or between earlier and later strata in the text, but between formal types of mishnaic segments. (It should be noted that line 3 on p. 124 in Neusner's book is probably intended to start with 'E', not 'D'.)

parameters of the situation in which the legal obligation applies from case to case. We have three situational parameters: the place from which the *get* is delivered in relation to the land of Israel; the ability of the person delivering it to give the verbal testimony; the availability of the *get*'s witnesses in the land of Israel. Here is the progression of the case schemata under these headings:[13]

PLACE	DELIVERER'S TESTIMONY	WITNESSES
from beyond the sea	available	(not necessary)
from province to province beyond the sea	available	(not necessary)
within the land of Israel	not necessary	available
from beyond the sea	not available	necessary

The transition from one case schema to the next consists of the variation of one of the three situational parameters at a time, or the introduction of only one totally new parameter at a time. That is what is meant by the formula 'minimal critical difference between protases' used above. We thus find the four case schemata to have the following features: their situational parameters, i.e. their *topics*, are very closely linked; and they stand in a relation of similarity and contrast to each other which builds a *progressive sequence*.

In this progression, the dispute segments contained in (1), the actual text of the Mishnah, create a *hiatus*. They do not change that sequential progress, except in one point: the opinion of the Sages in (1) actually adds, in the form of a single word, a whole new case schema: that of the person delivering a get from the Land to overseas (as opposed to from overseas to the Land).[14] That case is presented in total textual dependence on (a) as repeated by the Sages; it is not formulated by the provision of a new case schema, which is what happens for the cases (a)-(d) despite the amount of repetition of wording this involves; and there is no echo of this case schema anywhere else in the unit. Overall, therefore, the dispute materials make no contribution, and thus also do not modify the directionality of the case schemata to which they are

---

[13] The theme is set by the protasis, and only the protasis is represented. For each case schema the apodosis, 'in order to safeguard the validity of the *get*', is implied.
[14] The reversal of directionality is expressed by the participle מוליך, standing in opposition to מביא.

attached – they are detachable from the series of case schemata.[15] In order to understand the relationship of case schemata, the reader has to go back from the alternative apodosis to the complete case schema to which it is appended, and *from there* to the next complete case schema in order to construct the progress. We shall refer to this movement as the *loop* of reading involved in properly integrating the 'delaying' material (in this case the rival opinion) into the discourse progression.

The alternative apodoses need only be skipped, however, for construing the thematic progression of the discourse. For other, less linear, dimensions of the halakhic discourse they are vital. Thus, in our example, the dispute segments help to place the concept of 'beyond the sea' firmly into the context of the question of the various halakhic boundaries of the land of Israel (somewhat more clearly than the case schema (c) could do so on its own). In particular, the dispute segment ascribed to R. Eliezer has a striking effect. As the word 'even' (אפילו) signals, the place names of Kefar Ludim and Lod are felt to present a limiting case for the norm's application. This could be reconstructed from the text structures alone, without any reliable information on the geography of these places.[16] The 'even' segment makes it clear that at issue is not a distance, but the crossing of a boundary. This may provide an important clarification for the first formulation of the case schema, even where the alternative is rejected.[17] In other words, even what counts as a proper *disagreement* with the apodosis of a case schema helps to narrow down the valid interpretations of that case schema.[18] However, this is typical of disputes whose relationship with the case schema is defined by the term 'even'. For other types of dispute, the additional

---

[15] The words 'attached', 'detachable' here are not meant to contrast an original composition with later additions. In this paper we are interested in a synchronic understanding of these structures. The investigation of text history requires such synchronic understanding, and more besides.

[16] See further note 78 below.

[17] It does not even matter whether merely the extension of the 'boundary' principle to these two localities is rejected, or whether the interpretation of the point of the original case schema as 'boundary' is also rejected by such a rejection (and the principle of the case schema is identified instead as one of 'distance', for example). In both cases, the presence of an alternative helps to clarify what is at stake, as a matter of principle, in the original case schema.

[18] Compare with this the notion that one understands a philosophical or scientific hypothesis as soon as one understands what would constitute a counter-argument to it.

information that can be derived is not necessarily as rich as this, as the next passage (3) will show.

The alternative or rival apodosis makes no contribution to the movement of the discourse through the cases; this has to do with the fact that the protases, not the apodoses, carry the thematic identity. But often the alternative is even textually redundant, for the same words are used. Occasionally, the fact that alternative apodoses make no contribution to the thematic progress seems to have helped bring about a curious phenomenon: the text continues as if no alternative had been presented at all. This is what happens to R. Yehudah's dissenting opinion in the next passage (*mishnah* numbers in square brackets):

> (3) m. Bikkurim 1:1-2
> The one who plants [a tree] within what is his [property] and bends it [to continue growing] into his own, but someone else's path or a public path is in the middle, behold this one does not bring (הרי זה אינו מביא) [the first-fruits]. *R. Yehudah says: Such a one does bring [them]* (כזה מביא). [2] For what reason may he not bring them? Because of what is said, 'The first-fruits of your ground [you shall bring to the house of the Lord your God]' - [you may not bring them] unless all of the growth is from your ground.

The second *mishnah* starts with a sentence which presupposes the opposite of what R. Yehudah was just quoted as saying; it links back to the anonymous opinion expressed before, as if nothing separated it from that opinion.[19] Although this could point to secondary additions in the text, such a diachronic explanation is not really necessary. A strong assumption that any opinion marked by a rabbi's name, and presented as deviating from an opinion stated anonymously beforehand, is to be rejected, suffices to explain this structure. Functionally speaking, the mishnaic Dictum attributed by name stands not in opposition to the anonymous Dictum so much as to the Dictum *sanctioned* by collective tradition. On this basis it is explicable that the text in *mishnah* 2 directly links back to the anonymous opinion. This is supported by another observation concerning disputes. There is no signal to show that the text

---

[19] In another example of this phenomenon, m. Yoma 5:1, the alternative opinion (R. Yose) is even supported by a scriptural quotation. Cf. P. A. Pettit, *Shene'emar. The Place of Scripture Citation in the Mishna* (Ph.D.; Claremont Graduate School 1993), 191f. and 109 ('The fact which Yose introduces by his scriptural citation does not affect the progress of the Mishnaic discourse at hand.'). See also Y. Fraenkel, *Darkhey Ha-Aggadah weha-Midrash* (2 vols; Givatayyim 1991), 286, whose explanation is based on m. 'Ed. 1:6.

ascribed to a named rabbi (say, an alternative apodosis) has *ended*; the Mishnah knows of no equivalent of the 'unquote' sign. The reader is instead trained by the text to take any *shift* of topic as an indication that the speaking voice has reverted from a named rabbi to the anonymous tradition (what one might call the *stam* mode). Thus a new protasis coming after a named rival apodosis is likely to belong once more to the anonymous voice, not to the named rabbi's speech. So, dispute structures are regularly treated as having no impact on the thematic route of the mishnaic discourse.

Passages (1) and (3) exhibit the following structure: a case schema which is complete in itself is followed by a textual amplification[20] which contains or implies an alternative to the apodosis of the preceding case schema. The alternative opinion thus depends textually on the preceding case schema (the *protasis* of the latter retains its pertinence and is presupposed), while the case schema itself can be detached from the dissenting voice's text without injury to its grammatical integrity or comprehensibility. This is why we spoke above of case schemata as 'semi-independent' literary units. There are, however, cases where the dispute material is presented as part and parcel of the protasis-apodosis unit. As before, the protasis is shared; in the transition to the apodosis, however, there is an explicit signal that alternative apodoses are to follow. Here is an example of this dispute format, which in contrast to the loop might be called bifurcation.[21]

---

[20] This use of the word amplification is, I think, compatible with a technical meaning established in some recent work on rabbinic texts, in particular in H.-P. Tilly, *Zur Redaktion des Traktates Moed Qatan des Talmud Yerushalmi. Versuch einer formanalytischen Diskursbeschreibung* (Frankfurter Judaistische Studien 9; Frankfurt am Main 1995), pp. 57ff.; see also the work by Goldberg cited in note 29 below. It should again be noted that this terminology makes no diachronic claim. See above on parataxis and the construction kit model.

[21] In a different context, J. Neusner uses the term 'stich' of a dispute. See e.g., *The Memorized Torah* (note 4 above), pp. 70ff.: 'In order to spell out the character and distribution of declarative sentences of various sorts, I have taken *each stich of the apodosis of a dispute* and treated it as if it were a complete sentence. I thus add the protasis to one of the two (or more) stichs of the apodosis' (emphasis mine). The procedure here explained by Neusner is what we are going to do presently, but without 'deleting' the attribution as he does (op. cit., p. 71). See, however, the next note.

(4) m. Terumot 3:5

The person who said: Let the Terumah of this store [lit. heap] be in it!, and: Let its tithes be in it!, Let the Terumah of tithe be in it! -
- R. Shim'on says: He called it [by its proper] name,
- and the Sages say: [Only] as long as he says: [Let it] in its north! or: [Let it be] in its south!

If we make explicit the protasis-apodosis units that are contracted here we obtain the following (numbering the various protases using 'P', the various apodoses using 'A'):

(5)
I. R. Shim'on says:
    (P1) If a person says 'Let the Terumah of this store be in it'
    (A1) Then he has made a valid declaration regarding Terumah
II. The Sages say:
    (P1) If a person says 'Let the Terumah of this store be in it'
    (A2) Then he has made no valid declaration regarding Terumah
    but
    (P2) If a person says 'Let the Terumah of this store be to the north of it'
    (A1) Then he has made a valid declaration regarding Terumah.

The protases of the case schema envisaged by Shim'on (I.P1) and by part of the utterances of the Sages (II.P1) are identical; but the Sages withhold the sanction of approval from it, approving instead a critically different case schema, namely one in which the person utters a slightly expanded sentence. The two units, I and II, are mutually exclusive as presented; in other words, the movement of the discourse through the topic P1 goes through one or the other, but not through one after the other – the two cannot be added to each other when reading the text. The movement of the discourse, represented in italic print, is either

(6) the protasis with R. Shim'on's apodosis:
The person who said: Let the Terumah of this store be in it!, and: Let its tithes be in it!, Let the Terumah of tithe be in it! - R. Shim'on says: *He called it [by its proper] name*, and the Sages say: [Only] as long as he says: [Let it] in its north! or: [Let it be] in its south!

or:

(7) the protasis with the Sages' apodosis:
The person who said: Let the Terumah of this store be in it!, and: Let its tithes be in it!, Let the Terumah of tithe be in it! - R. Shim'on says: *He called it [by its proper] name*, and the Sages say: [Only] *as long as he says: [Let it] in its north! or: [Let it be] in its south!*

It is easy to see that a fairly normal-looking mishnaic text *without* bifurcation can be constructed by crossing out the small non-italic print in *either* (6) or (7).[22]

---

[22] As well as deleting the ascription to an individual rabbi. The reason for the latter deletion we have explained above: the functional meaning of the mishnaic use of a rabbi's name includes dissent.

Either (6) or (7) complete the halakhic theme of this case schema, namely: What happens under situational circumstances P1? But together they produce a redundant structure which treats the same theme, the same protasis, twice so that the progress to the next halakhic theme is 'delayed'. The path of topical progress is bifurcated into two, only for the two separate paths to merge again for the next case schema. This movement is given a generalized representation in Diagram 1:

Diagram 1: Bifurcation

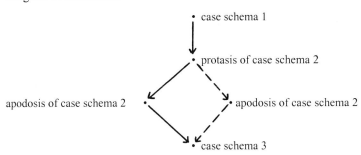

Through either of the alternative routes, one acquires the 'right' to proceed from case schema 2 to case schema 3. The text given in smaller print in (6), or that of (7), is redundant; they render each other redundant, once a decision between them has been taken. There are good reasons to assume that the Mishnah takes the possibility of such a decision for granted, and implies it by naming one position as that of the 'Sages'. The otherwise often economical Mishnah thus produces – conspicuous – redundancy: it does not present only the preferred apodosis, thus progressing faster to the next case schema or norm. What exactly would be lost if the dispute were removed? Below is the text without R. Shim'on's alternative, and with all conditional material (required by the Sages) transferred to the opening protasis:

(8)
If a person said: Let the Terumah of this store be in its north! or: Let it be in its south!, and: Let its tithes be in its north! or: Let it be in its south!, Let the Terumah of tithe be in its north! or: Let it be in its south! – he has called it [by its proper] name.

In this hypothetical version, there is no indication that it makes a critical difference to the validity of the utterance that the north or south be mentioned; the reader may surmise that it makes such a difference, but cannot be sure. In (4) it is absolutely clear that mentioning 'north' or 'south' makes the difference between valid and invalid utterance (for the Sages). This also means that there is less transparency in (8) than in (4) regarding the principle or reason that might stand behind the decision of the Sages. The underlying principles for deciding individual case schemata are mentioned very rarely in the Mishnah (see below). It seems that dispute structures can serve as implicit pointers to such principles.

II. The zero-sum condition as discourse bifurcation

We should here briefly mention another example of discourse bifurcation in the Mishnah, apart from the dispute structure illustrated by passage (4) above. Occasionally, the protasis of a case schema claims that a certain situational circumstance makes *no* difference to the apodosis. Our passage (14) below will provide an illustration of this.[23] In such passages, it is made clear that the apodosis applies regardless of whether a certain fact obtains or not. I shall call this as a zero-sum condition. Its presence in a protasis can be explained as addressing an *expectation* that a certain feature would affect the apodosis. It addresses such an expectation by explicitly rejecting it. In many cases, the presence of a zero-sum protasis creates textual links, in that the same expectation, for some other topic treated elsewhere in the Mishnah, is actually justified. Thus a contrast is implied between the case at hand and some other case (often but not always found close by). Here is an example of a zero-sum condition in a normative list:

(9) m. Maaserot 1:4

Among vegetables, cucumbers, gourds, water-melons, musk-melons, apples and citrons are liable *whether gathered in their earlier or later condition [of ripeness]*. R. Shim'on declares citrons exempt in their earlier condition.

The zero-sum condition (given in italics) is redundant at the point of its occurrence

---

[23] The zero-sum condition of (14) is (for the first two case schemata): whether one creates one or two threshing floors.

(cf. m. Maʿas. 1:2): it *denies* that the liability is affected by condition of ripeness. The words in italics could be excised from the text without jeopardizing the meaning of the norm as such. Its absence would make no structural difference. On a smaller scale than the dispute bifurcation, the zero-sum condition also produces a forking of paths. Our case above could be explicated by duplicating the norm: (9.1) 'Cucumbers ... gathered in their earlier condition are liable', (9.2) 'and cucumbers ... gathered in their later condition are liable'. Although both statements are valid at the same time (not only one of them, as in the case of a bifurcation of apodoses), they envisage mutually exclusive circumstances. And both situation 9.1 and situation 9.2 lead to the same obligation (liable). We thus have a disjunctive structure again: mutually exclusive protases lead to the same apodosis, while in (4) we have mutually exclusive apodoses given for the same protasis. This is a bifurcation of the textual sequence *within* a unified case schema, i.e. the link between the two forks and the apodosis that follows it is substantive (only together do they form a unit of meaning or information). By contrast, the forking into two rival apodoses does not require the next case schema to unify it; but if a further case schema follows, and if it is thematically related, such unification of paths is actually achieved in the larger textual entity (the series of case schemata).

III. The scriptural quotation as discourse loop

Our next type of redundancy is the biblical quotation, used as complement of one part (usually the apodosis) of the rabbinic case schema. We are speaking here of the scriptural quotation as reduplicating the Mishnah's own words, in contrast to the use of biblical words to express (only once) rabbinic ideas.[24] The quotation backs up, *in another person's voice*, the rabbinic formulation (the Dictum). This backing or support produces two formulations of the *same* message. The convergence of meaning or message is *the point* of such units of text (midrashic units), and thus redundancy is a necessary result. In the context of the Mishnah, the midrashic unit is

---

[24] For this distinction, see chapter 4 in my *Rabbinic Interpretation of Scripture in the Mishnah* (Oxford, forthcoming).

therefore a structure which can delay the progress from case to case. The double expression of the same rabbinic-biblical message creates a hiatus. At times, the redundancy is conspicuous on the surface of the mishnaic text because there is a *repetition* of words:

> (10) m. Sanhedrin 2:1 (Lev. 21:12)
> If a member of his family dies, he [the high priest] does not go out after the bier, but when they are out of view, he is seen, and when they are seen, he is out of view. And [in this manner] he goes out with them up to the gate of the city – these are the words of R. Meir. R. Yehudah says: He does not go out from the sanctuary, *as it is said: 'From the sanctuary he shall not go out [and he shall not profane the sanctuary of his God...]'*.

R. Yehudah's description of proper practice and the biblical commandment converge in meaning. Moreover, they converge in wording. R. Yehudah uses the very same words that Scripture uses to make his point.[25] The mishnaic position in which the scriptural segment is quoted ensures that its meaning and relevance is adapted from its biblical function to its rabbinic one; this positioning, not any reformulation, performs the hermeneutic work.[26] Redundancy within midrashic units in the Mishnah can be even more marked than in case (10) above, namely when the scriptural quotation is both preceded and succeeded by rabbinic formulations presented as converging with it.[27]

But quite apart from any repetition of words, the scriptural quotation together with its introductory formula (שנאמר) always creates a delay in the mishnaic progress from one topic to the next, if that progress is measured in terms of mutually differentiated case schemata. The midrashic unit (assuming for the moment that R. Yehudah represented the main conduit of the mishnaic discourse, not R. Meir) *dwells* on the fact that the high priest does not go out under these circumstances. It provides a hermeneutic warrant for it and thus expands on the information already given by the case schema (in Yehudah's version). As in the case of the rival apodosis discussed in section I above, the contribution the hermeneutic warrant makes to the case schema

---

[25] Here are the two formulations: ומן המקדש לא יצא (Scripture), and אינו יוצא מן המקדש (Mishnah: Yehudah).

[26] The hermeneutic mechanism is explained in chapters 3 and 4 (resource Topic2) of my *Rabbinic Interpretation of Scripture in the Mishnah* (note 24 above).

[27] Cf. *Rabbinic Interpretation of Scripture in the Mishnah*, chapter 12 end (reprise).

and to the mishnaic discourse is by no means negligible; but it does not concern the progress from case schema to case schema, the *pulse* of the mishnaic discourse.

Is the apodosis of a case schema dependent on the scriptural support attached to it? Or is the biblical quotation detachable not only textually speaking, but also in its discourse function? The latter is suggested by the fact that most mishnaic case schemata have no hermeneutic warrant while their functional form is identical with the ones that do have one. There are also disputes in the Mishnah whose point of disagreement is not the Dictum, but the identity or nature of its biblical support. There is thus some initial evidence for saying that, where an apodosis is supported by a biblical quotation, that quotation is an amplification of the case schema. Functionally speaking, the protasis-apodosis relationship is more fundamental than the relationship between apodosis (i.e. Dictum) and biblical quotation. This means that the contribution of the quotation to the case schema is limited to it, and presupposes its presence and validity.[28] Furthermore, in the overwhelming majority of cases,[29] the next case schema presented thereafter in the Mishnah arises not from any thematic link to the biblical quotation, but to the case schema which it supports. The following passage illustrates how the hermeneutic warrant sits *between* topically related case schemata without in any way managing the transition between them.

> (11) m. Shabbat 6:4 (Isa. 2:4)
> A man may not go out [on the Sabbath] with a sword, and not with a bow, and not with a shield, and not with a club, and not with a spear; and if he does, he is liable to a sin offering. And the Sages say: They are his adornments. And the Sages say: They are nothing but for reproach[30], *for it is said, 'And they shall beat their swords into ploughshares and their spears into pruning hooks; nation shall not lift up a sword against nation, neither shall they learn war any more'.*

The *mishnah* continues with the following words:

> A knee-band is clean and they go out with it on the Sabbath. Ankle-chains are un-clean and they do not go out with them. [5] A woman goes out with bands of hair...

---

[28] In chapter 12 of *Rabbinic Interpretation of Scripture* (note 24), I suggest that the rabbinic voice is simultaneously committed to the Dictum on the one hand, and to the interpretation which links the Dictum to Scripture on the other.

[29] See my remarks on the surplus of biblical quotations at the end of chapter 10 of *Rabbinic Interpretation of Scripture* (note 24); see also the narrative amplifications of Dicta discussed in A. Goldberg, *Rabbinische Texte als Gegenstand der Auslegung. Gesammelte Studien II* (ed. M. Schlüter and P. Schäfer [Tübingen 1999]), 116ff. (= *Frankfurter Judaistische Beiträge* 17 [1989], 51ff.).

[30] Some mishnaic texts have here the additional words: 'in the days of the Messiah'.

The larger topic at this point in the Mishnah is the question what constitutes the prohibited act of 'going out' (cf. Exod. 16:29) with a burden on the Sabbath. Chapter 5 of tractate Shabbat deals with the burdens that are permissible for animals to 'go out' with on the Sabbath. Chapter 7 starts a new section concerning what constitutes the prohibited act of 'working' on the Sabbath. This is how the discourse is shaping up from the beginning of chapter 6 (*mishnayyot* numbers in square brackets):

> 1. Items which, if carried despite being prohibited, do not incur liability for a sin offering:
>   1.1. For women: ... [1]
>   1.2. For men: ... [2]
> 2. Items which, if carried, incur liability for a sin offering:[31]
>   2.1. For women: ... [3]
>   2.2. For men: ... [4]
> 3. Items that are mostly allowed (acc. to first opinion): [4-10]

Our hermeneutic warrant comes at point 2:2. The overall structure, as well as the actual themes addressed in the mishnaic sentences before and after the scriptural quotation, fit into the thematic overview given above. There is no deviation to be discerned here, let alone one which could be linked to the theme of the verse used as hermeneutic warrant at 2.2.[32] Unimpressed by any reference to the end of days, the analogy between the Sabbath and the messianic age, or even the Sabbath-implications of pruning hooks, the mishnaic discourse ploughs on. The theme of the biblical passage when read in its own co-text is a stranger to this mishnaic landscape. So this biblical segment could not appear at this mishnaic point without being interpreted in the way our passage (11) interprets it. It is appropriated by the mishnaic discourse, while that discourse yields to it in nothing. Nothing thematic, at least: the verse's biblical meaning can in turn be unlocked by bringing to the mishnaic text a focus not

---

[31] In cases of disagreements, the first opinion favours liability.

[32] It is true that the discourse takes a slightly new direction after the hermeneutic warrant, but that is because it seems to be placed at the end of the case schemata concerned with what men can carry around on a Sabbath by way of ornaments. That may be important in itself; there may be a mishnaic tendency to place midrashic units at the 'end' of some thematic series (see chapter 1 of *Rabbinic Interpretation of Scripture*).

thematic in it.[33] The verse thus imparts its thematic flavour or implications in subtle ways to the mishnaic environment; but it does not contribute to the shape of that environment as a textual configuration. We have thus again a looping of the discourse: the reader is referred back to the preceding case schema, and proceeds from there to the next schema (not from the biblical quotation placed between the two), when it comes to construing the thematic progression.

Our midrashic units have so far been linked to the appearance of disputes in the Mishnah. This is not unimportant for determining the function of the hermeneutic warrant, and more than 200 midrashic units in the Mishnah (i.e. about one third) are integrated into dispute structures or play host to them. However, we also find biblical proof-texts without disputes. Our next passage exemplifies a loop produced by (two) such hermeneutic warrants.

> (12) m. Bava Metsia 2:10 (Exod. 23:5)
> If he has unburdened it [i.e. the donkey fallen under its load] and re-burdened it, unburdened it and re-burdened it, even four and five times, he is [still] obliged [to do it again], *as it is said, 'You shall surely loosen* (עזוב תעזוב) *[with him]'*. If he [the owner of the animal] went and sat down and said to him: Since a commandment is upon you, if you want to unburden, unburden!, he is free [from the obligation to unburden], *as it is said 'with him'*. If he [the owner] is old or ill, he is obligated.

The biblical verse receives two hermeneutic treatments in sequence, first linked to the case schema, 'If the animal breaks down again and again ...', then to the case schema, 'If the owner does not help himself ...'. The change in case schema makes the hermeneutic focus move from the verb (plus infinitive absolute) to the preposition עמו ('with him') in successive midrashic units. Yet here too the case schemata follow each other without actual dependency on the *biblical sequence* of lemmata.[34] One further element from the verse ('under its load'), which *precedes* both these lemmata, is investigated further down in the same *mishnah* (not translated above). For this, the biblical sequence of lemmata could not account. In fact, these four neighbouring case

---

[33] The notion of a similarity between the Sabbath and the time of redemption is one of the non-thematic, potential messages of this quotation. Such a link is made explicitly in m. Tam 7:4 (with reference to Ps. 91:2).

[34] The question addressed here has nothing to with the question whether the mishnaic norms were 'prompted' by the scriptural text as opposed to them serving as a 'peg' for pre-existing rabbinic norms. It is quite clear that the manner in which the mishnaic text is constructed is not determined by these alternatives. See further *Rabbinic Interpretation of Scripture in the Mishnah* (note 24), chapter 3.

schemata dealing with the topic of the overburdened ass[35] form a coherent set in themselves, and their formal features are indistinguishable from case schemata without proof-text. Also, the lemma 'with him' is used to support the notion that the owner must help. But in the very next mishnaic sentence, this expression is treated as if it did not exist. For that sentence stipulates that the owner need not help if he is old or ill. No attempt is made to apply the lemma 'with him' to that eventuality (which, after all, is taken to require the opposite apodosis), or to explain why it does not also apply there. Without the text containing its hermeneutic warrants, our passage would look like this:

> (13) If he has unburdened it and re-burdened it, unburdened it and re-burdened it, even four and five times, he is [still] obliged [to do it again]. If he [the owner of the animal] went and sat down and said to him: Since a commandment is upon you, if you want to unburden, unburden!, he is free [from the obligation to unburden]. If he [the owner] is old or ill, he is obligated.

The hermeneutic warrants make no discernible difference to the topical progression (unless to obscure it); they are each relevant only to the case schema which precedes them. Diagram 2 shows the loop which is necessary to link those parts of the text which constitute the progression.

Diagram 2: Loop in a series of case schemata

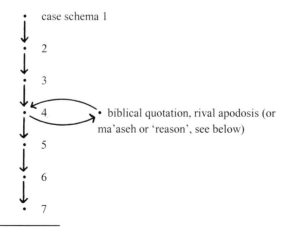

[35] They are: (a) the animal breaks down repeatedly; (b) the owner sits down and does not help; (c) the owner does not help but is old or sick; (d) the helper unburdens but does not burden again.

117

In Diagram 2, only one loop (at case schema number 4) occurs in a series or cluster of case schemata of seven members. But there can be several such amplifications, and the type of information contained in them can differ from one to the next, as in Diagram 3:

Diagram 3: Several loops in a series of case schemata

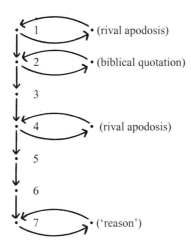

In the case of the biblical proof-text, the loop movement is linked to the inherent hermeneutic function, which postulates a convergence of meaning between two textual segments of different origin (one rabbinic, one biblical). The redundancy of this convergence, although much more tangible on the surface of the text of (10) than of texts (11) or (12), is part and parcel of the functional form midrash. However, hermeneutic convergence is merely a special case of the delaying effect any warrant (whether hermeneutic or otherwise) can have on the progress from case to case. Our next section attempts to place proof-texts into the larger context of reason-clauses.

IV. Reasons as discourse loops in the Mishnah

Several types of warrant creating a delaying effect can be found in the textual space between neighbouring case schemata. In all these structures, the progression leads from the case schema preceding the warrant to the case schema placed after it. In other words, the relationship between textual proximity and coherence is the same as in the case of the proof-text and the rival opinion (apodosis). The warrants now considered include arguments and reasons for norms, as well as what is sometimes called the rabbinic 'precedent' or *ma'aseh*.[36] We shall start with the *ma'aseh*, for its format admits conspicuous repetition of wording.

> (14) m. Peah 2:5-7
> The person sowing his field with one kind, even if he creates two threshing floors [for it], leaves one *Peah*. If he sows it with two kinds, even if he creates one threshing floor for them, leaves two *Peot*. The person who sows his field with two kinds of wheat, if he creates for them one threshing floor he gives one *Peah*, if two threshing floors, two *Peot*. *[6] A case happened that* (מעשה ש־) *R. Shim'on of Mitspah sowed [in this manner and came] before Rabban Gamliel; they went up to the Chamber of Hewn Stone and asked, [and] Nahum the Scribe the said: I have received from R. Measha, that he received from his father (or: from Abba), that he received from the 'pairs',*[37] *that they received from the prophets, a halakhah to Moses from Sinai, concerning the person who sows his field with two kinds of wheat: if he creates for them one threshing floor, he leaves one Peah; if two threshing floors, two Peot.* [7] If a field is reaped by non-Jews, or is reaped by robbers, or bitten off by ants, or broken down by the wind or cattle, it is free [from *Peah* obligation].[38]

If we look at the progress through the case schemata we obtain the following sequence: 1. the person sowing one kind (with a zero-sum condition concerning the number of threshing floors); 2. the person sowing two kinds; 3. the person sowing two kinds of wheat creating one threshing floor; 4. the person sowing two kinds of wheat creating two threshing floors. The new situational factor 'two kinds *of wheat*' is introduced in case schemata 3 and 4, and only for these does the number of threshing floors have *critical* effect, leading to opposite apodoses. The fifth case schema following in the sequence (in *mishnah* 7) deals with an entirely new set of hypothetical cases, namely fields for which there is no proper harvest or none by a

---

[36] The literature on the *ma'aseh* concerns mostly its place in the development of halakhah, or its role as a 'source' of law, not its textual function. Most relevant for our purposes is A. Goldberg, 'Form und Funktion des Ma'ase in der Mischna', *Frankfurter Judaistische Beiträge* 2 (1974), 1-38, reprinted in *Gesammelte Studien II* (see note 29 above); Ch. Albeck, *Einführung in die Mishna* (Berlin and New York 1971), pp. 136f., 178f., 447ff.; cf. also the work by Segal mentioned in note 41 below.
[37] זוגות , cf. m. Avot 1:4.
[38] For this *ma'aseh* and its function see in particular G. Mayer, *Ein Zaun um die Tora. Tradition und Interpretation im rabbinischen Recht dargestellt am Toseftatraktat Kil'ajim* (Stuttgart-Berlin-Köln-Mainz 1973), 15ff.

(Jewish) owner. The *ma'aseh* finds its place between the fourth case schema (to which it belongs thematically) and the fifth. But it makes not contribution to the transition between these two; it has no thematic link to the subsequent cases, only to the preceding two. It also repeats, mostly word for word, case schema 4 (and 3). By no means all mishnaic *ma'asiyyot* exhibit this level of verbal repetition.[39] Some are even linked to apodoses which contain the opposite decision from the one given in the *ma'aseh*.[40] However, it is clear that the *ma'aseh*, in its effects on the discourse, is quite similar to the hermeneutic warrant. It too goes over the same ground as the case schema to which it belongs, and constitutes some kind of support, warrant or source for a decision or norm.[41]

We come now to the most diffuse category of material delaying the progress from case to case. In contrast to disputes, hermeneutic warrants and *ma'asiyyot*, there is no fixed literary shape to 'reasons' given in the Mishnah. In other words, for this category we are totally dependent on our own classification of certain segments of mishnaic text. And that classification relies almost exclusively on a certain type of contents, namely anything that could constitute the answer to a 'why'-question (see below). So we have no reliable formal signal for the presence of a reason-clause,[42] and only a very general criterion for its contents. Still, there are examples which are intuitively clear as belonging in such a category. Here is one of them.

---

[39] According to Goldberg, 'Form und Funktion' (note 36 above), 8, the components of the *ma'aseh* are actually congruent with those of the protasis-apodosis unit.

[40] See in particular Goldberg, 'Form und Funktion', 32ff.; also Maier, *Zaun* (note 38 above), 24f.

[41] On the employment of the *ma'aseh* as a source of law, see in particular Goldberg, 'Form und Funktion' (note 36 above), 27ff. (he suggests it is secondary). Goldberg also draws the parallel to the midrashic unit. However, he only addresses the relationship between the *ma'aseh* and the mishnaic segments to which it is themtically linked, not the effect of the *ma'aseh* in slowing down the progress from one case schema to the next. Cf. also P. Segal, 'Jewish Law during the Tannaitic Period', in N. S. Hecht, B. S. Jackson, S. M. Passamaneck, D. Piattelli, and A. M. Rabello (eds), *An Introduction to the History and Sources of Jewish Law* (Oxford 1996), 101-40.

[42] Some of these clauses take the form of specifying the purpose of a norm, e.g., 'If she wore gold and chains ..., they took them from her *to shame her*' (m. Soṭ. 1:6). Cf. S. E. Fassberg, 'Constructions of Purpose and Intended Result in the Hebrew of the Mishnah', in Bar-Asher (ed.), *Studies in Mishnaic Hebrew* (see note 5 above), 153-63.

(15) m. Yoma 5:1
He [the high priest, after offering in the Holy of Holies] went out and came [back] the way he had entered. And he prayed a brief prayer in the outer room. He did not prolong [his prayer], *so as not to alarm Israel.*

The final Dictum in this segment requires the high priest's prayer in the sanctuary on the Day of Atonement to be brief. There is a reason given for this, introduced with 'so that ... not' (שלא): prolonged absence would alarm the congregation waiting outside. The assumption is presumably that the duty in the sanctuary was considered perilous and any mishap ominous for all of Israel, so there is an anxious wait for the high priest to re-emerge. There is no overlap in wording between the norm and the reason-clause (in bold print), so no verbal repetition. On the other hand, the reason clause does not set the theme for the topic mentioned next in the Mishnah (the stone 'Shetiyah'), or the next prescription (in *mishnah* 3). That prescription specifies the subsequent act the high priest is to perform, i.e. its appearance at this point in the text is determined by the sequence of required acts on the Day of Atonement.[43]

Yet, there is some kind of redundancy for reason-clauses. This can be seen from the fact that the reason for an apodosis can occasionally take the place of the apodosis itself, as in the following passage:

(16) m. Peah 5:4
A householder who was passing from place to place, and in need to take 'gleanings', 'forgotten' [sheaf], and *Peah*, and tithe of the poor, he may take [it]. When he returns to his house, he must repay – these are the words of R. Eliezer. And the Sages say: He was poor at that hour.

The Sages disagree with R. Eliezer's apodosis, but there is no direct presentation of their alternative apodosis, namely that the householder is not required to repay. The argument of the Sages is: since he was really poor *at the time* of taking – despite being a 'householder' at home, i.e. himself under a duty to give such agricultural alms – he need not repay them even after returning. And this argument for the apodosis is presented in place of the apodosis itself, as *implying* the apodosis.[44] Other types of

---

[43] Such chronological ordering, for which the tractate Yoma is the prime example, is an alternative principle of ordering for normative material to the series or cluster of case schemata. See my 'From Case to Case' (note 2 above).

[44] Danby spells out the implied apodosis: 'But the Sages say: [He need not make restitution because] at the time he was a poor man' (H. Danby, *The Mishnah* [Oxford 1933], 15).

clauses can also substitute for the apodosis, often in polemical contexts.[45]   But

passages such as (16) show that, given the reason-clause, the apodosis supported by

the reason can be so predictable as to require no separate expression.

The same can happen with biblical quotations, as in our next passage:[46]

(17) m. Hag. 1:5 (Deut. 16:17)

> He who has many eaters and few possessions brings many peace offerings and few
> whole offerings;[47] [he who has] many possessions and few eaters brings many whole
> offerings and few peace offerings; [he who has] few of these as well as those, about
> him they said [in *mishnah* 1:2]: a *meah* of silver, and: two pieces of silver; [he who
> has] many of these as well as those, about him it is said: 'Each man [shall give]
> according to the gift in his possession, according to the blessing of the Lord your
> God which he has given you'.

The formula used to introduce the biblical quotation here is עַל זֶה נֶאֱמַר.[48]   The

quotation occupies the place of the fourth apodosis of series of four case schemata.

The four protases are: many eaters/few possessions; many possessions/few eaters;

few possessions/few eaters; many possessions/many eaters.   As can be seen, the

fourfold structure is generated by a quasi-mathematical mechanism, namely a

permutation of the elements 'eaters' and 'possessions' with the quantifications 'few'

and 'many'.   For the final case schema, opening with the protasis 'many

possessions/many eaters', the apodosis is not given in the Mishnah's 'own' words at

all, but only by way of the biblical quotation.[49]   In other words, the biblical quotation

---

[45] Such as 'This is only an occupation for idlers' (m. Neg. 12:5), or 'Its only guarding is the knife'
(m. B.Q. 4:9).

[46] For more on this and similar passages, cf. *Rabbinic Interpretation of Scripture in the Mishnah* (note
24), final section of chapter 4 (Performance3).

[47] From the whole offering the person bringing the sacrifice does not benefit, but from the peace
offering he does. Changing the mix in favour of the latter takes account of the circumstantial factor
poverty. See further Fraenkel, *Darkhey* (see note 19 above), vol. I, 79f., who takes the biblical
expressions 'according to' as linked to parity (of whole offerings and peace offerings) and 'blessing'
as pointing to both children and the possessions. Cf. b. Hag. 8a on Deut. 16:10. Ms. Kaufmann
(Budapest) reverses the order in which the 'possessions' and 'eaters' are mentioned in the next clause,
but the sense is unchanged.

[48] Cf. N. A. van Uchelen, 'The formula עַל זֶה נֶאֱמַר in the Mishnah. A form-analytical study', in A.
Kuyt and N. A. van Uchelen (eds), *History and Form. Dutch Studies in the Mishnah* (Publications of
the Juda Palache Institute IV; Amsterdam 1988), 83-92; see also idem, *Chagigah* (see note 1 above).
Cf. also chapter 12 (final section) of *Rabbinic Interpretation of Scripture* (note 24). A similar use of
the deictic term זֶה ('this') in a non-halakhic case schema is found in m. Avot 3:2.

[49] See also note 24 above.

is not, as in most cases of hermeneutic warrants, *appended* to an apodosis.[50] Our last two passages thus show that both the hermeneutic warrant and the reason-clause can take over the function of expressing the apodosis.[51] In both examples, other textual structures contribute to the predictability of the apodosis: the dispute structure in (16), and the fourfold differentiation in (17).[52]

The *economy* achieved in (16) and (17) is one of ellipsis, i.e. the reduction of redundancy. What makes this economy possible is that the reason-clause, just as the quoted scriptural wording, speaks about the same topic as the apodosis to which it is attached, only from a different perspective. No new topic is broached, but a known topic is elaborated upon, the same ground is covered. Again the construction of coherence goes through a loop: from the reason-clause of the apodosis backwards to the apodosis itself and its protasis, and from there (not from the reason-clause) on to the next protasis.

The topic of 'reasons' for commandments has another dimension, which comes to the fore in post-talmudic Jewish discourse and is not directly linked to our problem. It is the question whether it is possible and desirable to speculate on the rationales of divine commandments.[53] Of more immediate relevance to our topic is the evidence of biblical texts. Here one finds occasionally clauses which appear to offer 'because'-statements, appended to the main clause of conditional precepts (i.e. apodoses) and also to apodictic precepts. They have been called 'motive clauses' in

---

[50] Elsewhere, על זה נאמר *is* used as part of a midrashic unit. See for instance m. Peah 7:3; m. Suk. 2:6; m. Hag. 1:6; m. San. 3:7.

[51] Very similar passages can be found for the *ma'aseh* also. As Goldberg shows, the attitude manifest in the Babylonian Gemara (e.g., b. Naz. 11a) that in such cases the mishnaic apodosis is missing and needs to be supplied shows that the *ma'aseh* was taken to be a reason or a source ('Form und Funktion', note 36 above, 36f.).

[52] It would be wrong to say that the redundancy is equally effective in both directions – the apodosis may be predictable from the reason and other structures in the co-text, but the reason is not from the apodosis; and the same is true for the hermeneutic warrant.

[53] See I. Heinemann, *Ta'amey Ha-mitsvot*, 2 vols. (Jerusalem 1966; fifth edition); cf. J. Maier, *Geschichte der jüdischen Religion* (Freiburg-Basel-Wien 1992), 282f. (with respect to the Maimonidean context in which the question acquires its virulence); L. Jacobs, *A Tree of Life. Diversity, Flexibility and Creativity in Jewish Law* (Littman Library; Oxford 1984), 33-42. E. E. Urbach synthesizes opinions from talmudic times in his *The Sages. Their Concepts and Beliefs* (trans. I. Abrahams; Cambridge, MA-London 1987), 365-99.

biblical studies.[54] Here is an example, from Deut. 24:6 (following the RSV translation); the motive clause is given in italics:

> (18) No man shall take a mill or an upper millstone in pledge, *for* (כי) *he would be taking a life in pledge.*[55]

The following topics are treated in the text surrounding Deut. 24:6: exemption from military service (verse 5), remarriage with one's former wife (verses 1-4), kidnapping (verse 7), scale disease (verse 8), and again with loans in verse 10. In the verse itself, we see internal redundancy, as in our mishnaic cases. But we do not find a thematic link with the immediately surrounding norms comparable to that found in a mishnaic series of case schemata. As to the type of reason given above in (18), it seems similar to those found in the mishnaic discourse. But the perspective of many other biblical motive clauses is that of a divine lawgiver speaking, and it is indeed 'motives' rather than 'reasons' which accompany the norm. These motives can be those of the lawgiver (e.g., 'jealousy'),[56] or the motivation of the group to which the norm is addressed (e.g., promise of 'length of days').[57] In either case, the relationship to the norm is quite different from that found mostly in the Mishnah and illustrated by passage (15) above.

Is it possible to construct a classification of mishnaic reason-clauses? Even a brief perusal of the mishnaic material will reveal a wide variety of relationships between the reason-clause on the one hand and the norm or apodosis to which it belongs on the other. Among them are what one might call implied[58] or explicit[59]

---

[54] Cf. B. Gemser, 'The Importance of the Motive Clause in Old Testament Law', *Copenhagen Congress Volume* (Supplements to Vetus Testamentum 1; Leiden 1953), 50-66. He also uses the German term 'Begründungssätze', and defines motive clauses as 'grammatically subordinate sentences in which the motiviation for the commandment is given' (p. 50). Cf. also B. S. Jackson, 'On the Nature of Analogical Argument in Early Jewish Law', in idem (ed.), *The Jewish Law Annual*, Volume 11 (Boston 1994), 137-68, here at pp. 139ff.

[55] On the meaning of this, see e.g. P. Dale, *Old Testament Law* (London 1986), 135.

[56] For instance, כי ... אל קנא הוא in Exod. 34:14.

[57] As in Exod. 20:12.

[58] For example, the principle that some legally effective factors are irreversible, as in m. Yev. 3:7 ('she is forbidden to him for all time since she was forbidden to him during a certain time'), or in m. Meg. 1:9 (the '[high] priest that was' is not demoted in sanctity).

values, priorities, or principles of halakhah; the removal of conflict between norms;[60] precautionary measures;[61] the reference to intention;[62] or the reference to a universal or local disregard for a norm.[63] All these and others are offered in the Mishnah to support, in some manner, a norm or apodosis. Add to these what has been called hitherto, with some deliberate vagueness, 'hermeneutic warrant'; note that the Mishnah uses the word *reason*, טעם, for the biblical quotation in m. Bik. 1:1f. (our passage (3) above). Add to these the mishnaic argument from halakhic analogy, or the inference *a fortiori*.[64] Furthermore, we need to include the *ma'aseh*, apparently a 'source' of the law. Also considered should be statements of the form, 'This is the rule' (זה הכלל), which are usually appended as generalizations to a concrete set of case schemata;[65] in other instances, a generalization is simply introduced by 'for' (-ש).[66] There is clearly much variety here. Can we learn something from the way the biblical material is classified? Here is Gemser's classification of biblical motive clauses according to contents: (1) the motive clauses of a simply explanatory character;

---

[59] Cf. the expression 'the sinner should not be rewarded' (אין החוטא נכשר) in m. Shevi. 9:9, the rule giving priority to local *minhag* in m. Suk. 3:11 (הכל כמנהג המדינה), the 'order of the world' in m. Git. 4:2 (מפני תקון העולם); cf. Albeck, *Einführung*, note 36 above, p. 395), or that one must not merely fulfil, but be seen to fulfil, certain commandments (e.g., m. Sheq. 3:2: ... שמא יעני ויאמרו מעון הלשכה העני).

[60] As in m. San. 2:1, where the prohibition of levirate marriage for the high priest is justified with reference to another norm (the high priest is forbidden to marry a widow). It is of some interest that the second, overriding norm is not supported by a hermeneutic warrant from Lev. 21:14; it underscores the fact that it is the Mishnah, not Scripture, which takes the decision on priorities here.

[61] Such as that the poor may not use sickles and spades when collecting the *Peah* from a field, so that they cannot harm each other (m. Pe'ah 4:4). Cf. also the famous aim to 'distance man from transgression' articulated in m. Ber. 1:1 as reason for a norm (in answer to the question למה). Sometimes, as in m. Ber. 5:4, the individual is empowered to decide whether or not the measure is necessary under the circumstances.

[62] For example, m. Suk. 3:14.

[63] Given as the historical origin for the introduction of the *prozbol* in m. Shevi. 10:3 (also a conflict of norms), and for the abolition of the ritual of the *Soṭah* and of the heifer whose neck is broken (m. Sot. 9:9); cf. also mention of the proclivities of young male Judaeans as 'reason' for a norm in m. Yev. 4:10/m. Ket. 1:5.

[64] Both can be used with or without reference to scriptural wording, and to the latter the scriptural quotation is always incidental; cf. *Rabbinic Interpretation of Scripture in the Mishnah* (note 24), chapters 7-8.

[65] For example, m. Meg. 1:10, cf. Albeck, *Einführung* (note 36 above), 259 s.v. כלל; Epstein, *Mavo Le-Nusah Ha-Mishnah* (2 vols, Jerusalem-Tel Aviv 1964; 2nd edn), p. 1039. Epstein points out that beyond the particulars mentioned in the cases to which it is appended, what is actually included in the 'general rule' is often left implicit (and object of a supplement in the Gemara, e.g., at b. Meg. 21a).

[66] For instance in m. Bek. 1:2: 'for what is born from an unclean (animal) is unclean ...'

125

(2) those of ethical contents, (3) those of a religious kind, cultic as well as theological, and (4) those of religious-historical contents.[67] These categories are very general; also, every single term here used to characterize the material (even 'simply explanatory') relies on culturally embedded differentiations which are unlikely to have been relevant to the biblical authors, while they are firmly rooted in modern western scholarship or theology. They certainly give little guidance for classifying reasons in the Mishnah.

The question of what counts as a 'reason' has also exercised modern philosophy, and the results are interesting. If the philosopher's net is cast wide enough over the different contexts in which reasons appear in ordinary conversation, quite disparate phenomena are caught in it. And that seems to be the best starting point for a comparison with the Mishnah, for here too plurality reigns. In accepting all sorts of observations as 'reasons', the Mishnah seems to reflect ordinary language use rather than a technical, abstract or philosophical discourse. The Mishnah is clearly technical in *some* aspects of its discourse, but not in the same sense technical with regard to reasons or warrants.[68] Here is a catalogue of what one modern philosopher, Charles L. Stevenson, counts as 'rational' reasons for norms:[69] (a) the properties of the item evaluated, (b) consequences of actions, (c) motives of agents, (d) consequences of generalizing an action, (e) authorities, (f) behaviour of the person claiming the norm's validity, (g) an account of the historical genesis of a moral position. Stevenson also has a list of what he calls 'persuasive' categories:[70] (a) persuasive definition, (b) reiteration of ethical terms, (c) metaphorical expressions, and

---

[67] Gemser, 'Motive Clauses' (note 54 above), 55f.

[68] Insofar as reasons or warrants imply values, this observation tallies with Max Kadushin's important clarification of the fundamental difference between the rabbinic discourse on values and the western philosophical discourse (see his *The Rabbinic Mind* [3rd edn; New York 1972], for instance pp. 46f; cf. also his *Organic Thinking: A Study in Rabbinic Thought* [New York 1938]).

[69] *Ethics and Language* (New Haven-London 1944), 111-29; cf. idem, *Facts and Values. Studies in Ethical Analysis* (New Haven-London 1963). See the summary, as well as the comparison with the later work of Hare, Toulmin, Lorenzen/Schwemmer and Habermas, in R. Alexy, *A Theory of Legal Argumentation. The Theory of Rational Discourse as Theory of Legal Justification* (trans. R. Adler and N. MacCormick; Oxford 1989 [German original Frankfurt 1978]).

[70] *Ethics and Language*, 139ff.

(d) didactic narrative. Anybody with some knowledge of rabbinic literature will recall or easily find examples for most of these types of reason, and some illustrations from the Mishnah have just been given in the footnotes. The Mishnah in any case does not seem to exert a systematic, conceptually based, control over what counts as 'reason'; instead of abstract notions we find contextual decisions or pragmatic plurality. Certainly the category 'authority' is present in the Mishnaic discourse, both with regard to scriptural quotations and with regard to rabbinic tradition; but it is far from being the only sort of observation that counts as a valid reason in its discourse.

V. A stratum signalling halakhic accountability

Let us consider all the Mishnaic phenomena of 'delay' together. The presentation of disputes seems to presuppose a certain attitude to halakhah in the Mishnah. It seems to allow *in principle* for alternative legal positions, i.e. it embodies an idea of law as open to human processes of conceptual exploration, persuasion, reasoning, rhetoric or negotiation.[71] The provision of arguments[72] or warrants, both inside and outside dispute structures, points in the same direction. They are quite incompatible with an idea of authority which claims indubitable knowledge in matters of correct conduct. Not *fiat*, but legitimation through tradition and argument underpin the mishnaic discourse on halakhah in many places. The impression is created that the mishnaic interlocutors accord each other the *right to ask* for reasons or warrants.[73] Scripture quoted as proof-text finds its place in this array of reasons, arguments or warrants. Its use moreover implies that the authority of the

---

[71] For this see in particular van Uchelen, *Chagigah* (note 2 above); cf. also A. Goldberg, *Mystik und Theologie des rabbinischen Judentums. Gesammelte Studien I* (ed. M. Schlüter and P. Schäfer; Tübingen 1997), 418.

[72] The *a fortiori* argument is a particularly clear example, see *Rabbinic Interpretation of Scripture* (note 24), chapter 7.

[73] Perhaps the most fundamental feature is that the text of the Mishnah is woven by a polyphony of voices, so that there can be 'interlocutors' *within* it. This is similar to the way in which substantive positions are distributed to different named voices in the Platonic dialogues. But it is not necessary to have named speakers in a text for achieving such a plurality of voices, as the discourse of the Gemara shows. Similar to the internal flow of argument and counter-argument in the Gemara are many texts of the western philosophical discourse (notable modern examples include Wittgenstein and Heidegger). The main signal for a switch of perspective is the appearance of a question.

mishnaic voices is ultimately derived, and that there is an external standard by which it measures itself. The realm of rabbinic knowledge or decision-making, while pragmatically and procedurally binding,[74] is not absolute but needs to assure itself of its own accuracy. We might say: in particular through the passages which delay the progress from case to case the Mishnah shows that it is appropriate to expect *accountability* from the halakhic discourse – even if the forms of that accountability are determined inside that discourse itself, not by some other discourse.

And yet, the Mishnah does not enunciate abstract principles of halakhah. What is thematic in the Mishnah is not developed from general notions or foundational statements.[75] Only very occasionally are there several layers of *conceptual hierarchy* in the mishnaic discourse. There is no sustained attempt to lead the reader gradually from universal principles to concrete legal norms or cases. Apart from some types of lists, comparisons and so-called 'general rules' (on these more below), there are hardly any statements in the Mishnah which could be considered to lie *above* the level of generality on which the case schemata operate. The more general forms just mentioned are not given the role of imposing a *shape* on the discourse, and are severely restricted in scope and generality. The case schemata themselves do in fact vary in the amount of situational detail they envisage. But there is no guarantee that for a certain protasis in which the same situational features apply as in a more general case schema but one more situational feature is added, the apodosis will remain unchanged.[76] In other words, there is no *hierarchical* relationship between the more detailed and the more general case schemata. In the sense that each case schema envisages in its protasis a *different and concrete* situation (or selects different situational features), they are all equally concrete or general. It thus emerges that the discursive or reflective function of passages which delay the progress from case to case is very important. For, insofar as they afford a glimpse of principles, arguments, warrants or reasons, they provide the bulk of such material in

---

[74] See b. B.M. 59a/b (oven of Akhnai).

[75] The comparison with Maimonides' Mishneh Torah is particularly instructive in this regard.

[76] Textually speaking, the opposite expectation operates in the Mishnah. See the principle of minimal critical difference formulated in section 1 above.

the Mishnah. They are not found at the beginning or end of larger units, i.e. at the strategic points for controlling larger textual structures. Instead, they are tucked away between smaller units (namely the case schemata). But that gives them a cumulative effect through repetition. They do not determine or explicate the thematic order of case schemata, i.e. what we have called the *pulse* of the mishnaic discourse; but their insistent if irregular recurrence sets its *tone*.[77]

Yet their position between neighbouring case schemata is not merely a stylistic fact. As a rule, they could not be moved to a more independent textual position without modifying their scope. The case schema does not only provide what one might call the 'point of attachment' for any material that interrupts a series of case schemata. It also often limits conceptually such material in its generality or scope. For example, in passage (1) above, on the boundaries of the Land of Israel, it is not the boundaries *in general* that are the topic of the dispute. Instead, it is the boundaries of Israel *with regard to the halakhah of writs of divorce*: 'R. Meir says: Akko is like the Land of Israel for the purposes of (-ל) the *get*.' This implies that for other halakhic questions, for example first-fruits, the boundaries might be drawn differently. A quick comparison within the Mishnah confirms this; in the context of other topics where the distinction is relevant, Kezib – not Akko – is confirmed as the northern boundary.[78] In other words, the conceptual background definitions which underlie a thematically related group of case schemata are not only textually, but

---

[77] Spinoza's *Ethics* offers a somewhat similar punctuation of tightly organized thematic progression ('mos geometrico') by units of discussion and comment. But these *scholia*, which interrupt the sequence of numbered 'propositions' and 'demonstrations' in the *Ethics*, are more obviously guided by a systematic concern; they also 'jump one to another, echo one another' (G. Deleuze, *Expressionism in Philosophy: Spinoza* [trans. M. Joughin; New York 1990; French original 1968], 344f.).

[78] For example, m. Dem. 1:3, m. Shevi. 6:1 and m. Ḥal. 4:8 identify Kezib as the point north of which the rules of *demai*, release-year produce and *hallah*, respectively, do not apply (cf. m. Dem. 6:11). In m. Shevi. 6:1 we find the formulation 'Three regions (ארצות) are to be distinguished in what concerns (-ל) the seventh year'. Also m. Shevi. 9:2, 'Three regions (ארצות) are to be distinguished in what concerns (-ל) the law of removal (of fruits)'. Cf. the excellent discussion of the tannaitic sources in P. S. Alexander, *The Toponomy of the Targumim with special reference to the Table of the Nations and the Boundaries of the Land of Israel* (D.Phil. thesis; Oxford University 1974), 234ff.; on the difference Akko-Kezib, see p. 237. Alexander draws attention to the co-existence of various *types* of definitions of the Land, with a variety of 'respects' introducing 'a refinement, or complication' ('only Israel in a weaker sense', p. 235). He says, 'effectively the boundaries can be moved from an exegetical basis unto a pragmatic [one]' (p. 240) and mentions points 'temporarily declared as outside' (p. 243).

conceptually, 'local' – tied to one topic.[79] And in many other cases, where there is no explicit indication of such a limitation of scope, the reader is left *uncertain* about the level of generality intended by an apparently unrestricted formulation. There is a pervasive ambiguity about the scope of general statements in the Mishnah. Even for rules whose wording is general[80] or those which appear repeatedly, it is by no means clear if their validity is as unrestricted as their formulation suggests, or how they are constrained by one another. Some of them are obviously not to be taken 'literally', for elsewhere in the Mishnah some restriction of their generality is presupposed. The *hyperbolic* (i.e. rhetorical) potential of general formulations educates the user of the Mishnah not to place absolute trust in them. Thus the reader is referred back to the case schemata in their concreteness. They are more definite precisely because they contain internally a structure of *conditional dependency* which, while limiting them, limits them explicitly. The apparently unlimited, 'absolute' formulations, by contrast, are also limited, but only tacitly. It is thus the case schemata which become the anchor of much of the information presented outside case schemata in the Mishnah. We could say, the 'absolute' wording of mishnaic generalizations is rendered vague and condi-tional by their textual function. Without knowledge of a larger context, the reader can only be sure about the validity of the general principles, reasons or hermeneutic operations *in their application to the very case schema* to which they belong textually. Their scope is thus controlled and limited by individual case schemata or the series of case schemata.

In this respect too the probative use of biblical wording in the Mishnah is similar. In particular, the methods by which rabbinic and biblical meaning are taken to converge are tied to specific acceptable interpretations. And Scripture is often not

---

[79] Compare the 'local' definition of the *minor* (a category used hundreds of times in the Mishnah), at m. Hag. 1:1. In that passage, the minor is defined in terms of the ability to make an assisted ascent up the temple mount during the pilgrim festival – which is the theme of the mishnaic discourse at that point.

[80] For example זה הכלל, or the phrase הכל כמנהג המדינה (m. Suk. 3:11). On *zeh ha-kelal*, see note 65 above. Cf. also the hermeneutic formula אין...אלא... which, despite its universal negation, is limited in scope and indeed used for *paradoxical* identifications (see W. Reiss, 'Wortsubstitution als Mittel der Deutung. Bemerkungen zur Formel אין...אלא', *Frankfurter Judaistische Beiträge* 6 (1978), 27-69; here 68f.).

quoted when a suitable proof-text is obviously available (or one is used elsewhere in rabbinic literature to support the mishnaic Dictum).[81] The conclusion to draw from this is: the authority of biblical wording is not admitted as *a universal principle*. And in their *selective* provision, hermeneutic warrants also fit the larger picture. For the same patchiness is found for reasons, generalizations and warrants appearing in the Mishnah.

Why does the Mishnah subdue or limit its provision of halakhic justifications in this manner, while at the same time suggesting (mostly through these) that the halakhic discourse is fundamentally 'accountable'? We shall venture a twofold, speculative answer. First, such limitation of the scope of principles renders the text of the Mishnah *insufficient* as the sole source of halakhic competence (ultimately binding it to a social context of learning or training). The ability to render new halakhic decisions or to contribute to the discourse of halakhah cannot be acquired from this text, or any text – this would be the implied message. Instead, that competence must be acquired by a process of learning and imitation which cannot be reduced to a verbal representation. No understanding of the principles can be gained except through experience of the way they are applied in many different circumstances. This throws light on the notion of 'Oral Torah'. The notion of orality (תורה שבעל פה) could point to a message which is fully articulated and verbally fixed, only not written down; and it is often understood in this way. More likely, however, is that it points to a competence ('Torah') or faculty of judgement which eludes exhaustive articulation but requires a context of doing,[82] similar to the way in which practical crafts cannot be wholly reduced to fixed verbal formulations. This is one explanation. Another one (partly compatible with the first) is that the principles are withheld from the user of the Mishnah, in order to prevent the unauthorized use of halakhic competence. In that case, the insufficiency of the Mishnah would be a means to ensure that the boundaries of the group whose members are competent to

---

[81] See on this *Rabbinic Interpretation of Scripture* (note 24), beginning of chapter 3, and chapter 15.

[82] Cf. M. Goodman, 'A Note on Josephus, the Pharisees and Ancestral Traditions', *Journal of Jewish Studies* 50 (1999), 17-20. The topic has wide ramifications, both in the history of knowledge in antiquity and in the philosophy of language. See for example W. Wieland, *Platon und die Formen des Wissens* (Göttingen 1982).

participate in the discourse of halakhah coincide with the boundaries of a specific social group, the rabbis. The Mishnah, while revealing much about the halakhah and making an important contribution to the training of halakhists, would then be designed so as not to jeopardize the monopoly of the rabbis as the sole source of halakhic competence.[83]

---

[83] The relationship between the literary structures of rabbinic literature and the historical triumph of rabbinic Judaism is discussed (from a different perspective) by A. Goldberg in 'Die Zerstörung von Kontext als Voraussetzung für die Kanonisierung religiöser Texte im rabbinischen Judentum'. The article appeared first in A. and J. Assmann (eds), *Kanon und Zensur. Archäologie der literarischen Kommunikation II* (Munich 1987); it can now be found also in Goldberg, *Mystik und Theologie des rabbinischen Judentums* (note 71 above), 413-25.

The Aramaic Targumim:
The Many Faces of the Jewish Biblical Experience

Moshe J. Bernstein

I. Preliminary Remarks[1]

Since the only area from which I was precluded from speaking (by very reasonable presidential prerogative) at the 1999 British AJS Conference was 'Biblical Interpretation at Qumran', I was still left with a great deal from which to select, and I chose to focus on my other central interest in Jewish interpretation in antiquity, the targumim or Aramaic versions of the Bible. However, rather than considering some suitably narrow corner of targumic studies, as would be my practice if this were a conference on targumic studies, I decided to view the Aramaic versions in this paper more broadly as reflecting a rather unique confluence of forms of Jewish biblical interpretation, and to judge for the purpose of my ensuing presentation how it is that the nature and history of the Aramaic versions enables them to encompass so many aspects of Jewish biblical interpretation. I am interested in this study not only in 'interpretation' in its narrowest sense, limited to the ways in which Jews have explained, translated and exegeted the narratives, laws and poetry of the Hebrew Bible. Rather, I include in addition to those obvious categories of 'Jewish biblical interpretation' some of the many other ways and contexts in which the Bible has been expanded, such as midrashic

---

[1] I take this opportunity to express my gratitude to the British Association for Jewish Studies, and, in particular, its 1999 President, my fellow Qumranite, Professor George J. Brooke for inviting me to the conference whose theme was 'Jewish Ways of Reading the Bible', and asking that I deliver a paper in an area of Jewish biblical interpretation which is of particular interest to me. The conference is memorable to me both for the level of intellectual discourse which it engendered and for the warm hospitality with which I was received. I have retained in this published form of my paper.some of its oral quality, while at the same time disfiguring it with the footnotes that are inappropriate to an oral presentation.

narratives, and employed, such as liturgy. In other words, I should like to map the Aramaic versions, their contents and contexts, against the broader field of Jewish biblical interpretation, its contents and contexts, that is, what I might call the 'Jewish biblical experience.'[2]

II. Introduction: What Do We Mean by 'The Aramaic Targumim'?

The term 'targumim', the Aramaic versions of the Hebrew Bible, covers many sorts of texts, and, once again, for the purpose of this discussion, I choose to cast the net labelled 'Aramaic versions' even more widely than usual. First, of course, there are the running Aramaic translations of all the books of the Hebrew Bible with the exception of Daniel and Ezra-Nehemiah. These both contain text in Aramaic and perhaps for that reason have no targum. The Pentateuch has several complete translations: Onqelos, recognized as official in Babylon (regardless of the location of its origin);[3] the

---

[2] I do not intend this paper to be a systematic introduction to targumic literature in its many aspects, but a selective survey of some the ways that targumic literature behaves and the roles which it plays. For general background and initial bibliography on the Aramaic translations as a group, see P. S. Alexander, 'Targum, Targumim', *Anchor Bible Dictionary* 6.320-331 and idem, 'Jewish Aramaic Translations of Hebrew Scriptures', in M. J. Mulder (ed.), *Mikra: Text, Translation, Reading and Interpretation of the Bible in Ancient Judaism and Early Christianity* (Assen-Philadelphia 1988), 217-53. A satisfactory systematic book-length introduction to targumic literature does not, in my view, exist.

[3] On the debate over the Palestinian or Babylonian *origin* of Onqelos, see Alexander, 'Targum', 321, where he concludes 'that *Onq.* originated in Palestine in 1st or early 2d centuries C.E. ... The Babylonian redaction of *Onq.* probably took place in the 4th or 5th century C.E.' On this theme, see most recently P. V. M. Flesher, 'Is *Targum Onqelos* a Palestinian Targum? The Evidence of Genesis 28-50', *Journal for the Study of the Pseudepigrapha* 19 (1999), 35-79. It is important that we should not view the arguments for a Palestinian origin for Onqelos as dissociating it too strongly from its traditional Babylonian context. The only 'critical' text of Onqelos is that found in A. Sperber, *The Bible in Aramaic*, Vol. 1 (Leiden 1959), although a more I do not intend this paper to be a systematic introduction to targumic literature in its many aspects, but a selective survey of some the ways that targumic literature behaves and the roles which it plays. For general background and initial bibliography on the Aramaic translations as a group, see P. S. Alexander, 'Targum, Targumim', *Anchor Bible Dictionary* 6.320-331 and idem, 'Jewish Aramaic Translations of Hebrew Scriptures', in M. J. Mulder (ed.), *Mikra: Text, Translation, Reading and Interpretation of the Bible in Ancient Judaism and Early Christianity* (Assen-Philadelphia 1988), 217-53. A satisfactory systematic book-length introduction to targumic literature does not, in my view, exist.

[3] On the debate over the Palestinian or Babylonian *origin* of Onqelos, see Alexander, 'Targum', 321, where he concludes 'that *Onq.* originated in Palestine in 1st or early 2d centuries C.E. ... The Babylonian redaction of *Onq.* probably took place in the 4th or 5th century C.E.' On this theme, see most recently P. V. M. Flesher, 'Is *Targum Onqelos* a Palestinian Targum? The Evidence of Genesis 28-50', *Journal for*

Palestinian Neofiti;[4] and the late, hybrid pseudo-Jonathan.[5] In addition, we now have,

thanks to Michael Klein's magisterial edition, a range of fragmentary Palestinian targum

texts from the Cairo Geniza, some of which are earlier than any other surviving targumic

texts and some of which, more significantly, do not necessarily derive from the same

circles which have transmitted to us the more fully preserved texts.[6] Furthermore, there

are the non-comprehensive and selective Fragment Targums of the Pentateuch,[7] the

complete targum Jonathan to the Prophets which is probably related linguistically and

exegetically to Onqelos,[8] and a melange of targumim on the books of the Hagiographa,

with differing exegetical agenda, translation techniques, and probably provenances.[9] All

the Jewish Aramaic targumim are theoretically eligible for my discussion; the only

significant text that I am not including is the Syriac Peshitta which, despite its Jewish

origins, cannot comfortably be described as a Jewish Aramaic version.[10]

I also wish to include under the rubric of the targumim not only the continuous

and non-continuous Aramaic translations of the individual books of the Hebrew Bible,

---

the Study of the Pseudepigrapha 19 (1999), 35-79. It is important that we should not view the arguments for a Palestinian origin for Onqelos as dissociating it too strongly from its traditional Babylonian context. The only 'critical' text of Onqelos is that found in A. Sperber, *The Bible in Aramaic*, Vol. 1 (Leiden 1959), although a more comprehensive edition, taking into account a fuller range of manuscript evidence is a desideratum.

[4] Neofiti (A. Diez Macho [ed.], *Neophyti I*, 6 volumes [Madrid-Barcelona, 1968ff.]) is a complete pentateuchal targum representing one branch of the Palestinian tradition, and is related to the non-complete texts mentioned immediately below.

[5] Pseudo-Jonathan, which is often included in discussions of the Palestinian tradition, is likely to be a combination of one or more Onqelos traditions, Palestinian material, and some elements of unknown provenance (D. Rieder [ed.], *Pseudo-Jonathan. Targum Jonathan ben Uziel on the Pentateuch*, [Jerusalem 1974]; reprinted in 1984 in 2 volumes with modern Hebrew translation and rabbinic cross-references; and E. G. Clarke et al. [eds], *Targum Pseudo-Jonathan: Text and Concordance* [Hoboken 1984]). It also appears to have been composed at a later date than the 'authentic' Palestinian targumim.

[6] *Genizah Manuscripts of Palestinian Targum to the Pentateuch*, 2 volumes (Hoboken 1987).

[7] The standard edition is M. Klein, *The Fragment Targums of the Pentateuch*, 2 volumes (Rome 1980). For a brief discussion of the issue of their evolution, see Alexander, 'Jewish Aramaic Translations', 221.

[8] Included in the edition by Sperber referred to in n. 3 above.

[9] There is no critical edition of most of the targumim of the Hagiographa; those which have been done properly include D. M. Stec, *The Text of the Targum of Job: An Introduction and Critical Edition* (Leiden 1994) and R. Le Deaut and J. Robert, *Targum des Chroniques* (Rome 1971).

[10] On the Jewish origin of the Peshitta, see Y. Maori, *The Peshitta Version of the Pentateuch and Early Jewish Exegesis* [Hebrew] (Jerusalem 1995) which will appear in the near future in an English translation.

but also ancillary Aramaic material, often of a liturgical nature, which was employed side-by-side with these versions in the synagogue service. Some of these texts are argumic poetic material, dating from as early perhaps as the fourth or fifth century CE.[11] Others belong to an ambiguous genre usually referred to as *toseftot*, aggadic segments (of apparently Palestinian origin) which were introduced into the version of Onqelos in certain liturgical contexts.[12] This broad characterization of the forms of targumic literature anticipates the varied roles which it plays in the Jewish biblical experience. I shall not have time to introduce material from each of these sources into the survey which follows, but feel that it is important to indicate the very broad scope of the 'targumic' corpus nonetheless.

While I generally try to avoid doing so in my scholarship, I am here 'clumping', or grouping together under a single rubric or heading, in this case 'Aramaic versions' or targumim, works which have clearly definable differences among them. I am by nature a 'splitter', searching for that which identifies and characterizes two things which appear to be alike as differing from one another. In the context of this paper, however, although there are profound differences among them in language, date, completeness, function, translation technique, theological framework, and prospective audience, the Aramaic versions are bound together sufficiently strongly that they can be considered as a single corpus. My goal is to demonstrate how that corpus functioned.

---

[11] On early targumic poems, see the introductory material in Y. Yahalom and M. Sokoloff, *Jewish Palestinian Aramaic Poetry from Late Antiquity: Critical Edition with Introduction and Commentary* [Hebrew] (Jerusalem 1999) and J. Heinemann, 'Remnants of Ancient *Piyyutim* in the Palestinian *Targum* Tradition' [Hebrew], *Hasifrut* 4 (1973), 362-75. On the targumic poetry preserved in the Cairo Geniza, see also M. L. Klein, 'Targumic Poems from the Cairo Genizah', *Hebrew Annual Review* 8 (1984), 89-99.

[12] On *toseftot*, see briefly Alexander, 'Jewish Aramaic Translations', 221-22 and more fully, M. L. Klein, 'Targumic Toseftot from the Cairo Genizah', in D. Muñoz León (ed.), *Salvación en la Palabra: Targum, Derash Berith: En Memoria del profesor Alejandro Díez Macho* (Madrid 1985), 409-18. On *toseftot* to the targum of the Prophets, see R. Kasher, *Targumic Toseftot to the Prophets* [Hebrew] (Jerusalem 1996). The texts of the *toseftot* in the Pentateuch are often identical with the aggadic expansions found in the Palestinian targumic traditions to be discussed later, and it is only their presence within a 'Babylonian' Onqelos tradition which makes them particularly worthy of notice.

The Aramaic versions of the Bible may indeed have begun their existence in the synagogue, the *bet ha-keneset* as is likely, or in the study-hall, the *bet ha-midrash*, which is less likely.[13] Since I am not concerned primarily with the history of the targumim, I shall not enter into the debate over whether free targumic renderings are earlier than literal ones. What is significant for our discussion is that the Aramaic translations have developed far beyond their probable beginnings as renditions of the Hebrew text, whether free or literal, into a variety of related literary forms set in a variety of liturgical and educational contexts. The key point is the fact that the targumim evolved, and not how they evolved, from straightforward translation into a variety of literary genres whose remains shed light on the whole spectrum of Jewish biblical interpretation as well as other aspects of Jewish thought and literature such as poetry, liturgy and intellectual history.

III. The Aramaic Versions and the Hebrew Bible

What allows the targumim to be the subject of a paper such as this one, which will survey a broad range of interpretive methods, both exegetical and eisegetical, as well as a spectrum of roles played by the targumim in Jewish intellectual life? The answer can probably be summed up in a single point: The targum(im) is/are not (a) translation(s) like other translations, ancient or modern. How are these translations, to borrow an ancient Jewish formula, different from all other translations? First of all they never became, nor were they intended to become, as far as we can tell, the 'Bible' of Aramaic-speaking Jewry. The term 'Aramaic Bible' which is often used in the titles of series or of a new journal is thus something of a misnomer from the standpoint of the actual

---

[13] A. D. York, 'The Targum in the Synagogue and in the School', *Journal for the Study of Judaism* 10 (1979), 74-86, gathers the rabbinic data for the contexts in which the targumim were employed. See also Alexander, 'Jewish Aramaic Translations', 238-41 and cf. the more recent discussions by A. Shinan, 'The Aramaic Targum as a Mirror of Galilean Jewry', and S. D. Fraade, 'Rabbinic Views on the Practice of Targum, and Multilingualism in the Jewish Galilee of the Third-Sixth Centuries', in L. I. Levine (ed.), *The Galilee in Late Antiquity* (New York-Jerusalem 1992) 241-51 and 243-86, respectively.

history of the targumim; the 'Bible in Aramaic', the title of Sperber's forty-year-old edition of the targumim is probably more appropriate.

Second, in order to explain why these works never became a 'Bible' in and of themselves, I point to the fact that the targumim never achieved an independent existence since they always circulated together with the Hebrew text. All of the audiences of the targumim, in whatever context, read, heard, or at least knew of, the Bible being read in its original language, especially in liturgical frameworks. Even if the Hebrew language skills of the Aramaic-understanding Jew were seriously deficient, he or she knew that the Bible was a Hebrew text, that the Pentateuch was read in Hebrew in the synagogue, and perhaps that Psalms were recited in Hebrew. It would therefore have been very difficult for the Bible in Aramaic to take on a life of its own as a 'biblical text.' This observation is not new with me. It has been made by others in the past, including James Barr and Sebastian Brock.[14] What I suggest is that, somewhat paradoxically, it was this attachment to the Hebrew text which enabled the Aramaic versions to range far and wide beyond the mere translation of the ancient Hebrew original, to be untrammelled, at times, by the constraints of the words of the Hebrew text, to add to that text units both large and small, and to become an educational tool in the hands of its composers in areas which at times maintain only the most tenuous connection to the biblical text. The Aramaic versions may have become authoritative as translation or interpretation, but not as biblical text. The Hebrew text remained, in some sense or other, a very elastic check on the Aramaic versions, allowing them to be literal, free, paraphrastic or even allegorical, without fear that the reader or listener would assume that the Aramaic words represented the *ipsissima verba* of the divine original.[15] The flexibility granted to the Aramaic

---

[14] J. Barr, *The Typology of Literalism in Ancient Biblical Translations* (MSU XV; Göttingen 1979), 31; S. Brock, 'Translating the Old Testament', in D. A. Carson and H. G. M. Williamson (eds), *It is Written: Scripture Citing Scripture. Essays in Honour of Barnabas Lindars* (Cambridge 1988), 92, and cf. Alexander, 'Jewish Aramaic Translations', 238-39.

[15] It might be suggested that the same constraint of the Hebrew text allowed the expansiveness and freedom of rabbinic midrash.

versions in this way enables them to do all of the un-translation-like things which we shall discuss shortly.

Can we imagine a similar development in the Septuagint? However free the Greek translation might appear to be at times, it still attempts to mirror or to maintain the form of the biblical text. It does not, as do the Palestinian targumim, interrupt the flow of the translation narrative, for example, to insert a midrashic expansion which elaborates the biblical story in dramatic detail. It does not flesh out biblical similes or implied similes through the introduction of both the vehicle and the tenor of the simile into the translation. It does not contain, or at least we do not possess, poetic passages in the style of the translation which were to be added to the Greek text when it was read liturgically. The Greek translators appear to have had far less freedom in departing from the shape of a very difficult verse in order to present something coherent and sensible to their readers than was available to the Aramaic versions in translating passages in Psalms, for example.

Since the Aramaic versions, in Jewish tradition, never took on the aura of a divinely inspired or enhanced document as the Septuagint did in both Jewish and early Christian tradition,[16] they remained versions of, commentaries on, and expansions of a text. This does not mean that some of the Aramaic versions did not achieve a certain canonicity of their own, especially Onqelos to the Pentateuch and Jonathan to the Prophets, but this was as canonical translation, not canonical text. The rabbinic halakhah which demands that a private individual complete the reading of the weekly portion of the Torah twice in Hebrew and once in Aramaic also points in the direction of characterizing the Aramaic versions as I have done.[17] I believe that this difference

---

[16] I disregard for the moment a peculiar comment by Rashi on b. Qid. 49a s.v. הרי זה מחרף which asserts the authority of Onqelos 'since it was given at Sinai.'

[17] b. Ber. 8a-b. I use the term 'reading' loosely; the Hebrew reads לעולם ישלים אדם פרשיותיו עם הציבור שנים מקרא ואחד תרגום, 'an individual should complete his [weekly Torah] portions with the congregation, twice the text and once the targum.'

between the Aramaic versions and the Septuagint can also be demonstrated using the Vulgate or any number of modern translations as a contrast with the Aramaic versions.

Even among Jewish translations, the qualities which I have described make the targumim stand out. In the Yemenite community alone, the tenth century translation of Rav Saadiah Gaon took on as central a role in liturgy and education as the targumim had done earlier. If I have exaggerated somewhat in my depiction of the unique nature of the Aramaic versions, it is only slightly, and the fundamental point remains, namely that the targumim were freer of the original text than the Septuagint or other versions because they were always connected to the text.

IV. The Jewish 'Biblical Experience' in Antiquity

Of what did that 'biblical experience' consist in antiquity? What were the faces or facets which the Bible presented to a Jew from the last centuries BCE to the first centuries CE? For the Jew of late antiquity, regardless of the subgroup of Judaism to which he or she belonged and the beliefs he or she held and the practices which he or she followed, the Bible stood at the centre of spiritual and religious life.[18] The Bible provided Jews with the history of their people and earliest ancestors, with the source for the laws which they observed in daily practice, and with some of the texts with which they might approach God on a personal level. It was the basis of the theology and practice of the Qumran sect, and of both the halakhah and the aggadah of rabbinic Judaism. The legal passages of the Pentateuch formed the foundation of Jewish law and their ongoing exegesis furnished the solutions to legal questions which were generated by new social and historical situations.

The Bible formed the framework around which the rabbinic *derashot* or 'sermons' were preached; its stories became the foundation for moral education and were expanded to fill in perceived gaps in the biblical narratives and even further elaborated

---

[18] My attempt at inclusive language does not mean that I think that the same opportunities for study, learning and worship were available equally to men and women during this era. They were not!

into a virtual full-scale history of Jewish heroes in the biblical period. The Bible was 'rewritten' or 'retold' by all Jews, with each group and each author choosing expansions and abridgements, characters and incidents to highlight or to de-emphasize, according to the goal of the retelling, its theological guidelines, the nature of the audience and the literary context.[19] The Torah and selections from the prophetic literature were read and interpreted publicly on a weekly basis in rabbinic Judaism. The Psalms were likely recited publicly, and certain other texts, such as the book of Esther (and later the book of Lamentations) were read on special occasions. The rabbinic literary genres of biblical interpretation other than the family of the Aramaic versions tend to be denoted by the term midrashim, and include halakhic midrashim, as well as exegetical and homiletical midrashim. But other Jews in antiquity, the authors of the Apocrypha and of Second Temple pseudepigraphical works, not to mention the writers of the Qumran scrolls, have left a broader range of literary *oeuvres* than the rabbis, including, the kind of rewritten Bible typified by Jubilees and similar works, and a spectrum of apocalyptic works with biblical links.[20] Some of these non-rabbinic genres may also find representation in the surviving Aramaic versions.

V. A. The Targumim as Translation: Narrative Prose

For the rest of this paper I shall attempt to survey how the Aramaic versions range over many, if not all, of the areas just mentioned. We are all aware that all translations are commentaries, but that we sometimes have to look closely at the rendering to extrapolate the comment which is implicit. Certainly the first level of interpretation of any text not written in an audience's native language will be translation, for it is through the straightforward process of translation that the reader/listener first

---

[19] The term which is commonly employed for this genre understood broadly is 'rewritten Bible', and was coined by Geza Vermes in *Scripture and Tradition in Judaism* (Leiden 1961). Examples include Jubilees, the Genesis Apocryphon (1QapGen), Josephus' Jewish Antiquities 1-11, and pseudo-Philo's Book of Biblical Antiquities.
[20] The works focusing on Enoch and the Testaments of the Twelve Patriarchs are typical of the apocalyptic type.

gains access to the words, sentences, ideas and message of the original text. In the realm of translation, the targumim themselves *are* the major representatives (other than LXX and Peshitta) of Jewish interpretation in antiquity. They are not cut from a single cloth in terms of translation technique, and, perhaps equally significantly, individual targumim do not exhibit the same mode of translation in all passages. One of the useful techniques in comparative targumic studies (of the versions of the Pentateuch) is the alignment of the various Aramaic versions side by side in passages which are difficult in some way (and sometimes even if they are not difficult) in order to study the translation techniques of the different versions. The version of Onqelos is often described as very literal, and perhaps it *is* in comparison with the exuberant expansions of pseudo-Jonathan. But an examination of Onqelos' version of even the non-poetic portions of the Pentateuch, which do not present the interpretive difficulties and the need for non-literal translation which the poetic portions do, will show clearly where, and how often, Onqelos moves from a literal formal equivalence in the direction of the non-literal explanatory 'translation'.

We must always bear in mind, however, that the targumim, like other ancient translations, did not have the flexibility of modern translations and commentaries. They could not present alternative translations in the body of the text and in footnotes; they could not write notes vindicating their choice of vocabulary or structure; they could not leave three dots in the text and note in the margin 'text hopelessly corrupt' or 'emendation yields'. They, like all the other ancient versions, had to place a rendering of the Hebrew in front of their reading or listening audience without any opportunity to explain or comment overtly. The translator as interpreter must also operate with much more subtlety than the writer of a commentary or a rewritten Bible. Since the targum is fundamentally bound to the shape of the Hebrew text, minor changes in word choice or in syntactical structure become virtually the only ways by which the translator can direct the reader to the 'correct' interpretation.

It is apparent that at least one Palestinian Aramaic text may owe its existence, in part, to the difficulty which is inherent in translating the biblical text. The so-called Fragment Targumim of the Pentateuch, whose best known representative is the targum

Yerushalmi printed in the standard Rabbinic Bibles, covers in all of its recensions a total of only about 850 verses of the Torah. At times, as we shall see later, it contains aggadic expansions of biblical narratives, shared with other representatives of the Palestinian targum tradition. But in other places, only a word or two survives from a verse, usually a difficult or obscure term which is particularly hard to translate.[21] This targum, if indeed it was composed at an early date (an issue on which is there is still no agreement among scholars), may point to the Aramaic versions evolving from translations of individual difficult words into full-fledged translations of a whole text.[22] Even though it is not a complete vocabulary list of hard words in biblical Hebrew, and even if it were to have come into being as a selection from a fuller running translation, this lexical focus of the Fragment Targum points to the use of targum on this basic level of interpretation side by side with the aggadic expansions of which we shall speak later.

When it comes to a running targum, such as Onqelos, the choices made by the translator are often geared toward selecting one out of several possible translation options, and these choices also represent interpretation on its most fundamental level. For the modern student of targum, the study of the variations among the Aramaic versions in their choices of vocabulary and meaning at a given location can give us insight into the exegetical diversity of Judaism in late antiquity, even without examining other rabbinic or non-rabbinic interpretive documents. But such profundities did not occur to the Jew who heard or, less likely, read the Aramaic version of the pentateuchal or prophetic reading in the synagogue; for him or her the Aramaic versions served a much more fundamental need, the laying out of the scriptural message in his or her language.

---

[21] For examples of this phenomenon, cf. the Fragment Targum in either of its recensions (Paris MS or Vatican MS) on Exodus 25-28, the chapters on the building of the tabernacle, where a good number of individual words are translated, but very few fuller units of text.

[22] Alexander, 'Targum', 324 and 'Jewish Aramaic Translations', 221, adopts the widespread view that Fragment Targum texts are excerpted from full versions of the Palestinian Targum. I am less certain of that fact and think that the alternative suggested by Shinan, namely that the Fragment Targum 'reflects fundamentally the foundations of targumic aggadah which circulated in the circles of the translators' and is the kernel around which the full Palestinian targum was formed (A. Shinan, *The Aggadah in the Aramaic Targums to the Pentateuch* [Hebrew] [Jerusalem 1979] 1.109). Unlike Shinan, I believe it possible that not only the aggadic material in the Fragment Targum, but also the individual translations of difficult words may be early.

Let us examine two examples of the targumim labouring at the task of reading the Bible. I have chosen them from cases where there is some disagreement on how to read a word or phrase, even a fairly simple one. After Moses has attempted to allay the fears of the Israelites at the approach of the Egyptians (Exodus 14:13-14), God addresses him in 14:15 מה תצעק אלי דבר אל בני ישראל ויסעו (Literally, 'why do you cry out to me; speak to the Israelites and let them set forth'). It appears that there was a targumic tradition not to render the first of these phrases literally. Onqelos translates it קבילית צלותך, 'I have heard your prayer;' pseudo-Jonathan has למא את קאי ומצלי קדמי הא צלותהון דעמי קדמת לדידך, 'why are you standing and praying to me? The prayer of my people takes precedence to yours;' Neofiti reads: עד אימת את קיים תהווי מצלי קדמיי שמיע הוא צלותך ברם צלותהון דבני ישראל קדמא לדידך, 'How long will you stand praying before me? Your prayer has been heard by me, but the prayers of the Israelites takes precedence to yours.'

Putting aside the fairly regular rendering of the Hebrew צעק by Aramaic צלי, it is clear that there are two free translations chosen by the Aramaic versions which retain the sense of the Hebrew, although not literally. Onqelos turns the rhetorical question into a statement, while Neofiti translates almost literally (if we allow 'how long' to be the equivalent of Hebrew מה), followed by the a translation parallel to that of Onqelos (but employing a different lexeme, שמע rather than קבל), followed by a statement about the precedence of the prayer of the Israelites, as if reading the verse 'why are *you* praying to me? [Your prayers are unnecessary.]' Pseudo-Jonathan appears to be a curtailed version of Neofiti, omitting the section parallel to Onqelos.[23] These are not aggadic expansions or 'paraphrastic' translations, but rather attempts to make the sense of the Hebrew clear to the audience, even at the expense of hyper-literality.

---

[23] One might have surmised that pseudo-Jonathan represents an original form of the Palestinian targum here, and that Neofiti has the later form, having integrated an Onqelos-type reading with the Palestinian, were it not for the fact that both MSS of the Fragment Targum have virtually the same reading as Neofiti. Of course, the lines of development and connection among targumic versions are not always easy to draw, so in this instance, as often, we can only ponder the relative likelihood of the two positions.

Sometimes the problem in translation goes beyond a choice of how to make the sense of a clear text clearer. Thus where Exodus 14:20 reads ויהי הענן והחשך ויאר את הלילה ('there was cloud and darkness, and it brightened the night'), the Aramaic translators were uniformly puzzled by the fact that 'cloud and darkness' apparently 'brightened the night.' They resolved their difficulty by a typical targumic technique of inserting extra language and creating new clause divisions which clarify the syntax in the sentence. The similarity of the resolutions employed in the different traditions, despite the fact that they are not identical linguistically, points to the likelihood that there is an early interpretive convention at work here. So Onqelos renders והוה עננא וקבלא למצראי ולישראל נהר כל ליליא ('*there was darkness and cloud* for the Egyptians, while for Israel, *it lit up the whole night*'). The Palestinian tradition, represented here by FT MS V, has והוה עננא פלגה נהור ופלגה חשוך נהורה מנהר על ישר' וחשוכה מחשוך על מצראי ('*there was cloud*, half light *and* half *dark*; the light *gave light* to Israel, and *the dark* darkened over the Egyptians'). This kind of technique represents an approach to the solution of syntactical awkwardness which is typical of the targumim and, I may add, of rabbinic midrashic readings as well. These two brief examples show the translators at work on the most fundamental level, conveying the meaning of the Hebrew prose in sensible Aramaic for their audiences.

V.B. The Targumim as Translation: Poetry

Biblical poetry poses a challenge to any translator, and the targumim chose varied solutions to the exegetical problems. At times they would adopt the approach which we saw in the narrative above, introducing into the version words which do not stand in one-to-one correspondence with the Hebrew, while still maintaining the shape of the Hebrew texts. At others, they would rewrite the Hebrew completely, dropping all pretence of literal translation, and telling their audience what the text was actually *supposed* to mean. There are biblical passages which are so ambiguous that the references in pronouns obscure the theology of the text and divergent readings can arise out of the obscurities. In these passages, more than in narrative or legal texts, the role of the targum as commentator in addition to translator is highlighted, because in order to make the Hebrew text meaningful to the audience the targum had to show what it meant in addition to translating its words. Once again, let us examine a couple of actual examples of how this works. My examples are chosen from Deuteronomy 32, the Song of Moses, an enigmatic Hebrew poetic text, the targumic versions of which I have been studying intensively for a number of years.

Biblical poetry is often obscure due to its terse modes of expression; in the following instances there is ambiguity in the referent in the biblical text which the some-what vague poetic context does not clarify. Deut. 32:34 reads הלא הוא כמס עמדי חתם באוצרתי ('Is it not stored up with me, sealed in my storehouses?'). Onqelos takes הוא, 'it', as referring to the iniquitous deeds of the Israelites הלא כל עובדיהון גלן קדמי גניזין ליום דינא באוצרי ('*Are* their deeds *not revealed before me, stored up* for the day of judgment *in my storehouses*?'). The Palestinian tradition, on the other hand, takes it as referring to the eschatological punishment of the wicked, הלא הוא כסא דפורענותא ממזג ומתקן לרשיעיא ליום דינא רבא באוצרי (Fragment Targum MS P; '*Is this*, the cup of punishment, *not mixed* and *readied* for the wicked *in my storehouses* for the great day of judgment?'). Note the commonality, despite the divergence in the first half of the verse, in assigning the latter half of the verse to the eschaton. Both readings can be said to make sense, in the difficult biblical context, and, whichever one the targumist chose is clearer than the ambiguous biblical original.

Similarly, in a case where the issue is the unpacking of a biblical simile, different targumim choose differing (and perhaps opposite) options. The Hebrew text of Deut 32:32 reads כי מגפן סדום גפנם ומשדמת עמרה ('For their vine is of the vine of Sodom and of the fields of Gomorrah'), but what is being described is not immediately obvious. For Onqelos the simile refers to the punishment of the Israelites ארי כפורענות עמא דסדום פורענותהון ולקותהון כעם עמורא ('For like the punishment of the people of Sodom is their punishment, and their smiting like the people of Gomorrah'), while for the Palestinian tradition it refers to the Israelites' actions and thoughts, ארום עמא האילין עובדיהון מדמיין לעובדיהון לעמא די סדום ומחשבתהון מדמיה למחשבתהון דעמא דעמורא (FT MS V; 'For the deeds of this people are compared to the deeds of Sodom and their thoughts are like the thoughts of the people of Gomorrah'). The elusive nature of the biblical text allows, and even compels, the translator to become a more active exegete than in a narrative prose context.

For the second example in this segment, I choose Deut 32:37-38:

ואמר אי א-להימו צור חסיו בו
אשר חלב זבחימו יאכלו ישתו יין נסיכם
יקומו ויעזרכם יהי עליכם סתרה

('He/one will say, "Where are their gods, the rock in whom they took shelter? The flesh of whose [pl.] sacrifices they would eat, drink their libation wine; let them arise and aid you, let him be a protection over you".'). Aside from the issue of the seemingly inconsistent singulars and plurals, who is the speaker, the subject of ואמר? And to whom are the words addressed? The option selected is not merely a choice among translations, but of the ultimate message of the chapter; it is the choice of a commentator (and theologian), not just a translator. Onqelos reads the subject of ואמר as 'God' (= 'the Lord' of LXX and 4QDeut[a])[24] who mocks the Israelites by suggesting that they call for aid on the multiplicity of divinities whom they used to worship.[25]

The Palestinian targumim choose a very different reading, where אומיא, 'the nations', are supplied as the subject of the verb ואמר,[26] because, in the reading which these Aramaic versions adopt for the broader context, the breach between God and Israel has begun to be repaired in the previous verses. The two verses under consideration become a mockery of God by the enemies of Israel, not a critique of Israel by its God. These 'fighting words' become a further impetus for God's response on behalf of His people in 32:39ff., beginning with ראו עתה כי אני אני הוא ואין אלהים עמדי ('See now that indeed I am He and there is no god beside me'). This reading happens to be shared by the Samaritan Pentateuch and Targum which read or render the singular Hebrew ואמר with a plural verb, thus guaranteeing that the subject is the enemies of Israel.[27] Both of these readings involve taking exegetical and theological positions, and illustrate the

---

[24] 4QDeut[q] reads [וא]מר יהוה; LXX has καὶ εἶπεν κύριος.

[25] The term דחלתהון (literally, 'their objects of reverence') indicates clearly that אלהימו refers to pagan deities. Onqelos does not resolve the problem of the lack of agreement between the singular number of בו and the plurals יקומו ויעזרכם, although the singular יהי of MT is rendered by the plural יהון, in agreement with the verbs יקומו ויעזרכם in the first half of verse 38.

[26] FT P reads עתידין אומיא למימר ('the nations will say in the future'), while Neofiti and FT V have the same phrase preceded by ואמר, probably dittography of the lemma. Pseudo-Jonathan belongs to this tradition, as well, supplying סנאה ('the enemy') as the subject of ואמר.

[27] SP reads ואמרו; ST ויימרון.

commentary aspect of the targumim in ambiguous poetic passages. In these poetic examples, as opposed to the prose examined above, the targumim have to work harder to accomplish their goal, and are compelled to supplement the text further and fill in more theoretical gaps in order to accomplish their goals. The clarification of the 'message' of the text is a necessary by-product.

V.C. The Targumim as Translation: Legal Material

Legal material presents a somewhat different set of difficulties to the would-be interpreter. Here we can presume that some of the time one of the problems or issues for the author of a targumic text is the relationship of the biblical text with its 'official' rabbinic interpretation. To what degree was the rabbinic reading 'binding' and authoritative for the translators? In a rabbinic text, whether Talmud or midrash, more than one view could be presented, but in the Aramaic versions there was no room for such niceties. Once again the biblical text had to be endowed with *a* meaning, *one meaning*. There is no single approach adopted by the various targumim to this issue, and rabbinic halakhah is not always seen to have control over the translation.

The subject of Onqelos' fidelity to rabbinic halakhah has been dealt with for more than a century and half, both by traditional scholars who start with the presupposition that an official targum such as Onqelos should not contradict classical rabbinic sources, and by modern students of rabbinic literature.[28] In halakhic passages, Onqelos seems to be willing at times to apply the rabbinic dictum אין מקרא יוצא מידי פשוטו ('the verse cannot escape its simple sense meaning'), and to translate in a way which does not conform to the halakhah. If the simple sense translation produced is at variance with classical halakhah, Onqelos cannot be blamed for being a translator and not a halakhist. The explication of the text

---

[28] For two recent contributions to this literature which contain references to previous discussions in traditional rabbinic commentators, see Yeshayahu Maori, 'The Aramaic Targumim of the Torah and Rabbinic Midrash' [Hebrew], *Proceedings of the Ninth World Congress of Jewish Studies: Panel Sessions Bible Studies and Ancient Near East* (Jerusalem 1986) 1-12, and Bernard Grossfeld, 'Targum Onqelos, Halakha, and the Halakhic Midrashim', in D. R .G. Beattie and M. J. McNamara (eds), *The Aramaic Bible: Targums in their Historical Context* (Journal for the Study of the Old Testament Supplement 166; Sheffield 1994), 228-46.

is still his first goal, and we perhaps should draw the inference that the straightforward translation of the text without regard to halakhic exegesis or practice was his initial responsibility. Despite the fact that the translation was to be declaimed publicly in the presence of a not necessarily learned audience, the teaching of halakhah seems to have been deemed to be secondary in this instance to the rendition of the Hebrew text.

Let us take a couple of brief examples from Exodus 21: Exod. 21:6 reads ועבדו לעלם which is rendered literally, ויהא ליה עבד פלח לעלם ('he shall be his servant, working in perpetuity'), not according to the halakhic interpretation (explicit in Leviticus 25) that Israelite slaves go free in the jubilee year. Exod. 21:24 'an eye for an eye', is translated verbatim, despite the virtually unanimous rabbinic interpretation of this verse as demanding monetary compensation.[29] When we stop to consider the nature of classical Jewish biblical interpretation as a whole, this seemingly trivial observation becomes quite significant, for it demonstrates that even in legal contexts the actual words of the biblical text could not be ignored, even if they were in conflict with the eventually accepted halakhah.

On the other hand, there are cases wherein Onqelos adopts renderings which are in line with rabbinic legal interpretation. The injunction against seething a kid in its mother's milk, which is repeated three times, is thrice rendered by Onqelos 'you shall not eat meat with milk' (Exod. 23:19; 34:26; Deut. 14:21) in agreement with rabbinic law. The biblical text of Deut. 16:2 וזבחת פסח לה' א-להיך צאן ובקר ('You shall sacrifice a paschal offering to the Lord your God, sheep and cattle') implies that the paschal sacrifice may be brought from either the flock or the herd and appears to contradict

---

[29] It has been argued by M. M. Kasher that Onqelos is following the view of R. Eliezer (his teacher according to rabbinic tradition in b. Meg. 3a) as expressed in b. B.Q. 84a understanding the biblical verse as עין תחת עין ממש, 'an eye for an eye literally' (*Torah Shelemah* [New York 1956] 17.262); for fuller discussion see I. H. Haut, 'Lex Talionis: Views, Ancient and Modern, Particularly Those of Maimonides', *Diné Israel* 16 [1991-92], 7-45, esp. 19-21 and n. 46). However, aside from the fact that such an interpretation of R. Eliezer is immediately rejected by the talmudic context, and that rabbinic tradition regards the day on which the 'rabbinic' exegesis of compensation triumphed over the 'Sadducean' one of literal talion worthy of celebration (Megillat Ta'anit 4), I believe that methodologically we should assume that literal translations by a targum or any other translator should be ascribed to the fact that he is a translator first and a legal exegete second. In other words, if Onqelos intended the view of R. Eliezer to be implied by his translation, we can never know it.

Exod. 12:5 which states that the offering is to come 'from sheep or goats.' Onqelos renders ותכוס פיסחא קדם ה' אלהך מן בני ענא וניכסת קודשא מן תורי ('You shall sacrifice the paschal offering before the Lord your God from sheep and holy sacrifices from oxen'); by separating the sheep from the oxen in this fashion, he interprets in the same fashion as the rabbinic tradition found in the first opinion in the Sifre on this verse.[30] The methodology of splitting the Hebrew and inserting modifiers is technically quite similar to the treatment of Exod. 14:20 which we examined above. When Onqelos renders the swearing of a true oath in the Torah *qayyem qeyama*, while designating false oaths by the choice of a different Aramaic lexeme for the same Hebrew one, it is commentary without remark.[31] What criteria affected Onqelos' choices between following the literal sense of the text or adhering to a halakhic reading still remains to be determined.

If this is true of Onqelos, it is even more true of the Palestinian targum tradition. Actually a good deal of the attention which has been paid to the halakhah of the Palestinian Aramaic versions has unfortunately been focused on a few very well-known passages in which their exegesis stands in sharp contrast to rabbinic exegesis or rabbinic halakhic rulings. These passages, such as Neofiti and the Geniza fragment at Exod. 22:4, or pseudo-Jonathan at Lev. 18:21, are unusual in their overt opposition to rabbinic interpretive tradition and halakhah.[32] But there are others which are less blatant and less well-known, although we should, for methodological reasons which will become clear later, exclude much of the halakhic material in pseudo-Jonathan from this portion of the discussion.[33] At times the targumim appear to interpret a text which is consonantally or vocalically different from MT, and, although some of these renditions can be treated as

---

[30] Sifre Deut. 129 (ed. L. Finkelstein; Berlin 1939 [repr. New York 1969], 187): צאן לפסח ובקר לחגיגה, 'sheep for the paschal offering and cattle for the festival offering'.

[31] I demonstrated this aspect of targumic translation technique in an as yet unpublished paper, 'Oaths and Vows in the Targumim', delivered at the European Association for Jewish Studies in July 1984 and at the Society for Biblical Literature in November of that year.

[32] Both of these passages have been subject to much discussion: for Exod. 22:4, see J. Heinemann, 'Early Halakhah in the Palestinian Targumim', *Journal of Jewish Studies* 25 (1974), 114-22; for Lev 18:21, G. Vermes, 'Leviticus 18:21 in Ancient Jewish Bible Exegesis', in J. J. Petuchowski and E. Fleischer (eds), *Studies in Aggadah, Targum and Jewish Liturgy in Memory of Joseph Heinemann* (Jerusalem 1981) 108-24.

[33] Cf. Maori's brief remarks, 6-9.

midrashic, others appear to indicate differing reading traditions among the authors of these versions from the ones reflected in MT.

I choose one example from Neofiti and its margins as illustrative. Exodus 22:12 reads ואם טרף יטרף יבאהו עד הטרפה לא ישלם ('If it be totally torn apart, let him bring it as a witness; he shall not pay for the torn animal'). Neofiti: ואין מטרפה יטרף ייתון סהדין קטילא לא ישלם ('If it is totally torn apart, let them bring witnesses; the torn one he shall not pay'); Margin I: מתקטלה יתקטל יתיה (יתי=) ליה מן אברוי שהד ('[if it is] indeed killed let him bring one of its limbs as a proof'). Both of these translate the masoretic text, although there is an interesting exegetical dispute regarding the nature of the proof which is required to exempt the bailee from payment. Is the torn piece of the animal sufficient proof, or are human witnesses demanded? But Margin II reads ימטינ]יה[עד גושמת חיובא (חיווא=) דתבירא ולא ישלם ('let him bring him to the body of the torn animal and he shall not pay'). This version seems to read עד הטרפה, a reading, incidentally which is found also in midrashic halakhic literature.[34]

Whether these readings represent a textual variant or an exegetical *'al tiqrê* is a discussion which will have to be postponed to another occasion. The larger question of the stances of the Aramaic versions in halakhic contexts remains one of the most vexed in targumic studies. Even assuming that the various targumim hold consistent and definable positions vis-à-vis the translation of legal material in the Pentateuch, it will require careful examination of each corpus individually, controlled by very careful methodology, against the background of other ancient halakhic interpretations to paint an accurate portrait.

VI.A. Expansion of Translation in the Palestinian Tradition: Narrative

When we look for large scale expansions of the biblical story in the targumim, we must leave Onqelos for the moment and focus on the Palestinian material and on

---

[34] The view of R. Yonatan in *Mekhilta de-Rabbi Yishmael* Neziqin 16 (ed. H.S. Horovitz and I.A. Rabin [Frankfort am Main 1931], 305) reads יביאהו עד הטרפה, יוליך את הבעלים אצל הטרפה ויהא פטור מלשלם ("'He shall bring him to [עד] the torn animal": he shall lead the owner to the torn animal and be exempt from repayment.')

pseudo-Jonathan. My remarks in this context are of course indebted to Avigdor Shinan who laid a proper foundation for the study of this material in both the common Palestinian tradition and in pseudo-Jonathan.[35] These aggadic elements, which often stand at the beginning or end of a triennial lection, represent the introduction of what we should generally characterize as midrash into the world of the targum. We are no longer confined to the shape of the biblical text, since the linkage of these targumic augmentations to the translation of the Hebrew verse is often merely formal, with a conjunctive phrase being inserted to connect the 'plus', as we often call it, to the actual targum. When we find a passage appearing in several of the Palestinian sources of targum, i.e., Neofiti and its marginalia, Fragment Targum, and Geniza Fragments (whether or not it is also found in pseudo-Jonathan), it very likely belongs, according to Shinan's convincing analysis, to the earliest stratum of targumic tradition.

We are thus dealing with midrash in this targumic guise at a fairly early stage of its 'literary' representation. I use the term literary with some hesitation, because these targumim, at the stage when these aggadic pluses were inserted, were almost certainly oral in nature, and there are traces within them of the 'live performance' which the *meturgemanim*, the synagogue translators, once gave.[36] But they *are* literary, in a sense, because each transcribed version of the Palestinian targum 'freezes' that version in time. I have selected as examples one from the beginning of a triennial *seder*, and one from an end, (and the choice out of a broad and rich inventory was difficult).

Genesis 15:1 reads אחר הדברים האלה היה דבר ה' אל אברם במחזה לאמר אל תירא אברם אנכי מגן לך שכרך הרבה מאד ('After these matters, the word of the Lord came to Abram in a vision, saying, "Do not fear Abram, I am your shield; your reward is very great"'). The

[35] A. Shinan, *The Aggadah in the Aramaic Targums to the Pentateuch* [Hebrew] 2 volumes (Jerusalem 1979); *The Embroidered Targum: The Aggadah in Targum Pseudo-Jonathan of the Pentateuch* [Hebrew] (Jerusalem 1992); *The Biblical Story as Reflected in its Aramaic Translations* [Hebrew] (Tel Aviv 1993) and numerous articles. By 'common Palestinian tradition', I mean the intersection of Neofiti and its margins, the Fragment Targum, and the fragments found in the Cairo Geniza (as well as pseudo-Jonathan, at times), as opposed to the aggadic material which is unique to pseudo-Jonathan and which therefore must be suspected to have had different, and later, origins.
[36] Cf. A. Shinan, 'Live Translation: On the Nature of the Aramaic Targums to the Pentateuch', *Prooftexts* 3 (1983), 41-49.

following aggadic expansion is shared by all of the Palestinian versions at this point (the translated text is that of Fragment Targum MS V); note how the translation itself almost gets lost in the expansion:

> *After these things*, after all the kings of the earth and the rulers of the countries gathered together and they engaged in battle against Abraham the righteous, and they fell before him, and he killed four kings of them, and he turned back nine camps, the righteous Abram thought to himself and said: 'Woe, now, unto me, perhaps I have received reward for the commandments in this world, and I have no portion in the world to come. Perhaps the brothers and relatives of these dead who fell before me, who are in their cities and countries, will join to themselves many legions, and they will come against me; or perhaps there were a few meritorious deeds in my hand the first time that they fell before me, and they already were spent on me; or perhaps some merit was found for me the first time they fell before me, but perhaps it will not be found for me on the second occasion, and the Name of heaven will be desecrated through me.' Therefore *there was a prophetic word from before the Lord upon Abram* the righteous *saying, 'Do not fear, Abram*, even if many legions gather together and come against you, *My memra is* spread as *a shield for you* in this world and protects you all day in the world to come; and even though I have placed your enemies before you in this world, *the reward* for your good deeds is established for you, before Me in the world to come.'[37]

The targumic midrash has gone far beyond the biblical text. God's words are now envisioned as a specific response to a particular concern which had been voiced by Abram. In order to show this, the targum introduces a speech by Abram preliminary to the dialogue in the biblical text, a speech which, although not alien to the context, is certainly not compelled by it. The introduction into the biblical story of theologoumena which we also know from rabbinic literature such as 'merits' and 'the world to come' is typical of the technique of the Palestinian targumim.

I next choose a briefer example from the end of a lection, Genesis 40:23, ולא זכר שר המשקים את יוסף וישכחהו ('but the chief butler did not remember Joseph, rather he forgot him'), once again in the version of Fragment Targum MS V, but shared across the tradition.

> Joseph abandoned the grace of above and the grace of below and the grace that had accompanied him from his father's house, and he trusted in the chief cupbearer, in transient flesh, and in flesh that tastes the cup of death; and he did not remember the Scripture that is written and is explicit, 'Cursed be the man who trusts in flesh and who

---

[37] I have taken some slight liberties with the text in the translation in order to produce a smooth text because my goal here is not close analysis of the language of the targumic passage.

> makes the flesh his power', and 'Blessed be the man who trusts in the name of the memra of the Lord', and therefore *the chief cupbearer did not remember Joseph, and he forgot him* until his fixed time had come to be redeemed.

The forgetfulness of the cupbearer is not accidental; it is a punishment to Joseph for a lack of faith. The religious message to the audience is unequivocal, man is to trust in God, not in human beings in these circumstances; every man, certainly Joseph, who elsewhere in rabbinic literature merits the epithet הצדיק, 'the righteous one', and should have known better.

Pseudo-Jonathan, with its admixture of Onqelos and other less easily identifiable materials, takes the notion of supplementing the biblical text with aggadic data further than any of the 'pure' representatives of the Palestinian tradition. In the course of his translation, he integrates into the biblical text far more midrashic remarks, both brief and lengthy, than any of the other Palestinian targumim, and he does not limit their location to the beginnings and ends of lections or the high points of a dramatic narrative. Especially in the cases of remarks interspersed within the translation of the biblical text, however, the translation remains clearly separable from the supplementation, as Philip Alexander has pointed out in his article in *Mikra*.[38] It is very likely that this version was never intended for synagogue use; Avigdor Shinan has playfully referred to it as the 'pseudo-targum according to Jonathan.'

Because it is fundamentally a literary, and not an oral, work, and because it covers the whole Pentateuch in this fashion, targum pseudo-Jonathan bears greater resemblance to the works of 'rewritten Bible' such as Jubilees or the Genesis Apocryphon which were produced in non-rabbinic circles earlier in the second temple period. Unlike them, however, it is constrained by having to maintain the shape of the biblical text around the interpolated expansions, but I have noted passages where the same compositional technique is applied in Jubilees, places where the language reflecting the biblical text of Genesis can be bracketed off and the supplements observed quite

---

[38] Alexander, 'Jewish Aramaic Translations', 229-34.

easily. It is important to realize that whereas this very late version clearly belongs to the targum family, it has close relatives in the rewritten Bible of an earlier era.

I choose one example to show how pseudo-Jonathan expands the text in a passage where none of the other, 'genuine', representatives of the Palestinian tradition do so. Exodus 17:8-9 reads ויבא עמלק וילחם עם ישראל ברפידם. ויאמר משה אל יהושע בחר לנו אנשים וצא הלחם בעמלק מחר אנכי נצב על ראש הגבעה ומטה הא-להים בידי ('Amaleq came and warred with Israel at Rephidim. Moses then said to Joshua "Select men for us and go forth and war with Amaleq. Tomorrow I shall stand on the top of the hill and the staff of God will be in my hand."'). Pseudo-Jonathan, including a variety of midrashic traditions in his rendering, writes

> [8]*Amaleq came* from the land of the south, and leaped in that night 1,600 miles, and because of the hatred which existed between Esau and Jacob *he came and did battle with Israel at Rephidim*. And he would take and kill warriors from the tribe of Dan whom the cloud [of glory] would not receive because of the idolatry which they possessed. [9]*Then Moses said to Joshua, 'Select for us men* who are mighty warriors and powerful in [observance of] the commandments and military battles, *and go forth* from beneath the clouds of glory *and set a battle array against* the camp of *Amaleq; tomorrow I shall stand* in fasting relying *upon* the merits of the patriarchs the leaders of the people, and the merits of the matriarchs who are compared to *the hills, and the staff* with which miracles were performed *from before the Lord* will be in my hand.'

This is a different sort of expansion from the single set pieces like the ones which we examined above which belong to the entire Palestinian tradition. The aggadah that is blended into the text enhances the story contained in the biblical narrative into something more interesting and exciting, while still maintaining faith with the underlying Hebrew. Of course the overlay consisting in part of theologically significant issues (the sin of idolatry causing the deaths of the Israelites at the hands of Amaleq, the need to choose warriors who were both pious and powerful, fasting and the merits of the righteous ancestors) can be found at times across the whole Palestinian tradition. But it is only pseudo-Jonathan who strews them so liberally across his whole translation. In these expansions, whether shared by the whole Palestinian tradition or unique to pseudo-Jonathan, the targumim link the literal translation of the text with the aggadic kinds of reading which we find in rabbinic midrash. It is more than the meaning of the Hebrew which is significant to the targum as it teaches the stories of the midrash as well as its value system to the listener or reader of the Aramaic text.

VI.B. Expansion of Translation in the Palestinian Tradition: Legal

Most of the halakhic material in the Palestinian targum is found in the running trans-lation of the legal portions of the Pentateuch, not in brief or lengthy supplements. What is perhaps interesting from the perspective of this discussion is the relative absence of supplementary halakhic material from the broad Palestinian tradition. We have seen that there exists a common aggadic tradition among the authors of the various Palestinian targumim and that it may be possible to identify early targumic material merely by the fact that it belongs to that stratum of the corpus. It seems that, for whatever reason, there was no coherent attempt made in the broad Palestinian targumic tradition to teach what I call 'nuts and bolts' halakhah. There are no supplementary passages detailing lists of prohibitions or describing the details of how positive commandments are to be carried out. Even the technical minutiae of biblical laws furnished by rabbinic literature are not to be found in the common Palestinian tradition. I note this omission because it underlines an unexpected lacuna in the employment of the targumim. I should have expected that the translators (and their rabbinic supervisors, if they existed) would have taken the opportunity, at key locations in the legal corpora within the Torah, to stress or highlight certain laws and to educate their audience regarding the proper way to observe them.[39]

The omission is thus quite striking, especially when compared with the practice of the pseudo-Jonathan targum (and a few passages in the marginalia to targum Neofiti) in this area. Pseudo-Jonathan covers his translation of the legal material in the

---

[39] I have discussed this issue in several unpublished papers: 'The Halakhah in the Common Palestinian Targumic Tradition', American Academy for Jewish Research, New York, NY, January, 1994; 'The Social Legislation of the Pentateuch in the Palestinian Targumic Tradition', Fifth Congress of the European Association for Jewish Studies, Copenhagen, Denmark, August, 1994; 'The Halakhah in the Palestinian Targumim of the Pentateuch: Preliminary Considerations', Society of Biblical Literature Annual Meeting, Boston, MA, November 1999; in December 2000, I shall present a paper on 'The Halakhah in the Fragment Targumim of the Pentateuch: Contents and Contexts' at the Association for Jewish Studies annual meeting in Boston, MA. I hope to publish a synthesis of this work in the near future.

Pentateuch with a wealth of halakhic details, usually lifted right out of rabbinic sources; his version consists of the Hebrew text with the rabbinic halakhah already integrated.[40] A perusal of the notes in the editions by Ginsburger and Rieder will show how much rabbinic literature has affected pseudo-Jonathan's version in halakhic contexts. Two brief examples must suffice: Exod. 21:7 כי ימכר איש את בתו לאמה לא תצא כצאת העבדים ('Should an individual sell his daughter as a maidservant, she shall not leave as do the servants') becomes in pseudo-Jonathan 'Should an Israelite *man sell his* minor *daughter as a maidservant, she shall not go out as do* Canaanite *slaves* who are freed by tooth and eye, but only through sabbatical years, and puberty and the jubilee year and the death of her master or monetary redemption.' Exod. 21:20 וכי יכה איש את עבדו או את אמתו בשבט ומת תחת ידו נקם ינקם ('Should an individual smite his slave or maidservant with a rod, and he die beneath his hand, he shall surely be avenged.') engenders 'Should an individual smite his Canaanite *slave* or Canaanite *maidservant with a rod and he die* on that day *under his hand he shall indeed be condemned* to the death penalty by the sword.' In each case, the details of rabbinic halakhah are made into a (separable) part of the translation.

What is, however, somewhat striking about the treatment of legal material by the common Palestinian tradition is the following: These Aramaic versions frequently take their opportunity to expand the translation in legal passages not, as I have commented, to teach practical halakhah, but to preach edifying messages, often of a social welfare nature. My survey of the material which is shared by the common tradition (by which I mean that it appears in at least three witnesses to the Palestinian tradition) has left me with the strong impression that these laws appear in a disproportionately large number of legal passages preserved in PT, including the Fragment Targum, and I think that the educational and hortatory role of the targum in the synagogue is responsible for this

---

[40] See Y. Maori, 'On the Relationship of the Pseudo-Jonathan Translation of the Torah to the Sources of the Halakhah' [Hebrew], *Te'udah* 3 (1983), 236-50. On the marginal readings in Neofiti which share the qualities of pseudo-Jonathan in halakhic passages, see my article, 'The *Halakhah* in the Marginalia of Targum Neofiti', *Proceedings of the Eleventh World Congress of Jewish Studies*, Division A, (Jerusalem 1994), 223-30.

distribution. Often there is not even an expansion of the Aramaic translation, and it is only its appearance in a variety of witnesses which makes it stand out.

Thus Deut. 15:11 reads כי לא יחדל אביון מקרב הארץ על כן אנכי מצוך לאמר פתח תפתח את ידך לאחיך לעניך ולאבינך בארצך ('For the poor shall not cease within the land; it is for this reason that I command you as follows, "Be certain to open your hand to your brother, the poor and the destitute, in your land".'). Once again, Fragment Targum represented by MS V: 'If Israel keeps the commandments of the Torah, there will be no poor among them. But if they abandon the commandments of the Torah, *the poor will not cease from within the land. Therefore I command you saying "Open wide your hand to your poor and needy brethren in your land".'* The interdependence of the keeping of the commandment of giving charity and the presence or absence of the poor in the land provides, in my view, another insight into the educational goals which shaped the employment of the targumim in the synagogue. The targumic exhortation to give charity is linked to the biblical text regarding the ongoing presence of the poor in the land. One could suggest that the synagogue's function as the venue of charity collection might have stimulated such a reference, but there are other, similar, expansions in contexts where the synagogue plays no specific role. If my observation is correct, then, while pseudo-Jonathan's halakhic supplementation endeavours to teach halakhic minutiae, some of the selections in the Fragment Targum adopt a different approach to halakhic material and appear to function in an exhortatory and educational role, whether in study hall or in synagogue.

VII. The Targum in the Synagogue: Supplementary Texts

The targumim were apparently an integral dimension of the weekly Torah reading aspect of the synagogue liturgy, but their role became expanded at a rather early date particularly in conjunction with the festival readings and those for special sabbaths. Not only were prose pieces added to the biblical narrative in an integrated fashion as we saw earlier, but more independent pieces, often poetry, written in Aramaic, and intended to dovetail with the translation of the text, began to be composed no later than the 4th century CE. That date has been suggested for the papyrus text of *'Ezel Moshe*, 'Go

Moses', an acrostic poem which was recited on the seventh day of Passover when the story of the crossing of the Red Sea and the accompanying song were the assigned reading.[41] These poems are midrashim in poetic guise, just as are some of the Hebrew *piyyutim* written by the Palestinian Hebrew poets of the Byzantine era who interspersed midrashim related to the Torah lection of each week within the poems they wrote for other parts of the liturgy. This material, which has been studied for over a century, especially by Heinemann, is often parallel or supplementary to that which we find in the formal targumim, but is couched in vivid poetry, often presenting a dialogue or a debate.

There are several targumic poems, for example, which survive to supplement the Torah reading for *parashat haHodesh*, one of the special Sabbaths before Passover, which begins with the words of Exod. 12:2 'This month is for you the beginning of months.' Some of these alphabetic acrostic poems present debates among the months of the Jewish year, arguing in which of them the redemption from Egypt was to take place based on merit alone, while others simply expand on themes related to the Exodus.[42] From a narrative perspective, these introductory poems do not have to be well-integrated into the story, but they clearly were intended to grab the synagogue audience's attention at the beginning of the reading and present them with historical or theological information not necessarily related to the biblical text or story.

The acrostic poem, *'Amar Yishaq*, from which I am selecting an example, was still being recited in medieval Franco-Germany, even after the practice of targum as a regular part of the synagogue liturgy had ceased in Europe. Cited in *Mahzor Vitry* by R. Simhah of Vitry (one of Rashi's students), it is one of several targumic poetic pieces (including *'Ezel Moshe*) to have maintained a role in the festival Torah reading liturgy where the expanded Palestinian targum of certain texts was used on special occasions,

---

[41] A version of this text on papyrus from the Fayyum, dated to about the fourth century, was published initially by Y. Yahalom in '*Ezel Moshe* in Papyrus' [Hebrew], *Tarbiz* 47 (1978), 173-84 and recently reprinted by him and M. Sokoloff in *Jewish Palestinian Aramaic Poetry*, 82-86. There are also two versions of this poem from the Cairo Geniza published in Klein, *Genizah Manuscripts of Palestinian Targum*, 1.237, 239, as well as other medieval copies.

[42] For the texts and translations, see Klein, *Genizah Manuscripts of Palestinian Targum*, 186-207.

rather than the version of Onqelos which would have held sway at all other times.[43] This survival shows perhaps that these pieces of Palestinian material had become integrated so tightly into the liturgical framework that no one thought to question their presence. The targumic *toseftot* which are individual pieces of Palestinian targum collected for liturgical integration into an Onqelos framework seem to have survived for similar reasons, although their survival is more difficult to explain since they are not associated with special sabbaths or festivals.[44]

Exodus 19-20, the giving of the Ten Commandments, is the liturgical Torah reading for the first day of Shavuot, and in the version found in *Mahzor Vitry* there are Aramaic poems preceding the targumic renditions of almost all of the commandments.[45] *'Amar Yiṣḥaq* serves as the introduction to the reading of the fifth commandment, honouring one's parents, presumably because Isaac displays filial piety toward his father Abraham who is about to sacrifice him. Heinemann, however, justifiably maintains that the poem originally belonged to the Torah reading for the second day of Rosh Hashanah on which the portion was Genesis 22, the Akedah.[46] The outline of this *piyyut* can readily be identified from the several parallels to it in the Palestinian targum translation tradition where it appears at the high point of the story, Gen. 22:10, as Abraham stretches out his hand to slaughter his son. The following are excerpts from the text of the poem:

> Isaac said to Abraham his father, 'How fair is the altar which you have built for me father. Quick stretch forth your arm and take your knife while I pray before my Master ... Like a cruel man, take your knife and slaughter me so that you do not disqualify the offering ... Open your mouth and recite the blessing, father, and I shall listen and answer "Amen".' The angels arose and begged their Master, 'Please have mercy on the child.' ... The mighty one responded, 'Fear not O youth, for I the redeemer shall redeem you.'

---

[43] S. Hurwitz (ed.), *Mahzor Vitry of Rabbenu Simḥah* (Nürnberg 1923), 341.

[44] See above, n. 11.

[45] *Mahzor Vitry*, 336-43.

[46] Heinemann, however, claims quite reasonably that the poem originally belonged to the Torah reading for the second day of Rosh Hashanah on which the portion was Genesis 22. See 'Remnants', 366-67, especially n. 17, where he writes, 'It was intended without a doubt to serve as an expansion of the targum of the section on the Aqedah (presumably on Rosh haShanah), and its place is after Gen 22:10 or in place of the targum of this verse.' Yahalon-Sokoloff, 124-31, print the text among the *piyyutim* for Shavuot.

This poem and its targumic parallels, in addition to creating a dialogue involving Isaac, the angels and God, retard the action of the drama at the key moment, as Abraham's hand holding the knife is poised to descend upon Isaac, engrossing the audience in suspense longer than the straight translation of the Hebrew text would have. In this fashion the poem makes the Torah lection a more moving and dramatic experience.[47]

VIII. The Non-Liturgical Targum as Textbook of Values

Another way in which the targumim helped shape the values and ideals of the communities in which they were promulgated was not dependent on the public use of the targum like the moralizing remarks in the common Palestinian legal tradition in the Pentateuch discussed above (see section VI B above). The Aramaic version of a text like Psalms, a work which as far as we know was not translated in public liturgy, furnishes a good example of the way in which 'values education' could be carried out. Probably a good deal later than the classical targumim which we have been discussing to this point, it is fundamentally a straightforward and minimally expanded Aramaic version. But if we examine the nature of some of the translation, the emphases in some of the paraphrases, and the subjects of some of the expansions, we see that the theological themes which the translator brings to the text are those which he wishes to teach his readers.

I choose an example from an article I published a couple of years ago entitled 'Torah and Its Study in the Targum of Psalms.'[48] I began with the observation that the Hebrew word תורה occurs a total of only thirty-six times in the Hebrew text of Psalms. If Psalm 119, often described as a wisdom psalm in praise of Torah and which contains the term Torah twenty-five times, is excluded from the tally, the number drops to eleven occurrences for the rest of the book. Despite the fact that the contents of Psalms are

---

[47] The major expansion in the Palestinian targum tradition at this point emphasizes the angels watching the sacrifice and commenting on the devotion of the father-son pair, while Isaac begs his father to carry out the sacrificial ritual correctly, as he does in *'Amar Yiṣḥaq*. Shinan, *The Biblical Story*, 84-85, remarks on the dramatic position both of the targumic additions and of this poem.

[48] 'Torah and Its Study in the Targum of Psalms', in J. Gurock and Y. Elman (eds), *Hazon Naḥum: Studies in Honor of Dr. Norman Lamm on the Occasion of His Seventieth Birthday* (Hoboken 1997) 39-67.

generically varied, including laments of individual and community, hymns in praise of God, His kingdom, and His creations, and psalms of thanksgiving by individuals and community, we do not find Torah or its study playing a prominent role in this biblical book. When we examine the text of the Aramaic version of Psalms, however, we find that אוריתא, the Aramaic equivalent of תורה, appears about *one hundred times* (with some variation within the manuscripts), and the synonymous נימוסא occurs twice. In addition, there are over twenty examples of אולפן, 'learning', some of which refer to Torah, and a half dozen of the term בית מדרשא = 'study hall (of Torah)'. Thus Torah and a variety of terms in its broad semantic category appear far more frequently in the targum of Psalms than they do in its Hebrew text.

According to our suggested method, this accumulation of language in the translation which does not appear in the original must reflect something of the targum's intellectual concerns. Some of these 'non-translation' occurrences of אוריתא appear as translations of terms other than תורה and belong to the intermediate range between translation and externally imposed ideology. Thus we are not surprised to find the Lord's 'saying', אמרת ה' (Ps. 18:31) and similar terms rendered as אורייתא, but we do not expect Ps. 29:11 ה' עז לעמו יתן ('the Lord grants *strength* to His people') to be translated with the same word, 'Torah.'[49] Probably the most extreme example of the substitution of אוריתא for a word in the Hebrew text is the rendition of Ps. 45:10 נצבה שגל לימינך ('*the royal consort* stands on your right') as בזמן דמעתד ספר אוריתא בסטר ימינך ('at the time that the *book of the Torah* is set on your right side').

As components of the exegetical world of the targum, these 'translations' contribute to our portrayal of the targum's *Weltanschauung*, but do not carry the independent weight which is borne primarily by material which is completely supplementary to the targum and which has no equivalent, literal or otherwise, in the biblical text. Thus, moving from the 'expected' to the 'unexpected', Ps. 13:4 האירה עיני פן אישן המות ('Enlighten my eyes lest I sleep in death') becomes 'enlighten my eyes

---

[49] In many cases there are parallels to the targumic exegesis in rabbinic literature; in this instance, cf. Midrash Tehillim 28:6.

with the Torah;' the jibe of the wicked at the righteous in Ps.127:2 שוא לכם משכימי קום *מאחרי שבת* ('woe to you who rise up early and *sit late*') refers to those who 'stay late at night sitting and studying Torah' (according to a *targum aḥer*); Ps 84:8 ילכו מחיל אל חיל יראה אל ה' בציון ('they go from strength to strength; it will be seen by God in Zion') becomes in the targum 'The righteous go from Temple to *bet midrash*; their toiling in Torah will be seen before God whose presence dwells in Zion.' And there are some Torah-supplements which are even less well-integrated into their verses than these are.

It seems reasonable to assume that the translator(s) of Psalms into Aramaic wrote for Jews who read or recited or even studied Psalms in a variety of circumstances. The effect of the translation is to supplement, and at times even to change, the theological and ideological message of the Book of Psalms, to make the content of the book more accessible and meaningful to its reader or student, perhaps to make it more 'rabbinic' in substance. The inclusion of a substantial number of supplementary remarks about the importance of Torah, its study, its significance in daily life, its teachers and its students, even if not done systematically, would have served to inculcate into the minds of the reader an idea which is one of the fundamental foundations of rabbinic Judaism. Since the Hebrew Book of Psalms does not proclaim that value, the author of the targum of Psalms was constrained to add it.

Whereas the targum of Psalms could teach rabbinic values through translating and supplementing the Hebrew text, the targum of Song of Songs could only present its theologico-historical message by not translating the Hebrew text. Treating Song of Songs as an encoded version of Jewish history emphasizing God's relationship with the Jewish people, this targum does not translate the Hebrew text in any immediately recognizable fashion, but rewrites it. This kind of reading is of a very different nature from the material which we have examined. Although it is occasionally referred to as 'paraphrastic', a careful reader of the targum can see the hooks in the Hebrew on which the Aramaic depends.[50] The mode of interpretation, however, can be said to anticipate, or at least to share common elements with, other allegorical forms of interpretation in Jewish tradition.

IX. Concluding Remarks

This survey has touched upon a variety of the contexts in which the Aramaic versions of the Bible are to be found and the ways in which they respond to the demands of the underlying Hebrew text and the contexts in which it was employed. They translate the Hebrew text, but their translation technique often depends on what sort of text lies before them. Poetry and prose, law and narrative present different sorts of interpretive and exegetical difficulties to which the Aramaic versions respond in different ways. In their effort to reflect the meaning of the Hebrew text they at times reflect the straightforward sense of the Hebrew, while at others they are beholden to interpretive traditions and methods familiar to us from rabbinic midrash. To borrow from the title of York's article referred to above, the targumim stretch from synagogue to school, but their roles overlap and intersect in the two cases. The liturgical, *bet ha-keneset*, setting of the targumim may have impelled them to be expanded in one direction with legal exhortations and midrashic insertions in both poetry and prose. On the other hand, they reach toward the rabbinic *bet ha-midrash* in some of their midrashic expansions in both halakhah and aggadah as well as in non-liturgical values supplementation. They straddle the territory covered by a number of other genres of Jewish exegetical literature, from re-written Bible to midrash to commentary to liturgical poetry, and thus present their student with a corpus both broad and deep which can be profitably investigated from a number of angles. From a chronological standpoint, despite the thorny difficulty of establishing specific dates for specific texts, there is no doubt that the targumim present

---

[50] For a brief but excellent characterization of this version with explication of a sample passage, see Alexander, 'Jewish Aramaic Versions', 234-37. He stresses, correctly in my view, the non-mystical nature of the symbolic reading.

us with a 'genre' which was productive over a long period of time and which can, with appropriate *caveats*, allow us to gain insight into exegetical development. Both as objects of study in their own right and in comparative work with other translations and commentaries, the Aramaic versions must continue to play a significant role in any discussion of how Jews read and have read the Bible.

Reading the Bible in the Mediaeval Age

Is Yhwh Yireh Jerusalem?

Clive Fierstone

Genesis 22:14 ostensibly records the name of the location that Abraham gave to the place intended for the sacrifice of Isaac: יהוה יראה.

This term has puzzled exegetes, classical, medieval and modern. We will consider the various solutions suggested and tentatively offer a different approach to the problem. In the first place I suggest that the verb יראה has been used in a circumlocutory manner. As noted by J. Skinner, 'In truth, it seems to be given as the explanation, not of a name, but of a current proverbial saying which can hardly be the original intention.'[1] The redactor of Targum Onqelos translated the phrase 'he said before the Lord, future generations will pray'.

M. Auerbach and B. Grossfeld have already shown in their edition of Targum Onqelos to Genesis[2] that the Hebrew root ראה was midrashically interpreted as ירא. This would indicate at a primary level 'fear' and by extended meaning 'pray'. Similarly, the redactor of Targum Pseudo-Jonathan introduced Abraham's prayer at this juncture and seemingly understood the verb ראה in the same manner as the redactor of Onqelos. The redactor of the Second Targum went as far as to associate the location with the future temple site. This tradition is no doubt based on 2 Chron. 3:1 which records that Mount Moriah is indeed the temple mount. As N. Sarna correctly states, 'It is clear that the narrative reflects both verbs r'h and yr' as popular etymologies for Moriah.'[3]

---

[1] J. Skinner, *Genesis* (International Critical Commentary; second ed.; Edinburgh 1930).
[2] M. Auerbach and B. Grossfeld, *Targum Onqelos to Genesis: A Critical Analysis Together with an English Translation of the Text* (Denver, CO 1982).
[3] N. A. Sarna, *Genesis* (Torah Commentary; Jerusalem 1989), excursus 16.

The Septuagint is similarly puzzled by the phrase. Whereas in Gen. 22:8 the verb יראה is translated as 'will provide', in 22:14 it is translated as 'has seen'. Rashi, the medieval scholar interpreted the phrase יהוה יראה in the latter source in a manner reminiscent of Targum Pseudo-Jonathan's interpretation of the parallel phrase in Gen. 22:8 (אלהים יראה), which was Abraham's rejoinder to Isaac's question as to the whereabouts of the lamb of the burnt offering. Thus Rashi translated the phrase as 'will choose and see (יראה) the place', whereas the redactor of Targum Pseudo-Jonathan translated Gen. 22:8 'will choose (cf. Hebrew יראה) for himself a lamb'.

The tension that Rashi felt is demonstrated by his repetition of the verb יראה. Rashi certainly realised that the phrase used in Gen. 22:14 replicated that in Gen. 22:8 but did not elucidate further.

Amongst Jewish medieval scholars it was Ibn Ezra who obliquely hinted that the phrase recorded in Gen. 22:14b, בהר יהוה יראה, was a scribal gloss reflecting an event yet to happen.[4] The replication of the root ראה, albeit in the *niphal*,[5] merely compounds the problem of how to treat the phrase under discussion.

Meyuhas ben Elijah, a yet undated Greek-Italian scholar,[6] was slightly more conservative (in medieval terms) in his view of Gen. 22:14b:

> It is the Torah that is relating the information about this place and directing a command concerning the Mountain of God and the place of his Divine Presence. This is indicated by utilising the passive verb ראה both here and in Exod. 23:17 and 34:23, where each Israelite male is commanded to appear (*yera'eh*) thrice yearly before the Sovereign, the Lord.

Thus Gen. 22:14b is clearly not seen as the word of Abraham but as a gloss to the text indicating a theological message.

---

[4] See his commentary on Deut. 34:1 where he refers to 'the secret of the twelve' which is a reference to Deut. 34:1-12. b. B.B. 15a admitted that the latter part of the chapter was an addendum to the Pentateuch. Ibn Ezra seemingly extended the idea of additional glosses to a small number of Pentateuchal references.

[5] My italics.

[6] Views range from the late eleventh to the fourteenth century. A. W. Greenup and C. H. Titterton, *The Commentary of Rabbi Meyuhas ben Elijah on the Pentateuch* (London 1909), 59.

That the name Yerushalayim is a literary embellishment is clearly demonstrated in Bereshit Rabbah 56.10:

Abraham called it יראה. Shem called it *Šalem.*[7]

The holy One, blessed be He, said 'If I call it יראה as Abraham did, the righteous Shem will complain. If I restrict the name to *Šalem*, Abraham will complain. I will combine both *yireh šalem.*'

The difficulty of the name was thus acknowledged and a quasi-histroical notion was constructed. We will explore this notion in more detail.

Abraham, son of Moses Maimonides, similarly connected the verb ראה here with its usage in later passages in Exodus (noted supra), but clearly acknowledged that the phrase under discussion was Abraham's wish for the present, whereas Gen. 22:14b was a prayer directed to God and reflected a future desire: 'May God be seen and ackowledged by future generations.' Although there is an acknowledgement of the intrinsic connection between both phrases in Gen. 22:14, the problem of understanding the phrase under discussion still remains.

Both Levi Gersonides and Abrabanel have suggested a more esoteric approach. For Gersonides it conveyed the message that the location was to be that which would attract the Divine influence to cling to it: 'O may the Divine One seek out a place for himself' (parallel to Gen. 22:8); 'O may God seek out (i.e. provide) a lamb for himself'. Abrabanel viewed the phrase as Abraham's inner feeling: 'the Lord sees what I intend to do'. Further he suggested that it may express an action in the past, 'the Lord has seen what I intend to do', as if it were an answer to his expressed wish to Isaac, 'O may God seek a lamb for himself'. Thus the imperfect verb יראה is used to express a future intention in Gen. 22:8 and a past action in Gen. 22:14.

E. A. Speiser almost encapsulated the mood of the text when he wrote concerning Gen. 22:14b: 'This parenthetical note embodies two separate illusions. Yir'eh (Gen. 22:14) points back to yir'eh (Gen. 22:8); the other is connected with the

---

[7] Melki Zedek, King of Šalem (Gen. 14:15) is associated with Shem, son of Noah, in midrashic literature; see b. Ned. 32b as an example.

Temple Hill in Jerusalem, Mount Moriah (Gen. 22:2)'.[8]

I now suggest a different approach. In the El Armana[9] letters, which record the fourteenth century BCE diplomatic correspondence between the kings of various Canaanite cities and their Egyptian overlords, there is recorded the allegiance of the land of Urusalim. Whether 'Ur' is the Sumerian[10] word for 'city', or derived from the Semitic root ירה, implying foundation, is not absolutely relevant to this argument. In addition it is almost probable that *salem* is a derivative of the deity Šulmanu.

I tentatively suggest that the phrase יהוה יראה has sublimated the original name Urusalim by utilising the three letter root ראה as a pun on either the Sumerian word *ur* or the Semitic root *yrh*, and by substituting יהוה for the deity Šulmanu. By implication this can be further extended to include the verbal root ירה as in Mount Moriah (Gen. 22:2), thus effecting the word play on the root ירה, but not on the deity at this stage. Thus in Gen. 22:14 only the tetragrammaton will suffice to effect the intended theological sublimation. Whereas in Gen. 22:8 the noun אלהים is of prime importance, there is a necessity to be more specific in Gen. 22:14.

Abrabanel indeed noted that we never find the term יהוה יראה used geographically or in a historical context. Indeed, I put forward the idea that the original name has been subject to a theological interpretation which became lost in the passage of time. This necessitated new and sometimes ingenious invention.

Once a geographical location has been theologically renamed to indicate a different theological stance, then the message will need further reiteration in other areas of the saga. I suggest that the phrase Mount Moriah (Gen. 22:2) was utilised to underpin the geographical renaming recorded in Gen. 22:14. The utilisation of Mount Moriah in 2 Chron. 3:1 as the name of the temple site would seem to indicate this trend. As a result, the phrase בהר יהוה יראה recorded in Gen. 22:14b further extended the theological message since, as indicated above, the *niphal* use of the verb ראה was

---

[8] E. A. Speiser, *Genesis: A New Translation with Introduction and Commentary* (Anchor Bible; New York 1987).
[9] D. Bahat and C. T. Rubins, *The Illustrated Atlas of Jerusalem* (Jerusalem 1990), 23.
[10] *Biblical Encyclopedia* (Hebrew; Jerusalem 1976), column 792.

utilised distinctly to indicate the religious necessity of the male population to appear at a specific time before the Lord. However, neither Exod. 22:17 nor 34:23 indicated a distinct geographical location. The verb *yera'eh* (Gen. 22:14b) is an obvious pun on the verb יראה (Gen. 22:14a). By cross-referencing the use of the verb *yereah* to the sources in Exodus, a geographical location is indicated for the centralised place of worship. Thus the implication of Gen. 22:14b is that the mountain of יהוה will be the communal place of worship for all male Israelites.

I further suggest that a passage from Bereshit Rabba 64.4 may well indicate this line of thought.

> Abraham even knew the futuristic name that the Holy One, blessed be He, was to call Jerusalem as indicated in Gen. 22:14. Abraham called the name of that place יהוה יראה. It is similarly recorded in Ezek. 40:35: 'The name of the city (the futuristic Jerusalem) shall be יהוה שמה (is there)'.

I suggest with Mirkin[11] that the adverb שמה indicated to the midrashic master the noun שם ('name') plus the pronominal suffix of the third person feminine singular. Thus the phrase was interpreted, midrashically, as 'יהוה is its name'. As a secondary proof, the midrashic passage quoted Jer. 3:17: 'At that time they shall term Jerusalem the throne of יהוה'. However, the continuation of the verse which is not quoted by the midrash would appear to be quintessential: 'all nations shall gather there for the sake of (לשם) יהוה to Jerusalem'. Once again we will suggest that implicitly the phrase לשם יהוה has been interpreted as 'the name of יהוה'. Thus this phrase has been equated with the geographical location of Jerusalem. The last clause of the verse may well have been interpreted as 'all nations shall gather there to Jerusalem to be known by the name יהוה'.

This midrashic trend has its parallel in a revealing comment made by the Spanish biblical exegete, R. Bahya ben Asher (died 1340) in his biblical commentary on Gen. 26:19. Inter alia, he quoted a midrashic text (seemingly lost to scholarship) which was a comment on 2 Sam. 5:7:

> 'David captured the fortress of Zion, the city of David ...' The city was given a name

---

[11] M. A. Mirkin, *Midrash Rabbah*, vol. 3 (Tel Aviv 1958), 28.

designated by Man, since it was built by human endeavour and will be destroyed by human endeavour. However, in the future it will be given a name designed by Divine intent.'

The proof text quoted was Isa. 60:14: 'The oppressed ones shall come to you bowed down. Those that reject you shall bow down to the soles of your feet. They shall call you the city of יהוה, Zion, Holy One of Israel'. Although the medieval interpreters refer this to the futuristic name of Jerusalem, this midrashic extract may well indicate the quintessential understanding of the name Jerusalem.

Why no Textual Criticism in Rabbinic Midrash?
Reflections on the textual culture of the Rabbis[1]

Philip S. Alexander

Why does rabbinic Midrash not resort to textual criticism as a method of exegeting Scripture?   Much classic rabbinic Bible commentary is explicitly or implicitly based on identifying and solving problems – linguistic, moral and theological – in the biblical text.   Why never once, as far as I am aware, and more persuasively as far as Saul Lieberman is aware,[2] does it propose that the problem has been caused by textual corruption and can be removed by conjectural emendation or by invoking a better reading from another manuscript?   Because it is so universal, the absence of textual criticism in Midrash has been taken for granted, and the significance of this fact has been missed.

---

[1] I am grateful to Moshe Bernstein, George Brooke, Julian Abel, Raphael Loewe, Sacha Stern, Alex Samely and Joanna Weinberg for criticisms of an earlier version of this paper. Their comments were valuable even when I could not agree with them. Aspects of the problem of the rabbinic attitude towards textual criticism are discussed by: Saul Lieberman, *Hellenism in Jewish Palestine* (2nd ed.; New York 1962), 20-46; Menahem Ben Yitzhaq, 'Qerei u-khetiv', *Ha-Ma'yan* 33/3 (1993), 49-55 [Hebrew]; Yeshayahu Maori, 'Rabbinic Midrash as Evidence for Textual Variants in the Hebrew Bible', in S. Carmy (ed.), *Modern Scholarship in the Study of the Torah: Contributions and Limitations* (Northvale, NJ 1996), 101-29; for an earlier Hebrew version of this essay see: M. Bar Asher et al. (eds), *Sefer Zikkaron le-Moshe Goshen-Gottstein* (= '*Iyyunei Miqra u-Farshanut* 3) (Ramat Gan 1993), 267-86; Sid Z. Leiman, 'Masorah and Halakhah: A Study in Conflict', in M. Cohen, B. L. Eichler and J. H. Tigay (eds), *Tehillah le-Moshe: Biblical and Judaic Studies in Honor of Moshe Greenberg* (Winona Lake, IN 1997), 291-306; and above all David Weiss Halivni, *Revelation Restored: Divine Writ and Critical Responses* (Boulder, CO 1997). I drafted this paper before I read Halivni. In revising it I found myself more and more entering into dialogue with his work. See further note 25 below.

[2] Lieberman, *Hellenism in Jewish Palestine*, 47: 'The Rabbis never suggest a correction of the text of the Bible. In the entire rabbinic literature we never come across divergences of opinion regarding Biblical readings. It is therefore obvious that the textual corrections of Greek classics practised by Alexandrian grammarians have no parallel in the rabbinic exegesis of Scripture.'

Jewish Ways of Reading the Bible

One might be tempted, rather hastily, to assume that there is no textual criticism in Midrash because it is unthinkable theologically that the rabbis should have admitted that the text of the Torah which they had in their hands was even to the smallest extent corrupt. This may seem axiomatic at first sight, but on reflection it becomes less obvious. The doctrine of the divine origin of Scripture, its inspiration by the holy spirit (*ruah ha-qodesh*), does not preclude textual criticism, as the history of the Christian use of the Bible shows. The fact that the original text may originally have been given under divine inspiration does not *ipso facto* rule out the possibility that that text may have subsequently been corrupted in transmission. Granted that serious corruption would have profound implications, and for this reason the doctrine of inspiration is usually linked to a doctrine of special providence whereby Scripture has been preserved so that its essential message remains available to the faith community down through the ages, but corruption at the margins, so to speak, can be safely admitted without detriment to scriptural authority.

It would be equally mistaken to suppose that textual criticism is a modern invention. Textual criticism in the sense which concerns us here, namely collation of manuscripts and conjectural emendation, can be traced back at least to the third century BCE to Zenodotus of Ephesus, the first head of the royal library in Alexandria and to his successors, Aristophanes of Byzantium and above all Aristarchus. These, and other Alexandrian scholars, solved many problems in the canonic texts of Greek literature, especially Homer, by correcting the text. They were particularly sophisticated in their understanding of the principles of emendation and raised emendation to the level of high art.[3] Every educated Greek probably knew something of their work through his study of Homer at school (though, significantly, only the *textus receptus* of Homer seems to have been used in the classroom). Textual criticism of canonic texts was an accepted part of Hellenistic textual culture in the time of the rabbis, a culture of which the rabbis were broadly aware and from which they may have derived some of their hermeneutical norms. And Hellenistic textual

---

[3] See Rudolph Pfeiffer, *History of Classical Scholarship: From the Beginning to the End of the Hellenistic Age* (Oxford 1968), 105-233.

criticism was taken over and applied specifically to the Bible by Christian scholars such as Origen and Jerome. All of which highlights the rabbis' lack of interest in it, at least with regard to the Scriptures.

As consumers of manuscripts the rabbis would have known only too well that it is impossible to transcribe any text absolutely accurately. Like all other scholars in antiquity, one of their first tasks on acquiring a new manuscript would have been to correct it. They were aware of variant readings in Bible manuscripts. Rabbinic tradition famously records the fact that Rabbi Meir's Torah read כתנות אור, 'garments of light', rather than כתנות עור, 'garments of skin', in Gen. 3:21.[4] The rabbis treated Samaritan and Jewish-Christian Sifrei Torah with deep suspicion, presumably because they knew that their texts differed significantly from the standard Synagogue scrolls.[5] They noted variations from the Synagogue text in the Septuagint, the Torah prepared for King Talmai (Ptolemy), though they tend to put these down to deliberate editing by the Greek translators.[6] They were aware that somewhat similar editorial changes had been introduced into their own Hebrew copies of the Torah in the so-called *Tiqqunei Soferim* and *'Itturei Soferim*. There were cases where what was read (*qerei*) differed from what was written (*ketiv*), where a word was read which had nothing to represent it in the consonantal text (*qerei ve-la' ketiv*), or where letters appear in the consonantal text when nothing at all was read (*ketiv ve-la' qerei*).[7] The

---

[4] Genesis Rabba 20:12, 'And the Lord God made for Adam and his wife garments of skin (עור), and clothed them. In Rabbi Meir's Torah it was found written, Garments of light (אור). This refers to Adam's garments, which were like a torch [shedding radiance], broad at the bottom and narrow at the top. Isaac the Elder said: they were smooth as a fingernail and beautiful as a jewel.' Note here how the Midrash in effect accepts both readings as correct, a procedure to which we shall return below.

[5] In certain places the phrase *Sifrei Minim* probably means not books composed by heretics, but Torah Scrolls written by heretics: see Philip S. Alexander, '"The Parting of the Ways" from the Perspective of Rabbinic Judaism', in James D.G. Dunn (ed.), *Jews and Christians: The Parting of the Ways A.D. 70 to 135* (Tübingen 1992), 11-15.

[6] y. Meg. I 5; b. Meg. 9a-b; Massekhet Soferim 1:7-8.

[7] On the Masoretic tradition in general see: Israel Yeivin, *Introduction to the Tiberian Masorah* (trans. and ed. by E. J. Revell; Masoretic Studies 5; Missoula, MT 1980). Still useful is C. D. Ginsburg, *Introduction to the Masoretico-Critical Edition of the Hebrew Bible* (London, 1897; repr. with Introduction by H. M. Orlinsky; New York 1968). For the *Tiqqunei Soferim* see Yeivin, pp. 49-51, where it is noted that most of the cases listed in the Masorah are mentioned already in classic rabbinic sources. C. McCarthy, *The Tiqqune Sopherim and Other Theological Corrections of the Masoretic Text of the Old Testament* (Göttingen 1981) argues persuasively that at least some of the *Tiqqunei Soferim* originated as genuine scribal corrections. For the *'Itturei Soferim*, see Yeivin, pp. 51-52 (cf.

Jewish Ways of Reading the Bible

Dead Sea Scrolls clearly show that widely divergent texts of the books of the Hebrew Bible circulated in the Second Temple period. There are no obvious grounds for thinking that this situation would have changed dramatically by the third century CE. Indeed, as every Yeshivah *bocher* knows, classic rabbinic literature from time to time quotes Bible in forms which differ significantly from the standard Masoretic text.[8] These variants are probably only the tip of the iceberg, since it is reasonable to suppose that many other aberrant quotations in the classic talmudic sources would have been 'corrected' by the mediaeval copyists to conform to the *textus receptus*. Even within the full-blown mediaeval Masoretic tradition, represented by the great master-codices of Aleppo and Petersburg, variants are to be found, as Kennicott, de Rossi and Ginsburg show.[9] The rabbis knew of the hazards of transmission and record the existence of highly accurate master-copies, like the Scrolls that had been deposited in the Jerusalem Temple.[10] There was, in short, a great deal of uncertainty about the text of Torah available to the rabbis which cried out for textual criticism, but textual criticism on any strict definition of the term was never applied.

---

b. Ned. 37b-38a). For *Ketiv/Qerei* see Yeivin, pp. 52-61 (cf. b. Ned. 37b-38a); further, Robert Gordis, *The Biblical Text in the Making: A Study of Ketibh-Qere* (Philadelphia 1937; repr. New York 1971).

[8] See Halivni, *Revelation Restored*, 38-42. These divergences are being collected by the Hebrew University Bible Project.

[9] B. Kennicott, *Vetus Testamentum hebraicum cum variis lectionibus* (Oxford 1776-80); G. B. de Rossi, *Variae lectiones Veteris Testamenti* (Parma 1784-88); C. D. Ginsburg, *Masoretico-Critical Edition of the Hebrew Bible*, 2 vols (Vienna 1894).

[10] Sifrei Deut. 356; y. Ta'anit IV 2; Massekhet Soferim 6:4. The Massekhet Soferim text reads: 'Rabbi Simeon ben Laqish said: Three scrolls of the Torah were found in the Temple court: the *Ma'on* scroll, the *Za'atutei* scroll, and the *Hu'* scroll. In one of these they found the expression *ma'on*, but in the other two it was written, "The eternal God is a *me'onah* (dwelling place)" (Deut. 33:27), so they adopted the reading of the two scrolls and discarded that of the one scroll (וקיימו שנים ובטלו אחד). In another of the scrolls they found written, "And he sent the *za'atutei* (youths) of the children of Israel" (Exod. 24:5), and in the other two they found written, "And he sent *na'arei* (the young men) of the children of Israel", so they adopted the reading of the two scrolls and discarded that of the one. In one of the scrolls *hu'* was written eleven times, but in the other *hi'* was written eleven times, so they adopted the reading of the two and discarded that of the one.' The eleven cases of *hi'* are the *exception* to the *Qerei perpetuum* rule. Note how the manuscripts were named after their distinctive readings (cf. 'the Vinegar Bible', 'the Breeches Bible'), and how the reading was established by majority vote among the manuscripts. Whether or not the latter was the case it shows that some rabbinic authorities believed that the *textus receptus* was an eclectic text which had been produced by applying rudimentary principles of textual criticism.

The Masorah illuminates vividly the paradox of the rabbinic position. The Masoretic notes, which, though only formalized in the gaonic period, were already being compiled in talmudic times, if not earlier, are broadly of the same type as the Alexandrian glosses to Homer, but in contradistinction to the Hellenistic tradition they involve, at least as traditionally interpreted, no emendation of the text. The Masorah's careful recording of the linguistic anomalies of the Hebrew would have been readily seen in Hellenistic scholarship as a necessary first step towards the correction of the text. The Masorah, however, seems to serve precisely the opposite function: it warns the scribe to curb his natural instincts and *abstain* from emendation, however obvious it might be. Thus the widespread use in the Torah of *hu'* for 3rd fem. sing. pronoun *hi'* – an anomaly already noted in Avot deRabbi Natan (A 34:5) and Massekhet Soferim (6:4) – is left intact and simply recorded as a *Qerei-perpetuum*, even though substituting *yod* for *vav* is graphically one of the easiest changes to make in Hebrew script, as any editor of the Dead Sea Scrolls knows. The position becomes even more strange when we note that within the Masoretic text and the Masoretic notes are signs of an earlier stage of Jewish textual scholarship in which textual criticism actually was applied.   David Kimḥi (ca. 1160-1235) suggested that the *Ketiv/Qerei* were variant readings which originated through collation of manuscripts (he thought the collators were the Men of the Great Synagogue).[11] The use of dots in the Qumran Scrolls to mark letters to be erased strongly supports the theory that at least some of the *Nequdot* in the Masoretic text originally served the same function.[12]   The *nun*s and inverted *nun*s probably

---

[11] See the introduction to his commentary on Joshua. Kimḥi has clearly been influenced by the texts quoted in the preceding note. It is not clear, however, whether he believed that his theory applied to the Torah, or only to the *Nakh*. Abarbanel (1437-1508) also believed that the *Qerei* was added in the time of Ezra. However, it does not contain genuine variants but only explanations of difficult words in the Bible which contain hidden meanings (see the introduction to his commentary on Jeremiah). Kimḥi's view, though supported by the Meiri (1249-1315), was criticized severely by later scholars (such as the Radbaz [1480-1574], the Maharal [1525-1609] and Malbim [1809-1879]), who increasingly took the view that both the *Qerei* and the *Ketiv* were *Halakhah le-Moshe mi-Sinai* – a view which can invoke good talmudic authority (note 23 below). See further Halivni, *Revelation Restored*, 42-44, 72-73; Ben Yitzhaq, 'Qerei u-khetiv'.

[12] On the *Nequdot* see Yeivin, *Introduction to the Tiberian Masorah*, 44-46. Further, R. F. Butin, *The Ten Nequdoth of the Torah* (Baltimore 1906; repr. New York 1969). The Dead Sea Scrolls are

originally indicated passages which an editor thought should be athetized. The suspended letters, and the large and small letters may also (sometimes) originally have indicated textual variants.[13] But all this has been ignored in the full-blown Masorah. The editorial marks have now become part of the inspired, unchangeable, divine text, and in the Midrash are given theological rather than functional, text-critical meaning.[14]

By way of contrast, the rabbis were prepared to countenance the use of textual criticism in *rabbinic* literature. The textual criticism of the Bavli, as David Goodblatt rightly notes, 'is as old as the study of the document itself.'[15] Gaonic commentators regularly solve problems in the Bavli both through collation of old manuscripts and through conjectural emendation. This trend continued into the middle ages and was a feature of the school of Rashi, some of whose corrections, as I have argued elsewhere, have actually been incorporated into the *textus receptus* of the Bavli.[16] And, of course, the standard Yeshivah edition of the Talmud prints an extensive and

[potentially of great significance in tracing the history of textual culture among Jewish scribes. Emanuel Tov is currently compiling what promises to be the definitive work on this subject. Meanwhile see his 'Scribal Practices Reflected in the Texts from the Judaean Desert', in P. W. Flint and J. C. VanderKam (eds), *The Dead Sea Scrolls after Fifty Years* (Leiden 1998), 405-29; 'Scribal Practices and Physical Aspects of the Dead Sea Scrolls', in J. Sharpe and K. Van Kampen (eds), *The Bible as Book: The Manuscript Tradition* (London 1998), 9-34; 'Correction Procedures in the Texts from the Judaean Desert', in D. W. Parry and E. Ulrich (eds), *Proceedings of the 1996 International Dead Sea Scrolls Conference, 15-17 July, 1996, Provo, Utah* (Leiden 1999).]

[13] On *nuns* and inverted *nuns* see Yeivin, *Introduction to the Tiberian Masorah*, 46-47. They probably correspond to the *sigma* and *antisigma* used by Greek textual critics to bracket out material which they thought was interpolated or in the wrong place in the text. See Lieberman, *Hellenism in Jewish Palestine*, 38-46 (following a suggestion by Samuel Krauss); further, Emanuel Tov, *Textual Criticism of the Hebrew Bible* (Assen-Minneapolis 1992), 54-55; Sid Z. Leiman, 'The Inverted Nuns at Numbers 10:35-36 and the Book of Eldad and Medad', *Journal of Biblical Literature* 93 (1974), 348-55. On the suspended, large and small letters, see Yeivin, *Introduction to the Tiberian Masorah*, 47-48.

[14] This move towards theologizing all aspects of the physical form of the Sefer Torah began comparatively early in the rabbinic tradition. Note how in b. Men. 29b it is God himself who adds the *tagin* to the Sefer Torah, because from them Aqiva would later derive mountains of halakhah. Typical of this theologizing is *Midrash Ḥaserot vi-Yeterot* (J. D. Eisenstein, *Otzar Midrashim*, vol. I [New York 1915], 194-201) which offers homiletic explanations of variations between *ḥaser* and *male'* spelling.

[15] 'The Babylonian Talmud', in H. Temporini and W. Haase (eds), *Aufstieg und Niedergang der römischen Welt*, II 19.2 (Berlin-New York 1979), 268-70.

[16] '3 Enoch and the Talmud', *Journal for the Study of Judaism* 18 (1987), 40-68.

highly sophisticated text-critical apparatus, including emendations by the Vilna Gaon and others. The rabbis were perfectly aware of the principles of text criticism, and competent to apply them. Why, then, did they not apply them to solve problems in the biblical text?

In the light of all these considerations the lack of textual criticism in Midrash can be seen to be problematic. The avoidance of textual criticism seems to have been a deliberate ploy, chosen for specific reasons rather than adopted by chance. Faced with variants in the available biblical manuscripts and with intrinsic linguistic problems in all extant forms of the biblical text the rabbis could have chosen one of three options.

First, they could have accepted the variants as divinely inspired. This is an approach which seems to have been taken, at least in part, by the Habakkuk Pesher from Qumran. It has often been noticed that the commentary element of this Pesher seems to accept readings different from those quoted in the lemma. It is possible that Paul also adopted a similar attitude towards variant texts of Scripture.[17] It is not clear how far either the author of Pesher Habakkuk or Paul would have taken this approach. As is well known there is great diversity in the biblical manuscripts from Qumran. Is it possible that the Qumran community would have accepted all these forms of the text as divinely inspired? This might explain why they seem so tolerant of diversity. On the other hand, there are alternative ways of explaining the diversity, and it seems, on the face of it, hardly credible that the Qumranites would have simply accepted any chance variant which they found in any manuscript as equally the word of God. What limits, if any, they may have imposed on this principle are unclear. Perhaps the provenance of the manuscript would have played a part. If it came with an acceptable pedigree, then its variants would have been treated with respect. It is also unclear how this rather strange position could have been defended. One might justify it from the standpoint of the doctrine of divine providence. If God has exercised providential care over the transmission of Scripture (a doctrine which, as

---

[17] See Timothy H. Lim, *Holy Scripture in the Qumran Commentaries and the Pauline Letters* (Oxford 1997).

we have already noted, is necessary to complement the doctrine of the inspiration of Scripture), then one might argue that, within certain limits, any variants which he has allowed to emerge within the text are in some sense revelatory. They could be seen as disclosing Scripture's potential.

There may be an analogy here to the rabbinic hermeneutical device of *'al tiqrei*. This seems to imply that divine revelation embraces a variety of vocalisations of the consonantal text and even homophones involving changes to the consonants as well. I find it hard to axiomatize this position. In some cases the *'al tiqrei* may be no more than wordplay used to drive home a homiletical point, but in others it seems more seriously intended and can be taken as implying that each word of Scripture is a sign pointing beyond itself to a more complex and nebulous entity. Behind the written text of Scripture stands, so to speak, a grander and more complex Torah which is accessed through the narrow door of the finite words written in the Sefer Torah. It may be significant that as a principle *'al tiqrei* is tends to be found early in the Midrashic tradition, and that later authorities had difficulties with it and effectively banned the invention of new examples. On the face of it, it seems to show the rabbis starting from a text, which in principle they regarded as inviolable and absolutely fixed, and, as it were, artificially creating textual variants! Their final position may not be all that far from the putative Qumranian view that extant textual variants may all equally reveal the mind of God.

There is a second response which the rabbis could have made towards textual variants in their biblical manuscripts. They could have set to and produced an eclectic text, choosing the best readings (guided at least in part by their own theological predilections) and emending where necessary. This may have been how the *textus receptus* of Homer came into being. And it is possibly how the Masoretic text was originally created. The origins of the Masoretic text remain unclear, but it is now evident that a form it goes back to Second Temple times. It must have been a text-form promulgated at some point by competent authority, and this may largely explain why it prevailed. It dominates numerically even at Qumran. The most plausible explanation of it is that it marks an edition of the Torah created in the wake of the Hasmonaean revolution, perhaps by priests in Jerusalem, who in effect published it by depositing master copies in the Temple. The Hasmonaean revolution forged a new definition of Jewish nationality and generated an intensification of religious norms. Defining a corpus of national literature to act as a focus of national identity and to rival the Homeric corpus of the Greeks makes a great deal of sense in this context, as does the suggestion that this work would have been undertaken by the Jerusalem priests or at least completed under their aegis.

An analysis of the Masoretic text against the early variants suggests that it is an edited, eclectic text. The exact nature of the choices exercised by the first editors is now hard to monitor, but some at least seem to have been driven by theological considerations. We may be dealing here with a conscious rewriting of the traditional literature, more than with a textual-critical process in the strict sense of the term, which involves only careful assessment of the readings of different manuscripts and conjectural emendation, where manuscript evidence fails, in order to arrive at the original text. However, the difference between rewriting and editing may be moot: where redaction-history ends and textual history begins can be blurred. It is possible that if we could have asked the creators of the Masoretic text what they thought they were doing they might well have answered that they were recovering the original Torah as given to Moses on Sinai. The main point is that the text which was finally declared authoritative seems to have been based on heavy editorial intervention. It did not involve taking one extant form of the text and declaring that form in all its detail as authoritative.

It was this latter strategy that was adopted by the rabbis. Of the available text-types they chose one, the Masoretic, and simply accepted it without more ado as authoritative. All other forms of the text were regarded as invalid. Textual variants could and did arise in the copying of the Masoretic text, and these had, of course, to be corrected, but once the 'original' Masoretic text had been recovered the process of correction abruptly stopped. That Masoretic text itself, with all its inherent textual problems which were carefully noted in Midrash and Masorah, was regarded as absolutely fixed and inviolable. As we have already observed the rabbis applied this strategy so literally and formally that they included as part of the unchangeable text of Scripture editorial marks and symbols that had been introduced for text-critical purposes into the manuscripts of this tradition at an earlier stage.

Why was this strategy adopted? What advantages did it offer? The possible reasons fall under three heads: (1) tradition, (2) apologetic, and (3) theology.

(1) Tradition. By the time rabbinic Judaism emerged in the post-70 period the Masoretic text-type had probably already largely prevailed among the Jewish communities of Palestine. It was already venerable and authoritative. The rabbis simply went along with tradition. One might be tempted to suppose that they consciously chose this text-form because it fitted best with their own theological standpoint, but actually this is far from certain. It is equally possible that this text-form shaped their theological position, or that they were in some sense the spiritual heirs of the circles that stand behind the Masoretic text and were in consequence naturally predisposed to accept it. The fact remains that the text came to them with great authority and they bowed to that authority.

(2) Apologetic. A second factor in the rabbis' choice may have been apologetics. Accepting one extant and time-honoured text is less controversial than deciding to edit and issue a new definitive version. The latter course raises sharply the questions of who has the authority to make such an edition, and whether the principles on which it has been constructed are valid. As the history of Christianity shows, creating new versions of the Scriptures can be divisive, even schismatic. It is easier to defend a venerable existing form of the text as representing accurately the original than a text which, however careful its editing or convincing its emendations, has been newly minted. And it silences the fears of the faithful that the text as originally given has been corrupted and that the Bible they have been following hitherto was an insufficient guide to faith and practice. These may all have been relevant considerations, but they were amplified by the polemical situation in which the rabbis found themselves. They were aware of alternative users of the Hebrew Bible – Jews, Christians and Samaritans – each with their own versions of it. It was polemically much stronger for the rabbis steadfastly to maintain that the text which

they had received was the true text, passed down faithfully by tradition, than to engage publicly in the hazardous exercise of re-editing it.

The rabbis' apologetic stance on this point proved rather effective at least towards Christianity. Greek-speaking Christianity had originally accepted the view of Alexandrian Judaism that the Greek text was inspired and of equal authority to the Hebrew.[18] Some Christian scholars, however, were inclined to see inspiration as residing only, or primarily, in the original Hebrew. They argued that it was necessary to emend the Greek to bring it into closer conformity to the Hebrew. For the Hebrew text, however, they turned to the Synagogue and effectively conceded the Synagogue's claim to possess the true form of this text. The most important early representative of this position was, of course, Origen, but the return to the *Hebraica veritas* was to be a recurrent theme in Christian biblical scholarship right down to modern times. One thinks of the way in which Franciscan scholars in the middle ages, such as Nicholas de Lyra, prioritised for theological reasons the historical sense of Scripture over the allegorical and used the *Hebraica veritas* to recover that sense. Or one thinks of the return to the original biblical languages, again for polemical purposes, by Protestant scholarship at the time of the Reformation. Arguably the appeal to the *Hebraica veritas* has, religiously speaking, done considerable mischief within Christianity. For example, by undermining the link between certain key New Testament passages and the Old Testament it has raised doubts about the basis of certain Christian claims, and forced Christian scholars to engage in some interesting theological gymnastics.[19]

---

[18] See M. Müller, *The First Bible of the Church: A Plea for the Septuagint* (Sheffield 1996).

[19] On the conflict between 'Hebraism' and 'Hellenism' within the Church see my essay '"Hellenism" and "Hellenization" as Problematic Historiographical Categories', forthcoming in Troels Engberg-Pedersen (ed.), *Paul: Beyond the Hellenism-Judaism Divide*. If one invokes the concept of a 'long' Reformation, then one can see the rise of critical biblical scholarship in the 19th century as a natural outcome of the return to the Scriptures in their original languages in the 16th century. But there are ironies here. The appeal to the Hebrew was initially effective in challenging the authority of the Vulgate, and of the Church which supported it, because the Hebrew text which the Protestants cited was seen as reliable and unproblematic. However, the line of inquiry which they inaugurated ended in challenging and 'dissolving' the Masoretic text. As a result it created a crisis of faith within Protestantism by calling into question the authority of Scripture itself. And the Synagogue, whose status had initially been raised by the Reformation, because it was seen as the faithful preserver of Scripture, found itself outflanked when Protestant scholars got behind the Masoretic text; it has had

(3) Theology. Theological factors may also have played a part. The granting of absolute authority to the Masoretic text-form chimes in well with the developing rabbinic doctrine of Scripture. It is not clear in this case what was the cause and what the effect. Was it the rabbinic doctrine of Scripture that led the rabbis to declare the Masoretic text as authoritative and unchangeable? Or was the doctrine, at least in part, a working out of the implications of that declaration? Or was there some sort of mutually reinforcing dialectic between the doctrine and the declaration? As it developed the rabbinic doctrine of Scripture located inspiration ever more precisely in the graphic form of the consonantal text as it is found in the Synagogue Sifrei Torah. These constituted the Written Torah. The vowels and the accents belonged to the Oral Torah. The Rabbis held a very high view of inspiration which effectively eliminated human agency: Scripture – the letters and their shapes – originated in the mind of God. In this context altering even one letter of the text becomes increasingly unthinkable. Textual problems – oddities of spelling or grammar or vocabulary which in other traditions or textual cultures would have cried out for emendation – were seen as deliberate, as divine signs of deeper meanings in the text. Textual anomalies were not smoothed away; they were theologized. And this approach fitted in well with one of the fundamental aims of Midrash, namely to maximize the potential of Scripture.[20]

These trends were further accentuated by an evolving doctrine of the cosmic significance of the Torah. Rabbi Hoshaiah was, according to Gen. Rab. 1:1,

---

increasingly to face its own crisis of faith as modernist ideas about the history of the biblical text have impacted on Judaism. There is a somewhat analogous situation in Islam, with similar, though as yet largely unrealised, potential. Early Muslim scholars such as Tabari were happy to consult Jewish sources, and particularly the Jewish Scriptures, to explain the Isra'iliyyat. They implicitly acknowledged the Isra'iliyyat as 'borrowings' from Judaism and so conceded the primacy of the Jewish sources. Later Muslim scholars, however, for theological reasons, generally found this objectionable, and today many Muslims would find even the term 'Isra'iliyyat' tendentious and unacceptable. See further my essay 'Jewish Tradition in Early Islam: The Case of Enoch/Idris', forthcoming in Jawid Mojaddedi et al. (eds), *Middle Eastern Studies in Memory of Norman Calder* (Journal of Semitic Studies Supplements; Oxford forthcoming).

[20] For some perceptive remarks on the rabbinic doctrine of Scripture see Arnold Goldberg, 'Die Schrift der rabbinischen Schriftausleger', *Frankfurter Judaistische Beiträge* 15 (1987), 1-15; repr. in Goldberg, *Rabbinische Texte als Gegenstand der Auslegung: Gesammelte Studien II* (ed. Margarette Schlüter and Peter Schäfer (Tübingen 1999), 230-41.

famously to declare that the Torah, and at least in the context of Genesis Rabbah this means the text of the Sefer Torah as found in synagogue, was the blue-print of creation: 'God looked into the Torah and created the world'. To alter the blue-print of creation could potentially have cosmic repercussions. There is a correlation between the correct performance of Torah and the stability of creation. Similar ideas may lie behind the Sefer Yetzirah, though there the basis of creation is something even more ultimate – the letters of the Hebrew alphabet, from which the Torah was formed. This doctrinal development reached its climax among the Hasidei Ashkenaz in the middle ages. They used it to argue against, not only changing the text of the Torah (that was no longer a live issue), but against changing the text of the canonical prayers. The text of the prayers were as inviolable as the text of Scripture, and to perform a changed text was to court cosmic disaster by breaking the threefold link between the prayers, the Torah and the created order. This is certainly an extreme position, but similar views were already being adumbrated in the talmudic period. It is fairly obvious that this intellectual climate is hostile to a culture of textual emendation.

We are constantly reminded these days that all *reading* of texts is culturally conditioned. I would suggest that this claim should be explicitly extended to cover all aspects of the *handling* of texts, even the most formal and apparently technical – how they are copied and how they are corrected, if they are corrected at all. The range of processes through which users put texts ostensibly to prepare them for reading are not neutral: the dichotomy between an 'objective' lower criticism, and a 'subjective' higher criticism is false. These pre-reading processes involve choices, a kind of prior reading which strongly conditions all subsequent acts of interpretation. It is no accident that textual criticism is absent from Midrash. Its absence was one of a range of strategies which together constitute the textual culture of the rabbis. Its absence is inextricably linked to the very essence of the midrashic enterprise.

I shall conclude by proposing a number of theses which attempt to synthesize the argument of this brief paper:

Jewish Ways of Reading the Bible

(1) The Torah of Moses lies at the heart of classic rabbinic Judaism, but what in precise, concrete, textual terms constitutes this Torah? The rabbis affirmed one of the textual forms of the Torah of Moses extant in their days (the 'Masoretic') as the true Torah of Moses, to the exclusion of all other forms.

(2) They were motivated to do so mainly because of the prestige and authority of this form of the text. But theological and apologetic reasons also played a part. Theologically it was less divisive and disturbing to the faithful to proclaim the accuracy of one well-respected text than attempt to produce a newly edited text based on the principles of textual criticism. This position was also more easily defensible apologetically against Christianity, non-rabbinic Judaism, Samaritanism and (later) Islam, all of which claimed that their versions of the Torah were true.

(3) The affirmation of this Masoretic text became ever more concrete and precise, till finally the Torah given to Moses on Sinai was identified with the exact graphic form of the consonantal text as contained in the Synagogue Sefer Torah – its *Ashurit* letter-forms, its orthography (whether *male'* or *ḥaser*) and its use of the *mantzapakh* letters. Somewhat surprisingly it also came in effect to embrace editorial scribal marks and conventions included in the Masoretic manuscripts, such as the *Nequdot*, the inverted *nuns*, the large and small letters, and the decorative *tagin*. This text was declared absolute and inviolable, and was supposed to be reproduced exactly in every Sefer Torah. Any omission rendered the Sefer Torah *pasul* – unfit for liturgical use. The full-blown doctrine of the inviolability of the Masoretic text probably did not emerge till gaonic times, but there are clear adumbrations of it in the talmudic period.

(4) The preservation of this text was ensured by the development of a set of external notes (the so-called Masorah), the function in part of which was to *prevent* the elimination of textual anomalies in the manuscripts. These notes began to emerge in the talmudic times, but only reached completion in the gaonic period.[21] The

---

[21] Of course the Masoretic tradition went on being studied, and to a degree elaborated, down to modern times, particularly in the great Masoretic handbooks, such as Norzi's *Minhat Shai* (1626, though not printed till 1742), which has been used to correct many modern printings of the Masoretic

inclusion in the text and in the Masoretic notes of scribal marks such as the *Nequdot*, is most economically explained by assuming that the full-blown Masoretic tradition goes back to a single master manuscript, perhaps a master scroll used in the School of Tiberias, which was effectively regarded as an exact copy of the Torah given to Moses on Sinai. The Masorah is ultimately a description of the exact content and conventions of one particular Torah scroll.

(5) However, the affirmation that the Masoretic text was identical to the Torah given to Moses on Sinai remained essentially a theological and polemical construct, because of the insurmountable technical problems of reproducing and disseminating absolutely exact copies of it. There are small, but numerous textual variants within the Masoretic manuscripts. Thus the 'Masoretic Text' remained in practice an ideal text, precisely and absolutely exemplified nowhere. Textual criticism was permissible to a limited extent to recover that ideal text, but once that ideal text was recovered, textual criticism abruptly ceased.[22]

(6) Within the textual culture of the rabbis textual criticism of the 'Masoretic Text' was impossible. Textual anomalies were usually seen not as evidence of textual corruption requiring emendation, but as signs of deeper meanings hidden in the text. They were theologized. This theologizing was one of the functions of Midrash. Midrash in its essence is opposed to textual criticism, since one of its major purposes is to obviate the need for emendation.[23]

---

text. Julian Abel at Manchester is currently researching *Minḥat Shai* to the opening chapters of Genesis.

[22] It is not clear when full-blown textual criticism of the 'Masoretic Text' first emerged within the Jewish tradition of Bible commentary. Since the concept of a fixed, inviolable text is the minimum requirement for the Midrashic method, one might have expected that when Midrash waned textual criticism would emerge. However, there is, in fact, little sign of it in Parshanut, even among philologians such as Kimḥi and Avraham ibn Ezra. Arguably the earliest evidence of it is in the writings of Samuel David Luzzatto (1800-1865). Even Azariah de Rossi (c.1511-1577), though he was strongly influenced by the textual scholarship of the Renaissance and Reformation, does not seem to propose emendations of the biblical text.

[23] As Halivni points out (*Revelation Restored*, 40-42) the closest the Midrash comes to actual emendation is through the application of the principles of *im eino 'inyan le-gufo, teneihu 'inyan l-* ('if the matter has no bearing on the subject at hand, apply it elsewhere'), of *'eiruv parashiyyot* ('interweaving of sections'), and of *seirus* ('transposition'). But, as he also points out, these remain hermeneutical rather than text-critical principles: the obvious step of emending the text is never taken, nor even apparently contemplated.

(7) However, problems remained. The manuscript tradition which the rabbis inherited contained within it signs of the earlier application of textual criticism to the text of the Torah. These were largely explained away, either by simply acknowledging them as indicating scribal changes (as in the *Tiqqunei* and *ʾItturei Soferim*), though no attempt was ever made to restore the unchanged text, or by giving the scribal marks *theological* significance (as in the *Nequdot*), or by applying a theory of polyvalency to Scripture, thus allowing variants to be accepted equally as the word of God (as in one interpretation of *Ketiv/Qerei*[24]). Rabbinic hermeneutics had a sufficient armoury of techniques to allow it to contain these problems and prevent them from breaching the basic principle of the absolute inviolability of the Masoretic Text.[25]

---

[24] This view is found already in the Talmud enshrined in the principle *yesh em la-masoret ... yesh em la-miqra* (b. Suk. 6b; b. San. 4a). See further note 11 above.

[25] Halivni's *Revelation Restored* offers an intriguingly different way of understanding the rabbinic evidence, one that is closer to modern critical scholarship. The Torah was originally given by God to Moses on Sinai, but, because of Israel's sin, starting with the incident of the Golden Calf, it was corrupted over the succeeding centuries. Then Ezra came and restored it, but the restoration was imperfect, as can be seen from the contradictions, repetitions and inconsistencies (what Halivni rather coyly calls 'maculations') which mar the existing text. Acknowledging these imperfections does not involve a denial of the doctrine of *Torah min ha-shamayim*. Halivni's argument is a theological *tour de force*, but I doubt if it is a defensible reading of the rabbinic evidence (Kimhi is one of the few authorities who comes anywhere close to it: see note 10 above). It is clearly motivated by a desire to seek an accommodation with modernist biblical scholarship and but for the influence of that scholarship would probably never have been proposed. Moreover the accommodation is limited. Halivni's position still seems to be that the Masoretic text (though imperfect) is, religiously speaking, the best text attainable. He does not appear ready to concede that it might be possible to get behind Ezra's imperfect text to a more original version of the Torah of Moses. To allow that possibility would be theologically devastating and run the risk of replaying within Judaism a version of the damaging Catholic-Protestant debate over Scripture (see note 18). And I doubt whether any major rabbinic authority would have been comfortable with the view that the original Torah was to a significant extent corrupted. The doctrine of *Torah min ha-shamayim* is usually seen as implying a high view of the providential preservation of Torah.

The Psychology of Oppositional Thinking
in Rabbinic Biblical Commentary

Brian L. Lancaster[1]

'*Nirin-veeyn-nirin* ['visible and invisible'] is the expression of transcendence.' So comments Marc-Alain Ouaknin in relation to a Talmudic discussion[2] of the staves attached to the holy Ark in the Tabernacle. The phrase נראין ואין נראין conveys the opposition between two biblical phrases quoted regarding the staves' visibility from beyond the Holy of Holies. Ouaknin further writes: 'The will to make the two opposites coexist at the same time, the refusal of the diachronization of the case, opens up a dialectic of the Visible and the Invisible that is not resolved by a third term and whose force and meaning arise in the infinite tension underlying it.'[3] This paper explores such use of what I shall refer to as oppositional thinking by rabbinic commentators and considers its psychological significance. Ouaknin's view, that the coexistence of opposites represents an expression of transcendence, will be elaborated in terms of contemporary psychological approaches to creativity and the unconscious.

That an emphasis on the sustaining of oppositions characterizes rabbinic literature has been argued, amongst others, by Boyarin.[4] Ambivalence and equivocation are key features of the midrashic elaboration of the biblical text. For

---

[1] Honorary Research Fellow, Centre for Jewish Studies, University of Manchester; Co-Director, Consciousness & Transpersonal Psychology Research Unit, Liverpool John Moores University.
E-mail: b.l.lancaster@livjm.ac.uk.
[2] b. Yoma 54a.
[3] M.-A. Ouaknin, *The Burnt Book: Reading the Talmud* (trans. L. Brown; Princeton, NJ 1995).
[4] D. Boyarin, *Intertextuality and the Reading of Midrash* (Bloomington, IN 1990).

Jewish Ways of Reading the Bible

Boyarin, rabbinic texts are distinctive in relation to comparable literature with regard to the extent to which oppositions are allowed to stand: '[T]he point is not that there was more or less dissent and controversy within the rabbinic culture than in the cultures of other forms of Judaism or Christianity but that in this culture, as in none of the others, it is precisely dissent that was canonized.'[5]

The famous Talmudic dictum, 'These and these are the words of the living God',[6] employed to sustain the validity of divergent opinions or arguments, is perhaps the crown of such canonisation. It is not simply that divergence of view is tolerated or even encouraged. Rather, for the rabbis, divergence of opinion is truly essential; without it the possibility of glimpsing the divine through the text would be eclipsed. Not only are the diverse views of different authors to be respected, but, as we will discuss later, the ability of the individual to entertain contradictory ideas, i.e., to engage in oppositional thinking, is encouraged. Such thinking may be necessary in order to comprehend the Unity within revelation – 'All is one on the side of the Giver but to us they [i.e. the two sides of the contradiction] seem different.'[7]

Why do we find this respect for ambiguity and opposition within rabbinic literature? I wish to propose two answers, one which attempts to reconstruct the rabbis' own understanding of their task, and a second, psychological, one which suggests that oppositional thinking predisposes towards those higher functions of the mind associated with Ouaknin's term 'transcendent'. Needless to say that, as a psychologist of religion, I am inclined to see these two answers as contiguous: that our contemporary psychological language of discourse merely 'unpacks' what is effectively intrinsic to the logic of rabbinic commentary.

The oppositional tendency may itself be inherent in the Hebrew language. The verbal root עקר, for example, gives rise to לעקר, 'to uproot', as well as עקר, 'root' or

[5] D. Boyarin, *Carnal Israel: Reading Sex in Talmudic Literature* (Berkeley, CA 1993), 29.
[6] b. 'Eruv. 13b; b. Git. 6b. For a recent discussion of the implications of this dictum, see A. Sagi, '"Both are the Words of the Living God": A Typological Analysis of Halakhic Pluralism', *Hebrew Union College Annual* 65 (1995), 105-36.
[7] R. Meir ibn Gabbai, cited in Sagi, 'A Typological Analysis of Halakhic Pluralism', 113.

'essence'. Munk[8] argues that the Hebrew roots were originally biconsonantal and notes that verbs deriving from the same biconsonantal root frequently have opposite meanings. He cites the example of נתן, 'to put into a place', and נתק, 'to tear from a place', both deriving from the root נת. From the rabbinic perspective, the Hebrew of the Bible is of divine origin (m. Avot 5:6) and therefore conveys in essence features of the divine mind which are more fully revealed in the Torah as a whole. The fact that a single Hebrew root can convey opposite meanings therefore lays the ground plan for the attitude to concurrent oppositions in which I am interested.

It is, however, more within the context of exegesis that the principle finds clearer expression. That the staves of the Ark were said to be 'visible and invisible' we have already noted. A second example may be drawn from the Jerusalem Talmud. An eagle hovering over its young, a biblical image alluding to the relation between God and man (Deut. 32:11), is described as נוגע ואינו נוגע, 'touching and not touching'.[9] Both of these examples concern the human-divine relationship. Interestingly, the only cases where the commentator, Rashi draws attention to seeming conflicts in the biblical narrative relate precisely to this relationship. The cases are: (1) the revelation at Mount Sinai where different verses imply that God both spoke from heaven and descended onto the mount; (2) God's speaking to Moses in the Tabernacle where there is a mutual contradiction between verses stating that God's voice emanates both from between the cherubim and from the tent of the congregation; and (3) Moses' entry into the tent of the congregation where there is a question whether the cloud did or did not prevent him from entering.

My concern is not with the details of these conflicts, but with the fact that Rashi emphasizes these specific instances. The general principle,[10] which entails sustaining oppositions, and not simply denying one of two alternatives, applies to a

---

[8] E. Munk, *The Seven Days of the Beginning* (Jerusalem 1974), 150.

[9] y. Ḥag. 9a

[10] In Rashi's words: שני כתובים המכחישים זה את זה בא שלישי והכריע ביניהם, '[Where] two verses oppose one another, a third comes and reconciles them.' This is one of the thirteen general principles of exegesis enunciated in the Sifra in the name of Rabbi Yishmael.

broader range of cases. By emphasizing these specific instances, Rashi seems to be drawing our attention to the value of oppositional thinking specifically in the context of the human relation to the transcendent.

Perhaps the most interesting of the oppositions is one enunciated in the Torah directly. The ashes of the red heifer are portrayed as having the paradoxical property of purifying the impure whilst rendering the pure impure. In Rabbi Akiva's words, על הטמא טהור ועל הטהור טמא.[11] Ritual purity and impurity appear to represent the core polarity of the Torah. Whilst topics such as heaven and earth, good and evil, light and dark, have their place, the fundamental orientation of the Torah is clearly towards ritual practice, and the categories of purity and impurity are therefore central. It seems especially strange therefore that there is a paradoxical blurring of the distinction between the two categories. Indeed, the ability to switch between the two is portrayed as the ultimate in human intellectual endeavour:

> R. Aha b. Hanina said: It is revealed and known before Him Who spoke and the world came into existence, that in the generation of R. Meir there was none equal to him; then why was not the halakhah fixed in agreement with his views? Because his colleagues could not fathom the depths of his mind, for he would declare the ritually impure to be pure and supply plausible proof, and the ritually pure to be impure and also supply plausible proof....[12]

This extract from the Talmud is particularly interesting in our context. Rabbi Meir was a pupil of Rabbi Akiva, whom we met above. The extract I have just quoted follows a statement concerning Rabbi Meir's function as a scribe. A second of his teachers, R. Ishmael is quoted as saying to him, 'Be meticulous in your work, for your occupation is a sacred one; should you omit or add even one single letter, you would destroy the whole world.' The juxtaposition is poignant indeed: as far as the written Torah is concerned, exactitude is essential; in relation to the commentarial tradition (i.e., the oral Torah) however, oppositional thinking is placed on a pedestal.

To an eye alive to the subtleties of talmudic style there is more to be gleaned in our present context from this discourse on Rabbi Meir. Rav is quoted as saying

---

[11] b. Yoma 14a
[12] b. 'Eruv. 13b

that the only reason why he himself is sharper than his colleagues is that he saw the back of R. Meir. Had he seen his front, he would have been sharper still! Another opposition then – back and front. Furthermore, there is considerable emphasis on Rabbi Meir's name, meaning 'enlighten'. 'Why was he called Meir? Because he enlightened the sages in halakhah', bringing light to the darkness – a third opposition. Note, however, that the text has just specifically stated that the halakhah was not fixed according to Rabbi Meir. Clearly, the enlightening we are dealing with here relates to the mind processes engaged in the work of the oral Torah, and not to the end result in terms of ritual practice. Moreover, as Kraemer points out,[13] this talmudic passage seems to allude to the sequence of events surrounding Moses' receipt of the Torah (specifically, the second set of tablets). First, Moses sees the back of God (Exod. 33:20-23), and second, following the forty-day spell on Sinai, his face shines with light (Exod. 34:29).

This talmudic passage on Rabbi Meir continues to state that one of his pupils gave forty-eight reasons for each detail of purity and forty-eight for each detail of impurity. Why forty-eight? At the risk of departing too far from the academic straight (and narrow) path, let me use some of the logic which anyone who has seriously studied the rabbis will surely recognize! In m. Avot we read that the Torah is acquired through forty-eight principles. Similarly in a Talmudic discussion of the way in which the Torah was to be established after the death of Moses, it is stated (in the name of Rabbi Akiva) that there are forty-eight covenants concerning the Torah.[14] I have little doubt that the editors of the Talmud were pointing to a significant relationship between these instances.[15] In essence, they seem to be intimating that the

---

[13] D. Kraemer, *Reading the Rabbis: The Talmud as Literature* (Oxford 1996), 63.

[14] b. Soṭ 37a-37b.

[15] In this context it is surely relevant to note R. Yannai's statement in the Jerusalem Talmud (y. San. 21a-21b):

> If the Torah were handed down cut-and-dried, [the world] would not have a leg to stand on. Why are we told "And the Lord spoke to Moses ..."? Said he to Him: "Master of the Universe! Teach me the detail of Halakha." Said He: "Follow the majority. When they acquit, acquit, and when they condemn, condemn, so that the Torah may be expounded in forty-nine ways in favour of ritual purity and in forty-nine ways in favour of impurity."

state of mind most appropriate to the kind of engagement with the Torah for which
they stood is one in which oppositional thinking has a major role to play.

Here, then, is my first answer to the question posed above concerning the role of ambiguity and opposition within rabbinic literature. It is not simply that by finding alternative interpretations for scripture, the rabbis were able to 'prolong [their] conversation' with God, as Stern argues.[16] There seems to be a more active, or psychologically deeper, dynamic in this feature of rabbinic exegesis. In this context, I think it important to note that the primary editors of the classical rabbinic texts most probably thought of them as teaching documents. Their interest lay not simply in preserving the content of debates and sermons, but more fundamentally in perpetuating a way of receiving the tradition. By encouraging the student to embrace oppositional thinking, I believe that the rabbis were leading him towards direct experience of the inner meaning of revelation. As the famous dictum in Sifre has it, 'If you wish to know the One who spoke and the world came into being, learn aggadah, for through that you will come to know the Holy One, blessed be He and cleave to His ways.'[17]

A more psychological perspective may be opened up by Faur's conception of the tension inherent within the tradition of rabbinic commentary, which seems to underlie the oppositions we have been considering. He argues that, 'The oral Law is grounded on the irreducible tension between the *oraculum* and articulation. Rather than suppress that tension, ... the oral Law accepts the tension ... as a constant.'[18] Faur holds that the term *oraculum* is the 'unprocessed original thought' prior to articulation into language. In psychological terms it is *preconscious* thought.[19] *The*

---

[16] D. Stern, *Midrash and Theory: Ancient Jewish Exegesis and Contemporary Literary Studies* (Evanston, IL 1996), 31.
[17] Sifre Ekev 13: דורשי רשומות אומרי׳ רצונך שתכיר מי שאמר והיה העולם למוד הגדה שמתוך כך אתה מכיר את הקב״ה ומדבק בדרכיו.
[18] J. Faur, *Golden Doves with Silver Dots: Semiotics and Textuality in Rabbinic Judaism* (Bloomington, IN 1986), 133.
[19] Freud used the term 'preconscious' to indicate thoughts, images and knowledge which, not being repressed and therefore unconscious, could be summoned into consciousness at will. In the light of the more recent emphasis in psychology on neural and cognitive operations involved in information processing, 'preconscious' generally refers to processes occurring prior to their entry into conscious-

tension is, then, between preconscious and conscious thought. For Faur, midrashic sources suggest that it was the *oraculum* which conveyed the inner totality of Torah to all those assembled at Sinai (and, by implication, to all who subsequently 'receive' the Torah through their study of the oral tradition). The *oraculum* is, seemingly, the point of connection between the human mind and the divine mind. We may suggest, then, that the rabbis extol oppositional thinking because it emphasizes this dynamic, as we would put it, between preconscious and conscious. The ground of the dynamic seems to slide between the Torah itself – that is, its visibility and invisibility or its conception of pure and impure – and the human mind.

The nature of this dynamic is considerably elaborated in the literature of the Kabbalah, where we find the revealed/concealed polarity becoming very much a central theme. Whilst the question of continuity here is, perhaps, contentious, the kabbalists themselves certainly viewed their ideas as implicit in the rabbinic sources I have been considering. In a typical passage the Zohar, for example, states that 'Throughout the entire Torah we find that the revealed co-exists with the concealed. So it is with the world, both this world and the higher world, everything is concealed and revealed.'[20] And for the Hasidic teacher, Rav Nahman of Bratslav, the Torah is related to the concept of *Tzimtzum* (The Lurianic teaching of God's contraction of Himself at the beginning of creation), in which 'Two opposites have to be accepted simultaneously: namely, "there is" and "there is not" (יש ואין).'[21] Earlier traditions seem to have been making the same point by emphasizing the duality inherent in the primordial nature of Torah – that it is constituted through black fire on white fire.[22] The text of the Torah, and – as Rav Nachman teaches – the very core of *makhloket*

---

ness. See N. F. Dixon, *Preconscious Processing* (Chichester 1971); for a discussion of the relation between preconscious and conscious stages in perception see B. L. Lancaster, 'On the stages of perception: towards a synthesis of cognitive neuroscience and the Buddhist Abhidhamma tradition', *Journal of Consciousness Studies* 4 (1997), 122-42.

[20] Zohar 2:230b

[21] Likutei Moharan 64:1

[22] y. Sheq. 13b. Nahmanides' Introduction to Commentary on the Torah. See also G. Scholem, *On the Kabbalah and its Symbolism* (trans. R. Manheim; New York 1965), 38, 47-50.

(Talmudic argument) itself serves to connect human to divine by dint of the recapitulation of the primordial opposition in *tzimtzum*.

In my reference to the conscious and the preconscious I have begun to give my second answer to the earlier question – the psychological answer. This psychological perspective may be developed further by reference to Rav Nahman's thinking. Rav Nahman asserts that the sustaining of opposites (ייש ואין) is a matter that reason cannot possibly grasp. He also states that the only means through which we can reach towards genuinely new knowledge involves accomplishing a *tzimtzum* in the mind. The *tzimtzum*, whereby two opposing ideas are conjoined in the mind, cuts the ordinary associations of ideas that well up seemingly automatically, clearing the ground – as it were – for new shoots to grow. Just as *tzimtzum* was the necessary preliminary to God's creation, so, for Rav Nahman, it is essential for our own aspirations to creativity.

At a simple level, oppositional thinking may be seen to go against the grain of the mundane function of mind: it runs counter not only to reason but to a whole range of cognitive processes that habitually function to limit uncertainty in ways which are clearly biologically adaptive. Any ambiguity in sensory signals, for example, is inhibited by the representational and interpretive processes of cognition. In unclear conditions, such as dusk, the mind generally insists on 'seeing' a specific object, even at the risk of error.

Oppositional thinking would seem therefore to encourage what Deikman refers to as deautomatization.[23] It forces the individual to refrain from those patterns of thought which act to maintain the status quo. In this sense, it resembles the effect of a Zen *koan*, which, as Austin puts it, is resolved 'in those deeper brain circuits which have suddenly become unconditioned.' Since the sense of 'I' is central to the conditioned nature of mind, he asserts that 'no egocentric *I-Me-Mine* self remains

---

[23] A. J. Deikman, 'Deautomatization and the Mystic Experience', *Psychiatry* 29 (1966), 324-38.

around in the resolution of the *koan*.'[24] Rabbi Akiva's על הטמא טהור ועל הטהור טמא ('it purifies the impure and defiles the pure') might well be described as a talmudic *koan*!

Whilst deautomatization is important to an understanding of oppositional thinking, a richer analysis may be advanced by considering the psychology of creativity. Rothenberg has proposed that two kinds of thought process are critically involved in creativity. They are the *homospatial* process, through which two or more discrete entities are actively conceived occupying the same space, and the *janusian* process in which two or more opposites or antitheses are actively conceived simultaneously. In a phrase especially redolent of rabbinic texts, Rothenberg characterizes the janusian process as, 'volitional, entailing multiplicity and contradiction together with rationality and elaboration carried out over extended periods of time.'[25] These conclusions are based on extensive interviews with creative individuals in addition to a number of empirical research studies. As an example of these thought processes at work, Rothenberg cites the famous case of Kekulé discovering the benzene ring.[26] According to Rothenberg, the homospatial process is evident in Kekulé's image of snakes superimposed on his image of carbon atoms, and the subsequent image of one of the snakes seizing hold of its own tail is janusian since mouths and tails are functionally and spatially opposite.

Csikszentmihalyi, another psychologist who has extensively researched creativity, argues that the oppositional tendency is evident not only in the thought styles of creative people but also in their personalities. He cites a number of personality dimensions characteristic of creative types and emphasizes the 'apparently antithetical traits that are often both present in such individuals and integrated with each other in a dialectical tension.'[27]

---

[24] J. H. Austin, *Zen and the Brain: Toward an Understanding of Meditation and Consciousness* (Cambridge, MA 1998), 113-14.

[25] A. Rothenberg, 'The Janusian Process in Scientific Creativity', *Creativity Research Journal* 9 (1996), 207-31, 221.

[26] A. Rothenberg, 'Creative Cognitive Processes in Kekulé's Discovery of the Structure of the Benzene Molecule', *American Journal of Psychology* 108 (1995), 419-38.

[27] M. Csikszentmihalyi, *Creativity: Flow and the Psychology of Discovery and Invention* (New York 1996), 57-58.

I consider Rothenberg's view of creative thinking particularly apposite to my analysis of the rabbinic approach to biblical commentary. Rabbinic texts clearly encourage janusian thinking. The reader is frequently required to entertain opposing views, or alternative interpretations, sometimes over fairly extensive portions of a text. More interesting than this, however, is the role of the homospatial process. Where exactly is it that the alternative interpretations occupy 'the same space'? Quite evidently it is *in the Torah itself*, for the whole edifice is founded on the polysemy of the revealed word.[28] We may draw a parallel between Kekulé visualizing the snake-like and the atom-like images in the same space and thereby understanding something new about the nature of benzene, and the *talmid* bringing alternate meanings of a word or phrase together and grasping something fundamental about Torah.

The point of the parallel is not simply that creative insight may dawn through oppositional thinking in the two cases. More fundamentally, the parallel leads us to consider the relation between the way in which we think of the mind and the conception of Torah as in some sense organismic, a view promulgated within the mystical tradition.[29] In order to pursue this relationship the following terms will be employed to elucidate the relevant parallels between the mind and the Torah: *unity*, *multiplicity* and *stability*. In relation to the mind, I use the term *stability* to refer to normal conscious images and thoughts.[30] The progression from preconscious to conscious entails the cognitive system generating unambiguous representations for each event or image involved. Of course, these representations are not generated in staccato-like fashion; they are enmeshed in the ongoing narrative – centred on the representation of self, which constitutes the stream of consciousness.[31] The precon-

---

[28] The verse comparing God's word to 'a hammer that shatters the rock' (Jer. 23:29) becomes the paradigm of the polysemy in scriptural words: 'just as this hammer is split into many sparks, so a single verse has several meanings' (b. San. 34a).

[29] Scholem, *On the Kabbalah and its Symbolism*, 1-86.

[30] See also G. O'Brien and J. Opie, 'A Connectionist Theory of Phenomenal Experience', *Behavioral and Brain Sciences* 22 (1999), 127-96. '[P]henomenal experience is identical to the brain's explicit representation of information, in the form of *stable patterns of activation*' (p. 138; italics added).

[31] I have discussed the role of self in the process whereby images and thoughts reach consciousness in Lancaster, 'On the Stages of Perception'; see also J. F. Kihlstrom, 'Consciousness and Me-ness', in J.

scious mind seems to be characterized by *multiplicity*. Studies have demonstrated, for example, that when words are presented to a subject, their multiple meanings are initially activated preconsciously (during the first 250 milliseconds). A single meaning will then be selected to enter consciousness, at which time the other, non-selected meanings are in some way inhibited.[32] As for the term *unity*, there seems to be accumulating evidence for the idea advanced by a number of contemporary psychologists and physicists that there is some form of transcendent root of the mind which is holistic in operation.[33] At the level of this transcendent root the mind may be described as unified but unconscious.

An instructive insight into the multiplicity at the preconscious level is given by the syndrome of synaesthesia, in which sensory modalities become confused – as when someone *hears colours*. On the basis of his analysis of the brain structures involved in the syndrome, Cytowic argues that it occurs when the normal multisensory preconscious activities are abnormally extended into consciousness.[34] In other words, the syndrome is evidence for the view that prior to their articulation as stable, meaningful objects and events in consciousness, preconscious images and thoughts are represented in multiple fashion. Such a formulation is supported by a variety of other lines of psychological enquiry.[35]

D. Cohen and J. W. Schooler (eds), *Scientific Approaches to Consciousness* (Mahwah, NJ 1997), 451-68.

[32] M Velmans, 'Neural Activation, Information, and Phenomenal Consciousness', *Behavioral and Brain Sciences* 22 (1999), 172-73 (and references cited there).

[33] D. Bohm, *Wholeness and the Implicate Order* (London 1980); J. S. Grotstein, 'The Numinous and Immanent Nature of the Psychoanalytic Subject', *Journal of Analytical Psychology* 43 (1998), 41-68.

[34] R. E. Cytowic, *The Man Who Tasted Shapes: A Bizarre Medical Mystery Offers Revolutionary Insights into Reasoning, Emotion, and Consciousness* (New York 1993).

[35] B. Lancaster, *Mind, Brain and Human Potential: the Quest for an Understanding of Self* (Shaftesbury 1991).

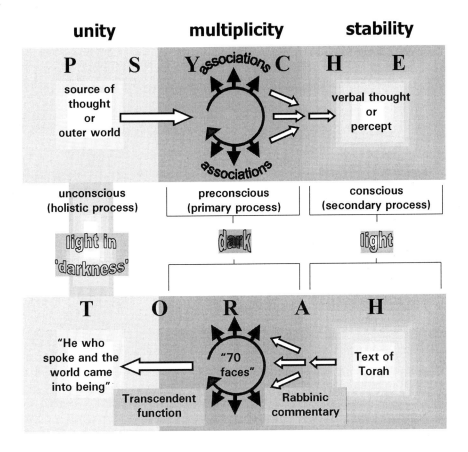

Figure 1: Rabbinic commentary and the transcendent function

What I am arguing is that, by exploring the multiplicity implicit in the text of the Torah, the Rabbis were paralleling the preconscious elaboration of images triggered when a root idea, be it the germ of a thought or sensory activation, enters the mind. The proposed parallels are presented in figure 1, in which I have also introduced the metaphor of light, since this is a universal symbol of transcendence. It will be clear that the normal direction of flow in mental activity – from root, to preconscious, to conscious – is reversed in the case of the Rabbis' exegesis of the Torah. Such exegesis encourages this reversal in two ways. Firstly, through its emphasis on polysemy it draws on the preconscious. Secondly, through the tendency to oppositional thinking it sensitizes the individual to the primordial opposition between conscious and unconscious, itself played out in the preconscious sphere of mind. In this formulation I am approaching Jung's conception of the transcendent function which he defined as 'a quality of conjoined opposites,' namely the 'union of conscious and unconscious elements.'[36] Parenthetically, let me note an important difference, however, between this Jungian perspective and that under discussion here, in that rabbinic exegesis works not towards the *union* of opposites but more to the goal of *sustaining* opposites, as we have seen. I am inclined to think that this distinction is itself highly significant for psychology, concerning, as it does, the relation between the unconscious and consciousness itself. This, however, is a topic for further consideration elsewhere.

Returning to my major theme, the rabbis' interest lay in the Unity which lies behind the multiplicity of interpretation. Just as the multiplicity of the preconscious underlies the stability of the conscious mind, so the multiplicity of interpretation underlies the stable outer form of the Torah. Oppositional thinking points behind such multiplicity towards the Unity at the root of Torah, which, as implied in figure 1, may be identified with the source of revelation. It is, in rabbinic metaphor, the One voice which manifests in 'seventy languages', giving rise to the 'seventy faces' of the Torah.

---

[36] C. G. Jung, 'The transcendent function', in *Complete Works*, vol. 8: *The Structure and Dynamics of the Psyche* (London 1916/1958).

The Structure of
Hymnic Insertions in the Statutory Jewish Liturgy

Raphael Loewe

The generalisation may be risked that no poem is without its context: and if the genius of the greatest poets may sometimes invest what they write with a power that sublimates it to independence of its *Sitz im Leben*, it is surely true that an understanding of its original occasion and purpose will, even here, enhance the reader's appreciation. Indeed, where less inspired writing is concerned such knowledge may be indispensable, and possession of it may sometimes redeem second or third-rate productions from being condemned as sheer banality. Nowhere is this more true than with regard to mediaeval Hebrew poetry, whether liturgical or social,[1] where the formal aspect is paramount: and since the first encounter of most readers and students (as distinct from worshippers) is with anthologized specimens, they are liable to depreciate or even to dismiss some of these because they are seen not as part of a concatenated series, but in isolation.

This paper offers nothing new (other than the English translations[2]) regarding the poems here to be considered. My purpose is merely to illustrate structure and inner coherence, taking as an example an integral series composed for the evening service introducing the seventh day of the feast of Passover. Like all post-biblical, pre-modern Hebrew poetry, it is saturated with biblical quotations and allusions, sometimes

---

[1] For the misunderstanding implicit in the conventional western translation of *šîrê ḥōl* as 'secular' poetry, as distinct from *šîrê qōdeš* (liturgical poetry), see R. Loewe, *Ibn Gabirol* (London 1989), 54ff.

[2] These versions were prepared for publication in the companion volume of the facsimile edition of *The Rothschild Haggadah* (i.e. of a portion of the Rothschild Miscellany, MS Jerusalem, Israel Museum, 180.51) (London 1999), and I am grateful to Mr Michael Falter of Facsimile Editions for his agreement to my reprinting them here.

reapplied, occasionally with audacious disregard of the meaning in their original contexts.[3] The modern reader (including probably a majority of Israelis) generally regards this feature as being but virtuosity, therein missing the point; its function may be compared with the use in music of a chord in preference to a pure note.[4]

The bulkiness of the Jewish liturgy in its current, so-to-say 'established' form is due to the self-assertive tenacity of cumulative tradition, which has incorporated into public worship items of study and psalmody, etc., that were originally a matter for private devotion or for groups of pietists gathering before or after the regular service. The original skeleton was quite small,[5] the nucleus of each of the three daily services being the series of benedictions – nineteen on weekdays, reduced on sabbaths and festivals – entitled *tĕpillah*, prayer *par excellence*, or *ʿămîdāh*;[6] this being preceded in the morning and evening services by the *šĕmaʿ* with its framework of three (or, in the evening, four) declarative paragraphs, all culminating in a benediction and the first also introduced by one. To this, scriptural pericopes were appended on the mornings of the sabbaths, festivals, and fast-days, as also a brief extract from the ensuing sabbath's *parašah* on Mondays and Thursdays. The high-lighting of climactic liturgical stations by introductory poems (*piyyûṭîm* > ποιητής) for festivals and special sabbaths began in Palestine, being first attested in the Byzantine period in or possibly before the sixth century,[7] if, for present purposes, we may leave Qumranic Judaism out of account.

---

[3] For a particularly bold example see below, p. 227.
[4] See R. Loewe, 'The Bible in Medieval Hebrew Poetry', in J. A. Emerton and S. C. Reif (eds), *Interpreting the Hebrew Bible: Essays in Honour of E. I. J. Rosenthal* (Cambridge 1982), 137-38.
[5] See, for a summary, L. Jacobs, 'Liturgy', *Encyclopaedia Judaica* 11.392ff., esp. 394; more fully, S. C. Reif, *Judaism and Hebrew Prayer* (Cambridge 1993), chs 3 (53-87) and 5 (122-52).
[6] Conceivably this term is but a calque on the Greek ἀκάθιστος, attached as a name to the popular Byzantine hymn in honour of the Virgin Mary attributed to Romanos (sixth century); see R. Loewe, 'Rabbi Joshua ben Ḥananiah: Ll.D. or D.Litt.?' *Journal of Jewish Studies* 25 (1974), 146, n. 48.
[7] See E. Fleischer, 'Piyyut', *Encyclopaedia Judaica* 13.573-602; I. Elbogen, *Der jüdische Gottesdienst in seiner geschichtlichen Entwicklung* (2nd edn; Berlin 1924), 208ff.; Fleischer, *ha-yōṣĕrōt bĕ-hithawwōtām wĕ-hitpattĕhūtām* (Jerusalem 1984); Reif, *Judaism and Hebrew Prayer* (n. 5), 133, 146, 162, etc.

Once these proemes had established themselves, as features that might be anticipated at specific locations, they came to constitute a series that invites comparison with the formal structure of musical composition. To be sure, the analogy is not one to be pressed too rigorously, but it seems to me to be an appropriate one, use of which will be made occasionally below.

The stations of the hymnic insertions into the morning service are termed collectively *yōṣĕrōt*,[8] since the first benediction to which they are attached is that which declares God to be the former (*yōṣēr*) of light and darkness:[9] although in the Sephardic rite there are also one or two preliminary stations near the end of the individual devotions. The complete series is as follows, the name given to each item being explained.

Preceding the *šĕma'*:

(i) *yōṣēr*, see above.

(ii) *'ōpān*, i.e. '[wheel-]angel', cf. Ezek. 1:16. Inserted in the body of the *yōṣēr*-paragraph, to lead up to the reference therein to the angels' doxology.[10]

(iii) *mĕ'ōrāh*, i.e. 'luminary', preceding the closing benediction of the paragraph (see n. 9)

(iv) *'ahăbāh*, 'love', i.e. as manifested in the divine election of Israel, preceding the climactic benediction[11] which immediately precedes the recitation of the *šĕma'*.

Following the *šĕma'*:

In the credal declaration that summarizes God's redemptive acts:[12]

(v) *zūlāt*, i.e. '[divine] exclusivism', following the words *wĕ-'ēn 'ĕlōhîm zūlātĕkā*.[13]

---

[8] Elbogen, *Der jüdische Gottesdienst* (n. 7), 210; Fleischer, *yōṣĕrōt* (n. 7), 149ff.; F. L. Cohen, 'Yozerot', *Jewish Encyclopedia* (New York 1906), 12.622ff.

[9] See, e.g., S. Singer, *Authorised Daily Prayer Book*[14] (London 1924), 128-29: ברוך אתה ה׳ אלהינו מלך העולם יוצר אור ובורא חשך עושה שלום ובורא את הכל (cf. Isa. 45:7) ... ב׳ א׳ ה׳ יוצר המאורות

[10] Singer, 131 (Ezek. 3:12): והאופנים וחיות הקדש ... משבחים ואומרים ברוך כבוד ה׳ ממקומו

[11] Singer, 131-32: אהבה רבה אהבתנו ... ב׳ א׳ ה׳ הבוחר בעמו ישראל באהבה

[12] Singer, 134-36: אמת ויציב ... ב׳ א׳ ה׳ גאל ישראל

[13] Singer, 135: מעולם הוא שמך ואין אלהים זולתך ...

206

(vi) *mî kāmōkā*, i.e. '[divine] uniquity', preceding the quotation of Exod. 15:11.[14]

[(vii) Some variations within the Ashkenazic rite may have included also an *'ădōnāy malkēnū*, preceding the quotation of Exod. 15:18.[15]]

(viii) *gĕ'ullāh*, 'redemption', preceding the climactic blessing of this section of the statutory liturgy.[16]

In modern Ashkenazic prayer-books in the west which print a translation parallel with the Hebrew text, many of these hymns are either omitted or relegated, without translation, to an appendix.   This reflects increasing resistance amongst western Ashkenazic Jewries in the nineteenth century to the continued recitation of lengthy poetic material which, because of the decline in Jewish educational standards, was incomprehensible to many worshippers.   As a result, in 1856 the French rabbinic authorities ruled that its inclusion was not obligatory, being followed some decades later by the English Chief Rabbinate.[17]   A number of such pieces by Sephardic liturgical poets are included in the Rylands Haggadah in Manchester, and have been translated into verse in the facsimile edition.[18]

No great insight is required to appreciate that the series as here tabulated constitutes a unity, its several parts each having its own characteristic flavour; readers, or worshippers, whose education has made a familiarity with the Hebrew Bible almost second nature will anticipate what sort of quotations and allusions are likely to be laid under contribution by the author of, e.g., a *mĕ'ōrāh* or a *gĕ'ullāh*. Each has its own specific colouring, and, if we are to resort to musical analogies, its *tempo*.

---

[14] Singer, 136: ... ‏ואמרו כלם מי כמוך באלהים ה'‎ ...

[15] Elbogen (n. 7), 211; but see Fleischer, *yōṣĕrōt*, 161-62.

[16] Singer, 136: ‏גאלנו ה' צבאות שמו קדוש ישראל‎ (Isa. 47:4) ‏ב' א' ה' גאל ישראל‎

[17] See Reif (n. 5), 269, 286; cf. Fleischer, *yōṣĕrōt*, 619. A. Ben-Baruch Créhange, *Prières des Fêtes à l'usage des Israëlites français, portugais et espagnols*, Passover volume (Paris 1861), preface, vii, footnote, records the ruling of the two Chief Rabbis of France. The concession by Nathan Adler, the English Ashkenazic Chief Rabbi, was promulgated in a private letter (printed for circulation) to Henry J. Kisch, dated 27th May 1880.

[18] Rylands Library, MS Heb. 6; R. Loewe, *The Rylands Haggadah* (London 1988), 38f.

The scheme as a whole may be viewed as a theological symphony, each of the four movements comprising sundry themes. *First*, creation (i-iii), the divine act not being a merely parochial affair concerning the universe of our immediate experience; it includes the creation of the angels that correspond with those cosmic forces outside our earth, of the existence and functions of which the daily re-emergence of light is at once the most constant reminder and the most spectacular example. A short, *second* movement (iv), concerning the election of Israel, both subordinates history to the providential element integral to the creative act, and, by leading directly into the recitation of the *šĕma'* and its injunction to love God with heart and soul (Deut. 6:5), insists upon the reciprocity implicit in election. A *third* movement (v-vi/vii) moves on to the articulation, in simple terms within the average reader's grasp, of what creation and the mutuality of God and Israel presuppose as regards the nature of the Godhead. Finally, the *fourth* movement (viii) proclaims the redemption of Israel, as a collective ethnic entity, evinced in the divine intervention in history that brought about the exodus from Egypt; this also typifying future redemption, faith in the ultimate actuality of which transcends awareness of all circumstantial realities. It is not difficult to descry similarities between this composition, when seen as a whole rather than the isolation of specimen parts, introduced as a token into anthologies of Hebrew poetry, and the construction of e.g., Beethoven's Emperor Concerto or the Seventh Symphony.

The corresponding, shorter series for the evening service of festivals, called *ma'ărîbot* or *ma'ărābōt*,[19] is constructed similarly. Sephardic liturgical poets did not, it seems, compose poems for this setting; and although no Ashkenazic *ma'ărābōt* gained a permanent foothold in any Sephardic rite, there is some evidence for short-term infiltration[20] of those composed by Me'ir b. Isaac *šĕlîaḥ ṣibbūr* (*sc.* precentor) of

---

[19] Elbogen (n. 7), 212; Fleischer, '*li-tĕkūnōt piyyūtê ha-ma'ărîb*', *Sinai* 69 (5731/1971) 123-34; *yōṣĕrōt*, 55, n. 50; *'hădāšōt lĕ-'inyan "rōš rāšê hodāšîm'''*, in E. Fleischer and J. Petuchowski (eds), *Joseph Heinemann Memorial Volume* (Jerusalem 5741/1981), 125f.

[20] The series of poems beginning ליל שמורים אותו אל הצה was included in the Rylands Haggadah (mid-fourteenth century, see n. 18), ff. 8rf., English translation 30f. In the so-called Barcelona Haggadah

Worms,[21] who died before 1096, for the eve of Passover. This divergence from the Sephardic norm was perhaps due to the magnetism of Passover night as a major feature of the Jewish calendar, which may have occasioned a popular demand for liturgical elaboration of the evening service that precedes domestic celebration.

The skeleton of the evening service into which *ma'ărābōt* were interwoven consists of four paragraphs with concluding benedictions.

Preceding the *šĕma'*:

(i) Insertion before the conclusion of the first benediction, which declares that the cause of the sun's setting is God's word.[22]

(ii) Before the benediction concluding the declaration of God's love for Israel.[23]

Following the *šĕma'*:

(iii) In the credal passage,[24] preceding the citation of Exod. 15:11 (cf. morning vi):

    (a) a longer poem, with alphabetic acrostic, elaborating on the biblical event which the festival commemorates;

    (b) a short piece leading into the quotation מי כמוך וגו׳

(iv) Preceding the citation of Exod. 15:18, ה׳ ימלך לעלם ועד (cf. morning vii).

(v) Preceding the benediction which affirms God's redeemership (cf. morning viii). See n. 16 (conclusion only).

(vi) In the prayer for a peaceful night (השכיבנו[25]), preceding the climactic benediction:

    (a) a prose passage, classified as [תוספת[26] בכור, is sometimes introduced; this is a halakhic piece, setting forth the ceremonial and other regulations for the celebration

---

(British Library MS Add. 14761), which is but slightly later (ed. J. Schonfield [London 1992]) it forms an addition to the nuclear MS (ff. 9vf., translation, companion vol., 83f.). M. Beit-Arié, p. 16, shows, from codicological evidence, that the manuscript has been supplemented.

[21] See A. David, *Encyclopaedia Judaica* 11, 1255; Fleischer, *yōṣĕrōt*, 766 (index); A. Grossman, *ḥakmē 'ashkĕnaz hā-rišōnim* (Jerusalem 5741/1981), 292-96, 453 (index).

[22] Singer, 113a: ב׳ א׳ ה׳ אלהינו מלך העולם אשר בדברו מעריב ערבים ... ב׳ א׳ ה׳ המעריב ערבים

[23] Singer, 113a: אהבת עולם בית ישראל עמך אהבת ... ב׳ א׳ ה׳ אוהב את עמו ישראל

[24] Singer, 113c-d: אמת ואמונה וכו׳. See nn. 12, 14.

[25] Singer, 114: השכיבנו ה׳ אלהינו לשלום ... ב׳ א׳ ה׳ הפורש סכת שלום עלינו ועל כל ישראל ועל ירושלם

[26] I have not seen any explanation for the use of this term ('firstborn') in this connection. Could it be intended to emphasise the primacy of the halakhic aspect of Judaism?

of the festival. If the musical analogy may be somewhat pressed, this may be said to correspond with a cadenza. A more apposite comparison, perhaps, may be drawn with a prominent feature of the Old Comedy in Greece, *viz.* the *parabasis*. This is a point at which the leader of the chorus lays aside his dramatic function and addresses the audience directly, rather than through the medium of the plot, on pressing issues of contemporary politics, etc.

(b) a poem leading into the benedictional affirmation of God's provision of peace.

We may now examine in detail a set of *ma'ărābōt* from the rite once current in Worms. They were written for the seventh evening of Passover, the pentateuchal reading on the morning following which tells of the Egyptian pursuit of the Israelites, the crossing of the Red Sea, and the sweetening of the waters of Marah (Exod. 13:7-15:26). In view of the crucial significance of this chapter of Jewish history, and of the graphic character of the biblical account, it is hardly surprising that the latter generated much midrashic elaboration, designed to underscore the miraculous aspect of Israel's divine deliverance: and these *ma'ărābōt* evince manifold allusions to the early rabbinic high-lighting of items in the biblical text, rather in the manner of script-writing for the production of a film.

The acrostic signature of the author, Menahem b. Jacob,[27] appears at the end of section (vi) (a) of the series of poems, and again at the beginning of (vii) (b). He lived in Worms, though possibly born elsewhere, his dates being 1120(?)-1203: as a member of the rabbinical court, he was a colleague of Qalonymus b. Gershom and Eleazar b. Judah,[28] the latter being the last major representative of the pietists known as *ḥasîdê aškĕnaz*.[29] Although no halakhic rulings are attached to his name, his scholarship is attested in his liturgical poetry, which includes some pieces occasioned by

---

[27] *Encyclopaedia Judaica* 11, 1305.
[28] *Encyclopaedia Judaica* 6, 92-94; Grossman (n. 21), 329.
[29] *Encyclopaedia Judaica* 7, 1377-83.

contemporary tragedies. His poem מצור באתה העיר[30] refers to the siege of Worms by Otto IV, a nephew of Richard I of England, in 1201, in the course of his war with Philip of Swabia, the rival claimant to the Empire. He also wrote elegies on specifically Jewish catastrophes: on the thirteen victims of a blood-libel disturbance at Boppard in 1179 and the massacre of the little Jewish community of Blois in its entirety in 1190.[31] The later portion of this (possibly, but improbably an independent poem) also laments the fate of the Jews of York who, in the same year, preferred self-immolation in Clifford's Tower to exposing themselves to the fury of the mob without.[32]

The text of the Worms liturgical poems will not, as far as I am aware, be found in accessible modern editions of the Ashkenazic liturgy. It is here reproduced from the scholarly edition of Daniel Goldschmidt,[33] the notes in which indicate the midrashic and talmudic sources. The numeration (i)-(vii) (b) refers back to the analysis of the structure of the *ma'ărābōt* above. The alphabetic acrostic (picked out here in larger type) runs through (i) and (ii) as far as *ḥet*, is resumed at (iii) (b) and continues to (v) (*ṭet-tau*). (iii) (a) has its own alphabetic acrostic, which is followed by the signature מנחם ברבי יעקב (the combinations of רבי and יע[קב] being contrived by resort to the second and third letters in the line concerned). (vi) (b) carries an acrostic signature, divided between the first stanza and the last two: מנחם in the first four lines of stanza 1, ברבי יעקב in stanza 5, while the initial words of stanza 6, חזק ואמיץ, intimate also the

---

[30] I. Davidson, *'ōṣar ha-širāh wĕ-ha-piyyūṭ*, 3 (New York 1930), 168, no. 2142.

[31] אללי לי כי באו רגע אלמון ושכול, Davidson, 1 (1924), 237, no 5154.

[32] The part of the elegy relevant to the York tragedy was printed, with a translation, by S. Schechter, 'A Hebrew Elegy', *Transactions of the Jewish Historical Society of England* 1 (1893-94), 8-14, from MS Vatican, ebr. 312. The complete poem was published by A. Berliner in Sammelband (קובץ על יד) 3 of the M'kize Nirdamim, 2nd pagination, 5-9. It is worth remarking that another contemporary elegy on the Jews of York, by Joseph of Chartres, contains much more specific detail; it was published by C. Roth, with a translation and notes, in *Transactions of the Jewish Historical Society of England* 16 (1952), 213-30.

[33] Daniel Goldschmidt, ed. J. Frankel, מחזור פסח לפי מנהגי בני אשכנז לכל אנפיהם (Jerusalem 5753/1993), 347-55. Goldschmidt may well be dependent on Heidenheim, to whom he refers (Heidenheim's הפיוטים והפייטנים [Hanover 1839] [Steinschneider, Bodleian Cat., 5197.8], is not immediately available to me).

imperative *ḥăzaq*, 'be strong!' which (occasionally as here reinforced by its synonym *wĕ-'ĕmaṣ*, cf. Josh.1:6) forms the conventional conclusion of an acrostic signature.

ב׳ א׳ ה׳ אל חי תמיד ימלך עלינו לעולם ועד

(i)

אורי וישעי[a34] על הים נגלה
בהחשיכו[35] צרי ולי האיר אפלה
גדלת מעשיו מפלאים[b] ונוראים להללה
ויהי הענן והחשך ויאר את הלילה[c]

God is my light,[a34] who, saving, at the sea
Revealed Himself, and darkness[35] o'er the foe
He cast, whilst beaming broad daylight on me,
His wondrous acts[b] in praises forth to shew:
    'Twixt cloud and darkness He made bright
    The sky, all lustrous turned the night'[c]

[a]Ps. 27:4; [b]cf. Ps. 119:14; [c]Exod. 14:20

ב׳ א׳ ה׳ המעריב ערבים

אהבת עולם בית ישראל ... ואהבתך אל תסיר ממנו לעולמים

(ii)

העיר ברית ישנים לשלם בנים גמולם
ויוצא עמו בששון[d] באברתו נטלם[e]
זכר **ח**סדו ואמונתו[f] בידידות לנהלם
באהבתו ובחמלתו הוא גאלם[g]

He woke that covenant, made long before
With sires asleep, whose sons their guerdon gained
When, leading forth his joyful folk,[d] He bore
Them on his wings,[e] mindful of faith engrained
    With mercy;[f] guidance friendship seemed
    'To those He lovingly redeemed'[g].

[d]Ps. 105:43; [e]cf. Deut. 32:11; [f]Ps.98:3; [g]Isa. 63:9

ב׳ א׳ ה׳ אוהב את עמו ישראל

---

[34] Cf. Midrash Lev. Rab. 21, 1, ed. Wilna, 1878, f. 29v. col. i.
[35] Cf. Mekiltā, *bĕ-šallaḥ*, 4, ed. I.H. Weiss (Vienna 1865), f. 36v. A parallel Hebrew and English text of the Mekhilta de-Rabbi Ishmael was published in the Schiff Library of Jewish Classics by J. Z. Lauterbach (3 vols; Philadelphia 1933f.).

אמת ואמונה ... ומלכותו ברצון קבלו עליהם משה ובני ישראל לך ענו שירה

(iii) (a)

נוראות על הים^{j} מעשיו ונפלאותיו במצולה^{i} **א**ודה חסדו הפלא^{h}

Thanks be to God, for wonders wrought
In mercy,^{h} deeds tremendous,^{i} fraught
   'With marvels at the sea'^{j}.

^{h}cf. Ps. 21:22; ^{i}Ps. 107:24; ^{j}Ps. 106:2

רוגע הים^{l} במושב זקנים^{k} אגדלה   **ב**קהל עם אהללה

Where folk foregather, let me praise
Him, yea, midst them on whom age weighs:^{k}
   'His will makes rough the sea'^{l}.

^{k}Ps. 107:32; ^{l}Isa. 51:15

ירעם הים^{n} גאו גלים נגדו^{37} **ג**זבר^{36} בנטות ידו^{m}

Moses^{36} but raised his hand,^{m} the roar
Of waves responded,^{37} ever more
   'Thunderous raged the sea'^{n}.

^{m}cf. Exod. 14:26; ^{n}Ps. 96:11

ויעמד הים^{o} אז נקרע בחלחלה   **ד**גול^{38} בכבודו נגלה

When God^{38} revealed his glory, past
Compare, the ocean quaked, aghast,
   'and stock-still stood the sea'^{o}.

^{o}Jon. 1:16

---

[36] b. Bek. 5a (R. Yoḥanan b. Zakkai): 'Moses our teacher was a faithful treasurer (גזבר), skilled in accountancy'.

[37] Cf. Mekiltā, ibid. (the sea resisted Moses' command, delivered in God's name, that it divide, until God revealed Himself).

[38] Solomon, the lover in the Song of Songs, described (5:10) as being *dāgūl mē-rĕbābāh*, 'outstanding in a myriad others', is in Jewish exegetical tradition allegorized as God, the beloved as Israel.

מה לך הים[p]   גאון גליך איפוא   **ה**שיבו[39] נאמן בזעפו

And Moses, God's true servant,[39] said:
'Where are thy boisterous billows fled?
     'What aileth thee, O sea?'[p]

[p]Ps. 114:5

אל תוך הים[r]   שרי יהודה רגמו[q40]   **ו**שבטי יה הממו

Then 'twixt God's tribes rose argument
Who should go first,[q40] till Judah went
     'Marching right through the sea'[r].

[q]Ps. 68:28; [r]Exod. 14:23

במצלות ים[t]   היתה יהודה לקדשו[s]   **ז**כה מלוכה להשרישו

And thus his seed to kingship[s] came,
Whose fathers praised God's holy Name
     'Where deep had flowed the sea'[t].

[s]Ps. 114:2; [t]Mic. 7:19

מעמקי ים[u]   דרך לעבור גאולים   **ח**צה לגזורים ומולים[41]

He split the depths, that those whose pride
Was circumcision's mark,[41] might stride
     'Ransomed right through the sea'[u].

[u]cf. Isa. 51:10

---

[39] Mekiltā, loc.cit. (Weiss, 37r). *ne'ĕmān*, 'faithful one', = Moses, so described at Num. 12:7.

[40] Mekiltā, 5 (Weiss, 37v; exegesis of Ps. 68:28). As a reward for their display of leadership, the territory of Benjamin embraced the site of the future temple, whilst Judah merited kingship.

[41] Mekiltā, 3 (Weiss, 35v); it was in virtue of circumcision that Israel merited the cleaving of the Red Sea (R. Simeon ha-temani). In Hebrew the stem *g-z-r*, 'cut', is used (Ps. 136:13) of dividing the Red Sea; Aramaic, which does not use *m-w-l* as a verb for 'circumcize', regularly uses *g-z-r* in this sense.

תוצהלו מים[v]   פתח באז זמיר   **טוב**[42] בכן שירתו

And then, inspired, did Moses[42] sing,
And all the people, answering,
    'Sang joyful from the sea'[v].

[v]Isa. 24:14

מושל גאות הים[x]   אחר אילים[43] מנגנים[w]   **ישרים** קדמו רוננים

First Israel, then, in answering strains[w]
The angels[43] sang to Him who reigns
    'O'er the majestic sea'[x].

[w]cf. Ps. 68:26; [x]Ps. 89:10

יכסו על ים[y]   ומלמעלה כמין כפה   **כבולוס**[44] צדדים הקפה

A solid block[44] of water froze
On each side, from o'er them rose
    'As covering the sea'[y].

[y]Hab. 2:14

קצוי ארץ וים[a]   אותותיו כי גדלו   **לכל** אפסים נגלו[z]

God's signs to earth's extremes did reach,
Revealed[z] beyond the furthest beach
    'Of the most distant sea'[a].

[z]cf. Ps. 18:16; [a]Ps. 65:6

---

[42] *tob* is here a surrogate for Moses, on the strength of Exod. 2:2.

[43] The angels who had disparaged mankind (Ps. 8:5) were constrained by Israel's song to join in their praise of God with the words of vv. 1 and 10. t. Sot. 6, 5 (ed. M. Zuckermandel [Pasewalk 1881], 304).

[44] Mekiltā, 4 (Weiss, 36r); God congealed the water in two parts, like lumps (βῶλος) of glass, and like a barrel-vault (מין כפה) overhead (*šīrāh*, 6, 48a).

הקורא למי הים‎^c   חסין בכח נהדר   **מי** כמוהו נאדר‎^b

Who, Lord, is like Thee,^b who bedecked
In power majestic, dost direct
      'The waters of the sea'?^c.

^bExod. 15:11; Ps. 89:9; ^cAmos 5:8

היא המחרבת ים‎^d   זרועו מחצבת רחב   **נהל** ידידיו באהב

His sword-arm's strength the monster clove:
Leading those whom He loved, he drove
      'A dry path through the sea'^d.

^dIsa. 51:9-10

הפך ליבשה ים‎^f   שבר ראשי תנינים‎^e   **סלעים** הפך זידונים‎[45]

Proud[45] waters, turned to rock, He brushed
Aside, and dragon's heads, all crushed,^e
      'Made dry land of the sea'^f.

^ePs. 74:13; ^fPs. 66:6

בקרקע הים‎^h   תהומות בהם נלחמו   **ערמות** מים נערמו‎^g[46]

Cunningly,[46] banked up^g waters fought:
The depths swamped Egypt's army, caught
      'On its bed neath the sea'^h.

^gcf. Exod. 15:8; ^hAmos 9:3

---

[45] One of the ten miracles effected at the Red Sea turned the water into a field of rocks, Mekiltā, 4 (Weiss, 36a); water is personalized in the poem, as the *arrogant* [element], cf. Ps. 124:5.

[46] נערמו מים, Exod. 15:8, is treated as a *double entendre*: first, the waters are 'piled' in *heaps* (ערמות), and secondly they are '[infused with tactical] *shrewdness*' (ערמה). Mekiltā, *šîrāh*, 4 (Weiss, 48r); cf. 5 (*bĕ-šallaḥ*) (Weiss, 46r), on v. 5.

כנד מי הם[k] | נד אחד[j] נצברו | פרורים[47] בעזו פוררו[i]

Crushed[47] as though rubble[i] by his power
There piled into a single tower[j]
    'All water of the sea'[k].

[i]Ps. 74:3; [j]Josh. 3:13; [k]Ps. 33:7

עד נבכי ים[l] | עולים ויורדים משלבים[48] | צמד סוסים ורוכבים

Rider and horse, as though compound
By joinery,[48] together drowned
    'Without trace, in the sea'[l].

[l]Job 38:16

על שפת הים[m] | קשוטי זהב ותורים | קלעם בזה מעטרים[49]

God flung them, with the jewels they wore
And gold embroidered spoils of war,[49]
    'Corpses beside the sea'[m],

[m]Exod. 14:30

בקע הים[n] | נגד אבותם עשה | רבה פלאיו לנוססה

That patriarchs thereon might feast
Their eyes, God wondrous signs increased,
    'Cleaving in twain the sea'[n].

[n]Ps. 78:12-13

---

[47] Mekiltā, 4 (Weiss, 36a).

[48] Mekiltā, šîrāh, 2 (Weiss, 43v), presses the copula of סוס ורכבו to effect a hendiadys of horse-and-rider, so closely fitted and responsive to each other as to constitute a single fighting machine (מגיד שהסוס קשור ברוכבו ורוכבו קשור בסוס).

[49] The Egyptian cavaliers went to war in bejewelled armour, destined to become booty for the Israelites' picking; Mekiltā, 6 (Weiss, 40a); Cant. Rab. on Song 1:11 (ed. Wilna, 11v), col. ii.

שביבילו ראו והליכותיו[o]   ולא נודעו עקבותיו[p]   אלהים בים[50]

They gazed upon his progress,[o] yet
No prints e'er showed where God had set
    Foot, walking[p] on the sea.

[o]cf. Ps. 68:25; [p]cf. Ps. 77:20

תמונת גבור נדמה[51]   יי איש מלחמה   ירה בים[q]

God, to men's fancy manifest
As warrior in armour dressed,[51]
    'Cast the foe in the sea'[q].

[q]Exod. 15:3-4

מפליא מקדם נוראות   עוד יראנו נפלאות[r]   ומטהו על הים[s]

He wrought dread deeds of yore: again
To show us wonders will He deign[r]
    'Like his rod at the sea'[s].

[r]cf. Mic. 7:15; [s]Isa. 10:26

נדחים ידריך בנעלים   והכה לשבעה נחלים   את לשון הים[t]

When He lets exiles dryshod go
Through seven rills, where once did flow
    'An inlet of the sea'[t].

[t]cf. Isa. 11:15

חפשים ידריר שירים   נשארים מאשור וממצרים   ומאיי הים[u]

Survivors, freed – from Egypt some,
Assyria, too, whilst others come
    'From islands midst the sea'[u].

[u]cf. Isa. 11:11

---

[50] אלהים בים is not a biblical quotation.
[51] Mekiltā, šîrāh, 4 (Weiss, 44vf).

מצפון ומים[w]　　　　ינטלם כימי עולם[v]　　　　**מ**ארצות יקבץ לגאלם

Assembled, with redemptive care
As long ago,[v] from everywhere –
　　　'The north, and from the sea'[w].

[v]cf. Isa. 63:9; [w]cf. Ps. 107:3

חצים אל הים[z]　　　　מים חיים וירפאו[y]　　　　**ב**חצרות אלהינו[x] יצאו

Healed[y] shall they be, by waters' gush
That springs from God's own courts,[x] to rush
　　　'With life, to either sea'[z].

[x]Ps. 92:14; [y]Ezek. 47:9; [z]Zech. 14:8

הולכים אל הים[b]　　　　ומן המקדש[a] מפכים　　　　**רב**ים מושכים והולכים

Forth from the shrine they flow,[a] in spate,
Bubbling, tumbling, animate,
　　　'Descending to the sea'[b].

[a]Ezek. 47:12; [b]Eccl. 1:17

קציריה עד ים[d]　　　　עצי מאכל לתרופה[c]　　　　**יע**לו על שפה

And on the banks grow herbs to pick
That nourish, and will cure[c] the sick,
　　　'Reaching the very sea'[d].

[c]cf. Ezek. 47:12; [d]Ps. 80:12

וירד מים אל ים[g]　　　　מגזע ישי[f] שרש　　　　**ק**צין עם[e] יפרש

From Jesse's stock[f] may God mark out
A leader[e] for his flock to sprout,
　　　'And rule from sea to sea'[g].

[e]Isa. 3:7; [f]Isa. 11:1; [g]Ps. 72:8

עשה את הים^i יקם יי את דברו^h **ב**ימינו יופיע הדרו

His glory in our days appear,
To prove God's word,[h] fulfilled, is here –
    'That God, who made the sea'[i].

[h]1 Sam. 1:23; [i]Jon. 1:9

(iii) (b)

טלאיו נהל^j כאומן מושיע וגואל^k

יקר זיוו ראו והכירו כבוד אל

כלכלם דבש מסלע^l החסם בצלו להצאל

במקהלות ברכו אלהים יי ממקור ישראל^{m52}

The lambs whom He redeemed[k] He, gentle, led,[j]
They knew his glory's lustre midst them stayed;
With honey from rock crevices[l] He fed
Them, shielded underneath his very shade.
    'Where men assemble, bless God's Name,
    The fount whence Israel sprang, acclaim'[m52].

[j]Isa. 40:11; [k]cf. Isa.49:26; [l]Deut. 32:13; [m]Ps. 68:27

בגילה ברנה בשמחה רבה ואמרו כלם מי כמוך באלהים ה׳

מלכותך ראו בניך בוקע ים לפני משה

(iv)

מפעל **נ**וראותיו^n **ס**פון מי לגדלהו

עוצם **פ**לאיו אשר הפליא למענהו^o

צמח **ק**דושיו אני ולי מורשה לקלסהו

זה אלי ואנוהו אלהי אבי וארוממנה^{p53}

How He effects his acts,[n] none may descry;
Who, then, shall priase that mystic power in deeds
Wrought for Himself?[o] 'Our heritage!' we cry,
Whose ancestry to holy forbears leads:
    'This is my God, Him will I praise,
    Lauds to my Father's God I raise'[p53].

[n]cf. Ps. 66:6; [o]cf. Prov. 16:4; [p]Exod. 15:2

זה צור ישענו פצו פה ואמרו ה׳ ימלך לעלם ועד

---

[52] The Israelite infants born in Egypt whom God (as exegesis of the verses quoted was deemed to show) had sustained with honey and concealed in the ground, were at the Red Sea the first to recognize his revealed presence, exclaiming 'this is my God' (Exod. 15:2; b. Soṭ. 11b); some, as yet unborn, broke forth into song from the very womb – from Israel's 'fount' (t. Soṭ. 6, 4 [Zuckermandel (n. 43), 303f.]).

[53] Since the seventh day of Passover involves no halakhah for ceremonial, beyond that current from the beginning of the festival, there is no occasion to introduce a běkōr piece (see above, pp. 209-10, (vi) (a)).

ונאמר כי פדה ה' את יעקב וגאלו מיד חזק ממנו

(v)

רכב על כרוב^q ברקים רב' מלכי
שלח ממרום המשני^s ממים המשיכי
תיומתי רעיתי פץ קומי ולכי^t
כי אמנם כי גואל אנכי^u

My king shot lightnings[r] from his cherub steed,[q]
Out heaven saved me, pulled from ocean clear,[s]
Then spake: 'Arise, beloved, come forth,[t] freed,
    'Tis I, bringing redemption, I am here'[u].

[q]cf. Ps. 18:11; [r]Ps. 18:15; [s]Ps. 18: 17; [t]cf. Song 2:10; 5:2; [u]Ruth 3:12

ב' א' ה' מלך צור ישראל וגאלו

השכיבנו ה' אלהינו לשלום ... ופרוש עלינו סכת שלומך

(vi) (b)

מתי אבוא ואראה פני אלהים^v להקבילה
נוי חומות מגיעות כסא כבוד⁵⁴ למעלה
חיל וארמון ומשפטו והעיר על תלה^w
מכלל יופי^x יופיע כעיר שחברה לה^y
במסלה בית אל עולה^z שרידי גולה להגילה
אלהים יכוננה עד עולם סלה^a

When, when shall I God's shrine restored as pilgrim greet,[v]
Its walls made fairer yet, reaching his very throne,[54]
Jerusalem rebuilt, her halls once more the seat
Of justice[w] – crown of beauty,[x] come into her own,
Concord within?[y] Seeking his temple,[z] exiles' feet
    The highway tramping, bring her joy, the day
    'When God shall once more stablish her for aye'[a].

[v]Ps. 42:3; [w]Jer. 30:18; [x]Ps. 50:2; [y]Ps. 122:3; [z]cf. Judg. 21:19; [a]Ps. 48:9

---

[54] A tannaitic dictum preserved in Cant. Rab., on Song 7:5 (ed. Wilna, 37r, i), asserts that in messianic times Jerusalem will extend not only outwards but also upwards, and will attain contact with the divine throne.

נכספה גם כלתה נפשי^b אל יופי מכלוליה^c
מדי חדשה ושבתה^d להראות תמיד עליה
בעלות כעב קרואיה^e לשלש פעמי רגליה^f
לסבב ציון ולהקיף ולספור את מגדליה^g
ברניות נוספים⁵⁵ לה למשמר נוי זבוליה
יקראו לירושלם כסא יי ונקוו אליה^h

For her fair diadem^c my heart each sabbath yearns,^b
Each moon,^d there to attend at feasts three times each year^f
Amid her guests, the throng that like a cloud returns,^e
To circle Zion, count each turret ringing her,^g
Defences doubled,⁵⁵ God's protection to confer,
      On splendid palaces, 'when men shall call
      Jerusalem God's throne, where gather all'^h.

^bPs. 84:3; ^ccf. Ps. 50:2; ^dcf. Isa. 66:23; ^ecf. Isa. 60:8; ^fcf. Deut. 16:16; ^gcf. Ps. 48:13; ^hJer. 3:17

חכיתי לייⁱ אותותיו כימי עולם למשמש
על אדום עשר נגעים עוד יחמש⁵⁶
תהו ובהו^j רומי לשמש
ועליך ציון כבודו יראה^k בקר ורמש
יי לאור יומם יהיה שחר ואמש
לאור עולם לא יהיה לך עוד השמש^l

I wait on Godⁱ for portents, like to those of old,
To bring on Rome primeval chaos^j as her fate,
Ten plagues which He, as then, shall multiply five-fold,⁵⁶
His glory meanwhile o'er thee, Zion, radiate^k
Even and morn, when God Himself, early and late,
      'For ever and a day shall make thee bright,
      And thou shalt no more need the sun for light'^l.

ⁱIsa. 8:17; ^jcf. Isa. 34:11; ^kcf. Isa. 60:1; ^lcf. Isa. 60:19

---

⁵⁵ b. B.B. 75b (Resh Laqish), on the fantastic enlargement of messianic Jerusalem. *bīrānī* is tentatively identified by S. Krauss, *Griechische und lateinische Lehnwörter*, vol. 2 (Berlin 1899), 146, as formed from φρουρά or φρούριον, but ?

⁵⁶ Pesiq. Rab. Kah., *wa-yĕhi ba-ḥaṣi ha-láylāh*, end (ed. B. Mandelbaum [New York 1962], 1, 133f.; ed. S. Buber [Lyck 1868], 67vf.) envisages the plagues of Egypt as each foreshadowing the ones to be inflicted on the enemy in the war preceding the messianic age. The device of R. 'Aqiba (Mekiltā, 6 [Weiss, 40v]) is then applied, the five items listed in Ps. 78:49 being treated as a multiplier for each of the ten plagues.

מאור משרתיו יזהיר כזהר הרקיע[m] להתחדש
הנותר בציון קדוש יאמר לו[n] להתקדש
אדיר יי שם[o] לא יעברנו טמא[p] להדש
לא יוסיף לבוא בו ערל[q] וקדש
שרידים אשר יי קורא[r] יכנסו לפרדס[57]
לבשי בגדי תפארתך ירושלם עיר הקדש[s]

His servants, new illumined, shall as heaven shine,[m]
Zion's survivors, each and all holy proclaimed,[n]
When none impure[p,q] shall dare, next majesty divine,[o]
Trample defiant, bent on purposes ill-famed:
That remnant, by God summoned,[r] each one holy named,
     To paradise:[57] 'with holiness for vest,
      Jerusalem, in glory be now dressed'[s].

[m]Dan.12:3; [n]Isa. 4:3; [o]cf. Isa. 33:21; [p]Isa. 35:8; [q]Isa 52:1; [r]Joel 3:5; [s]Isa. 52:1

בראש חמשה הרים[158] מקדש אל לכוננה
בית אלהים תחת זיו כבודו לגוננה
ירחיבו אהליה יריעות משכנותיה יטו[u] שכנה
עולה ומרחבת למעלה ונסבה ורחבה[v] בעליונה
קבוצי גליות מתקבצות ונחות[59] בבית מלונה
ופדויי יי ישובון ובאו ציון ברנה[w]

Her temple on five mountain peaks[158] will God restore
Beneath his glory's irridescence to protect
Their tents, spread ever wider, stretching more and more,[u]
The city rising higher,[v] heaven to reflect,
A lodge where exiles, gathered home,[59] in groups collect:
     'When those whom God redeems back He shall bring,
      And marching Zionward, for joy they sing'[w].

[t]cf. Isa. 2:2; [u]cf. Isa. 54:2; [v]cf. Ezek. 41:7; [w]Isa. 35:10

חזק ואמיץ לעינינו רוחו הטובה יעיר[x]
שנת גאולה[y] יראנו רב וצעיר
מיד בן נכר יפצנו[z] מיד בני שעיר
קול מהיכל קול שאון[a] מחריביו יסעיר
חומת אש סביב[b] לה שלם ישלם המבעיר[60]
התפללו בעדה ודרשו את שלום העיר[c][61]

---

[57] Cf. t. Ḥag 2, 3 (Zuckermandel, 234).
[58] Pesiq. Rab. Kah., *qūmî 'ōrī* (ed. Mandelbaum, 1, 321; ed. Buber, 144v), where one MS lists Mount Hermon alongside Sinai, Tabor, Carmel (and Zion).
[59] See n. 54.

May God in might before our eyes his spirit wake[x]
And show us, young and old, at last the year is near
For our redemption,[y] from the stranger's grasp to shake
Us free[z] from Rome. Then, from his temple, may we hear
The sound of war,[a] those who would raze it vanquished sheer.
    God fired her once, but, as her wall of fire,[b]
    Repays:[60] 'in prayer the city's peace desire'[c].[61]

[x]cf. Ezra 1:1; [y]Isa. 63:4; [z]cf. Ps. 144:11; [a]cf. Isa. 66:6; [b]Zech. 2:9; [c]cf. Jer. 29:7

ב׳ א׳ ה׳ הפורס סכת שלום עלינו ועל כל עמו ישראל ועל ירושלם

    We now survey briefly the poet's handling of the themes structurally associated with the 'movements' that constitute the *ma'ărābōt* as a conventional liturgical complex (see above).

    (i) *Sunset as part of the divine order.* The occasion for which this particular series was composed commemorates one of the two most spectacular, and indeed crucial chapters in Jewish history, the other being the theophany and law-giving at Sinai. Naturally enough, this circumstance colours each of the movements: it is integrated into the first by reference to the simultaneous presence, supernaturally effected, of light and darkness throughout the night of the Egyptians' pursuit (Exod. 4:20).

    (ii) *God's love for Israel.* History, as assumed to evince the hand of providence, constitutes one co-ordinate of Judaism, the other being Jewish response thereto in the light of a few, simply stated, matters of faith, i.e., in a nutshell, covenant-theology. This is here articulated by reference to the covenant with the patriarchs, and in particular the trust displayed by Abraham (והאמין בה'), in the face of adversity (Gen. 15:6), who was apprised by God of his descendants' 400 years' bondage and their ultimate deliverance by divine vindication (vv. 13-14).

---

[60] b. B.Q. 60b. R. Isaac Nappaḥa applied the law regarding restitution for conflagration (Exod. 22:5) to God, who, having Himself set fire to Zion (Lam. 4:11) will, in recompense, become her wall of fire (Zech. 2:9).
[61] See below, p. 226.

(iii) (a) *The historical reference of the festival.* The rich exegetical embroidery of the biblical account of the crossing of the Red Sea in the Mekiltā is exploited by the poet, who has succeeded in finding appropriate biblical quotations ending with ים, 'sea', to conclude every line of this section except for one, where he has had to improvise. At first sight, the concluding quotation from Jon. 1:9 ('God, who made the sea') would seem to be something of an anticlimax: but I suspect that it has been deliberately reserved as the keystone, in order to glance at the rabbinic theologizing of miracle as being in fact implicit in the laws of nature, as yet imperfectly understood. The formula by which this is expressed involves precisely the dividing of the Red Sea: 'Rabbi Jonathan (*v.l.* Yoḥanan) said, "[at creation] God imposed conditions (תנאין) on the sea, that it would be divided before Israel; the text (Exod.14:27) recording that the sea returned to its *normal flow* (לאיתנו) hints at לתנאו, according to God's stipulation".'[62] Despite the exegetical fantasies which, in the foregoing, are treated as poetically, if not indeed factually true, the cosmic order – the universe was not created by God as a chaotic entity (לא תהו בראה, Isa. 45:8) – remains uncompromised.

(iii) (b) *Divine uniquity* is correlated with its instinctive recognition and acknowledgement by Israel, exemplified here by the response of children as yet unborn (exegesis of Ps. 68:27).

(iv) *Divine sovereignty.* The historical dimension is highlighted by the climactic quotation from the Song of the Sea (Exod. 15:2). The notion that the miracles associated with the crossing of the Red Sea may, ultimately, tell us more about the transcendent nature of the Deity than about Israel's predicament, hemmed in between the shore and Pharaoh's army, seems to be hinted at in the citation of Prov. 16:4, which states that all God's works (including, that is, the wonders here rehearsed) are 'for Himself' (למענהו; see Rashi, *in loc.*).

(v) *Divine redeemership.* The miraculous 'stage effects' are almost reduced to a side-show, as it were the fireworks at the conclusion of a wedding reception, by

---

[62] Gen. Rab. 5, 4 (5) (ed. J. Theodor [Berlin 1903], p. 35; ed. Wilna, 17r, i).

reference to the reciprocity, of which conjugal love is the metaphor, of God and Israel, allegorically read into the Song of Songs and then 'historicized' in its targumic paraphrase[63] in terms of events beginning, effectively, with the redemption from Egypt.

(vi) *Peace*. From the Bible onwards the redemption from Egypt has been viewed as the prototype of future redemption from exile (see, e.g., Isa. 11:15-16; Mic. 7:15). That notion is taken up into the theme of the finale, *viz.* peace in its plenary sense, this being inconceivable without messianic restoration. Giving way to his yearning for this, the poet's reverie presents us with so to speak shots from a news-film of the *eschaton*, showing pilgrims converging on a divinely rebuilt Jerusalem, extended not merely terrestrially, but so spiritually renewed as to reach upward to touch the divine throne itself. An inevitable concomitant, from the standpoint of a European Jew at the time of the crusades, is the destruction of the arch-enemy, Rome, tacitly identified with Christendom: but the poet does not dwell on this aspect with any exuberant triumphalism, although, just before the close, the theme is briefly resumed. Rather he focuses on the purification and spiritual renewal which, he takes it for granted, will be integral to Israel's return to Zion, seen primarily as the fulfilment of the divine purpose rather than as the amelioration of Israel's material fortunes. Was not the land of Israel a land 'for which the Lord thy God careth (דורש), the eyes of the Lord thy God are always upon it' (Deut. 11:12)? It is this thought, surely, which has prompted his concluding crescendo, with Jer. 29:7 as its climactic chord – a brilliant stroke, and one of such astonishing boldness as to leave the reader dazed at first. Jeremiah's counsel to the Babylonian exiles to pray for the prosperity of the city of their domicile and to seek its peace (ודרשו את שלום העיר) has been taken for granted, as part of the civic stock-in-trade of the Jewish diaspora; it is here transmuted into an appeal to the poet's fellow-worshippers, to concentrate their prayers on the restoration of Jerusalem, in the name of which he will doubtless have assumed that the word שלום

[63] Outlined by R. Loewe, 'Apologetic Motifs in the Targum to the Song of Songs', in A. Altmann (ed.), *Biblical Motifs Origins and Transformations* (Studies and Texts 3; Cambridge, MA 1966), 169-73, whence summarized by M. H. Pope, *Song of Songs* (Anchor Bible; New York 1977), 95-96.

was integral. It would be hard to find a more spectacular example of the manner in which exegetical polysemy acts as a refracting mirror. Those who were trained in the school of Ishmael discovered a pointer to this in Jeremiah's own words (Jer. 23:29):[64] 'is not my word like a fire, saith the Lord, and like a hammer that breaketh the rock in pieces?' On which they remarked that in the same way that a hammer-blow can generate a plethora of sparks, so each divine utterance at Sinai was 'divided amongst' all the seventy languages. The ideal of the exegete is to emulate the methods of his Master.

This study has addressed itself to explaining the aesthetic structure of one particular form of mediaeval Hebrew poetry, and thus has concerned itself primarily with form. In conclusion, it is worth asking to what extent the content of the specimens studied here may be of significance to those whose interest lies in other aspects of Judaism, its values and its experience.

In regard to theology – that is, principles of faith as linked to ethnic identity in Jewish self-account – liturgical poetry is evidence, as William Horbury has explored,[65] of a tradition of devotion, conviction, and optimism articulated in terms of symbols first formulated in early rabbinic Judaism, and maintained intact in face of appalling catastrophe condoned by the misunderstanding, often the overt hostility, of western Christendom: a steadfastness, that is, which, on Christian premises, could not be accounted for otherwise than as the Jewish purblindness or, more charitably, the invincible ignorance[66] that formed part of the dispensation of providence. Such staunchness would have been dismissive of any temptation to jettison messianism in the light of contemporary realities, although a very few talmudic *dicta* might have provided occasion, perhaps even support for so doing.[67] The halakhah could operate

---

[64] b. Shab. 88b.

[65] W. Horbury, 'Suffering and Messianism in Yose ben Yose', in W. Horbury and B. McNeil (eds), *Suffering and Martyrdom in the New Testament* (Cambridge 1981), 143-82.

[66] For a bibliographical starting-point regarding this, see 'Invincible Ignorance', in F. L. Cross and E. A. Livingstone (eds), *Oxford Dictionary of the Christian Church* (2nd edn; 1974), 711.

[67] b. San. 99a, R. Hillel (II); 98b, Rabbah.

with efficient flexibility (within predetermined parameters) as a machine for maintaining the viability of Jewish diaspora existence in the light of economic facts and political conditions; what it firmly refused to do was to treat such arrangements, however established a convention they might become, as anything other than a temporary arrangement dictated by the paramount necessity of preserving Jewish identity and witness. Nor, in northern Europe, were its masters exposed, as was the Jewish intelligentsia of the Sephardic world, to the challenge of Aristotelian philosophy and science. To countenance any historical revisionism that would involve, as its corollary, theological reorientation, even though the Jewish concept of monotheism remained uncompromised, was something that neither rabbinical leadership nor popular instinct would have entertained.

At the same time, the historian would do well to exercise circumspection as to the evidential value of this type of writing in regard to social reality. This is not to ignore sentiments of hostility towards 'Esau' or 'Se'ir', i.e. Rome as symbolising Christendom, the virulence in the expression of which is scarcely surprising in a situation where outrages against local Jewish communities were a fact of life. Crusaders frequently harried those on their route; in Worms itself, in 1096, 800 were massacred or resorted to self-immolation, as did the Jews of York in Menahem b. Jacob's own lifetime (see above, n. 32). Whereas Judah Ha-levi, resident in Toledo after its conquest by Alfonso VI in 1085, could view both Chrisianity and Islam in terms of *praeparatio messianica* for the universal acceptance of Judaism,[68] amongst Ashkenazic Jewry a completely negative attitude to Christianity was deeply engrained. Nevertheless, to build this up into a notion of absolute *apartheid* between those living in the Jewish quarter and their fellow-citizens outside appears unwarranted. A substantial degree of social separateness was indeed the case, due not only to psychological reserve on either side, but not least to Jewish dietary considerations: the rabbinical toleration of joint drinking sessions of Jews and Christians in twelfth-century

---

[68] *Kūzārî*, 4, 23 (English trans. H. Hirschfeld, *Kitab Al Khazari* [2nd edn; London 1931], 200); cf. 1, 111 (Hirschfelld, 68).

England is recorded,[69] in a Jewish source, with astonishment. But Menahem b. Jacob and his fellow-worshippers can hardly have been unaware of efforts by royal officers and bishops to protect local Jewries from mob violence; in 1096 the Jews of Worms had taken refuge in the episcopal palace, but were overwhelmed. Jer. 29:7, deftly turned on its head by Menahem (see above, pp. 226-27), was generally acknowledged as enjoining loyalty to the secular authority, and the similar sentiments of R. Hananiah[70] would be adduced by R. Yehi'el of Paris as his last (reported) word at the disputation there in 1240.[71] Neither commercial relations with gentile clients seeking loans, nor administrative negotiations with the local authority, nor service on juries empanelling both Jews and Christians as recorded from England,[72] could have been conducted amid an atmosphere of constraint suggestive of that obtaining between prisoners and their guards: and the fact that such contacts were in general effective would seem to imply some degree of affability between Jewish and Christian fellow-citizens in the street. If, therefore, historical events commemorated at Jewish festivals linked up, as they naturally would, with awareness of great Jewish suffering personally experienced or within living memory, to give vent to an exuberance of liturgical imprecation directed at the gentile environment symbolised by [the Church and] Rome, one cannot safely extrapolate from it an accurate testimony to the day-to-day deals of Jews and Christians in the middle ages. To do so, would be analogous to concluding that, since annually on 5th November the pope is burned in effigy at Lewes, its Anglican citizens will have nothing whatsoever to do with their Roman Catholic neighbours.

---

[69] *Tōsāpōt* of R. Elhanan b. Isaac of Dampierre on b. 'A.Z., MS Montefiore, 65, 48v (now in the library of the London School of Jewish Studies), *Catalogue*, H. Hirschfeld (London 1904), 14; J. Jacobs, *The Jews of Angevin England* (London 1893), 269, where however the source-reference is incomplete.

[70] m. Avot 3: 2.

[71] J. D. Eisenstein, אוצר ויכוחים (New York 1928), 86.

[72] One such was convened in 1260; H. Loewe, *Starrs and Jewish Charters Preserved in the British Museum*, 2 (London 1932), citing *Calendar of Inquisitions*, 1, 242, no. 747.

Jewish Ways of Reading the Illuminated Bible

Eva Frojmovic

I. Introduction

In this paper, I propose to analyse the images in some illuminated Hebrew Bibles as Jewish readings. My argument is that these images gloss and amplify the biblical text in a way which is comparable to the work of Bible commentators and preachers. They are not just simple text illustrations, i.e. a direct transposition of the text into images; even less are they purely 'decorative'. Of course, they can also be decorative, often very pleasing to the eye; and they can likewise be text illustrations. But there is more: images also interpret for the reader. They constitute creative readings of the text with which they are coupled within the bindings of a book. They can also be readings of other images which preceded them. They speak a language of their own, full of visual codes and clues. Whereas this is sometimes a problem for us, it was a strength for the contemporary reader/viewer who could understand them on his/her level, even where that reader was not a scholar.

Readings through commentary, sermon and image create new meanings. It is in fact such readings which make an ancient text meaningful at all. I propose to ask how we can interpret these medieval documents and monuments in terms of their cultural meanings. Such cultural meanings are specific to their time, since cultures change all the time. Hence we are looking for the meanings illuminated Bibles would have evoked for their contemporaries or near contemporaries, be they scribes, painters or readers/viewers. Such a line of enquiry cuts across the quest for pure origins and lines of descent and development. Some scholars have assumed that themes which are tracable to prototypes in talmudic times retain their meaning unchanged across a millennium.[1] I prefer to follow the working assumption that they take on new meanings for each generation of readers.[2]

A further layer of fascinating readings is that provided by modern scholars. In what follows I will first look briefly at an Ashkenazi manuscript, and then at a well-known group of Sephardi manuscripts. All of them have been studied by eminent scholars, and in reviewing the literature I have found it revealing to follow the modern Jewish readings offered by these scholars.

II. The Schocken Bible

> Until Abraham arose, the Lord of the Universe used to judge the world with strictness: the generation of the flood he punished with a flood of water; the men of the tower [of Babel] he dispersed from one end of the world to the other; the inhabitants of Sodom he destroyed with fire and sulphur. It was only with Abraham that suffering was created to be atonement... (Sifrei Deut. 311)

My first example is the Schocken Bible, located today in Jerusalem.[3] I have chosen this manuscript because of its apparently indeterminate status. It is a Jewish text, but is its illumination Jewish? The question has been posed in terms of the author of the 'work of art' and the 'influences' which s/he was presumably subject to. But that is a very nineteenth century way of looking for meaning, positing anachronistic, because bourgeois notions of artistic authorship onto a period where such standards are not appropriate or certainly not self-evident. Instead, I will try to locate meaning in the reader.[4]

But to find the reader, we must first take some clues from what is known about the scribe and presumed illuminator. The Schocken Bible probably originated

---

[1] As suggested by G. Sed-Rajna, *Jewish Art* (New York 1997), 224, following C. Roth, 'Jewish Antecedents of Christian Art', *Journal of the Warburg and Courtald Institutes* 16 (1953), 24-44.
[2] As suggested briefly by Revel-Neher, 'L'alliance et la promesse', *Jewish Art* 12/13 (1986/7), 135-46, p. 146. I will elaborate on this methodological problem (iconographic tradition versus contemporary context) in an expanded version of this research, to be published in E. Frojmovic (ed.), *Imaging the Self, Imaging the Other*, forthcoming.
[3] Jerusalem, Schocken Library Ms 14840. See B. Narkiss, *Hebrew Illuminated Manuscripts* (Jerusalem 1992; 1st edn. 1969), 102.
[4] Cf. M. Bal, 'Ethics of Reading', in M. Bal (ed.), *Anti-Covenant: Counter Reading Women's Lives in the Hebrew Bible* (Sheffield 1989), 11-18, and A. Manguel, *A History of Reading* (London 1997).

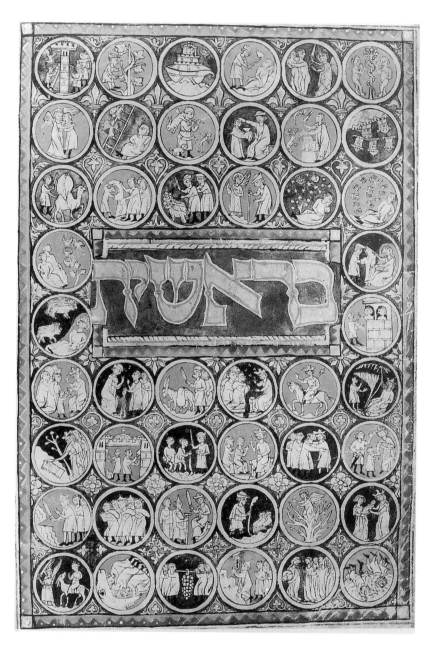

Schocken Bible, Jerusalem, Schocken Library MS 14840
South Germany, ca 1300, fol. 1

in South Germany ca. 1300. It was executed by a scribe called Hayyim, since this name is decorated throughout the Bible text. Also, the formula *Hayyim Hazak* is inscribed at several Explicit places in the manuscript. A scribe of this name is well known at the time: he or his workshop produced the Duke of Sussex Pentateuch and the so-called Tripartite Mahzor.[5] Hayyim, the scribe of the Tripartite Mahzor, apparently had links with the Maharam of Rothenburg, the spiritual leader of thirteenth century Ashkenazi Jewry. Thus the Schocken Bible probably emerged from a scribal workshop with close intellectual links to the religious leadership of Ashkenazi Jewry of the late thirteenth century. This should at least give us some indication of the type of readership which the scribe might have had in mind.

The Schocken Bible contains only one illumination: a full page frontispiece on fol. 1v features forty-six narrative medallions arranged in nine rows around a central panel containing the initial word *Bereshit*, 'In the beginning'. The initial word is highlighted by the application of gold, while the medallions and the scenes which they enclose follow a distinctive colour pattern: the figures are outlined in black ink on a white or parchment ground with barely an indication of colour (cheeks and lips, Benjamin's shirt). These are the colours of writing on parchment: the figures and their features are inscribed rather than painted. The plain background alternates between red and blue.[6] The overall effect of this regular and simple colour scheme is on the one hand strikingly decorative (enhanced by the floral fillers between the medallions). And at the same time, the result is a clear and eminently *legible* page, proposing an aesthetics of legibility and hence reading.

The iconographic programme encompasses, always from right to left (the same sense as Hebrew writing and reading), biblical history from Adam and Eve at

---

[5] B. Narkiss, *Hebrew Illuminated Manuscripts*, 102.

[6] There are two interesting exceptions where the medallion ground is bi-coloured: Joseph and Potiphar's wife and Pharaoh's first dream. In both, red is used to outline the bed on which the reclining figure is lying. In the former scene, this device has the effect of indicating the moral distance of the saintly Joseph from his temptress. In the latter, it indicates the ontological distance between the dreamer and his dream.

the tree of knowledge to Balaam's prophecy, with special emphasis on the stories of the Patriarchs and Moses.

This page has been described in the following terms by Bezalel Narkiss in his authoritative *Hebrew Illuminated Manuscripts*:

> Within the roundels are biblical illustrations, the subjects of which are arranged chronologically from right to left and top to bottom, covering the entire Pentateuch – beginning with Adam and Eve and ending with Balaam and the angel. These roundels resemble arrangements in stained glass church windows of the 13th century. There is evidence that such stained glass also existed in synagogues in the southern part of Germany. The iconography of the pictures, however, could be either Jewish or Christian.[7]

The effect of this description and interpretation is to diminish the Jewishness of this work through, firstly, a formal comparison with church *vitrailles*, and secondly, the assertion that the subject matter is not specifically Jewish, and could in fact be Christian. The two arguments reinforce each other to imply some form of cultural assimilation – a 'German-Jewish symbiosis' *avant la lettre*? A further implication is that the illuminations of a Christian Bible would not have looked that much different.

Let us look at these contentions and their implications in detail. First, the formal comparison with church stained glass windows. This is prima facie compelling since such windows are often organised in roundels. But roundels were not specific to church windows, since they were the result of the available techniques of glassblowing. Narkiss attenuates the link with churches by referring to stained glass windows in synagogues, which however are lost. Yet it seems in any case unlikely from what we know that these would have included narrative scenes of this kind, thought they would have been constructed from roundels. However synagogue windows are not the only ones lost to us: thirteenth-century windows of secular buildings, whether public or private, do not survive either. My point here is that it is not necessary to assume that this page is linked to Christian religious buildings. The

---

[7] B. Narkiss, *Hebrew Illuminated Manuscripts*, 102.

composition of a page from roundels was probably a neutral and shared cultural resource.[8]

Next, the *Bereshit* frontispiece is the only illustration in the book. This would be unthinkable in a Christian Bible of this time, which would of course include not just the 'Old' but also the New Testament. In fact, manuscripts containing only the unmediated Bible text are very rare – most Christians would have known only a fragmented Bible in the form of selected parts inserted in liturgical and exegetical works,[9] such as Petrus Comestor's *Historia Scholastica*, and the *Bible Moralisée*. Any Christian illustrative programme invariably culminates in the crucifixion. Further, the sequence is from right to left, again an extremely unlikely orientation in a Christian Bible or a work of biblical exegesis. The centrepiece of the Schocken Bible's frontispiece is the Hebrew initial word *Bereshit*, 'In the beginning', whose golden letters float on a turquoise field. They float, or hover above the page, because they breach, in a moment of creation and birth, the boundaries of the frame which is supposed to contain this doubly initial word: beginning of the book, beginning of the world, the first cause of the book and its illumination. With all its abundant pictorial narrativity, it is a word-centered page, returning us ever to the act of reading.

'The iconography of the pictures, however, could be either Jewish or Christian'. Finally, the 'iconographic programme' is more than a 'chronological coverage of the entire Pentateuch'. The forty-six medallions are a selection, and, I would argue, a conscious one calculated to convey a meaning. This meaning, however, is dependent on the act of reading by a specific, a Jewish reader. Theoretically, the very same forty-six scenes *could* have been read in a Christian sense by a Christian reader. Or could they? How many Christian readers were used to reading the unmediated Old Testament? How many would have been able to

---

[8] It may be relevant to recall that medieval Ashkenazi synagogues also rely on non-Jewish building types, but not on mainstream church types. Instead the two-nave prayer halls seem to have appropriated a 'neutral' type: the double nave hall used in chapter houses, halls of meeting, hospitals, governmental buildings such as town halls and royal palaces; cf. C. Krinsky, *Synagogues of Europe* (New York 1996).

[9] See J. Trebolle Barrera, *The Jewish Bible and the Christian Bible* (Leiden-Grand Rapids MI 1998).

decipher these scenes without the habitual aid of christocentric teleology to which they were used in the great pictorial typologies which they found in manuscripts, church windows, and cathedral sculptures?

Yes, it is true, if you look at each individual scene separately, that you can find many 'missed opportunities' to introduce 'traditional' Jewish (i.e. midrashic) traits. But midrashic elements were occasionally used even in Christian Bibles.[10] The absence of midrashic elements, and the reliance on the literal sense of the text, does not make this frontispiece Christian. In order to appreciate the Schocken Bible as a Jewish Bible, let's consider for a moment Christian (pictorial) readings of the Bible. Not only would we there find anthropomorphic representations of the Divinity, but the Hebrew Bible would be systematically reconstructed as the 'Old Testament' through Christological references.

The frontispiece of the Schocken Bible does include the anthropomorphic representation of the angels in the Joseph story, the Moses and Balaam episodes. But on the other hand, such anthropomorphism is restricted to angels and is quite common in medieval Jewish artefacts. These scenes are far removed from the overt Christian interpretations and uses of the events of the 'Old Testament'. Such Christian visual interpretations tended to favour scenes which patristic exegesis had understood in a christological sense. This sense was further imposed by representing God as Christ with a cruxifixion halo.

Christian readings of the Jewish Bible relied on the exegetical method of typology, that is the teaching that each event of the Hebrew Bible is a prophesy and foreshadowing of the New Testament, thereby erasing any independent Jewish sense of scripture. There are countless examples of this method in Latin exegesis and art. Perhaps the triumph of typology is the Bible moralisée (Paris 1230-40), where the body of text we call the Hebrew Bible is totally dismembered and in fact incorporated

---

[10] C. O. Nordstrom, *The Duke of Alba's Castilian Bible: a Study of the Rabbinical Features of the Miniatures* (Uppsala 1967).

into a Christian salvific scheme.[11] Typology was the justification of the doctrine of supersession, which claimed that not only was the Old Testament a prophecy of the New Testament, but that the Church (*not* the Synagogue) replaced the Temple.

But we know that the Schocken Bible was intended for Jewish readers, and our own reading must take this relationship between scribe/painter and intended reader into account. Needless to say, the Jews in medieval Europe were not in a position to counter, by openly representing the future coming of their Messiah, in a similarly blatant fashion. However, there were other ways of claiming a Jewish reading.

Narkiss' conclusion that the iconography of the Schocken Bible's 'religious identity' is indeterminate is probably based on the absence of midrashic elements. Such midrashic images would be unambivalently and explicitly Jewish ways of representing the biblical narrative. In contrast, the Schocken Bible represents the stories as the Bible tells them, without any midrashic material – hence there is supposedly nothing Jewish about them. Instead, I would propose that the absence of midrashic material is consistent with one specific Ashkenazi tradition of Bible interpretation. I am referring to Rashi's classic Bible commentary with its emphasis on *peshat*, the plain meaning of Scripture, and its sidelining of midrashic material. I am not here proposing to match the scenes of the Schocken Bible to Rashi's commentary, but rather to see the Schocken Bible as following a strategy of reading analogous to the commentary according to *peshat*.

In the following, let us go through the subjects again, with attention to the selection made for this remarkable page from among the many hundreds of biblical events. What then are the subjects?

The first row is devoted to the history of the first human beings: Adam and Eve's disobedience; their expulsion; Cain's fratricide; Noah's ark; Noah pruning his

---

[11] On this work, see now S. Lipton, *Images of Intolerance: The Representation of Jews and Judaism in the Bibles Moralisées* (Berkeley, CA 1999).

vine; the tower of Babel. Note that 'in the beginning' is not the creation of the world, but Adam and Eve's disobedience.

In the second row, we are transported into the world of the patriarchs: the destruction of Sodom and Gomorrah; the binding of Isaac; Isaac's blessing of Jacob; Esau returns from the hunt; Jacob's ladder; Jacob wrestling with the angel. Again, note how the row begins with a scene of (transgression and) punishment.

The third to seventh rows are devoted to the story of Joseph, beginning with his dreams and ending, in the middle of the seventh row, with Jacob and Joseph finding favour before Pharaoh; but this climax of success in exile is immediately followed by the slave labour of the Israelites, whose redemption is announced in the scene of Moses' finding by Pharaoh's daughter.

The eighth row is devoted to Moses' childhood, youth and the Exodus from Egypt, culminating with Moses parting the Red Sea.

Lastly, the ninth row depicts the Egyptians drowning in the Red Sea; Miriam's dance; the revelation at Sinai; the spies carying the giant grapes of Eshkol; the company of Korah swallowed by the monstrous mouth of the earth; and the non-Jewish prophet Balaam on the she-ass encountering the angel with the sword.

I have already pointed out some of the peculiarities of the cycle, such as its emphasis on transgression and punishment, which are meted out to the transgressors of God's laws and the laws of Noah. Punishment likewise follows the transgression of the Sodomites, the Egyptians at the Red Sea and the party of Korah. Significantly, two scenes in the first row refer to expulsion/dispersion: the expulsion from Eden and the dispersion of Babel. Rows two through nine are devoted to the patriarchs and Moses, the great Jewish heroes of the Pentateuch. As such, they directly frame and narrate the exile in Egypt and the Exodus from this exile. Thus certain thematic strands emerge, focussing on God's justice, which account both for Exile and for Exodus. We are left to imagine how such themes would have resonated with Jewish readers in medieval Germany. There seems to me to be no doubt that the selection of scenes places emphasis on the central Jewish experience of Diaspora, as well as on the articles of faith relating to the punishment of transgressions.

Finally, there is the curious ending. Why Balaam's prophecy? On the face of it, this is a strangely down-beat ending – why not end with the Hebrews conquering the land of Israel? Many answers are possible. One might point to the pressumed reticence against an overtly triumphalist ending and a preference for the ethical teaching of obedience and punishment. But it seems significant precisely that Balaam was a non-Jewish prophet who praised Israel. This brings to mind passages such as the one in *Sefer ha-Likkutim* (4:65a): "'And no prophet arose further in Israel who could be compared to Moses" – in Israel none arose, but among the peoples there arose one, so that they could not say: had we a prophet like Moses, we also would serve God. But who was their prophet? It was Balaam'.[12] Perhaps the choice of Balaam was a response to the Christian polemic against Jews who remain stubborn although, unlike pagans, they cannot claim ignorance of the new dispensation: Jesus was sent to the Jews, but they rejected him in their stubbornness. The use of Balaam in the *Sefer ha-Likkutim* seems the mirror image of this argument: the non-Jews were sent Balaam, so they cannot plead ignorance, for they rejected the (Jewish) truth. The Christian commentaries, on the other hand, interpreted Balaam's prophecy, particularly the final verses ('I shall see him, but not now; I shall behold him, but not near: a star will rise out of Jacob, and a sceptre shall rise out of Israel') as a prophecy of Jesus' birth at Bethlehem. Needless to say, the reader of the Schocken Bible was expected to recall Jewish, not Christian interpretations.

I hope the above provide some suggestions of how the scribe and illuminator of the Schocken Bible could be sure that his Jewish readers would read his handiwork Jewishly: by choosing biblical episodes which highlight the stories of exile and exodus, i.e. the familiar redemptive story of the Passover Haggadah, which would have had a deep resonance in the present exile of medieval Germany. The common

---

[12] M. J. Bin Gorion, *Die Sagen der Juden* (Berlin 1935), 516.

doctrine of exile as punishment would have been balanced by the theme of divine justice against rebels and enemies, and prophetic motifs such as the giant grapes of Eshkol and Balaam's prophecy would have alluded to Israel's greatness and redemption without risking censure. Such a reading takes into account not just the author but also the reader, for whom certain images would have had a specific meaning, a Jewish meaning even without visible 'Jewish elements'. The haggadic elaborations of the Balaam story stress the importance of the non-Jewish prophet blessing Israel.[13] These commentaries thus register the desire for a different relationship between Jews and non-Jews than that which was obtained in reality. In other words, they amplify the biblical text's fantasy of Jewish acceptance and superiority.

III. The Sanctuary Vessels: the Politics of Jewish Memory

'There is no difference between this aeon and the Days of the Messiah, except for the subjugation [of Israel] to the nations' (b. Ber. 34b)

My second case study is a well-known group of Hebrew Bibles from Spain. These manuscripts open with double-page spreads, sometimes even two double-page spreads of the implements of the sanctuary.[14] It is not without meaning that these Bibles were called *mikdashiyah*, 'sanctuary of God', by their contemporaries.[15] These temple vessel pages have been described and classified by Thérèse Metzger in a groundbreaking study.[16] From her research, it would appear that various types emerged in quick succession, between the third quarter of the thirteenth and the early forteenth century.

---

[13] M. J. Bin Gorion, *Die Sagen der Juden,* 513-17; J. T. Greene, *Balaam and his Interpreters* (Atlanta 1992).

[14] See E. Revel-Neher, *Le témoignage de l'absence : les objets du sanctuaire à Byzance et dans l'art juif du XIe au XVe siècles* (Paris 1998).

[15] Thus for example in formerly Letchworth, Farhi Bible pp 1-2 and plate 16, and London, BL Kings I, fol. 2v. See Wieder, '"Sanctuary" as a Metaphor for Scripture', *Journal of Jewish Studies* 8 (1957), 169-73; cf. J. Guttmann, 'The Messianic Temple in Spanish Medieval Hebrew Manuscripts', in J. Guttmann (ed.), *The Temple of Solomon* (Missoula MT 1977), 144 n. 33. See B. Narkiss, *Hebrew Illuminated Manuscripts,* p. 72.

[16] T. Metzger, 'Les Objets du Culte: Le Sanctuaire du désert et le Temple de Jérusalem dans les Bibles Hébraïques Médiévales Eluminées, en Orient et en Espangne', *Bulletin of the John Rylands Library* 52 (1969-70), 397-436; 53 (1970-71), 167-209.

The earliest datable example known is a Bible copied in Toledo in 1277 (Parma, Palatina 2668).[17] Others come from elsewhere in Castile as well as Catalonia and Aragon, and continued to be produced into the early fifthteenth century. More than twenty are known to survive.[18] Considering the known large-scale loss of Hebrew books through a history of persecutions, expulsions and migrations, this is still a very substantial group. Indeed I would agree with Cecil Roth that it must have been almost obligatory to preface your Bible with such a double page – if you were of a certain level of wealth.[19] That these Bibles were treasured family possessions long after they had been written and illuminated is suggested by their subsequent history: several of these were taken to Istanbul when their owners were forced to leave Spain.[20]

In 1953, Cecil Roth drew attention to the group for the first time. He constructed a continuous iconographic tradition reaching back into antiquity: from the embroidered synagogue textiles of the early modern period to the synagogue mosaics of sixth-century Palestine, via the Spanish sanctuary vessel pages and the Leningrad Bibles of the tenth century. The endpoint of his philological quest was a hypothetical archetype (lost, of course): an ancient Hebrew illustrated Bible. This reading is an implicitly apologetic one: it shows that not only have Jewish artefacts been unjustifiably marginalised, but that in fact Christian representations of the Old Testament derived from Jewish antecedents. Roth inserted Jewish art into a privileged position in the genealogy of Western art from which it had been excluded by the indo-germanic and aryan ideologies in the writings of Strzygowsky and his

---

[17] There appears to be some suspicion that the illuminated frontispiece to this Bible was added much later. I have been unable to verify this.

[18] See Appendix

[19] Roth, 'Jewish Antecedents of Christian Art', p. 26. There is also an isolated example in a Catalan Mahzor of ca. 1280, JNUL 8.6527 (*Books from Sefarad*, pp. 61, 65).

[20] Paris BN hebr 7 (bought by the French ambassador to Constantinople before 1620); Paris BN hebr 31, from Colbert's library, was acquired in Constantinople in 1676; see M. Garel, *D'une main forte: Manuscripts Hébreux des collections Français* (Paris 1992), 73; two copies are today in Istanbul's Karaite synagogue. I have been unable to verify the provenance of the other copies.

like.[21] A side-effect of the 'continuous hypothesis' was to create a vision of a unified and continuous, quasi-national cultural tradition for Judaism. A continuous tradition has also been assumed by Carl Nordstrom, who however showed some awareness that the continuity thesis and the thesis of medieval rabbinic inspiration (see below) contradict each other. These scholars trace iconography as a disembodied, almost metaphysical entity or substance. The Jewish lack of territory (prior to 1948) is compensated by a national art. But what is the meaning of this national art? Roth conceptualises Bible 'illustration' as purely artistic, a 'convention' of decoration.

This continuous historiographic thesis has been challenged by Joseph Gutmann and Thérèse Metzger on the grounds that the monuments from different periods do not display the same iconography. According to these scholars, the ancient synagogue mosaics represent synagogue interiors with festival symbols; the tenth-century Bibles are illustrated with plans of the Tabernacle in the Wilderness; the Spanish Bibles are prefaced with images of the Temple of Jerusalem. Gutmann and Metzger accordingly stress the innovative nature of the Temple vessels iconography, linking them to the exegetical and halakhic works of Rashi and Maimonides.

Gutmann suggested an interpretation in terms of Jewish messianic belief, based on extensive midrashic source material.[22] Hence, according to him, the Spanish Bibles contain images of the messianic Temple of the future. He supports this assertion by citing exegetical material linking the Mount of Olives motif present in many manuscripts with the vision of the prophet Zechariah. Elsewhere, Gutmann interpreted these images in terms of the 'medieval Jews'... predominant concern – salvation in the world to come'. He concludes: 'Eminently symbolic, their forms, like those of contemporary Christian art, were always conceived of as the vehicles of deep

---

[21] See Zofja Ameizenowa's discussion of Strzygowski's *Spuren indogermanischen Glaubens in der bildenden Kunst* (Heidelberg 1936), in her essay 'The Tree of Life in Jewish Iconography', *Journal of the Warburg and Coutauld Institutes* 2 (1938-9), 326-45.

[22] He quotes Midrashim according to which the temple vessels were not really lost, but hidden, to be restored to the messianic temple: J. Guttmann, 'The Messianic Temple', 129.

spiritual meaning'.[23] Gutmann thus incorporates these images into the realm of (comparative) religion, stressing the links between Jewish and Christian religiosity on an individual level.

Metzger presented a painstakingly detailed descriptive analysis of the Hebrew manuscripts containing representations of sanctuary vessels, from the Egyptian Bibles of the tenth century to the Spanish ones of the thirteenth to fifthteenth centuries.[24] She was perplexed by the variety she found – a variety which resists her attempts at an ordered typological tree according to the principles of classical philology defined in Weitzmann's 'archeology of the image'.[25] She was thus forced to conclude that the various types she describes were all created around the same time (late thirteenth century) and in the same place (Toledo). Her iconographic analysis is focussed on the taxonomic identification of objects and their attribution to either the tabernacle in the wilderness or the Solomonic temple, while she rejects any evidence of messianic elements such as the frequent inclusion of the Mount of Olives and messianically inspired inscriptions (see below). Her most remarkable attempt at interpretation is tucked away in a footnote: 'These were pages of commentary to the text which, by forming a vehicle for rabbinic teachings, constituted a kind of guide for the reading of the chapters of Exodus to which they referred'.[26] But elsewhere, she resists the notion that the double pages were anything other than incomplete illustrations of the biblical narrative.

We are thus left with numerous open questions, not all of which can be addressed here: was there a continuous tradition of symbolic representations of implements of the sanctuary, reaching back to ancient Palestine via Islamic Egypt? Do the various versions of sanctuary vessels constitute types in the philological/archeological sense, i.e. types which form family trees? Do the objects

---

[23] J. Guttmann, 'When the Kingdom Comes: Messianic Themes in Medieval Jewish Art', *Art Journal* 27/2 (1967), 168.

[24] T. Metzger, 'Les objets du culte', 433.

[25] K. Weitzmann, *Illlustrations in Roll and Codex* (Princeton, NJ 1947).

[26] T. Metzger, 'Les Objets du Culte', 433 n. 4.

represented signify the tabernacle in the desert or the temple, or could it be a mixture of both? Where these pages devotional images? Did they have a (political?) message?

They were not 'book illustrations', simple textual illustrations, since they did not appear in the place in the book where the text described the constructions of the tabernacle. The pages of temple vessels are frontispieces. Most of the debate has centred around the identification of various objects, and whether they refer to the tabernacle of the wilderness or the Solomonic temple, or even the messianic temple. This is in my view a realism not appropriate to the period. It is perhaps not surprising that Thérèse Metzger found to her disppointment that many of the splendid double pages are not arranged in a recognisable textual order, and appear to include many mistakes in relation to the authoritative source texts. But such disappointment presupposes that these images were read in the same way in which modern scholars read written texts. More likely these images could be produced and consumed within a wide range of readerly attitudes, ranging from scholarly attention, meditation and devotion to proud conspicuous consumption and the pleasure of gazing at dazzlingly abundant gold leaf. It seems to me then that questions about the cultural meaning of the Sephardi thirteenth to fourteenth century Bibles cannot be reduced to a matter of iconographic continuity.

One way of approaching the questions of meaning is through the framing inscriptions which we find in roughly half of the surviving examples. Arguably, these inscriptions frame the image in more than one sense: they gloss it, they provide a key to understanding, both to the medieval reader and to the modern scholar.[27] The Bible of Perpignan, (Paris Hebr 7, dated 1299) and the Bible of Copenhagen Ms II (dated 1301) both employ the identical inscription. The right hand page, showing the tables of the law and cherubim, the Menorah, the table of shewbreads, the vase of

---

[27] The framing inscriptions have been ignored in Roth and Nordstrom; Metzger discusses them purely for the purposes of identification of objects. Only Guttmann has devoted considerable attention to them, and has used some of them for his interpretation. See J. Guttmann, 'The Messianic Temple', in J. Guttmann (ed.), *The Temple of Solomon* (Missoula, MT 1977).

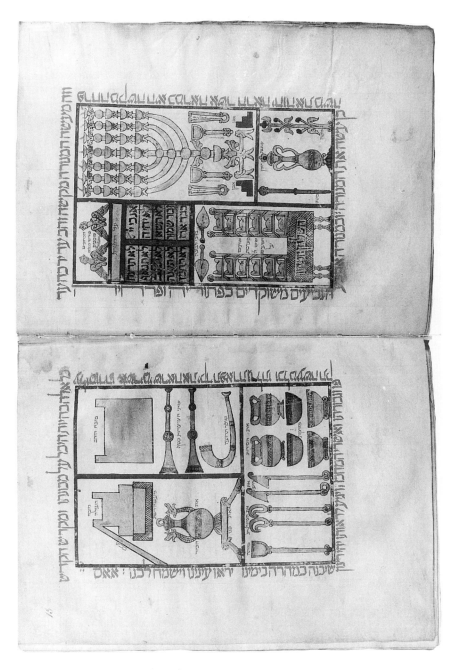

Bible, Perpignan 1299, Paris BN hebr. 7, fols 12v-13

manna, and the dry and flowering rods, is framed by a montage of verses from Numbers and Exodus: 'Now this was how the lampstand was made, out of hammered work of gold. From its base to its flowers, it was hammered work; according to the pattern that the Lord had shown Moses, so he made the lampstand' (Num. 8:4); 'on the lampstand itself there shall be four cups shaped like almond blossoms, each with its calyces and petals' (Exod. 25:34). The description of the Menorah of beaten gold, the textual basis of the wealth of gold leaf in all the sanctuary vessels pages, is combined with Numbers' insistence on the divine inspiration of its making. Implicitly, so I would argue, the inscription establishes also its divine authority and authorship, creating a 'chain of tradition' which bypasses the skilful artist Bezalel in favour of Moses and God himself. The chain of tradition also bypasses the recent rabbinical authorities whose commentaries contributed so much to the specific details of these pages. It thus asserts the substantive identity of rabbinic exegesis with the divine will. This inscription establishes a claim for authenticity.

The opposite page shows the two altars (for the incense and the animal sacrifices), the Levites' basin, the silver trumpets of the Levites, the shofar and various other instruments related to sacrifices. This inscription is an even more complex and original montage of biblical and liturgical allusions: 'All these existed while the Temple was upon its site and the holy Sanctuary was upon its foundation (alludes to the *Avodah* for Yom Kippur). Happy was he who saw the splendor of the beauty of its greatness and all the acts of its power and its might (cf. Esth. 1:4). And happy is he who waits, and lives to (cf. Dan.12:12) see it. May it be your will that it be speedily rebuilt in our days (see daily *Amidah* prayer) so that our eyes may behold it and out heart rejoice.'[28] The inscription links the memory of the temple (as enacted through study and prayer) with messianic expectation.[29]

---

[28] For a slightly varying translation see Ibid.

[29] For other expressions of messianic hope in material culture, see Ibid., 128 and F. Cantera Burgos, *Sinagogas espanolas* (Madrid 1955), 123.

Particularly notable is the triple emphasis on 'seeing' as past and future bliss, relating directly to the visuality of the image.[30] In the past, when the temple stood, those who witnessed the temple worship were blessed. In the messianic future, seeing the restoration of the temple, for which the sanctuary vessels are a metaphor, will be the bliss of the world to come. In the meantime, the bliss of the present is in seeing the painted sanctuary vessels in these two pages. While the colophon of the Copenhagen manuscript is damaged, the colophon of the Paris manuscript allows us to know more about the original reader who contemplated this devotional image: Solomon ben Raphael of Perpignan wrote the manuscript for his own use. Whether or not he also illuminated it, as Michel Garel has suggested,[31] there can be no doubt that this was a book with a personal meaning for its first owner, not a commodity.

But while the scribe and first owner of the Paris Bible BN hebr. 7 produced the copy in an act of personal choice, the message transmitted is implicated in more than an individual's wish for personal salvation. This is suggested by the fact that at least one other copy was made with the same inscription (Copenhagen Ms II). Together, the illuminated pages with their inscriptions encapsulate some of the great forces of religious Jewish culture in Christian Spain, with all its struggles and conflicts. One has to ask oneself: what did messianic restoration and the insistence on the authenticity of rabbinic traditions mean in a Christian country which insisted that Jesus was the Messiah and which did everything possible to undermine the Jewish belief in a restorative Messiah while simultaneously challenging rabbinic authority?

The second type of sanctuary page which Therese Metzger identified in her ground-breaking study, is represented here by two examples: Parma Palatina 2810,

---

[30] Though compare a very similar formulation in Judah Halevy's Ode to Zion 'O Zion, will you not ask how your captives are' whose last stanza begins with the verse 'Happy is he who waits and lives to see your light rising'. See D. Goldstein, *The Jewish Poets of Spain* (Baltimore 1971), 133. Metzger tried to ignore the evidence of this inscription by seeing text and image as disjointed elements: 'this new idea [of the restauration of the temple] does not translate itself other than in *a text which is secondary to the image*, while the iconograhy, absolutely unchanged, remains that of the tabernacle': T. Metzger, 'Les Objets du Culte', 433. Emphasis mine.
[31] M. Garel, *D'une main forte*, 74.

fol. 7v-8r (Catalonia 1340-50), and Brit. Lib. Add. 15250, fol. 3v-4r (Catalan, 1350-70). Both show what distinguishes this type: they place greater emphasis on the menorah, and they include an icon of the Mount of Olives. In both examples the tablets of the law have been shifted to the page opposite the Menorah. T. Metzger has attempted to explain away any messianic meaning by arguing that the Mount of Olives is shown only to indentify the miniatures as representations of the temple rather than the desert sanctuary. However, I feel that it is impossible not to connect the combination of prominent Menorah and Mount of Olives with Zechariah's vision of a time when the Menorah will be lit from the oil provided by the two olive trees which represent the kingdom and the priesthood of the messianic era. Furthermore, the Farhi Bible (1366-82) shows the olive tree standing on the Mount of Olives which here is clearly represented as hollowed out by a large cave; this corroborates the midrashic interpretation briefly proposed by Guttman, according to which the dead of Israel will arrive in the Holy Land in the days of the Messiah via the underground caves of the Mount of Olives.[32] The Mount of Olives of course was a contested site between the world religions, since it was hallowed to Muslims who believed that the resurrection of the dead would take place there, and especially to Christians since Jesus was believed to have ascended from there to Heaven.[33] It seems significant that miniatures incorporating messianic elements such as the Mount of Olives continued to be favoured well into the fifthteenth century. In my view, this success is explicable through the appeal of Zechariah's promise of messianic restoration.

What makes this a Jewish reading is not just the iconography of the sanctuary-temple. After all, Christian Latin mansucripts also represented the sanctuary. As Cecil Roth already found, such representations can be traced as far back as Cassiodorus' *Codex Grandior*.[34] Herrad of Landsberg's *Hortus Deliciarum* of the late twelfth century, which contains a map of the tabernacle in the wilderness, points to

---

[32] J. Guttmann, 'The Messianic Temple', in T. Guttmann (ed.), *The Temple of Solomon,* 132 and n. 30, without mention of the Farhi Bible which however confirms his interpretation.
[33] 'Oelberg', *Lexikon der christlichen Ikonographie* III (Freiburg 1971), 342-49.
[34] C. Roth, 'Jewish Antecedents of Christian Art', 26.

the central issue of disagreement in Jewish and Christian theology. In the Hortus, a bust of Christ appears above the tablets of the law. At issue is the supersession of Jewish faith by the Christian faith, pivoting around the concept of the Messiah.

This was to become the central issue in the Jewish-Christian debates of the thirteenth century and after. For the first time in Barcelona in 1263, Nachmanides had to confront the Christian attempts to prove that the Messiah had already come, that he was divine, in short: that Jesus Christ was the true Messiah. Interestingly, the attack by Pablo Christiani links the Messiah with the temple through the Midrash on Lamentations:

> A certain man was ploughing and his cow lowed. An Arab passed by and said to him: 'Jew, Jew, untie your cow, untie your plough, untie your coulter, for the Temple has been destroyed.' He untied his cow, he untied his plough, he untied his coulter. The cow lowed a second time. The Arab said to him, 'Tie up your cow, tie up your plough, tie up your coulter, for your Messiah has been born'.[35]

But Nachmanides rejects the christological interpretation of this Midrash. Pablo Christiani then engages him in a debate about the correct interpretation of the numerical calculations in the Book of Daniel, which, as Hyam Maccoby has pointed out, were the subject of debates by 'reckoners of the end', i.e. apocalyptic calculations of the end of the world. While Pablo interprets this also christologically, Nachmanides proceeds to offer his own calculation of the end:

> ... from the time that the daily burnt offering was removed until God will render desolate the abomination which removed it – and that is the people of Rome who destroyed the Temple – will be 1290 years; ... And then Daniel says, 'Happy is he who waiteth and reacheth to 1335 days' (Dan. 12:12), thus adding 45 years. And the meaning is that at the first date the Messiah will come, and he will cause the abomination, which worships that which is not God, to be desolate and destroyed from the world; and after that he will gather the dispersed of Israel to the 'Wilderness of the Peoples' (Ezek. 20:35) ... and he will bring Israel to their land, as did Moses our teacher, on him be peace, who was the first Redeemer; and this will take 45 years. And after that, Israel will rest on their land and rejoice in the Lord their God and in 'David their king' (Hosea 3:5), and 'happy is he who waits and reaches those good days' (Dan. 12:12). Now the present date is 1,950 years from the Destruction; so 95 years are lacking from the number given by Daniel. We may expect, then, that the Redeemer will come at that time, for this interpretation is firm, fitting and easy to believe.[36]

---

[35] I quote from the version in the Vikuah of Nachmanides, after H. Maccoby, *Judaism on Trial: Jewish-Christian Disputations in the Middle Ages* (London date), 110.

[36] This translation of the Vikuah of Nachmanides is found in Maccoby, *Judaism on Trial*, 125-27.

Jewish Ways of Reading the Bible

In this remarkable passage, Nachmanides predicts the coming of the Messiah for the year 1358, and the final redemption for 1403. Nachmanides' *Vikuah* was widely circulated in the Jewish community, since it was intended as a help in warding off further Christian missionary activity. The thinly veiled anti-Christian attack (Rome = the abomination which worships that which is not God) was presumably intended for Jewish eyes only.[37] I would like to draw attention to Nachmanides' double reference to the verse from Daniel which is also employed in the inscription of the illuminated sanctuary vessels in Paris BN hebr. 7 and Copenhagen Ms II. One can observe that the 'date' is actually missing in the inscription: '*And happy is he who waits, and lives to...* (Dan.12:12: literally: reaches to...) see it. May it be your will that it be speedily rebuilt in our days'. Instead, the exact date is left open, and combined with the daily prayer for the restoration of the temple, 'speedily in our days'. It is difficult not to draw a connection between this messianic interpretation by Nachmanides, the religious leader of Spanish Jewry at the time, and the use of Daniel in a messianic inscription in the Paris and Copenhagen manuscripts.[38] And beyond that to connect the entire group with a collective messianic hope which at that particular period in that particular place had a specific political edge. Is it then a coincidence that the earliest Bibles with double pages of the temple vessels began to be produced soon after Nachmanides had proposed this interpretation, and that the Paris and Copenhagen manuscripts originated in the kingdom of Aragon, Nachmanides' home country? The extant examples proliferate, it would seem, around the messianic date, and seem to abate after the date predicted for the final redemption. The catalan scribe Vidal Sartori's Saragossa manuscript (Paris BN hebr. 31: scribe Vidal Sartori,

---

[37] The Ramban used the same arguments in section four of the *Sefer ha-Geulah* (*Book of Redemption*). Ch. Chavel (ed.), *Kitvei Rabbenu Moshe ben Nahman* (Jerusalem 1963), vol. 1, p. 291. Cf. Chazan, *Daggers of Faith: Thirteenth Century Christian Missionizing and Jewish Responses* (Berkeley 1989), on the larger theme of Jewish rebuttals of christological readings of the Bible.

[38] On Nachmanides see I. Twersky, *Rabbi Moses Nahmanides (Ramban): Explorations in his Religious and Literary Virtuosity* (Cambridge 1983).

Saragossa 1404), written and illuminated in the year of the 'final redemption', marks in some sense the endpoint of this tradition.[39]

In conclusion, it is probable that the double page of the sanctuary implements could look back to a tradition of remembering the temple which might have reached back into antiquity. However, the religious, cultural and political meaning of this theme is unlikely to have remained unchanged. Like Jewish readings of the Bible, each and every generation rewrote the meanings attached to the memory of the sanctuary. The theme carried very specific meanings in late medieval Christian Spain. The leading idea then would have been that Jewish messianic belief would not be shaken, even in the face of concerted conversionist attempts.

---

[39] For this MS, cf. Sirat and Beit-Arie, *Mss medievaux* (1979), vol. 2, no. 45. A. Blasco and D. Romano, 'Vidal Satorre, copista hebreo', *Sefarad* 51/1 (1991), 3-11. In fact, the famous Kennicott Bible of 1476 is the only dated later example. It is doubtful whether any other mss are later than 1403-1404.

Jewish Ways of Reading the Bible

Appendix

The first list includes only Bible manuscripts which contain(ed) double page spreads (or multiples thereof) of the sanctuary vessels. The second list adds related manuscripts of a different text or with a different but related iconography. Photographic reproductions are indicated in brackets.

1. Cairo, Karaite Synagogue

2. Copenhagen, Royal Library Codex Hebr. II (dated 1301), fols 11v-12r (Roth Plate 6a-b)

3. Florence, Laurenziana Plut. 2.1. (Ferrara 1396), fols 106, 107v (Nordstrom figs 18, 20)
Frankfurt: see New York

4. Istanbul, Karaite Synagogue (1336), pp. 18-19 (Gutmann 1977: figs 37-38)

5. Istanbul, Karaite Synagogue, fol. 3v-4

6. Jerusalem, JNUL 4.5147, fol. 6v (*Books from Sefarad*, p. 17)

7. Formerly Letchworth, Sassoon Collection No 368 (Farhi Bible, scribe Elisha ben Abraham ben Benveniste ben elisha Crescas, dated 1366-82), pp. 1823, 186-7 (Narkiss, *HIM*, and Roth plate 7a-b)

8. Formerly Letchworth, Sassoon Collection no. 16: Rashba Bible, scribe Vidal ben Saul Sartori, Cervera 1383, pp. 6-7 (*A further thirty-three highly important Hebrew and Samaritan manuscripts*, Sotheby's Zurich 21.11.1978, p. 26; Metzger Plate III)

9. London BL Add 15250, fol. 3v-4 (Nordstrom fig. 9-10)

10. London BL Harley 1528, fols 7v-8 (Nordstrom figs 7-8)

11. London BL Kings 1, (1385), fol. 3v-4 (Nordstrom figs 5-6)

12. Milan Ambrosiana MS C. 105 sup.fol.1v-2 (Nordstrom fig. 15-16)

13. Modena, Biblioteca Estense Cod. a.T.3.8., fol. 26v-27 (Metzger Plate II, *Arte e cultura ebraiche in Emilia-Romagna*, p. 177)

14. Modena, Biblioteca Estense Cod. M.8.4., fols 9v, 10, 11 (Metzger Plate II)

15. New York, Private Collection (Formerly, Frankfurt, Stadtbibliothek, Ausst. 4), fols 25v-26 (Nordstrom figs 13-14)

16. Paris BN hebr. 7 (Perpignan 1299), fols 12v013 (Nordstrom, *D'une main forte*, pp. 74-75)

17. Paris BN hebr. 31 (Vidal Sartori , Saragossa 1404), fols 2v, 3r, 4r (Metzger Plate IV, figs 11-12, Gutmann 1977, fig. 39)

18. Paris BN hebr. 1314-15, fols 1v-2 (*Synagoga* [Frankfurt 1961], No. B 18 fig. 47; *Israel a travers des ages* [Paris 1968], no. 551, *Tresors d'Orient* [Paris 1973], no. 59; see M. Garel, *Bulletin de la BN* III/4 [1978], 158-66)

19. Paris, Saint-Sulpice 1933 (Foa Bible), fols 5v-7 (Sed-Rajna, *Jewish Art* [New York 1997], figs. 404-7)

20. Parma Pal. 2668 (Toledo 1277), fols 7v-8 (Nordstrom figs 11-12)

21. Parma Pal. 2810-11, fols 7v-8 (Metzger Plate III, *Manoscritto ebraici della Biblioteca Palatina de Parma/Hebrew Manuscripts from the Palatine Library*, Parma [Jerusalem 1985], front and back covers)

22. Roma, Comunita israelitica No 19 (Barcelona 1325), fols 214v and 216

Sassoon 16 (Rashba Bible): see Letchworth

Sassoon 368 (Farhi Bible): see Letchworth

Related manuscripts:

1. Jerusalem JNUL 8.6527 (Mahzor, Catalan use, prefatory pages in micrography of Psalms and 2 Samuel 23) (*Books from Sepharad,* figs on p. 65)

2. Lisbon BN Ms 72, fol. 60 (Menorah), fol. 316 (Menorah between the olive trees) (Metzger fig. 13-14)

3. London BL Or. 2201 (Toledo, 1300), fol. 2 map of the temple, based on rabbinic exegesis: (Nordstrom fig. 25)

4. Oxford, Bodl. Kenn. 1 (La Coruna 1476), fols 120v-121 (Nordstrom figs 17, 19; C. Roth, *The Kennicott Bible* [Oxford 1957], pl. 8)

5. Oxford, Bodl. Kenn. 2 (Joshua ben Abraham ibn Gaon, Soria 1306), fols (*Convivencia* fig. 48)

Reading the Bible in the Modern Age

'Eshet Ḥayil or *'Ishshah Zarah*:

Jewish Readings of Abigail and Bathsheba, Both Ancient and Modern

Heather A. McKay

I. Introduction

This paper aims to penetrate the ambiguity in the descriptions of Abigail and Bathsheba in the writings of Jewish authors and compare the two women against the biblical criteria for womanly excellence and its opposites. The women's stories state that both became wives of David closely after the deaths of their husbands. The behaviour of each husband was in some way 'wrong', inimical to the success of David's life – from the point of view of the narrator – and each husband's name had an attribution of regional identity attached to it. Each wife had the aura of this marked identity attached to her name more than once in the Hebrew Bible and the different types of 'wrongness' and regional identity of the two deceased husbands taint or tint each of the two women in subtly different ways. Also, their roles as strikingly beautiful wives of David are quite distinct.

Because both women are described in superlative terms in the biblical and secondary accounts of them, albeit in different ways and with different degrees of approbation or disdain, I have chosen to assess them against the two extreme descriptions of 'types' of biblical women: the *'eshet ḥayil* and the *'ishshah zarah*. To aid my study, I will explore the nuances of the attribution of the epithet *'eshet ḥayil* to women in the Hebrew Bible, identifying the qualities that define a 'woman of worth' to discover whether that term could properly be applied to Abigail and Bathsheba. Thereafter, to set that definition more clearly in context, I will distinguish the spectrum of meanings attributed to the term *'ishshah zarah* ('strange' or 'deviant woman') sitting, as it does, uneasily between the term *nokriyyah* ('foreign woman') and the term *zonah* ('prostitute').

The primary source of readings of the two women is the Hebrew Bible, closely followed by its translations[1] and interpretations. I shall first study the biblical text to see how it constructs the natures of the two women by means of the complimentary and less than complimentary phrases or innuendos that are used about them and their origins. Thereafter, in accord with the theme of this collection of essays,[2] I shall look at writings of a range of Jewish scholars from the earliest times and from the twentieth century.

II. Attribution of Delightful Womanly Qualities

The phrase *'eshet ḥayil* occurs only three times in the Hebrew Bible: Ruth 3:11, where it is said of Ruth herself, and in Prov. 12:4 and 31:10, where it is said of an ideal type of woman. I will now analyse the description given of this ideal woman.

A. The Woman of Worth in Proverbs 31

The keynote specification of a woman of excellence or wealth or quality, an *'eshet ḥayil*, is given in Proverbs 31.[3] This woman is reliable above all else, but her loyalty and productive efficiency are coupled with charm and kindliness. She is not said to be beautiful; in fact, her qualities are contrasted with the 'vain' types of charm and beauty (31:30). Implicitly, those personable physical attributes are only of value when linked with the sterling qualities she possesses in abundance. Her qualities, therefore, may be summarized under five main headings. She is (i) reliable, loyal and well-intentioned (31:11-12); (ii) successful in merchandising yet charitable (31:13-22, 24, 27); (iii) charming, cheerful, confident, wise and kind (31:25-26); (iv) loved and

---

[1] The main translation in use is the RSV; the use of other translations will be indicated.
[2] Based on presentations made at the British Association for Jewish Studies Conference, Manchester, July 1999.
[3] See also Prov. 12:4: 'a good wife is the crown of her husband, but she who brings shame is like rottenness in his bones'.

respected by her children and neighbours (31:28-31); and (v) free of misdemeanours and scandals (31:23).

Of course, this description is of an 'ideal' woman, not of any particular 'real' woman, but it does present a more or less rounded and complete picture of the 'perfect' wife in the eyes of the writers of Proverbs. Descriptions of 'real' women in the Hebrew Bible narratives present fewer specific details, but they can, nonetheless, be measured against this set of criteria.

B. Other Respected Women

By piecing together a picture from a variety of biblical and later accounts of Hebrew women who are admired and desired, I find that personal beauty does have a definite role in their characterization. The most highly prized women are beautiful, as well as wise, gracious and persuasive in speech, gesture and action. The women most commonly considered to fit into this category are: Sarah (Gen. 12:11, 14), Rebekah (Gen. 24:16; 26:7), Rachel (Gen. 29:17), Abigail (1 Sam. 25:3), Bathsheba (2 Sam. 11:2), Tamar (2 Sam. 13:1), and her niece and namesake, Tamar (2 Sam. 14:27), Abishag (1 Kgs 1:3, 4), Vashti (Esth. 1:11), and Esther (Esth. 2:7).[4]

Among these ten women, the diplomatic skills of ingenuity and persuasiveness are attributed to four only: Rebekah (Genesis 27), Abigail (1 Samuel 25), Bathsheba (1 Kings 1-2) and Esther (Esther 5-7). But only one woman within the whole Hebrew Bible has the term 'eshet ḥayil applied to her, and that is Ruth. The compliment is given to her in the voice of Boaz (Ruth 3:11): 'for all my fellow townsmen know that you are a woman of worth' (RSV); 'for all the city of my people doth know that thou art a virtuous woman' (KJV); 'all my fellow townsmen know that you are a woman of noble character' (NIV); 'since the people at the gate of my town all know that you are a woman of great worth' (NJB); 'as everyone in town knows, you are a fine woman'

---

[4] *Pace* Loius Ginzberg, *The Legends of the Jews* (trans. Henrietta Szold; Philadelphia, PA 5728/1968), not Rahab (vol. 4, 117), Jael, or Michal (vol. 6, 273). Note also that David is described as beautiful in similar terms in 1 Sam. 16:12.

(TEV); 'for all the assembly of my people know that you are a worthy woman' (NRSV).

As we can see, however, the different translations indicate to us the range of meanings implied by the Hebrew of the verse, for the meaning differs depending on whoever are implied as 'knowing' it. For, if those who 'know' it were male, Ruth would be understood to be a chaste, well-mannered and desirable woman. If they include the female citizens, Ruth would have to obey a slightly harsher behaviour and dress code, that set for a newcomer by the women of the town. Either way, it is clear that Ruth acquits herself in ways that meet the Bethlehem community's rigorous standards.

C. Ruth the Moabitess, a Woman of Worth

Throughout the story that bears her name, the qualities that Ruth has are manifold and are remarked upon by others: Naomi, Boaz, the people of the town and the women of the town – perhaps the strictest judges! Analysis of the portrayal of Ruth's character yields a second, slightly different, set of criteria for an *'eshet ḥayil.*

(1) Gracious and reliable in family matters. Ruth deals well and faithfully with her mother-in-law, Naomi, in Moab, and has persisted in, and insisted on, continuing to do so after Naomi decides to return to Bethlehem (1:8, 18).

(2) Beautiful and desirable, modest and chaste. Ruth's beauty and desirability are no more than implied but implied they certainly are, for although on his arrival at his harvest fields near Bethlehem Boaz first of all greets his workers, immediately after that he asks not about the success of the harvest, but about the provenance – and ownership – of Ruth (2:4-5). Thereafter, realizing that she is very attractive indeed, and appreciating in advance the devastating effect her beauty will have on his work force of casual day labourers, Boaz makes arrangements for her protection (2:8-9). In the subsequent narrative a significant amount of concern is voiced that Ruth be not 'molested', that her sexual integrity can be vouched for (2:21-23). It is during the incident on the threshing floor that Boaz retells the town's evaluation that Ruth is an

'eshet ḥayil (3:11) and after the incident he takes care to preserve her flawless reputation by sending her home in the half-light before dawn (3:14). One can almost hear the gnashed teeth of the disappointed Bethlehem gossips, the women of the town!

(3) Diplomatic and deferential. Ruth knows when and how to humble herself at the appropriate moment, so gaining more favour from Boaz, and also to speak diplomatically to him with a proper regard for the difference in their station in life, going so far as to prostrate herself on the ground (2:10, 13).[5] Ruth uses the truth about her circumstances humbly and convincingly but from her lips it functions as effective flattery.

(4) Successful in the production of healthy, male offspring. After this quasi-betrothal scene, events in the story move quickly (3:18) and near the end of the story the most glowing accolade of all, by male standards, is given to Ruth after she gives birth to Obed. The women of the town congratulate Naomi on having both Obed for a 'grandson' and Ruth as a daughter-in-law and give Ruth the highest accolade that could be given to a woman – in patriarchal terms: she is a woman who is worth more than seven sons (3:14). This is praise indeed!

Measuring Ruth's character and behaviour against the criteria taken from Proverbs 31 shows that she meets them point for point, though the attributes are differently clustered in the two formulations.

Proverbs 31	The Book of Ruth
Reliable and loyal, no misdemeanours and scandals	Gracious and reliable in family matters
Successful in housekeeping	Beautiful and desirable, modest and chaste
Charming, cheerful, confident, wise and kind	Diplomatic and deferential
Loved and respected by her children and neighbours	Successful in the production of healthy, male offspring

---

[5] We should also note that the noted beauty, Queen Esther, also employed prostration tactics when making her most demanding request of King Ahasuerus (Esth. 8:3).

Jewish Ways of Reading the Bible

However, there was one problem that Ruth had to overcome before she could be fully incorporated into Bethlehem society: the problem of 'foreignness', what I will call 'inappropriate ethnicity'. Throughout the story her Moabite origins are stressed repeatedly, particularly in the way she is named. However, her excellent behaviour and demeanour coupled with beauty and charm somehow removed or were able to wipe out that threatened stumbling block to her marriage to Boaz. But for other biblical women that obstacle was not so easily overcome.

III. Attribution of Appropriate Ethnicity

Women who present a character profile other than that of the 'ideal' woman may be indicated in several ways using words whose meanings seem to overlap at times, and at other times to slide into each other or be used as euphemisms for each other. The words used are derived from the roots נכר, meaning 'foreign', as in coming from a different ethnic, geographical or political location;[6] זר, meaning 'strange', as in other or different, not of our group;[7] and זנה meaning 'to practise prostitution'.[8] Whether genuine, ethnic 'foreigness', neutrally regarded and carrying no political or cultic overtones, is ever implied in the biblical narrative is a moot point.

Throughout the Hebrew Bible, foreigners – who are usually males – are considered to be 'other' and to merit different treatment, treatment that is usually less gracious or less generous than that meted to the Israelites' fellow countrymen,[9] in matters of commerce, politics, ritual practices, and marriage.[10]

---

[6] See R. Martin-Achard, 'nekar, stranger', in E. Jenni and C. Westermann (eds), *Theological Lexicon of the Old Testament*, vol. 2 (trans. M. E. Biddle; Peabody, MA 1997), 739-41.
[7] See R. Martin-Achard, 'zr, strange', in E. Jenni and C. Westermann (eds), *Theological Lexicon of the Old Testament*, vol. 1 (trans. M. E. Biddle; Peabody, MA 1997), 390-92.
[8] See J. Kühlewein, 'znh, to commit harlotry', *Theological Lexicon of the Old Testament*, vol. 1, 388-90.
[9] See Gen. 17:12, 27; 31:15; Exod. 12:43; Lev. 22:25; Deut. 14:21; 15:3; 17:15; 23:10; 29:22; Judg. 19:12; Ruth 2:10; 2 Sam. 15:19; 22:45, 46; 1 Kgs 8:41, 42; 2 Chron. 6:32, 33; Neh. 9:2; Ps. 18:44, 45; Prov. 20:16; 27:13; Isa. 2:6; 56:3; 60:10; 61:5; 62:8; Ezek. 7:21; 11:9; 28:10; 31:12; 44:7-9; Obad. 1:11. The only contrary example is Isa. 56:6 that promises that, in the future, some foreigners will be fully accepted into the community.
[10] However, there seems to be a distinction made between a prohibition for a man from 'outside' marrying an Israelite woman and the permitting of the opposite case where a foreign woman marries an Israelite man; Deut. 21:10-13.

In Proverbs (2:16; 5:3, 20; 6:24; 7:25; 23:27) a generalizing view of, mainly female, foreigners is taken. Female foreigners suffer somewhat more stigmatization than males, and perhaps more so in translation. For, possibly as a result of the frequent occurrence of parallelism between different combinations of two or three terms (2:16; 5:20; 6:24, 26; 7:5; 23:27), the noun for a female foreigner, *nokriyyah*, from the root נכר, is translated not as foreigner or immigrant, but as 'adventuress' and the term *'ishshah zarah*, not as incomer or traveller, but as 'loose woman'. *Nokriyyah* is also used in parallel with *zonah*, 'prostitute' (Prov. 23:27), implying something more than the merely alien and exotic in the use of 'foreign' as a descriptor. The three words, in their feminine forms, function as a linguistic cluster, so that whenever one is used, the meanings of the other two are activated.

Generally speaking, foreigners are regarded throughout the Hebrew Bible as deviant and possibly dangerous; and foreign wives likely to be doubly so. Jezebel, for example, is credited with persuading Ahab to worship Baal (1 Kgs 16:31), killing the prophets of God (1 Kgs 18:4), and re-introducing autocratic government (1 Kings 21). Later, she is accused by Jehu of 'harlotries and sorceries' (2 Kgs 9:22) and by the narrator of titivating herself before her death (2 Kgs 9:30), but perhaps a tinge of bathos may be noted there.

Foreign women are apparently regarded as acceptable as wives of Solomon; he marries the daughter of Pharaoh, along with Moabite, Ammonite, Edomite, Sidonian, and Hittite women (1 Kgs 11:1). But in Nehemiah (13:26, 27) Solomon also is castigated for having taken foreign wives and so 'sinned'. Numbers Rabbah takes time to explain that the indolence and lethargy brought about in Solomon by his pleasure-loving Egyptian wife led him to sleep through the daily sacrificial rites; fortunately his mother, Bathsheba, came and woke him and set him to rights.[11] Moreover, in Ezra (10:2, 10, 17-18) women of alien ethnicity are regarded as bringing danger or disaster,

---

[11] H. Freedman and M. Simon (eds), *Midrash Rabbah*, vol. 4 (London 1939), Numbers vol. 1, X.4, 352.

and the males, especially the sons of priests and Levites, are made to divorce their 'foreign' wives.

Throughout the Hebrew Bible certain ethnic groups are always given a bad name or a 'bad character'. With some tribal names the attribution seems to be no more than formulaic with no particular details or reasons given for the animosity: Peruzzites, Jebusites, Ammonites (though Rehoboam's mother was an Ammonite, 1 Kings 14:21), Moabites (though Ruth was a contrary example), Amorites and Canaanites (although the women *may* be acceptable as wives since they can usually be assumed to adopt the loyalties of their husbands; Exod. 6:15; 1 Chron. 2:3).

Some Hittites especially can acquire different degrees of acceptability. Abraham, Jacob and Joseph were buried in a grave that lay in the field of a Hittite (Gen. 25:9; 49:29, 30; 50:13), but the local Hittite women 'wearied' Rebekah (Gen. 27:46) and she did not wish Jacob to marry one of them, although Esau did so (Gen. 36:2). In Exod. 23:28 the Hittites are earmarked to be driven out, but, on the other hand, David has faithful soldiers who are Hittites: Ahimelech (1 Sam. 26:6) and Uriah (2 Samuel 11). In Ezekiel 16 (16:3, 45), where the personified Jerusalem is castigated and harangued by God for her sins, the blame is partly laid upon her parentage: she had an Amorite father and a Hittite mother. It appears that the naming of a person as a Hittite is not enough per se to mark him or her as dangerous, but definitely indicates the possibility of danger.

The use of 'Calebite' of Nabal, Abigail's husband (1 Sam. 25:3) seems to function less as a geographic marker than as a pun on *keleb*, 'dog', implying that he was snappish and ill-natured, a further insult than his given name which means 'fool',[12] though that name can also imply a 'vicious, materialistic and egocentric misfit',[13] the 'typical bait of "wisdom" literature',[14] to use the words of Jon Levenson. Moshe

---

[12] See M. Saebo, 'nabal, fool', *Theological lexicon of the Old Testament*, vol. 2, 710-14.
[13] Jon D. Levenson, '1 Samuel 25 as Literature and as History', *Catholic Biblical Quarterly* 40 (1978), 13-17.
[14] Jon D. Levenson and Baruch Halpern, 'The Political Import of David's Marriages', *Journal of Biblical Literature* 99 (1980), 510.

Garsiel draws further inferences from Nabal's name through the likeness of the consonants to Laban's name, and their repetition in his death notice (לב and לאבן).[15]

This admittedly brief survey shows that sometimes foreignness is not regarded as a danger and at other times it is. The evaluation seems to be determined by factors other than the mere ethnicity of the person; though their gender can also be a relevant factor. This leads me to the final characteristic of an 'eshet ḥayil.

(5) Of appropriate or acceptable ethnicity. Ruth is clearly a foreigner; her different ethnicity is a key feature of the story. The narrative tells of Naomi's journey to Moab and of her return to Bethlehem with the determined Ruth accompanying her. There is reference not only to the two lands, but also to the differnt gods of the two lands (Ruth 1:16). Throughout the Book of Ruth Ruth is five times referred to as 'Ruth the Moabitess', three times in the voice of the narrator, and twice in that of Boaz, and the name of the land, Moab, is mentioned seven times in the book. Yet Ruth's foreignness does not, as so often is the case in biblical narratives, render her dangerous or deviant.. Her behaviour and ways make her acceptable to the Bethlehem community in general as expressed in the voices of the women and to Boaz, the wealthy landowner. Outsider ethnicity is evidently not an insuperable barrier to total acceptance within Israelite society and scripture.

IV. How Do Abigail and Bathsheba Match this Profile?

In the narratives of the Hebrew Bible there are similarities and differences in the accounts and evaluations of Abigail and Bathsheba as if the narrator were measuring them against characteristics similar to those identified above from Proverbs 31 and the Book of Ruth. Also, the similarities and differences between Abigail and Bathsheba seem to have caught the attention of a variety of writers through the centuries and many compare, or, at least, juxtapose the two women.

---

[15] Moshe Garsiel, *The First Book of Samuel: A Literary Study of Comparative Structures, Analogies and Parallels* (Ramat-Gan 1985), 127.

Jewish Ways of Reading the Bible

My selection of Jewish authors cannot include Philo, since he mentions neither of the women. However, Josephus writes of both, although he does not draw comparisons between them.

Of modern authors, Joseph Heller in *God Knows* writes extensively of the two women throughout the book which is cast in the form of King David's reminiscences as his life draws to a close.[16] Throughout the aged king's rambling memories, Heller's David continually compares and contrasts these two women. When I first read this book, I was constantly driven to look up the Hebrew Bible to see if ambiguities and gaps in the Hebrew narrative could permit his readings – and very often they did. Since working on this essay, I have discovered that many of his other extravaganzas have their bases in readings and interpretations of later Jewish writers. Few are pure inventions by Heller himself. And, of course, he rolls them into his narrative together with quotations from the Hebrew Bible, Shakespeare and others in his own inimitable, hilarious style.

Other modern, and more scholarly, writers that I have surveyed are Adele Berlin, Moshe Garsiel, Meir Sternberg, Jon Levenson and Baruch Halpern. All of these, Garsiel,[17] Levenson,[18] Sternberg,[19] and Berlin,[20] recognize the comparison and contrast between Abigail and Bathsheba.

I will now arraign these two women against the criteria I have collected.

(1) Graciousness and reliability in family matters.

Abigail. In his adaptation of the story Josephus accepts the point of view of the biblical narrator,[21] and, in fact, accentuates it. For example, he writes of David's considerate and protective treatment of Nabal's shepherds, which on close scrutiny is

---

[16] Joseph Heller, *God Knows* (London 1984).
[17] Garsiel, *The First Book of Samuel*, 140.
[18] Levenson, '1 Samuel 25 as Literature', 23-24.
[19] Meir Sternberg, *The Poetics of Biblical Narrative: Ideological Literature and the Drama of Reading* (Bloomington, IN 1985), 357.
[20] Adele Berlin, *Poetics and Interpretation of Biblical Narrative* (Bible and Literature; Sheffield 1983), 30-34.
[21] Christopher T. Begg, 'The Abigail Story (1 Samuel 25) according to Josephus', *Estudios Bíblicos* 54 (1996), 5-34.

actually doing nothing, or doing no more than leaving them alone. The only good that David has done them is to refrain from damaging them! But there is no irony or exaggeration in the biblical story as far as Josephus is concerned. Events turn out as God wills and the good woman, Abigail, is helped by God to her new life (Ant. 6:301-20). As far as Josephus can see, she does nothing to accelerate Nabal's death by the ruthless manner of breaking the news of what she has done in spite of him. The ambiguity of her actions and words, effectively masking the extent of her duplicity or self-interest, which is left tantalizingly apparent in the Hebrew text, is smoothed out and smoothed over by Josephus.

Heller's David, on the other hand, praises Abigail for the timely telling to Nabal of what she had done so that Nabal had no more than time enough to feel the joy of not being killed by David, the brigand, before dying of a heart attack or stroke in about ten days.[22] David does, however, wonder whose life it was that Abigail was trying to preserve by her appeasing actions with the food supplies and with her honeyed words.[23] Thereafter, Abigail provided a sweet, soothing and organizing influence in David's life; while travelling about bivouacking and camping, she not only produced wonderful meals but remained also a carefully made-up beauty.[24]

Jon Levenson describes the Bible's account of Abigail as being in 'overtly evaluative language' and concludes that the pointing out of an intended contrast between her and her husband and an intended likeness to descriptions of David's beauty are part of the narrator's purpose in setting out the scene.[25] Levenson believes that with her beauty, intelligence and rhetorical powers Abigail is portrayed as the 'ideal woman'.

And we find that, in a similar vein to Ruth, Abigail acquires a superordinate standing in the writings of the Sages, though not in the Hebrew Bible itself. According to R. Simeon a man [meaning King David] should not multiply wives to himself, 'even

---

[22] Heller, *God Knows*, 266.
[23] Heller, *God Knows*, 251.
[24] Heller, *God Knows*, 267.
[25] Levenson, '1 Samuel 25 as Literature', 17-18; see also Garsiel, *1 Samuel*, 126.

such as Abigail'.[26] Abigail is the wife *par excellence*, but even she might turn a man's heart away from the Torah.

Bathsheba. Bathsheba's entry in *The New Standard Jewish Encyclopedia* gives no information about her except that she was married first to Uriah and then to David. Her brief seven line entry refers to the males in her life, her husbands and sons, but to her not at all.[27]

The *Encyclopaedia Judaica* gives a more substantial account of Bathsheba, consisting of a slightly paraphrased (and interpreted) outline of the biblical story that also names her children.[28] Reference is also made to the possibility of her being the granddaughter of Ahithophel the Gilonite (2 Sam. 23:34), which deduction can be used to explain Ahithophel's animosity towards David, but the consensus view (un-attributed) is that Bathsheba came from a Jerusalem family.

In the matter of family reliability, opinions are divided about Bathsheba. Texts seek either to exonerate or excoriate her in her role as Uriah's wife.[29] She is subjected to criticism over her sexual encounter with David, but the fact that she properly acknowledged the loss of Uriah by fulfilling a mourning period is also taken into account in her favour, for example, by Josephus (Ant. 7:146). Moshe Garsiel finds Bathsheba guilty of little more than obedience when she obeys the king's command to go to the palace and believes that she did not inititiate the sexual encounter and had, in fact, returned to her home – and role as Uriah's wife – on her own initiative.[30] He also believes there is a hint of physical coercion in the series of verbs of which David is the subject and Bathsheba the object in 2 Sam. 13:15-18. He regards the repetition of her title, wife of Uriah, as a textual indicator of her continued loyalty to her husband, rather than as a continual reminder of her unfaithfulness.

---

[26] Ephraim E. Urbach, *The Sages: Their Concepts and Beliefs* (trans. Israel Abrahams; Cambridge, MA – London 1987), 375-77, with notes on 839 referring the reader to b. San. 74a, y. Shevi. 4.2.32a, and y. San. 3.6.21a.
[27] C. Roth and G. Wigoder (eds), *The New Standard Jewish Encyclopedia* (revised ed.; London 1970), 321-22.
[28] *EncJud*, vol. 4, 73-74.
[29] Genesis Rabbah 32:1, 249.
[30] Moshe Garsiel, 'The Story of David and Bathsheba: A Different Approach', *CBQ* 55 (1993) 256.

In her later life, however, most writers surveyed regard her political mani-
pulations on behalf of her son Solomon as justified and accredited by their success and
his subsequent glorious achievements.[31] Thus, for example, Josephus (Ant. 7:348-53)
paints Bathsheba as a vital and positive agent, and ally of Nathan, in the securing of
Solomon's succession by persuasion and the smoothing over of relations with
Adonijah. He sees her, perhaps, as somewhat of a doer of diplomatic dirty work, for
example, in acquiring Abishag for Adonijah (Ant. 8:3-7), and quite clearly considered
her to be effective in that type of 'diplomatic' activity. Here we can appreciate the way
that Josephus characteristically praises those characters in whom he recognizes
himself.

Over and over again the Midrash refers to her positively in her role as
Solomon's mother.[32] And, as mentioned above, she is credited with having brought
him back to his religious duties when he had been distracted by his 'foreign' wife,
Pharaoh's daughter.[33]

(2) Beauty and desirability, modesty and chastity – including avoiding
misdemeanours and scandals[34]

Abigail. Adele Berlin notes that while Bathsheba apparently did nothing to
save her (too good) husband, Uriah, Abigail did a great deal to try to save the wretch,
Nabal, and that, in contrast with Bathsheba's participation in illicit sex, 'there is no hint

---

[31] Berlin, *Poetics and Interpretation of Biblical Narrative*, 27-30.
[32] Exodus Rabbah (n. 11), 579; Leviticus Rabbah 159-60; Numbers Rabbah, vol. 1, x.4, 352, 420, 473;
Ruth Rabbah, 21; Ecclesiastes Rabbah, 121; Song of Songs Rabbah, 173.
[33] Numbers Rabbah (n. 11), vol. 1, x.4, 352.
[34] The RSV consistently describes Abigail as the 'widow of Nabal of Carmel' while the Hebrew could
equally well be translated 'wife of Nabal' (1 Sam. 30:5; 2 Sam. 2:2; 3:3). This elective translation
functions as a means making sure that readers avoid picking up the possible negative connotation of her
being too keen to shed her husband and join with David. The merest hint of her indulging in an
adulterous relationship during Nabal's lifetime has been eliminated from her sobriquet by the delicate
and tasteful use of the word 'widow'. The Hebrew text plays no part in this change of perspective but
portrays Abigail as the woman/wife of Nabal throughout her lifetime. On the other hand, the RSV
consistently translates the same Hebrew construct phrase, *'eshet* plus a male proper name, as '*the wife of
Uriah (the Hittite)*' for Bathsheba (2 Sam. 11:3, 26; 12:10), indicating that throughout the narrative, even
in her widowhood and after her marriage to David, the translator wishes his readers to regard her as
properly speaking the woman-of-Uriah. The translation of each of these phrases, in this standard Bible
version, is an interpretation and a guide to the reader as to how to evaluate these two women; but we
should bear in mind that the Hebrew Bible makes no distinction between them in this way.

of unseemly behaviour' between David and Abigail; she is portrayed as a 'model wife and modest woman'.[35] Abigail is, however, in Berlin's view not portrayed in the biblical text as a fully rounded character. Instead, she is no more than a 'type' with 'a limited and stereotyped list of traits and ... represents the class of people with these traits.'[36]

Heller regards the first meeting between Abigail and David as fraught with veiled sexual desire, certainly on David's side,[37] but portrays Abigail in her later life in the role of modest wife and dutiful housekeeper.[38] Of the dealings of the 'stunning woman' herself with David at the time of Nabal's refusal to pay 'protection money', Heller has David use the words of Prov. 11:22 to say that Abigail was 'a jewel of gold in a swine's snout',[39] meaning that Abigail was the jewel attached to Nabal's 'snout', and that Nabal – by implication – was a pig, who did not 'appreciate or deserve so fine a wife'.[40] We might note, however, that the rest of the verse makes it clear that it refers to a woman with 'a rebellious disposition'. Is Heller by this means implying that there is something darker in Abigail's character, a quality that remains beneath the surface of the narrated story?

Moreover, Heller's David says that, for their first meeting, Abigail had 'rouged her cheeks and lips, made up her eyes, and brushed and tied her dark hair ... attired herself in a robe and mantle of brilliant desert scarlet' and insists that there was mutual desire and longing between them throughout their long dialogue.[41] But, in spite of these details – or perhaps because of them – Abigail remains his ideal woman, for David says, 'None of my other wives came close to Abigail in elegance, taste, and intelligence ...'[42]

---

[35] Berlin, *Poetics and Interpretation of Biblical Narrative*, 30, 31.
[36] Berlin, *Poetics and Interpretation of Biblical Narrative*, 32; see also Sternberg, *The Poetics of Biblical Narrative*, 328.
[37] Heller, *God Knows*, 82.
[38] Heller, *God Knows*, 106, 110, 143.
[39] Cf. Prov. 11:2 (KJV) where a woman without discretion is described in this way.
[40] Heller, *God Knows*, 246-49 (see also 221).
[41] Heller, *God Knows*, 249, 268.
[42] Heller, *God Knows*, 269.

Bathsheba. As far as her beauty, desirability, modesty and chastity are concerned, Bathsheba apparently has the first two in plenty, and the second two less so, at least at the beginning of her life with David. As Adele Berlin suavely says, 'it is not for nothing that we are told that Bathsheba was beautiful'.[43]

Josephus declares that Bathsheba was 'very beautiful to look upon and surpassed all other women', but he gives no other evaluation of her (Ant. 7:130). It is surprising that he finds none of the cunning in her that he recognizes in Rebekah – the cunning similar to his own (Ant. 1:245-48, 269).[44] Perhaps, however, this more devious aspect is represented when Josephus adds to the narrative the detail that Bathsheba asked David to save her from scandal, and possible death by stoning, likely to result from her inappropriate pregnancy (Ant. 7:130).

Bathsheba's behaviour in committing adultery with David, often regarded as a sin on his part,[45] is not always seen as a sin on hers.[46] Adele Berlin takes this stance, but explains this evaluation by reminding readers that she sees the character of Bathsheba being created by the narrator 'as a complete non-person' with the result that Bathsheba is not, and cannot be, 'an equal party to the adultery, but only the means whereby it was achieved'.[47]

Heller devotes a long section to retelling the whole grisly narrative from seduction to marriage, giving full interpretational power to Bathsheba's desires and to David's machinations to pass the pregnancy off on Uriah and then to arrange that Uriah fall in battle.[48] But he also portrays King David's love for Bathsheba as long-lasting and tells of his longing again for Bathsheba at the end of his life; David desires her still,

---

[43] Berlin, *Poetics and Interpretation of Biblical Narrative*, 34.
[44] See also Heather A. McKay, 'Eve's Sisters Re-Cycled: The Literary Nachleben of Old Testament Women', in Athalya Brenner and Jan Willem van Heuten (eds), *Recycling Biblical Figures: Papers Read at a NOSTER Colloquium in Amsterdam, 12-13 May 1997* (Studies in Theology and Religion 1; Assen 1999), 169-91.
[45] Berlin, *Poetics and Interpretation of Biblical Narrative*, 26.
[46] Numbers Rabbah, vol. 4, Numbers vol. 1, xi.3, 420.
[47] Adele Berlin, 'Characterization in Biblical Narrative: David's Wives', *Journal for the Study of the Old Testament* 23 (1982) 73.
[48] Heller, *God Knows*, 344-65.

the mature and comfortably spreading Bathsheba, though not with quite the fire of youth.[49]

Jewish legend explains away the criticism that David and Bathsheba committed serious wrong by adducing the so-called 'custom' of soldiers' divorcing their wives before going off to war.[50] If that custom were indeed the case, then there would have been no adultery since the attribution of 'adultery' in the Hebrew Bible depends not at all on the marital status of the adulterous man. The explanation elaborates matters further and claims that 'God Himself brought him [David] to his crime, that He might say to other sinners: "Go to David and learn how to repent".'[51] This seems to be somewhat tortuous special pleading, but whether on God's behalf or David's I cannot say.

Meir Sternberg takes the view that the rabbis had to find a way of exonerating David – king of Israel and writer of the Psalms – from the sin of adultery.[52] He finds that all the responses they make take the form of gap-filling and each one provides a reason or excuse or extenuating circumstance for David's seemingly law-breaking adultery, for example, by saying that Uriah had divorced Bathsheba before the campaign began, so David was guilty of the lesser crime of wife-stealing. Sternberg deftly describes the Hebrew Bible narrator as '[o]mniscient but far from omnicommunicative'.[53]

Sternberg further notes, while discussing David's predeliction for beautiful women, that Bathsheba is described merely as 'very good-looking' (טובת מראה מאד) while Abigail is 'of good understanding and good-looking' (טובת שכל ויפת תאר) and adjudges that 'David's own character would appear to be reflected in each instance or stage by the female company he chooses to keep, let alone the terms and consequences

---

[49] Heller, *God Knows*, 108-109.
[50] Louis Ginzberg, *The Legends of the Jews*, vol. 4, 103; see also Garsiel, 'David and Bathsheba', 244-62.
[51] Ginzberg, *The Legends of the Jews*, vol. 4, 103; vol. 6, 264-5.
[52] Sternberg, *Poetics of Biblical Narrative*, 188.
[53] Sternberg, *Poetics of Biblical Narrative*, 190; but see also below for the further layer added to this point by Sandra R. Shimoff, 'David and Bathsheba: The Political Function of Rabbinic Aggada', *Journal for the Study of Judaism* 24 (1992-93), 246-56.

of involvement'.[54] The side of David he defines as exisitng through his life with Abigail is characterized as 'devout, resolute, far-sighted, self-controlled, a shrewd judge of men, and yet a loving parent to the last.'[55] Sternberg believes that side to be lost to David after the encounter with Bathsheba. I go further and say that the difference in the two women predicates, and creates and delineates for the reader, these two distinct sides of David's character. The women function as living mirrors in which the readers can see David more clearly than through his own words and deeds.

(3) Diplomacy and deference.

Abigail. Abigail's character and person are summed up in a three and a half line entry in *The New Standard Jewish Encyclopedia* by the sentence: 'She won David's pardon for Nabal's churlishness by her gifts and conciliatory words.'[56] We note that, here, her beauty of face, figure or character are ignored and only her wealth and diplomacy are praised. This appeasing feature of her dialogue with David is also noted by Garsiel; in particular he comments that 'when he encounters Abigail he rapidly recovers from his transport of rage ...' because of Abigail's 'deliberate adoption of a tactic of deference for the sake of appeasement'.[57]

Genesis Rabbah treats Abigail as the ideal type of a maidservant, which suggests that deference and obedience are perceived to be qualities she has in abundance.[58] Adele Berlin, somewhat wryly, suggests that Abigail's story 'could be reduced to: "fair maiden" Abigail is freed from "wicked ogre" and marries "prince charming"', but concludes that the story functions as 'a strong endorsement of David's destiny to become the chosen favourite of God.'[59] Abigail is hardly relevant, even in her own story; her character is subsumed in the overall plan of the plot.

---

[54] Sternberg, *Poetics of Biblical Narrative*, 357-58.
[55] Sternberg, *Poetics of Biblical Narrative*, 358-60.
[56] *The New Standard Jewish Encyclopedia*, 7-8
[57] Garsiel, *The First Book of Samuel*, 132-33.
[58] Genesis Rabbah, vol. 2, 75:12-13, 699.
[59] Berlin, 'Characterization in Biblical Narrative: David's Wives', 77.

The *Encyclopedia Judaica* gives a more substantial account of Abigail's personality.[60] Abigail is beautiful and wise, and David is impressed by her sagacity. The account of Abigail to be found in Jewish legend embellishes and enhances her stature; her beauty, wisdom and power of prophecy are lauded.[61] (The power of prophecy is attributed to her on the grounds that she avowed that David would become king [1 Sam. 25:30-31].)

But Jewish legend also finds that not even Abigail is 'free from the feminine weakness of coquetry.'[62] The evidence of this is her use of the phrase 'remember your handmaid' which the writer believes to be inappropriate in a married woman of good financial standing, interpreting it as a type of attention-seeking wheedling.[63] However, the account of Abigail concludes by saying that she supervises one of the seven divisions of the women's Paradise, an exceptional honour that she shares with Sarah, Rebekah, Rachel and Leah.[64]

Sternberg believes that the biblical narrator laconically paints Abigail's prolixity in an 'unflattering light',[65] which indicates that he believes that the description of her long dialogue with David has something of the ironic in it. The ambiguity inherent in the biblical account of Abigail's dialogue with David certainly makes it amenable to all these varied interpretations.

Bathsheba. Bathsheba's skills in politics have been partly dealt with above under family matters as evidenced by the skill with which she operated on behalf of her son, Solomon. However, these same political skills may also be praised for their deviousness.[66] Heller's Bathsheba alternately entreats and cajoles David to get what she wants, unashamedly using *her* sexual desire to manipulate David, or else beating

---

[60] *EncJud*, vol. 2, 73-74.
[61] Ginzberg, *The Legends of the Jews*, vol. 4, 117; vol. 6, 272, 275; see also Heller, *God Knows*, 251.
[62] Ginzberg, *The Legends of the Jews*, vol. 4, 118.
[63] See also my different interpretation of this linguistic usage in Heather A. McKay, 'She Said To Him, He Said To Her: Power Talk In The Bible, Or Foucault Listens At The Keyhole', *Biblical Theology Bulletin* 28 (1998), 45-51.
[64] Ginzberg, *The Legends of the Jews*, vol. 4, 118.
[65] Sternberg, *Poetics of Biblical Narrative*, 155.
[66] Heller, *God Knows*, 18-29, 118.

him into submission by means of irony and unfavourable military and sexual comparisons of him with other men.

Taking the opposing position, Moshe Garsiel believes that Bathsheba is not at all 'a woman full of cunning'.[67] He believes that the debacle of the story of her first pregnancy with David reveals her to be someone of little astuteness and claims that this view is not overturned by her naive dicing with death in her dealings with Adonijah. He concludes that she is a 'tragic figure'.

Adele Berlin regards the Bathsheba of 1 Kings 1-2 as a 'real person' and 'one of the central characters, important in affairs of state as well as in family matters'.[68] But she also finds that character to be naive in her dealings with Adonijah,[69] echoing the evaluation of Sternberg, above. Nonetheless, she does not rule out the possibility of a 'scheming' Bathsheba, possibly playing at being naive.[70]

(4) Production of healthy, male offspring.

Abigail. Abigail bears a son, Chileab, to David (2 Sam. 3:3), but no more is heard of him in the Hebrew Bible.

Jewish legend makes good this 'deficiency' by telling of Chileab's good looks and intelligence, identifying him as a 'son worthy of his mother Abigail.'[71] According to Jewish legend, he was like his father in appearance – a point perhaps deduced merely from his name – and so 'silenced the talk against David's all too hasty marriage with the widow of Nabal.' Presumably, the writer of the legend would have preferred an appropriate delay to prove the child was not Nabal's rather than relying on the looks and intelligence of the child. Furthermore, he praises Chileab for his piety and states that as a result of it he entered Paradise alive.

In contrast, Heller's David speaks of miscarriages for Abigail followed by the delivery of the short-lived Chileab to whom he attributes Down's Syndrome.[72] He

---

[67] Garsiel, 'The Story of David and Bathsheba', 254.
[68] Berlin, 'Characterization in Biblical Narrative: David's Wives', 74.
[69] Berlin, 'Characterization in Biblical Narrative: David's Wives', 75.
[70] Berlin, 'Characterization in Biblical Narrative: David's Wives', 76.
[71] Ginzberg, *The Legends of the Jews*, vol. 4, 118.
[72] Heller, *God Knows*, 283, refers to Chileab as 'mongoloid'.

callously remarks that even the changing of the child's name to Daniel, in 1 Chron. 3:1, did not help him to achieve anything of note.

Bathsheba. Bathsheba first bore a son who sickened and died on the seventh day; the child, therefore, had no name and was mourned in his nameless state.[73] Thereafter she bore Solomon (2 Sam. 12:24), possibly, alongside Moses, Jacob and Joseph, one of the most successful sons of all the Hebrew Bible narratives. 1 Chron. 3:5 lists three other sons of Bathsheba: Shimea, Shobab and Nathan.

It seems as if Bathesheba's life had two parts: the part of seductive adulteress during which she is admired only by David, and that of successful queen and mother during which many commentators try to rehabilitate her and praise her.[74] The glorious career of Solomon does much to give Bathsheba a high status.

(5) Appropriate or acceptable ethnicity. In a similar way to the literary treatment of Ruth, there is evidence of moves to shield Abigail and Bathsheba from attributions of the dubious epithets, such as 'foreign women' or 'strange women', which could be applied to, or implied of, 'ethnically' or 'culturally' foreign females.

Abigail. As was noted above, the Hebrew Bible consistently refers to Abigail as the woman of Nabal of Carmel; the possible negative connotation of Calebite – earlier applied to him – has been eliminated from her identification.

This different geographical attribution reminds the reader both of Nabal's region of origin and of his immense wealth. Levenson argues that David's marriage to Abigail, in this way, authenticated his claim to kingship in Hebron, as also did his marriage to Ahinoam, the widow of Saul.[75] Identifying and naming the woman in terms of Abigail's deceased landowner husband gives some credibility to David's claim to the land and the marriage to Ahinoam did the same for his claim to kingship.

Bathsheba. The casual reader might assume that the 'wife of Uriah' would be a Hittite and that as such Bathsheba could be regarded as technically 'foreign'. On this

[73] 2 Sam. 11:27; 12:14, 24.
[74] Interestingly, Alice Bach, *Women, Seduction and Betrayal in Biblical Narrative* (Cambridge 1997), 7, identifies the first of these as the continuing portrayal of Bathsheba.
[75] Levenson, '1 Samuel 25 as Literature', 24-28.

point, Jewish legend reiterates a rabbinic suggestion that because of his giving of soldierly help to David to loosen the dead Goliath's armour, Uriah is able to petition to marry an Israelite wife.[76] The legend further hints that this was not an appropriate action on David's part and that he was, therefore, punished for it through the Bathsheba incident.

This anecdote implies that Bathsheba was an Israelite woman, and so could be seen as a counter to questions that suggested she was not. It possibly picks up on, and certainly parallels, the suggestion from 1 Chron. 2:3 that she (or Bathshua) was a Canaanite and, so, 'foreign'. Joseph Heller carries that notion further in his story of King David and makes Bathsheba a sexually proactive woman – with close friends and mentors among Canaanite prostitutes – as well as a politically powerful one.[77]

Whatever the reasons behind the ethnic markers attached to the two women, they continue to underscore the subtle difference in the way the two are evaluated. Foreignness is no more than a confirmation of a so-called truth that was already known. The rhetorical question, 'Well, what else can one expect from a ***-ite?' functions equally well to praise or censure a person of distinct ethnicity or area of origin depending on the point of view *already assumed.*

Excursus: reasons behind rabbinic accretions to biblical narratives

Painting an altogether different picture of the reasons for the hints and biases in rabbinic haggadic writing is Sandra Shimoff who finds that certain of the main biblical characters are regarded as eponymous ancestors of key rabbis involved in debates in those times could be easily and safely achieved by adding a twist to the biblical story of that eponymous ancestor and so honouring or discomfiting one's latter-day inter-locutor.

---

[76] Ginzberg, *The Legends of the Jews*, vol. 4, 88, 103; vol. 6, 252, 265.
[77] Heller, *God Knows*, 67, 110; Bathsheba claims to have learned her sexual tricks from friends who were Canaanite whores.

The examples she provides come from the rabbinic responses to the impasse of David's having sinned so patently with Bathsheba.[78] She notes that the responses are as follows:

(1) R. Samuel b. Nahmani, in the name of R. Jonathan, gave the explanation of the wartime divorce of soldiers.

(2) Raba taught that David sinned, not through lust, but to provide God with a justification for another punishment he had levied upon David.

(3) Rabbah b. Bar Hana, in the name of R. Johanan, said it was better that David cohabit with a woman of questionable marital status (and be executed by strangulation yet retain his share in the world to come) than that he shame his neighbour.

(4) Rab Joseph read Prov. 6:23 as Torah in accordance with teachings of R. Menahem son of R. Jose, and so David's non-defeat at the hands of Doeg and Ahithophel proves he had not broken the commandment.

(5) R. Johanan, in the name of R. Simeon bar Yohai, said that Ps. 109:22 implies that David had conquered his inclination to sin and that the apparent adultery acted as a didactic tale to prompt others to believe in the successful outcome of repentance.

(6) Raba taught that Bathsheba had a tragic role because, although destined for all time to be with David he had taken her before 'she was ripe'. This is an interpretation from a post-biblical reading of her name.

At the time of the writing of these rabbis the option 'to defend David in Palestinian academies was equivalent to defending the Patriarch, his lineal descendant' on the female side.[79] However, the Babylonian academies were keen to support the Exilarch, whose claim to Davidic descent was superior, being through the male line.

On close analysis of the passages, Shimoff finds that all the responses mentioned above function to exonerate David, from whatever source they come and no

---

[78] Shimoff, 'Rabbinic Agenda', 248-51.
[79] Shimoff, 'Rabbinic Agenda', 251.

matter which leader their responses aim to support. Of more interest, then, might be those responses that seek to denigrate David. But none of them refer to the incident with Bathsheba; they refer to other ambiguous episodes in David's life.

We can, therefore, conclude that the exoneration of David from the sin of adultery, and, with it, the references to Bathsheba in the haggadot, serve purposes other than description of Bathsheba's 'true' character, purposes that serve the current debating needs of the authors.

V. Conclusions

I have chosen to compare and contrast Abigail and Bathsheba because of the teasing contradictions they present to the reader of the Hebrew Bible. They are alike; they are very alike in many ways. Yet, in each of the ways that they are alike, they are also different. They are both wives of David, but in the similar situations they find themselves with David they produce a different response in him and help to 'create' a different David.

How are they alike? They are both candidates for the appellation *'eshet ḥayil*, being beautiful and desirable women with claims to being wise, persuasive and effective on David's behalf. They both marry David shortly after being widowed. Each brings the possibility of friendship with a clan or group in the surrounding countryside: Carmelites and Hittites. There is a hint of difference about each of them: each could be regarded as an *'ishshah zarah*. They are both persuasive of speech and skilled in arguing for their desired outcomes. They both bear at least one son. They both bring out manly qualities in David.

How are they different? David's desire for Abigail is restrained till they are married; his longing for Bathsheba is not. Both women are conveniently widowed as a result of David's words and actions, but David is less innocent of engineering the death of Uriah than the death of Nabal. Abigail's son plays no part in the narrative of Israel's history; Bathsheba's son, Solomon, plays a monumental role. The qualities Abigail brings out in David are those of a great leader, while Bathsheba stirs his libido and also bears his most famous son.

Both women are likened to the best of womanhood in beauty and persuasive power, but Bathsheba's picture is always somewhat tainted compared with her 'squeaky clean' sister-in-law; unless one accepts – as I do – the reading of Joseph Heller which indicates that Abigail was by far the more subtle and cunning of the two women.[80]

Careful scrutiny of the biblical and subsequent narratives shows that Abigail begins her interpretative history with more features in common with Ruth, a distinguished *'eshet ḥayil*, than does Bathsheba. And the subsequent history of their character descriptions – or character assassinations, some might say – while some tinkering with aspects and features of their profiles takes place, tends to confirm that view.

Throughout all the centuries of discussion, Abigail remains close to Ruth in all-round acceptability and Bathsheba remains just that little bit tainted. Literary analyses cannot rehabilitate her as they often identify her as a 'type' or mere 'agent'. Only as Queen Mother is Bathsheba supreme. If Abigail is the royal wife par excellence, Bathsheba is the Queen Mother par excellence. Perhaps a feminist re-envisioning of the narratives from these women's perspectives, giving the reader access to their possible inner thoughts, could equalize our perceptions of the two women. But these 'fictive biographies' have yet to be written.

---

[80] See also McKay, 'She Said To Him, He Said To Her'.

Theodicy, the Flood and the Holocaust

Moshe Ish-Horowicz

I. Introduction

I have chosen this subject because my parents and most of my family perished at the death camp of Treblinka II and the question 'where was the merciful and just God?' has haunted me ever since. It was the mainspring for my dissertation.[1] I was interested in discovering whether the rabbis had ever faced an event as challenging to their worldview as the Holocaust. I concluded that, despite major differences, the massive scale and harshness of the biblical flood offered some sort of analogy. Analysis of the rabbinic traditions concerning the flood led me to the realisation that the Prophets and Sages had never accepted evil or cruelty in silence, as Noah did when told about the flood, according to the narrative of Genesis. Noah's silence could be viewed as sinful. Rather, by way of example, according to the author of the book that bears his name, the prophet Samuel did not remain silent when faced with the great wickedness of his time, the people's demand for a king: 'God forbid that I should sin against the Lord in ceasing to pray for you'.[2]

Although the rabbis criticised the Almighty for the flood, they also searched for answers to justify Him. The rabbis were thus engaged in theodicy. God's apparent injustice may be considered the vulnerable spot of religion, its Achilles' heal. The discourse of theodicy tries to remove this weakness by seeking ways to vindicate God. For Jews the apparent paradox is that, on the one hand, the Torah appears to reveal God as merciful perfection, but on the other hand, injustice and

---

[1] This paper is based on my PhD thesis presented to the University of Manchester, England. Many more papers would be needed to cover the whole subject in some detail.
[2] 1 Sam. 12:23.

suffering are seemingly visible everywhere and appear incompatible with His attributes of righteousness and majesty. In addition, sometimes theodicy is concerned with the conflict which may arise between various ethical virtues, for instance, between the opposing demands of justice and mercy, and sometimes it is more obviously concerned with real life issues, such as when the wicked seem to prosper and the righteous suffer, whether as individuals or communities.

It is significant that in Jewish tradition doubts about divine providence have been explicitly expressed by some of the most important personalities. According to the Genesis account, Abraham, the founder of the faith, alleged unjust divine punishment of the pagan Sodomites in his challenge: 'Far be it from You to slay the righteous with the wicked ... Shall not the Judge of all the earth do justice?'[3] According to the narrative of Exodus Moses himself protested several times, and, after the sin of the golden calf, is even portrayed as changing the divine intention to destroy His people, 'Turn from Your fierce wrath and repent of this evil against Your people.'[4] Similarly, in Numbers 14:20, at the rebellion of the spies, God is portrayed as relenting, 'I have pardoned according to your word'. The existence of divine providence is also questioned in the entreaty: 'My God, my God, why have you forsaken me?'[5] Perhaps it is Jeremiah who formulated the most explicit criticism: 'Righteous are You, O Lord, when I plead with You; yet let me talk with You of Your judgements. Why does the way of the wicked prosper? Why are all they happy that deal very treacherously?'[6] Many other sources pose the same argument.[7] The Book of Job discusses in depth the suffering of an innocent man: what justification was there for God agreeing to Satan's evil instigation against him? Thus the characters in Scripture itself raise many of the issues which theologians discuss under the heading of theodicy.

---

[3] Gen. 18:25
[4] Exod. 32:11-12
[5] Ps. 22:2
[6] Jer. 12:1
[7] Hab. 1:13; Mal. 3:15; Eccl. 7:15; b. Ber. 7a; b. Shab. 55b; b. Hor. 10b.

Poets and writers of many ages have also grappled with the way in which the imperfections of this world can be understood as criticisms of divine providence. Alfred Tennyson in his 'Idylls of the King' describes his perplexity as follows:

I found God in the shining of the stars
I marked Him in the flowering of His fields
But in His ways with men I find Him not ...
As if some lesser god had made the world,
But had not force to shape it as he would
Till the High God behold it from beyond,
And enter it, and make it beautiful.
Or else as if the world were wholly fair
But that these minds of men are dense and dim,
And have not power to see it as it is ...

Indeed, why should not the righteous always be rewarded and the wicked punished in conformity with what is recorded as the divine promise in the Torah of just reward and punishment? Why should injustice exist at all? Is evil compatible with the existence of a good, merciful and just deity? Why should not human beings be good and happy, enjoying eternal bliss without hardship, disabilities, sorrow, cruelty and all other injustices and suffering? Cannot God bring about now the ideal kingdom envisaged in the post-messianic era? Why then does He not create such a righteous and happy world without evil and injustice?

But would this be possible, or even desirable? If all people were created only good, there would not be any inclination to either good or evil. Put simply, people would be like puppets without free will to choose good or evil, without reward or punishment, without purpose or drive to mend themselves and the world, and without repentance or forgiveness, etc. So, in place of straightforward yearnings for a perfect world, the discourse of theodicy attempts to address the issues surrounding why God has apparently created an imperfect world.

In addressing these enormous issues, a basic starting point in the rabbinical reply was 'Do not lose faith in just retribution'.[8] Some Rabbis even concluded that Gehenna is very good because the fear of it prevents people from sinning.[9] However,

---

[8] m. Avot 1:7.
[9] E.g., Gen. Rab. 9:8 and 5.

it was also recognised that suffering, such as that of Rabbi Akiva at his martyrdom, need not necessarily be retribution for evil.

II. Theodicy, the Flood, and the Holocaust

Theodicy, the analysis of the righteousness of God, was the main, if not the only, factor that motivated rabbinical discussion of the cruelty and injustice of the flood, even if the sages had to maximise the enormity of the crimes of the generations, in order to render their evil commensurate with the enormity of the punishment on the basis of 'measure for measure'. Nowadays, too, any theological or philosophical analysis of the flood narratives has to include most of the major religious and ethical themes concerning God and humanity, themes which still remain contemporary.

The story of the flood seems distinctive in several ways, some of which may facilitate some comparison with the Holocaust and modern reflection on it, though there is not room for those reflections to be worked out in this paper.

(1) The biblical text does not include any protests against this greatest ever destruction. We may ask whether protest is a suitable response to the Holocaust.

(2) It is the only episode in Scripture in which God Himself is portrayed as if he regretted His verdict; as the narrative goes, this regret does not originate in any human criticism. On all other occasions in Scripture in which God expresses regret, there is always some kind of intercession, by Abraham, Moses, the Prophets, or others. We may ask whether it is appropriate to talk of God regretting the Holocaust.

(3) The narrative of the flood describes an enormous destruction of life, both human and animal, by drowning. Although it is true that the flood might be considered as less cruel and cunning than the Holocaust, nevertheless the Deluge is reminiscent of the Holocaust because of the amount of destruction.[10]

---

[10] It must be remembered throughout this comparison that, whereas the Flood is described as divinely motivated, the Holocaust was a devilish methodical genocide using sophisticated technology for mass extermination; this was all accompanied by perverse ideological and psychological evil, sadism, brutality, humiliation and perfidy.

(4) The narrative of the flood concerns all humanity in its collective commonality; in a perverse way the targeted destruction by the Nazis on the basis of an obscene racist ideology was a denial of the commonality of all human beings.[11]

(5) The biblical version of the story of the flood is the only one which is known to explain the flood on ethico-religious grounds as a divine punishment for mankind's wickedness.[12] Is there a religious explanation for the Holocaust?

(6) There is an extensive post-biblical literature on the flood which is critical of God; the earliest elements of this come from the rabbinic reflections of the mishnaic period. In what ways might the post-Holocaust literature be suitably critical of God?

(7) Beyond these criticisms of God, the story of the flood continues to raise complex moral issues and a wide range of concepts relevant in debates concerning theodicy today. Much in the narrative raises questions concerning divine righteousness, providence, and the status of the Torah as the revelation of the divine will. The Holocaust raises the same or similarly complex questions.

III. Righteousness and Theodicy

Both the flood and the Holocaust provoke various questions in the mind of the reflective person of faith. In light of those questions it is important to make a few comments about righteousness.

Conceiving of divine righteousness remains problematic in any generation. Even though there can be a commitment to thinking matters through incisively, for the person of faith, human theories, opinions and criticisms may be misconceptions of the limited human mind. Human limitations cannot be over-emphasised, especially when it is a matter of formulating an appropriate definition of a concept like the righteousness of God for which it is all too easy to suppose that a human counterpart

---

[11] Common humanity is asserted in b. San. 37b-38a, based on m. San. 4:5.
[12] See C. Westerman, *Genesis* (Biblischer Kommentar, Altes Testament 1/1; Neukirchen-Vluyn 1974), 536. According to J. G. Frazer, *Folklore in the Old Testament* (New York 1923), there are about 250 versions of the Flood worldwide.

may give an adequate understanding. As it is variously put in the Book of Isaiah: 'to whom can you liken God?'[13] 'no man can fathom His understanding';[14] 'as the heavens are higher than the earth, so My ways are higher than your ways and My thoughts than your thoughts'.[15] The faithful enquirer also has to take into account the way in which the tradition in the form of the second commandment prohibits the formation of divine images, both concrete and abstract, so that the very quest for an adequate conceptualisation of divine righteousness could be seen as flawed from the start.

Nevertheless, a start can be made through considering human righteousness. According to Leviticus 19:2 God commands Israel through Moses: 'Be holy because I the Lord your God am holy.' According to this section of the Torah it is clear that God orders Israel to imitate Him in righteousness. Righteousness might be understood as God's supreme attribute, as is implied in Isaiah, 'the Holy God shows himself holy by righteousness.'[16] The appropriateness of the human imitation of God is implied also in the way in which human beings are created in the ethical and spiritual 'image of God', and a key component of that imitation involves righteousness as Genesis goes on to imply: 'to keep the way of the Lord, to do righteousness…'[17]

Righteousness thus seems to be an overarching category which can be defined in relation to human beings as encompassing faith, mercy, justice, purity and all the other ethical and religious virtues, values and duties. As an overarching category righteousness refers to what provides ideal guidelines and criteria for evaluating the deeds and behaviour as well as the reward and punishment of human beings. It is possible to move from such a description to propose that God's ways and decisions can be evaluated and criticised as well as vindicated or defended by the same criteria of righteousness.

---

[13] Isa. 40:18.
[14] Isa. 40:28.
[15] Isa. 55:9.
[16] Isa. 5:16.
[17] Gen. 18:19.

Other concepts can also be introduced to help further define righteousness, especially divine righteousness. Righteousness seems to refer to something dynamic, not static. In biblical tradition, one can conclude that God has been shown to be dynamic in a way which admits and even invites challenge and defiance, for the sake of righteousness. According to the pentateuchal narrative, the flood is followed by the establishment by God of a covenant, which has a moral element. The narrator knew all too well that the flood did not put an end to mankind's wickedness, the inclination to evil and the old, imperfect order of things. The dynamic of the created order reasserted itself at every level.

Righteousness can be further defined through the combination of the concepts of justice and mercy. It can be argued that in its search for justice Judaism does not tolerate the strict application of inflexible law unless it is curbed and mollified by mercy. One might label these two principal facets of righteousness as moral justice, i.e. equity, which is manifested for instance in the rabbinical rule of לפנים משורת הדין. According to this principle, rabbinic legal decisions are to be made in the ethical spirit of the law and not in accordance with the strict letter of the law.[18] On this basis the sages criticised, for example, God's apparent cruelty in the destructive flood, destroying all life on land, and His injustice in drowning innocent children and animals, and in planting the inclination to evil in human beings. They even challenged the indiscriminate killing of the righteous with the wicked, both in the flood itself and with respect to the future unborn progeny of the victims of the flood.

That righteousness involves mercy can also be seen in a reading of the narrative of the flood. According to the story no longer was there to be universal collective responsibility, since after the flood, God, at His own decision and initiative, and without anybody's prompting, pledged never again to bring a flood on earth, never again to destroy total life on the ground and never again to curse the ground for human sins. His pledges signify the predominance of mercy over the static rigidity of

---

[18] b. Ber. 7a; b. B.M. 24b.

judgement, despite the fact that the evil of mankind,[19] which had caused and was punished by the flood, did not disappear. The story makes it abundantly clear that the inclination to evil continued to afflict mankind even after the flood, as is manifested by the stories of Noah's drunkenness and Ham's misconduct.[20]

Genuine repentance is another dynamic concept associated with mercy. By divine love and mercy, God accepts the sinner's contrition, changes His decree, and unconditionally forgives all past transgressing.[21] Of course, a person's repentance should emanate from genuine regrets for past misdeeds, and from the person's desire for divine nearness.[22] This was exemplified by R. Dordia's sincere soul searching and his pardon only a few hours before his death.[23] But God may also be understood as sometimes forgiving purely out of grace, without repentance, as He forgave the children of Israel instead of destroying them after the affronts of the Golden Calf[24] and the Spies.

In Jewish tradition theodicy bases some of its arguments for defending and justifying God on His infinite righteousness and perfection as follows. (1) Theodicy gives priority to divine grace and love in the very act of creation and in the giving of the Torah. (2) Theodicy indicates humanity's limitations and inability to comprehend divine ways. Anthropomorphism and anthropopathism, the attribution of human forms and feelings to God, are recognised as not adequately describing divine reality, though they are also seen as essential means for teaching the Torah, for explaining the divine will and demands in a human tongue.[25] (3) Theodicy commonly has an eschatological element involving the afterlife: present injustices for the righteous will be compensated by their ultimate bliss in the messianic era and in the world to come. (4) Theodicy cannot do without the concepts of human free will and the inclinations to do evil or good, although the divine command is always represented as an order to

---

[19] Gen. 6:5
[20] Gen. 8:21
[21] Ezek. 18:32; Pes. Rabbati 44:2
[22] Ps. 145:18
[23] b. 'A.Z. 17a
[24] Exod. 32 11-12
[25] Sifre Shelah 112.

choose the good. With free will the responsibility for any action resides with the individual. A few remarks on each of these four aspects are in order.

In giving *priority to grace and love* in the act of creation and the giving of the Torah, righteousness, the all-important quality of the Deity, remains the mainstay and measure of all aspects of Jewish religion. Divine commandments, mitzvot or halakhot, should not manifest unrighteousness. Any observances which become unrighteous as a result of changed circumstances and/or perceptions should be altered in the righteous spirit of Torah. Thus righteousness is not considered to rest with God alone. The authority to update rules and practices was perceived as having been granted in the Torah itself[26] and was considered to have been handed on to contemporary rabbinic courts and rabbis by the chain of tradition described in the Mishnah.[27] The rabbinic powers to legislate were also established in the Gemara,[28] in which there is description of how the Sanhedrin made decisions and established rulings democratically by a majority vote.[29] It dared to ignore even the Heavenly Voice, which supported the opinion of a minority headed by R. Eliezer ben Hyrkanos. For 'the Torah was not in heaven'[30] any more, since it had been handed down to the Israelites on Mount Sinai. According to a legend, the prophet Elijah told R. Nathan that, 'at that time' the Holy one 'laughed (amused or with joy)' and conceded: 'My sons have defeated me, My sons have defeated me'[31] – a remarkable assertion of rabbinic authority.

The assertion of rabbinic authority may also be apparent in the way in which a challenge can be mounted against the assumption that God always remains interested in the created order. This can be put in a straightforward way: while good deeds reflect divine immanence, bringing the divine presence (שכינה) closer to the truly pious, the inclination to evil and sin drives away the divine presence so that God is

---

[26] Deut. 17:8-11.
[27] m. Avot 1-2; Rambam, Hilkhot Mamrim 2:1.
[28] b. B.M. 59b.
[29] Exod. 23:2.
[30] Deut. 30:12.
[31] b. B.M. 59b.

displeased and distanced, eclipsed in His own transcendence. Put more boldly, R. Meir attributed to God Himself the saying in Job 34:29, 'When He hides His face who then can behold Him?' R. Meir protested against God, arguing that in hiding His face, God was declaring that He did not care for His world.[32] This was a remarkable statement, refuting divine providence and care, and it outraged his fellow rabbis who silenced him.

However, criticism of God is the parent of theodicy, provided humanity's limitations and *inabilities in comprehending divine ways* are remembered. In its attempts to vindicate God, theodicy is a critical search and demand for an explanation of any alleged injustice. Thus theodicy is indebted to criticism for its very existence. Many rabbis considered such questioning inadmissible, even blasphemous; others contended that it was God's desire to have His deeds and conduct criticised and even altered; in the words of the prophet Micah: 'O, my people, what have I done to you ... testify against Me.'[33]. Many sages and prophets expressed such criticisms. Rabbinical criticism emanates from reverence, love and faith in God on the one hand, and on the other hand, from people's suffering from poverty, drought, etc. and foreign domination. Evil also operates outside the sphere of human influence. Natural calamities, such as earthquakes, infirmity, premature death, drought and other painful disasters and tragedies may be God's instruments of retribution, but then why does He afflict also the righteous and innocent? Does compensation associated with the hereafter provide the only answer? Does it satisfy everyone? Two prominent rabbis, Rabbi Hiyya bar Abba and Rabbi Eleazar openly declared that they wanted neither suffering in this world nor reward in the world to come.[34]

In contrast with dynamic criticism, total religious submissiveness and passive inertia imply the belief that divine providence is perfect and cannot be improved; such an attitude stifles all criticism of God. Even if one believes that everything will be sorted out justly in *the world to come*, in reality, all forms of petitionary prayer,

---

[32] Lev. Rab. 5:1.
[33] Mic. 6:3.
[34] b. Ber. 5b.

however humble, contain seeds of dissatisfaction and defiance. Even the most submissive rabbis make entreaties for betterment and salvation.

A fundamental argument of theodicy asserts that the majority of the worst evils are man-made, resulting from *human free will* choosing to follow the 'inclination to evil', be it a wicked person, or a Nazi ruffian. Despite the need to recognise the place of free will in the order of things, when faced by destruction of the order of the Holocaust, the question still haunts us: 'could not God have stopped the Nazi outrage before it reached its heinous proportions?' Is it really the case that the only appropriate option is to trust His perfect but impenetrable ways? For,

> The Rock, His work is perfect;
> For all His ways are justice.
> A God of faithfulness and without iniquity,
> Righteous and upright is He.[35]

---

[35] Deut. 32:4

'It's difficult to understand'
Dealing with Morally Difficult Passages in the Hebrew Bible

Harry Lesser

If, as in Jewish tradition up to the modern period, the Torah, Prophets and Writings are all taken as divinely inspired in the strong sense, i.e. as containing a pure divine message in everything written, as opposed to a divine message at times corrupted by human error and misunderstanding and at other times never intended to be taken literally, there is an obvious moral difficulty. The difficulty is that all three parts of the Bible, even the Torah itself, contain several passages that appear to endorse, or even command, either cruelty or bloodshed or dishonesty or sexual practices now forbidden. This occurs in various ways: by approval of what is done by a particular character, by its being attributed to a divine command or to the direct act of God, or by its being actually one of the specific commands of the written Torah. Jael's murder of Sisera (Judges 5), the putting to death of Saul's descendants because of his murder of the Gibeonites (2 Samuel 21), the destruction of Sodom and Gomorrah (Genesis 19) and the extermination of the Amalekites (Deut. 25:19) are respective examples.

The recognition of this problem is not new, but seems to be as old as the Jewish tradition of interpretation itself. For this tradition is different from both the academic reading of Scripture and a true fundamentalist reading. The academic reading treats these writings as essentially human documents like any others, and has no expectation or requirement that they should always be morally edifying, or morally acceptable. The fundamentalist reading treats the text as an account of the commands and acts of God which themselves set the moral standard: if what God says or does offends our moral sensibilities, then so much the worse for those sensibilities; and if what He says or does is different on different occasions, for no discernible reason, then again that is His decision and judgement, and that settles the matter. The traditional Jewish reading, like the fundamentalist one, assumes that what is in the text is divinely inspired, and therefore both true and morally right, but assumes also that this means that the text must be interpreted and understood in a way that is both internally consistent and in accordance with commonsense and our normal understanding of what is right and just. Hence, wherever there is a departure from what is usually required by the Torah, or (which for the tradition is the same thing) from commonsense and justice, we must look for the reason why what is or was apparently right in this instance is something normally to be condemned and by no means to be imitated.

In this paper, I want to draw attention to four contrasting ways in which Jewish tradition has dealt with this problem. The first of these, which cannot be applied to God's acts or commands, but can apply to the behaviour of biblical characters, is to say plainly that the act was wrong. There is here an important difference between Jewish and Muslim interpretation. Muslim interpretation requires us to assume that the behaviour of the heroes of the Koran and Bible was impeccable, and sets a standard for us to follow. For Jewish tradition, there is no presumption that even those people described as 'righteous' were free from sin: indeed there is a presumption that they were not. Sometimes, in fact, the presumption seems to be precisely that they were not, at least initially, any better than the rest of us, and that there is therefore all the more to be learnt from the study of what they finally achieved. Moreover, from the fact that something is recorded in the Torah or Prophets all that can be inferred is that there is a lesson to be learnt from the incident: one cannot infer that the incident sets a standard to be followed in similar circumstances.

My first example of this is, even within the tradition, controversial. It is Abraham's lie, told at least twice (Genesis 12 and 20), that his wife was his sister. The mediaeval commentator Nachmanides (1194-68) says that Abraham 'committed a great sin', the offence according to Jewish belief, being greater when committed by a man of Abraham's spiritual stature, since the greater the person the more strictly

293

they are judged.   The nineteenth-century rabbi and philosopher Samson Raphael Hirsch defends Abraham against Nachmanides, but he agrees that the mere facts that the act was performed by Abraham and recorded in the Torah give not the slightest ground for saying that it was not a sin: 'The Torah never presents our great men as being perfect' and we should never 'whitewash the spiritual and moral heroes of our past',[1] but on the contrary regard only God as presented for imitation and learn from the human figures how to resist imperfection.   The Midrash takes a middle view, holding that Abraham took a risk but got away with it: 'had adultery [between Pharoah and Sarah] occurred – [according to tradition it did not] – Abraham would have been held guilty'.[2]

Three other examples may be given.   The first is the treatment of Hagar by Sarah and Abraham (Genesis 16 and 21).   Again, there is a difference of opinion: some commentators think this was a legitimate way of dealing with an insolent servant, but Nachmanides, once again, says 'Sarah our Mother acted sinfully in thus ill-treating Hagar, and Abraham in permitting it'.   A second example is Jael, whose action has been more widely approved, though not held up for imitation, but in whose case there are some commentators who regard 'Blessed above women shall Jael be' (Judg. 5:24) as referring to the excellence of her intentions and motives and the act itself as questionable: 'a transgression that is done for the sake of heaven is greater than a commandment which is not done for the sake of heaven' (b. Hor. 10b). Finally, Jewish tradition has been unanimous in condemning Jephthah for sacrificing his daughter to fulfil a rash vow (Judges 11), and has even interpreted the statement in Judg. 12:7 that he was buried in 'the cities of Gilead' as meaning that as punishment he died horribly, with his limbs rotting off, so that he was buried in several different places (Gen. Rab. 60:3).

A second, very different approach, found mainly with regard to marriage and sexual behaviour, has been to see the conduct as being at that time not forbidden. Thus Abraham's marriage to his half-sister, Jacob's marrying two sisters, and Judah's

---

[1] S.R. Hirsch, *Genesis* (New York 1971), 236-7.
[2] Gen. Rab. on chapter 12.

visiting a prostitute (Genesis 38) (as he thought), are all seen as taking place before these things were forbidden. Those who took the early chapters of Genesis literally would add Cain's evident marriage to his sister, since on a literal interpretation there is no other explanation of how he found a wife. Interestingly, this view accords with what is widely felt to be a principle of natural justice, that the law, and particularly the criminal law, must be made public and must not be retro-active, a principle which appears in Jewish jurisprudence as 'no punishment without a prior warning': this principle was used both in interpreting Torah, when the question would be asked, 'Here is the punishment: where is the warning?' and in limiting the infliction of capital punishment to situations in which a person has been warned that what they intend to do is wrong and carries the death penalty. The view also goes with a distinction which is often drawn between actions which are wrong in themselves and actions which are wrong because they have been forbidden (though it would also be held that there was a good reason for the prohibition). Thus, in the sexual sphere, rape was held to be intrinsically wrong, whereas which relatives one was forbidden to marry was a matter of God's decision.

However, neither 'it was wrong' nor 'it wasn't yet forbidden' will serve when the action is performed or commanded by God Himself. Here we find particular ways of reading the text, or supplying additional information that show, or attempt to show, how apparently cruel acts were nevertheless just. Thus Josh.11:19: 'There was not a city that made peace with the children of Israel, save the Hivites the inhabitants of Gibeon' was interpreted, in the Jerusalem Talmud, as indicating that Joshua did not simply invade Israel, but gave all the inhabitants the chance to make peace or emigrate, rather than fight, as a result of which the Girgashites emigrated to North Africa, as well as the Hivites making peace. Again, the repeated statements that God 'hardened Pharaoh's heart' are interpreted as meaning that initially Pharaoh himself 'hardened his own heart' and refused to repent, and it was only after he had done this several times that he was denied a further opportunity: according to one account, this happened when even after five plagues he failed to repent (Exod. Rab. 11:6).

So the interpretations seek to show that all those who were punished or who suffered at the hands of God or of humans acting on God's instructions were given an opportunity to save themselves. It is also argued that only the guilty suffered. Thus Joshua 7 tells us that, when Achan was stoned to death for stealing property after the destruction of Jericho, his sons and daughters were stoned with him; the Pirqe Rabbi Eliezer (38) says that this was because they were accessories: 'they knew and did not tell'. The descendants of Saul who were put to death by the Gibeonites as a reprisal for Saul's murder of their tribesmen (2 Samuel 21) were similarly held to have been implicated in the murder: 'Passersby would say . . . "what did they do?" "They stretched forth their hands against proselytes who had not been admitted"' (i.e. semi-converts to Judaism) (b. Yebam. 79a).

The attempt to show that only the guilty suffered is, it must be said, something that is more convincing in some contexts than others. There is an attempt to reduce (though admittedly not to deny) David's guilt in bringing about the death of Uriah (2 Samuel 11) by arguing that Uriah had committed treason by referring to Joab as 'my lord' and refusing to obey David's order to return home (2 Sam. 11:11), so that David was entitled to have him put to death, though not in the way that he went about it (b. Shab. 56a). But it is perhaps creditable that the attempt is made, even where it is very unconvincing!

Not only is it argued that those who suffer have been given a fair warning and are guilty; it is also argued that their guilt is very great. A particular example is the destruction of Sodom (Genesis 19). The text itself simply says that the inhabitants of Sodom were 'wicked and sinners against the Lord exceedingly' (Gen. 13:13), and gives one example – the attempted homosexual rape of two strangers to the town, who were in fact angels. Jewish tradition puts little emphasis on the homosexuality, and very much more on the breach of hospitality: the Midrash has a number of stories about how wealthy strangers were robbed and exploited and poor strangers left to starve to death, those who helped them being horribly executed.

Apart from the emphasis on the full responsibility and extreme wickedness of the victims, in these stories of revenge, there are two other features of the traditional reading. One is the extent to which the action is seen as necessary for future protection, and is not a pure act of vengeance. Thus the Amalekites are spoken of, not explicitly but by implication, as still sharing in the crime of their ancestors, who made an unprovoked attack on the Israelites in the desert (Exodus 17; Deuteronomy 25), i.e. as still retaining an implacable hatred for Israel and therefore still dangerous. Their extermination is thus seen as necessary for Israel's survival: Saul's failure to carry this out, and particularly his sparing of the Amalekite King Agag (1 Samuel 15) is held to have enabled Agag to beget a child who became the ancestor of the Jews' 'arch-enemy' Haman (called 'Agagite' in the Book of Esther).

Indeed, there is one story (b. Yoma 22b) that on this occasion a heavenly voice spoke to Saul, quoting Qoh. 7:16, 'Do not be over-righteous', which is explained as 'Do not try to be more righteous (more generous or charitable) than your Creator'. Nevertheless, given the general approach of the tradition, this does not seem to mean that God defines what is just or generous by fiat, but rather that Saul, having received a divine command, should have realised that God knew best what needed to be done. It might also be argued that, if the Amalekites, as a group, really were that dangerous, to exterminate them might be justified, but to kill some and not others, as Saul is aid to have done, could only be mass murder. We are also told that when Saul killed the priests at Nob the heavenly voice spoke again, using the other half of the same verse, 'Do not be over-wicked'. The conclusion is specifically drawn, that Saul's career shows that a person who is merciful when they should be severe will end by being cruel when they should be merciful.

One may say, perhaps, considering all this, that in Jewish tradition the apparent cruelties ascribed in the Hebrew Bible either to God or to men acting on God's orders are seen as justifiable and necessary severities. They are held to be necessary for two reasons: they are deserved, and they are required for the protection of the people and the religion. Sometimes, only one of these applies: usually, they both apply. In either case, what is being maintained by implication, and with regard to Saul explicitly, is that without this severity there would be more cruelty in the world, rather than less.

The final feature of the traditional interpretation is that these incidents are always seen as taking place under special circumstances, and not in any way to be imitated. Thus the descendants of Saul put to death for the murder of the Gibeonites, in the story already mentioned, were left to hang on the rock for the duration of the summer, instead of being buried on the day of their execution, as the Torah requires (Deut. 21:23). This was done, according to the passage in b. Yebamot already quoted, because 'it is good that one word of the Torah be uprooted in order that the Name of Heaven may be sanctified publicly'. This is explained by the fact that the passers-by would be deeply impressed to see that members of the royal family could be executed for crimes against people in the lowest rank of society, who were public slaves and not even regarded as full Israelites. The need to emphasise that no victim is too humble and no criminal too grand to prevent the law taking its course justified the breach of one commandment.

Another kind of example relates to the treatment of various heathen tribes: the instructions to exterminate the Amalekites (already discussed), to liquidate the population of any Canaanite city that refused to make peace or emigrate, to allow no marriages between male Ammonite or Moabite converts and women of full Israelite status. These were all regarded as applying only to the tribe(s) in question: there was no question of drawing any inference as to how other people should be treated. Also, the displacement and moving around of tribes and peoples undertaken by Sargon II of Assyria after the destruction of the northern kingdom of Israel, and described in 2 Kings 17, was seen as mixing up the nations so that, for example, the Ammonites and Moabites were no longer the same people, and the law no longer applied. Mishnah Yadayim 4:3-4 has an account of the discussion of this point, which ends with Rabbi Joshua's view prevailing over that of Rabban Gamaliel, and Judah, an Ammonite proselyte, being allowed to 'come into the congregation', i.e. to marry a full Israelite.

This last case brings us to the fourth area where the tradition has had to deal with moral problems – those laws in the written Torah which appear to command unjust or cruel behaviour. Some of these, as indicated, could be dealt with in the way indicated above, as being intended to deal with a particular situation and having become in practice obsolete. For although it is a fundamental principle that the Torah does not change, this means that what is right under certain circumstances will always be right *under those circumstances*. If those circumstances cease, the law will in practice be suspended, like the large number of laws that apply only when there is a Temple standing. If they cease and cannot occur again, because, as here, they concern a people that no longer exists, the laws are in theory in force but in practice will never have any application – unless they relate simply to remembering the past, as with the commandment to remember Amakek, or they are given a metaphorical interpretation, such as to blot out the spirit of Amalek, i.e. the spirit of gratuitous cruelty and enmity. It should be noted that, for Jewish tradition, even if a law has no practical application, one may still acquire merit by studying it.

In these instances, the work of rendering a potentially cruel or unjust law inoperative has been done by history. But in other cases, the work has had to be done by the interpreters. Thus, according to the written Torah a total of thirty-six offences should carry the death penalty. In no case was this questioned, but the interpretation of the circumstances under which the penalty should be carried out proceeded in such a way as to limit this as much as possible. First, there had to be two actual eyewitnesses to the crime; secondly, they had to be reliable male witnesses (I am not defending this limitation, but in capital cases it must have made conviction harder); thirdly, the criminal had to have been warned, in front of two witnesses, that what they were going to do was forbidden and punishable by death.

Not only were the standards of proof raised to the maximum. There was also an effort made to narrow down the definition of the crime. Thus blasphemy was a capital crime only if the Divine Name itself was used in the blasphemy, and similarly cursing parents (m. Sanhedrin 7). Again, Lev. 21:7 says that the daughter of a priest who 'plays the harlot' is to be burnt. This was interpreted as applying only to adultery, and only to adultery while she was betrothed but not yet married: when Rabbi Akiba pointed to a superfluous letter *vav* in the text, and argued that this extra *vav* ('and') indicated that the law should include the married as well as the betrothed, he was asked 'Are we going to burn a woman to death because of an extra *vav*?' But there is no doubt that if an equally small linguistic point could be used in the direction of restricting the infliction of the extreme penalty, then it would be.

One very good example is the case of the 'stubborn and rebellious son', who is to be stoned (Deuteronomy 21 and m. Sanhedrin 8). It was first argued that this could not apply either to a grown man, who is not under his parents' authority, or to a child, who is not morally responsible: this left, it was eventually decided, a period of three months after his thirteenth birthday. It was then argued, from the words 'a glutton and a drunkard', that he had to commit the specific offence of stealing meat and wine from his parents and eating it. Thirdly, for his first offence he was to be warned and beaten, and stoned only if he repeated the offence. Finally, if he ran away before sentence was passed and then the period during which this law applied came to an end, he was then exempt: and these are not the only restrictions (see m. Sanhedrin 8). It is not surprising that, though one sage claimed to have known a case, the general opinion was that 'there never was a stubborn and rebellious son [in this sense] and never will be'.

This account of various ways of dealing with moral difficulties in the Torah and generally in Scripture is not of course exhaustive. There are, for example, other incidents where a person's misfortune is not treated as retribution: Uzzah (2 Samuel 6), who touched the Ark and died, and is called 'a righteous man who suffered the fate of the wicked', seems to be treated less like someone who was punished and more like a man who was, so to speak, careless enough to touch a high-voltage cable. But I have tried to provide a range of examples, of various types; and they suggest one or two general conclusions. These are conclusions about *how* the tradition has operated. Whether it was necessary to take Scripture so literally, and how successful the attempts to deal with the resultant moral difficulties have been, though both very important questions, are outside the scope of this paper, though readers may well wish to give some thought to them. My concern here is with the way in which Jewish tradition has viewed Scripture, and particularly the historical and legal parts of Scripture, which are those most involved with the details of human behaviour.

There are, I think, parallels in the reading of stories and the reading of instructions. As regards stories, biblical history is seen neither as ideal history, in which the behaviour of great men and women is displayed for admiration and imitation, nor as straight academic history, where the important thing is simply what happened. Essentially, biblical history, for the tradition, is the record of those incidents from which one can learn something moral or spiritual, and it is assumed that one learns from the mistakes and even crimes of great men as well as from their virtues and virtuous acts.

Analogously – though the analogy should not be pushed too far – the legal and moral instructions of the Torah are not ideals, but requirements as to how best to behave in the world as it is. This means, both as regards stories and as regards instructions, that attention has to be directed towards the exact circumstances surrounding the action in question, wether it is an action which took place or an action which is commanded. It is necessary to learn exactly what is required and exactly when, and also to realise precisely what happened and why – halakhah fills out the first and haggadah the second.

Crucial here are the third and fourth ways of dealing with moral difficulties: the first two, involving simply the recognition that an action either was wrong or took place before a prohibition existed, are more straightforward. The third and fourth ways of approaching the problem involve, as we have seen, many different ways of dealing with history and with law: but they have in common that they involve an exact understanding of the details of the situation or the details of the requirement. The point here, I think, is that the need to look at the details becomes most acute when one is dealing with severity, in history or in law. To act generously or charitably requires no justification; to act with severity obviously does. Hence attention to detail becomes crucial: first, in order to understand why the severity is or was necessary, and secondly in order to understand exactly when it is required, so that one is not led into cruelty or injustice by imitating the wrong features of the action or misunderstanding the instruction.

In short, for Jewish tradition, one who wishes to understand Scripture must, as Blake said of one who wishes to do good to their neighbour, understand it 'in minute particulars'. Sufficient attention to the minute particulars, to the exact features of the situation or the exact requirements of the commandment, will in the end remove moral difficulties. But it must be noted that this does not simply involve minute analysis of the details of the text: as the story of Rabbi Akiba shows and similarly the whole approach to the 'stubborn and rebellious son', it is minute analysis informed by humanity and commonsense, so that it is already given in which direction interpretation should go – we look, for example, for ways of limiting capital punishment, not ways of increasing it.

The tradition does not, like the truly fundamentalist tradition, simply bow before the wisdom and justice of God and take the text as defining what is just and sensible. It acknowledges that human commonsense and feelings of justice can be transcended, but takes it that they cannot be utterly wrong and that the justice of God cannot be utterly different from human justice. To return to the point I made early on in this paper, we may say that for the fundamentalist, a thing must be right because it is in Scripture; for a non-traditional interpreter a thing cannot be right if it clearly goes against justice and commonsense. The complexity of traditional Jewish interpretation arises partly because it accepts both of these propositions, and when faced with scriptural passages that do not seem to meet normal moral requirements endeavours by close study to find an interpretation which will. This paper has tried to bring together some specific examples of ways in which people working in the tradition have tried to do this. It is a matter of opinion whether the enterprise always succeeded, but it was an honourable enterprise. The sages' response would probably be 'If you think we didn't succeed, go away and try to do better'!

The Bible in Contemporary Jewish Sermons

Christine M. Pilkington

An exploration of Jewish ways of reading the Bible tends to focus on biblical commentary. So far as the faith community is concerned, however, it is preaching rather than commentary which, it may be argued, should be the focus of attention. After all, far more Jews will be present in a synagogue on Shabbat than will attend a shiur. Assuming that this is minhah, then the Torah and Haftarah will be read and a sermon will be preached. (Whether or not everyone actually listens to or in any way engages with the readings and the sermon may be another matter.) It is in the context of worship that one comes close to what most Jews believe.[1] If, as is traditionally the case, sermons in some way relate to the readings, it is reasonable to suppose that an insight into contemporary Jewish belief, both about the Bible and deriving from it, may be gained from examining some modern anthologies.

It is easy to denigrate preaching and to lament the poor quality of biblical exegesis which it may offer. Before we neglect it as an important expression of Jewish thought and spirituality, however, especially in relation to the Bible, the advice of Saperstein, the pre-eminent scholar of mediaeval and early modern Jewish preaching might be heeded. 'Most investigations of exegetical issues focus exclusively on the commentary, a genre formally dependent upon another text and devoted almost entirely to its interpretation. I argue that sermons must also be recognised as an integral part of the history of Jewish hermeneutics.'[2] Furthermore, it

---

[1] A similar point is made about the Siddur reflecting 'popular Judaism' by P. S. Alexander, *Textual Sources for the Study of Judaism* (Chicago 1990), 6.
[2] Marc Saperstein, *'Your Voice like a Ram's Horn'* (Cincinnati 1996), xii.

has been contended that 'there is no creative Jewish community anywhere, at any period, in which homiletical literature did not hold a central place.'[3]

Saperstein's starting-point lies in the generally accepted interpretation of Neh. 8:8: 'So they read from the book, from the law of God, with interpretation. They gave the sense, so that the people understood the reading'. This is taken to include commentary and application rather than mere translation. This ancient tradition determines Saperstein's purpose as 'to foster an appreciation of the preaching tradition that contemporary rabbis represent by demonstrating how predecessors molded sacred texts to address the intellectual, social, and spiritual problems of their own time.'[4]   Saperstein admits that such dynamics as the reactions of the congregation – or lack of them –, the charisma of the preacher, the interaction with topical concerns and events cannot be captured by the anthologies he examines. Such would require a videotape and more.[5]   However, in an attempt to establish the peculiar genre and value of sermons, he does try to confine his attentions to material that has actually been preached. [6]   The same principle will here apply to a modest selection of contemporary anthologies, though brief reference will be made to homiletic literature, in the sense that it too represents an act of creative, communal interpretation even if not actually delivered orally to a congregation.

The aim of this study is threefold. Firstly, to consider how the Bible is used in a range of denominational traditions, that is, what different approaches to the Bible are found in contemporary Jewish sermons? Secondly, to establish the purpose of the sermon, as distinct from other biblical interpretation, that is, how do the preacher's aims affect his methods of interpretation?[7]   Thirdly, to return to the initial claim that

---

[3] Joseph Dan, *Sifrut ha-Musar we-ha-Derush* (Jerusalem 1975), 26.
[4] Marc Saperstein, *Jewish Preaching 1200-1800* (New Haven 1989), xi.
[5] Saperstein, *Jewish Preaching 1200-1800*, 7-9.
[6] Saperstein, *Jewish Preaching 1200-1800*, 3. In this he differs from a survey of the same field by Israel Bettan, *Studies in Jewish Preaching: Middle Ages* (Cincinnati 1939).
[7] 'His' is used advisedly, since no anthology of sermons from or including women in Progressive Judaism has been available.

sermons are a rich source of Jewish thought, that is, what central concerns of Judaism are expressed, perhaps even ideally expressed, in contemporary sermons?

The first area establishes the different schools of thought reflected in the examples selected. The obvious sidra with which to begin is Bereshit. Something of the variety of ways of handling the Bible in a homiletic context can be seen by noting some characteristics of three different treatments of a portion of this sidra. In the introduction to a collection of what are referred to as 'discourses' or 'talks' of the Lubavitcher Rebbe, Jonathan Sacks comments that they are 'addressed with relentless clarity to the contemporary Jewish condition.' Their purpose is to lead 'from the present moment of confusion to the timeless lucidity of Torah, beyond the clouds to the Infinite Light.'[8] We already begin to get the feel of an essentially mystical approach and this is spelt out in the foreword to the new edition, where different levels of reality and a journey inward 'toward integration of the human personality' and 'the Oneness that pervades all spiritual truth' are said to characterize the anthology.[9] It is through mystical spectacles then that we approach Bereshit in this volume. The main question raised is why light was created first when there was nothing to benefit from it. The answer is given, by way of Talmud, Midrash, and the Zohar, that the whole purpose of creation is captured in the opening phrase, 'Let there be light.' The heavenly world is hidden in the lower world and each Jew's purpose is to transform 'his situation and environment to light ... by changing the darkness itself to light, by positive commitment to good'.[10] Thus, Sacks claims, the Rebbe 'weaves together the results of many centuries of traditional Jewish scholarship focusing them through the prism of his intense Chassidic spirituality'.[11]

We may contrast the approach of the leading modern Orthodox rabbinical authority of the second half of the twentieth century, Soloveichik. His perspective is

---

[8] Menachem M. Schneerson, *Torah Studies* (Brooklyn 1996), ix.
[9] Schneerson, *Torah Studies*, xi-xii.
[10] Schneerson, *Torah Studies*, 1-5. It is interesting to note that this discourse ends with a quotation from Isaiah, though not, in fact, the Haftarah portion for Bereshit. This is the reverse of the traditional method of starting from the Haftarah and ingeniously working back to the Torah to demonstrate the unity of the Bible.
[11] Schneerson, *Torah Studies*, xi.

not mystical but existential. So, of Bereshit, he asks, 'Why did the world in its totality come into existence?'[12] Soloveichik refers to four major discrepancies between the two accounts of creation in Genesis.[13] Instead of following the rabbinic tendency to harmonise them, as exemplified by Nahmanides, he uses them to develop two perspectives corresponding to two dimensions of existential truth. There is a type of biblical analysis here, but Soloveichik uses it creatively to contrast not so much two stories of creation but two Adams. The first is the creative theoretician. The second 'explores not the scientific abstract universe but the irresistibly fascinating, qualitative world, where he establishes an intimate relation with God.'[14]

A quite different way of wrestling with 'the conflicting claims of tradition and modernity during the second half of the twentieth century' is to be found in the first of a three-volume collection of sermons 'much as they were delivered' at St John's Wood Liberal Synagogue, London.[15] Here Rayner describes his approach to biblical interpretation as one of 'reverence for the Jewish past combined with a spirit of free inquiry and critical evaluation as demanded by the present.'[16]

In the foreward, a fellow Liberal Rabbi, David Goldberg, describes the volume as an outstanding example of the 'largely lost craft of homiletics'.[17] It will, therefore, be drawn on heavily for examples of Liberal scholarship combined with tradition. When it comes to Rayner's treatment of Bereshit, one would expect to see the universalism and social idealism of Liberal Judaism and he does not disappoint.

---

[12] Joseph Soloveichik, *The Lonely Man of Faith* (Revised edition; New York 1992), 21. Though not strictly a sermon, this treatment of Genesis is essentially homiletical.
[13] Soloveichik, *The Lonely Man of Faith*, 10-11.
[14] Soloveichik, *The Lonely Man of Faith*, 23.
[15] John D. Rayner, *An Understanding of Judaism* (Oxford 1997); Rayner's own words in the Preface. Having been present at one of Rayner's *shiurim* at the Leo Baeck College where some of the material, viz. the midrashic comment in Genesis Rabbah, given in his sermon on *Toledot* featured, there might be a tendency to disbelieve Rayner's claim that all his anthology was actually preached. A more sensible conclusion to draw, however, is that too sharp a distinction between study and sermon should not be pressed. Particularly where text and its interpretation is concerned, the same material could well occur in both without there being much difference either in content or even style.
[16] Rayner, *An Understanding of Judaism*.
[17] Rayner, *An Understanding of Judaism*, xviii.

Dealing with Genesis 3 rather than Genesis 1-2, he draws from what his title describes as 'The Myth of the Garden of Eden' the Jewish emphasis on freedom of choice as given in Eden rather than taken away. He quotes Chief Rabbi J. H. Hertz as saying, 'Instead of the Fall of Man ... Judaism preaches the Rise of Man; instead of Original Sin, it stresses Original Virtue ... The Golden Age of Humanity is not in the past, but in the future.'[18]

A striking feature of this, and indeed of most of Rayner's sermons, is the knowledge of Hebrew which he assumes in his congregation. For a branch of Judaism which deems the vernacular to be so important for everyone's understanding the liturgy, this is surely remarkable. In his sermon on Shabbat Bereshit, Rayner has an interesting discussion of the Hebrew for 'the tree of life' and for 'the tree of good and evil', the implications of the word דעת occupying at least a quarter of the sermon. This, together with other examples both from Rayner and from others well to his right on the Jewish biblical spectrum, raises the question of how far examination of Semitic words and their meaning remains an important feature of contemporary Jewish sermons and, if so, whether it is an end in itself or rather a means to an end, aimed at 'translating' the central beliefs of Judaism into action.[19]

This takes us further into our second area of consideration, viz. the purpose of contemporary Jewish sermons. In his two seminal works on Jewish preaching already referred to, Saperstein attaches much importance to the prophetic tradition of rebuke – hence the title of one these works, taking words from Isa. 58:1.[20] Since Rosh Hashanah and Yom Kippur constituted the main occasions (apart from Pesach) for sermons in the eras to which Saperstein's study relates, it is not surprising that what

---

[18] Rayner, *An Understanding of Judaism*, 3-7.

[19] See, for example, Stefan C. Reif, 'Aspects of the Jewish Contribution to Biblical Interpretation', in John Barton (ed.), *The Cambridge Companion to Biblical Interpretation* (Cambridge 1998), 150-55, where an emphasis on textual criticism in Jewish biblical interpretation is contrasted with source criticism and systematic theology as found in 'the Protestant world of scholarship'.

[20] Michael Fishbane, in 'The Hebrew Bible Tradition: Reflections and Reconsiderations', a paper read to The Society for Old Testament Study (Oxford 1997), stressed the purpose of *teshuvah* in the homiletical biblical tradition. He saw evidence of a highly developed rhetorical style not only in Isaiah 58, read as the *Haftarah* on *Yom Kippur*, but also in Isa. 56:1-8. He concluded that homilies as injunctions to penitence already took place in late antiquity.

he calls the prophet's task of 'ethical and religious rebuke' looms so large.[21] There may well be a danger of overemphasising this function. This study deliberately avoids the crucial penitential period and seeks to take further examples of contemporary Jewish sermons from anthologies specifically dedicated to following the weekly sidrot in the one-year or three-year lectionary. Both the style and content of these examples leads to the conclusion that the purpose of contemporary Jewish sermons is both to articulate belief and to inspire action, not always of a penitential nature.[22] Again, a comparison of sermons on the same sidra, but from different theological perspectives, may be informative.

It is perhaps cheating to draw on what is subtitled *An anthology of the weekly Masorti guide to the weekly Torah readings and to Jewish Life*.[23] For this collection is not, strictly speaking, one of sermons, but rather of short articles 'reflecting week by week on the synagogue parasha'.[24] Beginning Shavuot 5,755, these became 'an accepted part of every Masorti synagogue', giving the members 'something in synagogue that they could glance at during the service' (so much for the gripping nature of the sermon, one might be excused for concluding!), 'which would give them some background into the weekly Torah reading and which would provide additional information on many of the rich and varied Jewish traditions.' I choose an example from this anthology, not only because I could not obtain sermons representing the British Conservative movement, but also because each 'reflection' includes a discrete

---

[21] Saperstein, *'Your Voice like a Ram's Horn'*, 2-3.

[22] A useful source of information on this might be manuals or course notes on homiletics from, for instance, the Yeshivah University and the Jewish Theological Seminary of America. Specific homiletical training used to be offered until about 1990 at what was Jews' College, London. Ingenious structure and what might be called the 'craft of the sermon' were at the heart of this training. Now more emphasis is on commentators. Generally, and not just in a study centred on the Bible in preaching, it would seem logical to assume that whatever methods of biblical study feature in rabbinic training will be what flow into the resultant sermons. On the other hand, a preacher may know certain things about the Bible but not carry them through into sermons.

[23] Harry Freedman (ed.), *Reflections of the Year* (London 1997).

[24] Freedman, *Reflections*, 7, 8.

section headed 'From the Midrash', which is a significant feature in itself.[26]   I give here some details of the entry for Lech Lecha, a parasha on which I want to draw later in this study.

The author of this particular entry, Zvi Berger, takes the very opening, 'Go from your country and your kindred and your father's house to the land that I will show you' and contrasts it with the appearance of God to Abram in Gen. 12:7 and 17:1.   In Gen. 12:1, there is not even an appearance described, but starkly and suddenly a voice confronting Abram with a command, Lech Lecha.   An immediate break with the past is what is demanded.   Berger, following S. R. Hirsch, takes הלך, 'to go', as being connected to חלק, 'to be divided'.   The extent of this total separation is spelt out in the words about land, birthplace, and 'father's house'.   What is required of the man of faith is an immediate leap, admitting neither quiet reflection nor turning back.[27]

Berger goes on to make an interesting comparison of this 'test' with later tests of Abraham, notably the Akedah.   In Genesis 22, the actual phrase, Lech Lecha, recurs. The gravity of the situation, as in Genesis 12, is similarly spelt out: 'your son, your only son Isaac, whom you love'.   The difference lies, however, in the type of faith now required.   Abraham has three days of anguished reflection and the break demanded is not with the past but with the future.   Whilst Lech Lecha provides us with a paradigm of faith, the Akedah demonstrates faith of a kind 'which passes the prolonged and terrible tests of overriding all other emotions, reflections, and moral considerations.'[28]

Berger then turns to the Midrash to answer the question of what was so special about Abraham that God chose him.   In Bereshit Rabbah 39:6, R. Azariah uses Ps. 45:8 to emphasise Abraham's righteousness.   R. Azariah then explains this text with

---

[26] By contrast, North American and Canadian Conservatism are well-represented in an anthology of sermons 'from all denominations': Saul I. Teplitz (ed.) *The Best of Jewish Sermons* (New York 1996). These are considered to represent the best from twelve volumes of sermons collected over the years. Despite its title, which is perhaps only marginally preferable to *Rabbis' Greatest Hits*, this anthology constitutes a serious and informative source of some 51 sermons.

[27] Freedman, *Reflections*, 58-59.

[28] Freedman, *Reflections*, 58-59.

Gen. 18:25, where Abraham seeks to defend the righteous at Sodom. R. Levi introduces a new idea linking the verse from the Psalms with the opening of Lech Lecha, quoting Abraham's, 'Shall not the Judge of all the earth do what is just?' (Gen. 18:25). The argument runs that absolute justice would mean that the world could not exist. Since there is a desire for the world to continue to exist, there has to be mercy and this is why Abraham argues with God. Thus it is Abraham's 'love for humanity that earns him his special status.'[29]

Two observations need drawing together at this point, one about purpose and one about hermeneutics. The aim of the sermon clearly determines the method of biblical interpretation. Though not necessarily to rebuke, it is nonetheless intended to influence the attitude and behaviour of the Masorti faith community. Midrash is called upon to answer a question which those who have 'heard' the sermon may be asking, viz. 'What is so special about Abraham?' Even so, the matter is not purely academic. 'You too should show mercy and cultivate a love for humanity with all its flaws' is surely the message to the congregation. Whether the text is biblical or midrashic, individual words and phrases are explored both out of interest in their own right and out of a desire to encourage faith, of one kind or the other, in each listener.

A brief comparison of the Lubavitcher Rebbe's treatment of the same sidra may serve to reinforce this important, if rather unremarkable, conclusion.[30] He maintains that the inner content of the whole of Lech Lecha is summed up in its name. Literally, 'go to yourself', he says, connotes moving 'towards your soul's essence and your ultimate purpose, that for which you were created'. The Rebbe examines the apparent contradiction between Abraham's 'going up' in the sense of ascending towards his destiny and his 'going down' to Egypt. He sees in this the foreshadowing of subsequent Jewish history and thereby offers Abraham as a type in the sense of an inspiration. The notion of the centrality and continuity of typology in Jewish sermons will be developed in the conclusion to this study. It is immediately

---

[29] Freedman, *Reflections*, 60.
[30] Schneerson, *Torah Studies*, 10-15.

obvious, however, that this treatment of the sidra has the purpose of inspiring certain attitudes and even more so actions. Jewish people are to remember that 'the end is implicit in the beginning', that God's presence should be felt in 'the most intransigent of places', that exile is 'a preparation for redemption ... an integral part of spiritual progress'. The final paragraph sums up the message and purpose of this sermon, 'Whatever a Jew's situation, when he turns towards his true self-fulfillment in the injunction of Lech Lecha, he places his life and his actions in the perspective of Torah, and takes his proper place in the bringing of the future redemption.'

Midrashic comment is employed in this sermon to the same end. So in Bereshit Rabbah 40:2, Abraham, when faced with famine in Egypt and the seeming pointlessness of his journey 'was not angry and did not complain' and, in 39:2, Abraham's wanderings are compared with the shaking of a spice box. In order to reach all corners, whether of the then-known world or of a room, some movement is necessary.

In a wide-ranging anthology of sermons already referred to, the editor, Saul Teplitz describes the sermon as the rabbi's 'prime instrument to instruct the congregation of the truths of Judaism and uplift them spiritually by quickening their conscience.'[31] A clear example of this comes in the sermon by Samuel Chiel on the sidra Vayikra. The second verse of Leviticus 1 is explored in relation to a variety of texts from the Nebi'im and Ketubim.[32] The apparently superfluous מכם in the phrase אדם כי יקריב מכם קרבן ליי is examined in order to establish that the key to acceptable sacrifice is, as the sermon's title has it, 'giving of yourself'.[33] Chiel draws on Jewish and world history up to modern times for his exemplars of such giving, but his 'types' from the Bible are the most numerous, since, as he says, the Bible 'is replete with

---

[31] Teplitz, *Best Jewish Sermons*, ix.

[32] Teplitz, *Best Jewish Sermons*, 60-67.

[33] Schneerson, *Torah Studies*, 153-57, also on *Vayikra*, similarly emphasises the 'of you', developing the well-known Hasidic interpretation that it is the person offering who is the sacrifice. Not surprisingly, in his treatment of *Vayikra*, Rayner, *Understanding*, 51-54, tackles the whole question of physical sacrifice and uses biblical and rabbinic tradition to repudiate the practice and any hope of its restoration.

stories of self-sacrifice and with examples of such wholehearted unequivocal giving of oneself.'

A second example from the same volume of sermons is one by Israel H. Levinthal.[34] From an Orthodox background, Levinthal taught homiletics at the Conservative Jewish Theological Seminary in New York and became famous, both there and in his volumes of sermons, for combining originality and tradition in his biblical interpretation. The opening words of his sermon on Acherei Mot doubtless reflect his vast experience: 'It is not easy, my friends, for anyone to preach these days.' The cause of his gloom is, in fact, the subject of this sermon, 'the generation gap'. He perceives the first such gap as exemplified in the incident in Leviticus 16 and he draws on the Midrash, for example Leviticus Rabbah 20:7, to try to establish the nature of the אש זרה which, according to Lev. 10:1-2, Nadab and Abihu brought to the altar. It does not take very much imagination to guess how Levinthal develops, in terms of American life, two traditions represented in Leviticus Rabbah, firstly that Nadab and Abihu entered the sanctuary drunk and secondly that they entered it naked. The main point to note is that the aim of the sermon is, as Levinthal puts it, to recall the congregation to 'the sacred ideals of true religion, ethical religion, the ideals of the prophets and sages and saints of old'.

The complex structure of the rabbinic derashah, especially petihah and to a lesser extent hatimah is not much in evidence in contemporary Jewish sermons.[35] Nevertheless, the midrashic notion of the biblical text as open and to be exploited is present in all the examples considered here. Just as in the past, exegesis and eisegesis were not easily separated in the homiletic midrashim, across the spectrum of Jewish preaching today, the Bible is commented on and applied to the questions and practical concerns of Jewish living.

---

[34] Schneerson, *Torah Studies*, 217-22.
[35] On the importance of the synagogue for homiletic midrashim, see P. S. Alexander, 'Midrash', in R. J. Coggins and L. Houlden (eds), *A Dictionary of Biblical Interpretation* (London 1990), 455-57, and Gunter Stemberger, *Introduction to the Talmud and Midrash* (2nd edn; Edinburgh 1996), 240-45.

Unable to locate any anthology of sermons from Reform Judaism, I turn to Jonathan Magonet, one of Reform's best popular interpreters of the Bible and Principal of the Leo Baeck College for the training of Reform and Liberal rabbis, for some concluding thoughts on the relationship between the Bible and Jewish experience.[36] In a chapter on the biblical roots of Jewish identity, Magonet considers what he describes as 'archetypal events of Jewish self-understanding'.[37] 'The Hebrew Bible', he writes, 'is not merely a history book indicating our origins and roots as a people or a religious community. Just as in the past, it continues to create and shape Jewish existence whenever we open ourselves to it and accept the challenge it provides to us.'[38] It is for this reason, I believe, that what Saperstein maintains about sermons as a central expression of Jewish literature remains true of contemporary Jewish preaching. Though sometimes of poor quality and failing in their aim, sermons, as we have seen, can be of a high quality and a means of inspiring the faith community to live as the people of God.

This is the line taken by Jonathan Sacks when, in what was originally a series of broadcasts for the BBC World Service on Jewish spirituality, he describes the Bible as 'a way of experiencing history'.[39] He continues, 'To a remarkable degree, scenes that occur in the Hebrew Bible *recur* at critical moments in post-biblical Jewish history and continue to do so to the present day.' If we define Jewish typology as treating critical moments in the biblical narrative as recurrent in later Jewish experience, then we can easily see why sermons may give us a unique insight into Jewish ways of reading the Bible.

In his examination of preaching, Saperstein argues that typological interpretation, following Nahmanides' methods, continued to be widely used.[40] From our examples of contemporary Jewish sermons, the same can still be said. The method is not allegorical, but essentially historical, where a passage, normally a

---

[36] See, for example, *A Rabbi Reads the Psalms* (London 1994).
[37] Jonathan Magonet, *The Subversive Bible* (London 1997), 95.
[38] Magonet, *The Subversive Bible*, 105.
[39] Jonathan Sacks, *Faith in the Future* (London 1995), 171.
[40] Saperstein, *'Your Voice like a Ram's Horn'*, xii, 23-35.

narrative, 'seems complete in its own terms but which is shown to indicate something beyond itself.'[41]   The impact of Nahmanides on Jewish sermons in relation to the Bible is still felt, and not only in the patriarchal narratives. It is no accident that one of Sacks' principal images of Jewish spirituality revolves around the sidra exemplified earlier, Lech Lecha.[42]   The American Reform rabbis behind the Columbus Platform of 1937 defined Judaism as 'the historical religious experience of the Jewish people'. If they were right, it follows that the sermon, a genre which par excellence endeavours to attach religious significance to present experience in relation to that recorded of the past, may have much to say about contemporary biblical interpretation.[43]

---

[41] Saperstein, 'Your Voice like a Ram's Horn', 24.

[42] Sacks, Faith in the Future, 173-74.

[43] I am grateful to Rabbi Professor Marc Saperstein for several helpful observations made on the points raised in this study.

Index of Biblical References

Index of Classical Sources

Index of Modern Authors

323